TRAUMA CARE

HELICOPTER EMERGENCY MEDICAL SERVICE (HEMS) • LONDON

Editor: Richard Earlam

Saldatore Ltd

Published by Saldatore Ltd
Millars Three, Southmill Road, Bishop's Stortford, Hertfordshire CM23 3DH

Printed and Bound by Spottiswoode Ballantyne Printers Limited
Hawkins Road, The Hythe, Colchester, Essex CO2 8JT

ISBN: 0 948047 08 9

Front and Back Cover Photographs:
© A D Chandler
AC Photographics, 5 The Court, Cascade Avenue, London N10 3PS

ACKNOWLEDGEMENTS

I would like to thank the authors and photographers for their contributions to this book, especially realising that they are experts in their own field and have an extremely busy life. An attempt has been made to unify and collect this specialised knowledge for the benefit of all concerned with trauma care.

The project has taken over two years and during this time I have had continuous help from Shirley Wan. The photographic department at the Royal London Hospital have been extremely efficient and reliable with Ian Berle and Bob Tupper. If short of data and facts I could always rely on Clive Kirk and the body of experts on the helipad including all the pilots. In the A&E department there has been similar expertise provided by Alastair Wilson, Judith Fisher and Tim Coats. My present secretary Parveen Saleem has also been involved with the work recently.

At Saldatore, our publishers, Malcolm Allan has always been supportive in all things large and small; no detail escapes him. Kathy Day in the last hectic months has been very efficient combining text with illustrations on the computer in a meticulous fashion.

My thanks also go to my wife Roswitha and our children Melissa and Caroline for putting up with the presence of the editor working hard at home for most of the weekends of this year.

Richard Earlam
Consultant Surgeon
Royal London Hospital

November 1996

United Newspapers plc

Ludgate House
245 Blackfriars Road
London SE1 9UY

From The Chairman
The Lord Stevens of Ludgate

The creation of many projects is based on coincidence, or fortunate circumstances. Express Newspapers involvement in the Helicopter Emergency Medical Service arose from the fact that I had known Richard Earlam for some years. He phoned me at home one night and mentioned his ideas about this service and asked if I could help. I immediately thought it was a good idea and said I would reflect on it. As a result of that phone call we, at Express Newspapers, decided that it was a worthy cause not only to save lives but also to shorten the length of time that patients spend in hospital, since the sooner they arrive in hospital the less time is spent there. We decided to back the project for a period of four years. Without our friendship and that phone call this project quite literally might never have got off the ground. I am delighted that all the hard work that has been put into the project by the Royal London Hospital, the support of the National Health Service, the Wolfson Foundation and of Andrew Cameron and his team at Express Newspapers has enabled the helicopter service to be at the forefront of life saving in the United Kingdom. I hope that this service will be the forerunner of a nationwide service over the next few years.

Photo: Express Newspapers

Le Dauphin est arrivé

Lord Stevens (right) and Mr Richard Earlam FRCS celebrate the arrival of the helicopter flown in by Captain Alan Rock to Battersea Heliport, London on 15th December 1988

TRAUMA CARE

HEMS • LONDON

CONTENTS

LIST OF AUTHORS

Andersson L	Department of Plastic and Reconstructive Surgery	Section 8F
Baldry-Currens J	Rehabilitation (co-author)	Section 8K ii
	Measurement of Disability: The Functional Independence Measure (FIM)	Section 8K iii
Beale, Sir P	The British Red Cross Society	Section 4G
Bradbury G	A Six Year Perspective on Intensive Care at the RLH (co-author)	Section 7F
Brazier J	Economic Evaluation in Brief (co-author)	Section 9D
Bristow A	Interhospital Transfers by Helicopter	Section 3B iv
Budden G	Search and Rescue Helicopters and Civil Air Ambulance Units	Section 3B iii
	The Anatomy of a Call Out (co-author)	Section 5
Cameron A	Daily Express Involvement (1988-96)	Section 2B
Cannell H	Maxillofacial Department (co-author)	Section 8E
Canning I	Paramedics	Section 10C
Caple L	Air Ambulance Operations in England	Section 3B v
Chalk W	The Anatomy of a Call Out (co-author)	Section 5
Chan O	Value of the Spiral CT Scanner in the A&E Department (co-author)	Section 7D
	The Role of the Radiologist (co-author)	Section 8H
Chapman J	Haematology Department/Blood Transfusion Laboratory (co-author)	Section 8I
Coats T	Ambulance Services – The Future (co-author)	Section 4I
	Examples of Standard Operating Procedures (SOP)	Section 6B
	Pre-Hospital Analgesia and Anaesthesia (co-author)	Section 6F
	Entrapment and Release	Section 6H
	Hospital Trauma Team Organisation (co-author)	Section 7B
	Nuts and Bolts – Head Injury Management in the HEMS System(co-author)	Section 8B
	Outcome following Head Injury Treated by the HEMS System	Section 9C
Collins G	The Metropolitan Police Service	Section 4B
Colvin P	The Anaesthetic Department (co-author)	Section 8A
Cross F	Who Owns Trauma? The Patient	Section 8L
Crossfield S	Post Traumatic Stress and Counselling	Section 8K iv
Davies G	The Future of Pre-Hospital Care	Section 10I
Davis H	The Emergency Theatre Service	Section 7E
Dorey N	Raised Helipads at London and Leeds	Section 3B viii
Dyer P	Maxillofacial Department (co-author)	Section 8E
Earlam R	Introduction	Section 1
	Editorial Comment: 'The Patient who Talked and Died'	Section 6M
	Costs	Section 9 F
	Purchasing and Reimbursement of HEMS Costs	Section 11D
Fairhurst R	'The Patient who Talked and Died'	Section 6M
	The Faculty of Pre-hosptial Care at the Royal College of Surgeons of Edinburgh	Section 10H
Faulding P	Confined Space and Special Rescue Training	Section 6J
Fenton R	Case Histories 1:A Light Aircraft Crash	Section 6C
	Case Histories 2:A Bad Fall	Section 6E
	Case Histories 3:The Cyclist	Section 6G
	Case Histories 4:Under a Train	Section 6I
	Case Histories 5:Multiple Trauma in a Motorcyclist	Section 6N

Fleminger S	Psychiatry and the Trauma Patient (co-author)	Section 8K i
Field I	Night Flying in the HEMS Role (co-author)	Section 11B
Fisher J	The British Association for Immediate Care: BASICS	Section 4D
	The Most Venerable Order of the Hospital of St John of Jerusalem	Section 4E
	Training Doctors for Major Incidents	Section 4F
Goldhill D	A Six Year Perspective on Intensive Care at the RLH (co-author)	Section 7F
	Data Collection in the ICU and Trauma Unit: APACHE II (co-author)	Section 9B
Goode T	The Academic Future for Trauma (co-author)	Section 11G
Goodier D	Fractures of the Pelvis	Section 8D
Green C	Economic Evaluation in Brief (co-author)	Section 9D
Greengross P	Purchasing HEMS in the Internal Market	Section 9E
Griffiths M	The Anatomy of a Call Out (co-author)	Section 5
Gurney D	The Anatomy of a Call Out (co-author)	Section 5
	Notar Helicopters – Look No Tail	Section 11A
Hadjimichael P	Pre-Hospital Analgesia and Anaesthesia (co-author)	Section 6F
Harris J	Nuts and Bolts – Head Injury Management in the HEMS System(co-author)	Section 8B
Healy M	The Anaesthetic Department (co-author)	Section 8A
	Massive Blood Transfusion following Traumatic Surgery	Section 8J
Hoefliger C	Swiss Air Rescue: REGA	Section 3C iii
Huguenard P	Services de l'aide medical ungent en France: SAMU	Section 3C ii
Jeffs G	JAR-OPS – A New World: The Civil Aviation Authority (CAA) and the Joint Aviation Authority (JAA)	Section 11C
Joyce J	Psychiatry and the Trauma Patient (co-author)	Section 8K i
Kirk C	The First 1,000 Patients Admitted to the RLH via HEMS	Section 2C
	HEMS Missions from the RLH Helipad in Six Years	Section 2D
	Outcome	Section 9A
Kugler G	Concept of the Air Rescue System in Germany (ADAC)	Section 3C i a
Lackner C	Arbeitskreis Notfallmedizin und Rettungswesen (ANR): The Centre for Emergency Medicine and Rescue Service, Ludwig-Maximilian University of Munich (co-author)	Section 10F
Landon M	The Anatomy of a Call Out (co-author)	Section 5
	Night Flying in the HEMS Role (co-author)	Section 11B
London PS	The Birmingham Experiment - What Happened?	Section 3B i
	William Gissane (1898-1981)	Section 3B i
Machesney M	Pre-Hospital Management of Burn Injury: The HEMS Experience	Section 6K
Mahoney P	EMS Systems, Trauma Centres and Trauma Systems in the USA (co-author)	Section 3A
	Selection and Training of the HEMS Registrar	Section 10A
	Training in the USA – Multimedia for HEMS	Section 11E
Marsden A	Patient Air Transport in Scotland – An Integrated Service	Section 3B vi
Morley A	Pre-Hospital Phsyiological Monitoring of HEMS Patients	Section 6D
Moss R	Planning and the RLH Emergency Department (co-author)	Section 7C
Neal W	Diasters: Lessons to be Learnt	Section 4H
Newton A	EMS Systems, Trauma Centres and Trauma Systems in the USA (co-author)	Section 3A
Newland A	Haematology Department/Blood Transfusion Laboratory (co-author)	Section 8I
Oakley P	Stoke-on-Trent Trauma System	Section 3B ii
Pooley J	London Ambulance Service NHS Trust	Section 4A

Paterson M	Nails and Screws – Department of Orthopaedic and Trauma Surgery	Section 8C
Porz W	Gargantuan Efforts in Tiny Luxemborg	Section 3C iv
Purkiss S	Thoracic Surgery Department (co-author)	Section 8G
Rock A	Selection of G-HEMS: The Dauphin	Section 2A
Rushton D	Rehabilitation (co-author)	Section 8K i
Ryan J	The Future of Trauma Training in the United Kingdom	Section 10G
Samra G	Paediatric Trauma: The HEMS Experience	Section 6L
Schmidbauer S	Arbeitskreis Notfallmedizin und Rettungswesen (ANR): The Centre for Emergency Medicine and Rescue Service, Ludwig-Maximilian University of Munich (co-author)	Section 10F
Scolari M	Value of the Spiral CT Scanner in the A&E Department (co-author)	Section 7D
Schweiberer L	Arbeitskreis Notfallmedizin und Rettungswesen (ANR): The Centre for Emergency Medicine and Rescue Service, Ludwig-Maximilian University of Munich (co-author)	Section 10F
Seager J	The Anatomy of a Call Out (co-author)	Section 5
	Firecrew Training	Section 10D
Sherriff H	MAGPAS: The Cambridge Way with GP Immediate Care	Section 3B vii
Shuttleworth R	The Anatomy of a Call Out (co-author)	Section 5
	Night Flying in the HEMS Role (co-author)	Section 11B
Skinner D	The Advanced Trauma Life Support (ATLS) Course	Section 10F
Stolpe E	The First Air Rescue Service in Germany: Christoph 1	Section 3C i b
Strunin L	The Academic Future for Trauma (co-author)	Section 11G
Teh W	The Role of the Radiologist (co-author)	Section 8H
Watkins S	An Application of EMS Lessons: Formula One Grand Prix Racing	Section 3D
Watson L	Vehicle Entrapment Rescue: HEMS Interactive 'Workshops'	Section 4C
Whitbread M	The Resuscitation Officer	Section 10E
Williams J	Dispatch Protocols	Section 6A
	Trauma Nursing	Section 10B
Wilson A	Ambulance Services – The Future	Section 4I
	The Emergency Room (1990)	Section 7A
	Hospital Trauma Team Organisation (co-author)	Section 7B
	Planning and the RLH Emergency Department (co-author)	Section 7C
Withington S	A Six Year Perspective on Intensive Care at the RLH (co-author)	Section 7F
	Data Collection in the ICU and Trauma Unit: APACHE II (co-author)	Section 9B
Wood A	Thoracic Surgery Department (co-author)	Section 8G

SECTION 1: INTRODUCTION

THE ROYAL LONDON HOSPITAL / DAILY EXPRESS/ HELICOPTER EMERGENCY MEDICAL SERVICE PREFACE TO FIRST EDITION 1992

Richard Earlam

The London Hospital celebrated its 250th anniversary in 1990 and was then granted the Royal Charter by Her Majesty the Queen who has been patron of the hospital since 1953. In 1948 with the start of the NHS it was under a Board of Governors, but like all teaching hospitals it was eventually converted into a District General Hospital (T) and placed under control of the North Thames Region with first area and then district administration. The Royal London Hospital (RLH) has been granted trust status from the 1st April 1991. It is hoped that the hospital will continue to serve the local community in the future as for the past 250 years and that like the Vicar of Bray it will survive in a similar fashion regardless of politicians, as it has done since it was founded by local doctors in 1740.

The hospital will eventually have all its acute services on one site and the anomaly of a second acute site at Mile End with its own A&E department one mile away will finally be rationalised as we lose the last relic of the previous Metropolitan board hospitals. Mile End Hospital will then serve as a new geriatric, psychiatric and rehabilitation centre in close conjunction with the RLH. Our district facilities comprise the usual District General Hospital (DGH) services and in addition the regional specialties of neurosurgery, cardiothoracic, cardiothoracic and maxillo-facial surgery, and trans-plantation. The ICU has 13 beds, there is a regional blood transfusion service and the largest haemodialysis unit in the NE Thames.

This hospital is not a designated trauma centre because there are no trauma centres in the UK. It is a University Hospital in the East End of London which has expressed a desire to raise the standards of care given to emergencies and trauma patients, because such cases comprise over half of the work load and their present treatment must be greatly improved.

This special book contains a series of short articles on the different aspects of the RLH and the associated Helicopter Emergency Medical Service (HEMS). Each of the different aspects is written by a separate expert which demonstrates that our approach is multi-disciplinary and depends for its success on many people each with his or her own expertise. It does not include all of the components but only those which require emphasis. The fact that there are no separate chapters about orthopaedic surgeons or the maxillofacial surgeons from our dental institute, does not indicate that they are unimportant. On the contrary they are almost essential; their absence in these articles indicates that they are running extremely well and efficiently, and for this service have not actually had to change. The articles, in general terms but with mixed emphasis, are all based on the three main features of any successful system:

- places
- people
- organisation

Places are capital goods and things whether they be helicopters, helipads, new A&E departments, emergency rooms or trauma units.

People include all the doctors of all ranks, nurses, paramedics, ODAs, radiographers, physiotherapists, occupational therapists, administrative staff, accounts and secretaries. We especially consider that the training of nurses is very important so this has a separate chapter. Pre-hospital care is absolutely essential and articles are dedicated to each of the three groups of the emergency services – ambulance, police and fire brigade.

Organisation implies the proper, correct and efficient use of the two main resources, namely places and people, so there are chapters on such organisations as the Advanced Trauma Life Support course, the Trauma Team, committees and protocols. These are all part of a system which should exist and evolve in every DGH and which are there to be copied and improved.

The helicopter is an integral but separate component of this system. It is stationed on the helipad above the roof at the Alexandra Wing of the RLH. This wing contains the A&E department on the ground floor, radiology on the first, operating theatres on the second and third, and academic university units on the fourth and fifth floors. The helipad is connected to the ground floor by a separate lift. There is a control room on the roof integrated with the London Ambulance Service (LAS) by telecommunication.

The LAS is responsible for calling out the helicopter to appropriate emergencies in the approximate area bounded by the M25 ring road although much of the motorway itself is covered by the neighbouring county ambulances. Use of the helicopter by the county ambulances is still sparse but is also coordinated by LAS control. Details of the helipad building (the first in the UK), the helicopter, the LAS control and cooperation with the police and fire brigades are all so important that they have separate chapters.

The helicopter does not belong to the Royal London Hospital. It was bought by the *Daily Express* and is owned by their charitable trust. The running expenses of pilots, co-pilots, operations controllers, fuel and repair costs have all been donated for a fixed period by the *Daily Express*. Nobody and, in particular, no patient is charged for transport or the saving of his life. The service covers the four Thames Regions. The whole of this area with its numerous hospitals can call upon the helicopter for either primary rescue or urgent secondary transfer through the LAS control room. Over 60 of the hospitals have CAA approved landing sites into which the helicopter can bring emergencies or transfer them to specialist centres. Only a minority of patients are brought to the RLH and there are about 12 recipient hospitals into which we regularly fly carrying the multiply injured: e.g the Brook; or specialised single system trauma, e.g paraplegia to Stoke Mandeville. The helicopter and the money for its running costs were provided through the initiative of one person - Lord Stevens of Ludgate, Chairman of *United Newspapers*. He was so impressed by the fact that every modern western country, except for the United Kingdom, had helicopters to assist land ambulances in the pre-hospital care, that he quite simply said that the country should have such a service and acted. Obviously the *Daily Express* cannot be asked to fund this forever so it is clear that this is a pilot study and must be shown to be of benefit. Evaluation of this project by the Government commenced in July 1991 and will be completed by December 1993. It is being carried out by Professor Brian Williams, Department of Community Health in Sheffield, and will concentrate on the costs and the benefit therefrom. The costs can be carefully calculated.

The benefit is quite simply measured as lives saved. However there will be additional costs from those whose lives have been saved because some will be permanently disabled. On the other hand the cost of a death lies between £500,000 and £600,000 if calculated correctly from other sources. This controversial subject is described in the last article and should be of great interest to everyone because the future of any UK helicopter service will depend on it. The trouble is that the DOH pay for the health costs and other government departments pay for subsequent costs in social security or loss of taxation, but they do not talk to each other nor cross-transfer money. In which case the moral and ethical standards of the medical profession should override mere economics and we should save as may lives as possible.

This present book does not just describe a helicopter transport service, it represents a change of present attitude to everyone in order to improve trauma care. It does not only involve the RLH, it integrates all the pre-hospital care with all the hospitals in London.

The contents of this book describe the system and why such radical changes and improvements had to be made.

TRAUMA CARE • HEMS • LONDON PREFACE TO THE SECOND EDITION 1997

Richard Earlam

The First Edition of this book was prepared while we were developing a trauma care system and contained our plans and strategy. The Second Edition, five years later, is to celebrate what has been achieved. The service is now established and all those involved have learnt a lot. Success comes from individual efforts being combined and organised as a total service in which no-one is more important than anyone else. From any person who delivers the first aid establishment of an airway at the accident scene, through to the physiotherapist who continues work six months after the initial injury, each individual is essential. This Second Edition has contributions from many of the teams of the Royal London Hospital, but most importantly it also has statements by experts outside this hospital who are clearly leaders in their field from whom we have learnt and copied.

How about leadership?

To be first in the field does not imply that this system is the best. If the second dedicated hospital helipad – built in Leeds five years after ours at the London Hospital by the same constructional engineer – is not an improvement, we are not advancing. If the design of emergency rooms built after ours, which was completed in 1990, helped by a grant from the Wolfson Foundation, with a Siemens overhead x-ray gantry, automated film development and anaesthetic services for each of the five bays, to compete with the facilities in the main theatres, is not better, other architects have learnt nothing. The last of our original demands has taken all the five years to achieve. In the First Edition we stated the case for a CT scanner in the A&E department available both for trauma and other hospital patients, but could not convince any administrator of its necessity. This is in spite of every international hospital connected with Formula One Grand Prix racing insisting that CT scanning should be immediately available in the 30 different countries that host the races. Such standards are described by Professor Sid Watkins, Emeritus Professor of Neurosurgery and the first chairman of our Helicopter Committee. Finally with the help of our present administration we have obtained a fast spiral CT scanner which can scan heads in 15 seconds and a whole body in 30 seconds. In retrospect this quantum leap forward to reduce CT scanning time to only seconds will have been worth waiting for. But the essential point is that it must now establish CT scanning as normal for other A&E departments who should not have to wait as long as us.

To catch up is easy, as the man said, but to lead is difficult. Before we started, the UK had no integrated helicopter emergency medical service and nobody in central government was remotely worried that we were the last in Europe to start such a system. There was an excellent Search and Rescue helicopter service for sea and mountain rescue which, combined with the Royal National Lifeboat Institute, funded entirely by charitable donations, deals with coastal emergencies. But neither of these efficient services caught the imagination so much that the public should demand that pre-hospital care of accidents and emergencies on the roads and on land should be similar. Luckily examples of successful helicopter services lie nearby in Germany (originated by the ADAC – their equivalent to the AA), in France (SAMU) and in Switzerland (REGA). All have been running for over 25 years and as our team visited them it was clear that few from Britain had paid the same compliment, so we really were isolated. In the USA there is a similar concentration of expertise on wartime experiences gained in Korea and Vietnam. Anybody who is interested in trauma care must read the *Journal of Trauma*, started in 1961, and will quickly realise how advanced they are in America. This includes training and the introduction of the Advanced Trauma and Life Support teaching courses. The importance of learning from these experts elsewhere is reflected in the chapters on those subjects.

Have we actually Caught Up?

The contents of this Second Edition embrace the emergency services in London, the complex mechanisms of 'call out' integrating them with transport to appropriate hospitals, pre-hospital care, and the spectrum of treatment in hospital. There is a section on data and outcome, describing the collection of information about our patients and the arguments surrounding how the outcomes of mortality and morbidity should be measured. The majority of the methodology is American because they are the best and have been at work the longest, but it remains controversial. We have analysed our data and think that we compare favourably with other helicopter services. But in the final analysis those who criticise HEMS because it costs money should answer the question what is money for but to provide a better service to self or society on this earth. As the danger of futile wars recedes through better diplomacy and less nationalism, there should be money enough, extracted by governments from the people, to pay for a helicopter service which can provide quick transport, a specialist doctor and London Ambulance Service man, on scene care, and a ten minute flight to the best hospital, all for the cost of less than £1,000 per patient compared with his average hospital bill of £10,000. Our data suggests that we have actually caught up other countries in providing good trauma care. This is not unnecessary competition entailing elimination of the inefficient because other countries are not actually competing with us and in the UK the London helicopter service is not fighting with others because each part of the country should be equally well looked after in a National Health Service. This is why we are so pleased to see other UK services developing in Scotland, Leeds, possibly Oxford and hopefully in many other centres. Copying is the best form of flattery.

What are our Plans for the Future?

Such elements of our system may indicate leadership but that is only temporary because any sensible advance should be immediately copied. Of more importance is a system of research and development based on busy activity, good data collection and teaching which attracts dedicated staff who can forever deliver new ideas and techniques. That is why there is a futuristic chapter on a possible Trauma Research Institute which could combine all the essential expertise at the Royal London Hospital into a united research and development unit, because that is what a University Hospital should offer and that is what should be our aim after the first eight years of learning about trauma care.

SECTION 2: HEMS LONDON THE FIRST EIGHT YEARS

G-HEMS: The French built Aerospatiale SA 365N – The Dauphin

SELECTION OF G-HEMS: THE DAUPHIN

Alan Rock

The Helicopter Emergency Medical Service (HEMS) was given the green light in March 1988 and *Express Newspapers* agreed to provide a helicopter in the EMS role, together with the pilots, operations staff and all running costs for 3 years – approximately £3 million. Three doctors would be provided and funded by the National Health Service (this has subsequently been increased to four) and the paramedics would be taken from the London Ambulance Service. To provide the aircraft with an operations base, the Department of Health agreed to finance the building of a rooftop helipad on top of the Royal London Hospital (RLH) with a dedicated lift from the helipad to the resuscitation room, operating theatres and intensive care unit.

The choice then had to be made of a helicopter which best met the needs of such an important and new arm for the emergency services. The requirements that had to be met were:

a) It must be a twin engine helicopter capable of operating to Instrument Flight Rules (IFR)

b) It must be large enough to carry 2 pilots, a doctor, a paramedic and up to 2 patients with one hour's fuel plus reserves.

c) A Civil Aviation Authority (CAA) approved profile with acceptable performance to be able to operate safely to an elevated helipad on top of the RLH which is situated in a congested part of East London.

d) Bearing in mind the requirements at c), the helicopter should be one with a proven track record for safety and reliability.

Three helicopters were considered – The Sikorsky S.76, the Aerospatiale SA 365N, and the Bolkow 117 – but only one was able to meet all the requirements within the time scale envisaged. This was the French built Aerospatiale SA 365N – the DAUPHIN. It first appeared in service in the early 80s and has proved to be one of the most reliable and safe helicopters ever built. The United States Coastguard has 90 Dauphins (they call them Dolphins!), Maryland State Police have 11 in the EMS role, and others are flying in the North Sea in support of the oil and gas industry. Many are being used in the corporate business aviation industry. The French armed forces use them as a weapon platform and in anti-submarine warfare. The Dauphin chosen for HEMS is an ex-Aerospatiale demonstrator with low hours. It was completely refurbished by the manufacturer to the extent that the airframe hours were zeroed. All engines and gearboxes were guaranteed less than half-life expired. The aircraft spent six months at the Aerospatiale factory near Marseilles in France undergoing the major refit to make it into an EMS helicopter. It finally left the factory late on 14th December, 1988 and flew into Battersea Heliport the following day.

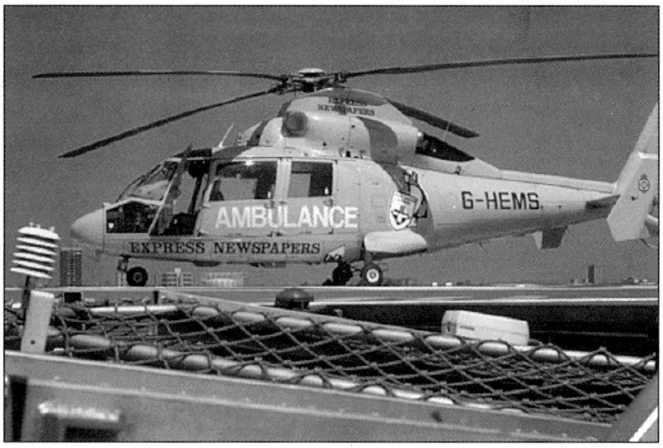

Photo: author

As to the capabilities of the Dauphin a few technical details may be of interest:

- It possesses two Turbomeca Arriel 1C engines producing 586 Horse Power (HP) at maximum continuous power.
- Maximum contingency power for 2.5 minutes on one engine is 700 HP.
- Maximum gross weight is 4000 kgs.
- Normal operating weight with 2 pilots, 2 medical crew, 2 patients with 1 hour's fuel plus reserves is 3450 kgs.
- Normal cruise speed at 3425 kgs is 150 knots (kts) giving a radius of over 50 nautical miles.
- Maximum fuel load is 915 kgs giving a range of over 400 nautical miles.
- The main navigation equipment is a KNS 81 working from VOR/DME beacons giving excellent accuracy to

within 0.5 of a nautical mile. In June 1994 a GPS (Satellite) navigation system was installed in the aircraft improving accuracy to less than 50 metres.

- The aircraft has a duplex Autopilot together with a Coupler which gives the facility of heading, height, airspeed and vertical speed control plus automatic VOR tracking and the ability to carry out an automatic instrument approach to land down to 80 feet above ground level.
- Two major safety factors of the aircraft which play an important part when operating in close contact with the general public are firstly the high ground clearance of the main rotors and secondly the enclosure of the tail rotor within the main fuselage.
- In October 1991, during the aircraft's major annual maintenance inspection, a Skyshout system was installed. One of the uses of this system is to warn the public to stay clear during the landing phase.

Since December 1988 the aircraft has flown 3000 hours to date (July 1996) averaging some 420 hours per annum. As a measure of the aircraft's reliability only 14 complete days have been lost to unserviceabilities in that time. Routine maintenance is carried out at night except for the 500 hour check when the aircraft is off line for two weeks. A replacement helicopter, a Twin Squirrel, is used during this maintenance period to ensure that there is no interruption in the Service.

Pre-hospital Costs

For the first three and a quarter years the pre-hospital costs of HEMS were mainly funded by *Express Newspapers*. The elements that were not met by the newspaper were the salaries of the doctors and paramedics, medical equipment used on missions, maintenance of the helideck and facilities, and some administrative costs. Since 1st April, 1992 the burden of all costs has been met by the Royal London Hospital Trust through the Department of Health. The way in which this has been provided has changed on occasion and is due one further major change by the 1st April 1997 with the re-structuring of the Health Authorities within London and the Greater London areas.

The vast majority of the costs are fairly stable and only vary with inflation. For example, the total number of personnel involved is 20 and looks likely to remain at this figure for some time. The aircraft hours are steady at 420 per annum and therefore fuel and oil, insurance, and maintenance costs are also fairly steady. The one expenditure that is inconsistent and can vary enormously from year to year is the component maintenance. All the major moving parts of the helicopter such as engines, gearboxes and transmissions have a finite life in respect of cycles (number of engine starts and large power changes) and/or aircraft hours. The life of these components is different from each other. For example, the main rotor gearbox has a life of 3000 hours. With a usage of 420 hours per annum this part is only changed once every 7 years. In that time some of the engine modules will have been changed 3-4 times. All of these items are extremely expensive.

Another expenditure which cannot be forecast is the unserviceabilities that occur. The aircraft has a reliable reputation but from time to time items do fail and have to be replaced. Nothing is cheap on an aircraft – even the clock cum stopwatch costs £2000!

In order to give a representative figure of cost per mission the pre-hospital costs for the last four years have been taken and divided by the number of missions. These costs have taken the salaries of the doctors, paramedics and firemen into account. A representative figure has been estimated for the medical equipment, helideck maintenance and administrative expenditure. The last four years of operations (1992-95 inclusive) are also more representative of the helicopter's usage with a work efficiency rate averaging 77%.

There are approximately 12 million people either on or inside the M25 motorway during our hours of operation, which represents 20% (one fifth) of the population of Great Britain and Northern Ireland. Any one of them can be reached by our medical team in less than 15 minutes. On the basis of the above costs, it works out at 10p per head per annum. **This is cheap medical health care.**

1992 - 1995	
Estimated Pre-hospital costs	£4,645,530
Total number of Missions	4362
Cost per Mission was £1065	

Selection and Training of Pilots

The company lays down a certain minimum of flying qualifications and experience for both captains and co-pilots as follows:

Captain	Co-pilot
Current ATPL(H) and Medical	Current CPL(H) and Medical
2000 hours total flying time	1000 hours total flying time
1500 hours Pilot-in-Command	750 hours Pilot-in-Command
1000 hours on Helicopters	750 hours on Helicopters
Current Instrument Rating	

There is no shortage of helicopter pilots in the aviation world who meet these professional requirements and the majority of applicants would demonstrate their flying skills to an entirely satisfactory standard. However, unlike

Photo: Mark Landon

most commercial operations there is an additional pressure applied to the EMS pilot. The very nature of his job is as a member of a team dedicated to saving life. This can apply undue pressure to fulfil a mission and in so doing put the aircraft and its occupants in danger. This 'press-on-itis' attitude was the cause of several EMS accidents in the United States some years ago where pilots continued a mission in worsening weather resulting in either a collision with an obstruction or an inadvertent entry into cloud and a subsequent loss of control. It is therefore important to assess the character of a prospective HEMS pilot at the interview stage as to his/her suitability. This may be difficult, but the last pilot you need is the excitable, over-enthusiastic, domineering type.

The training towards qualification as a HEMS captain or co-pilot is extensive. Full conversion training to the Aerospatiale Dauphin, including ground school as well as flying, will get the aircraft type on to the pilot's licence. Emergency and Survival training would form part of that conversion training. This would be followed by instrument training and subsequent instrument rating test. Finally there would be a 'line training' programme to train the pilot in the HEMS role. After a brief period of training the trainee would be certified competent and safe for line training with passengers. Training would then continue on actual missions under the supervision of a line training captain until he is assessed as competent to continue in his full capacity without further supervision.

HEMS always flies with two pilots. Great emphasis is placed on crew duties and co-operation throughout training. The average sector time of a HEMS mission is 6.7 minutes. In that time the aircraft has to be flown and navigated to a precise address in a congested urban area, possibly in indifferent visibility. There could be a requirement to use 4 different radios. On arrival overhead the scene a suitable landing site has to be located, a full recce made as to its suitability with regards to size, shape, slope, surface, surrounds and obstructions. Finally a safe landing has to be made without endangering persons or property. To achieve all this there has to be a precise delegation of duties between the two pilots and complete trust in each other's ability to fulfil those duties professionally.

Operating in the capital city with over ten million people within our main area of operations, HEMS has a high profile and it is essential to maintain the highest professional standards. The doctors and paramedics change at regular intervals, but the pilots are a permanent feature and provide the continuing link within the service. Being a small unit of pilots, all of whom have served since the virtual beginning, there is an excellent *esprit de corps* and dedication to the service. Motivation is not a problem. In addition, to help achieve that high standard a member of the Civil Aviation Authority flies as a co-pilot three to four times a month. Working closely with the regulating authority ensures that there is a constant monitoring of the operation.

As with any company operating to public transport standards there is a regular check of all pilots as laid down by the Air Navigation Order. Approximately every 6 months all pilots are tested on their knowledge of and ability to deal with emergencies, and their ability to fly by sole reference to instruments. Once a year each pilot is tested in their HEMS role. All this flying has to be fitted into the schedule without exceeding the allowable duty hours of the pilots. This often means that the aircraft has to be taken off line from HEMS duties in order to achieve this necessary testing.

There is no more rewarding role for a helicopter pilot than HEMS. There are others that bring more flying time in the log book but none that can give the same amount of satisfaction.

HEMS Operations

As one might expect with a new service of this nature it got off to a slow start in 1989. Making the emergency services aware of our existence and capabilities whilst determining a suitable protocol for its use takes time. Many liaison visits were made to hospitals, ambulance service headquarters and police traffic centres to publicise the service. Several demonstrations were carried out for the media. Too many of our early call-outs were to incidents which could be quite adequately dealt with by the ambulance crews on scene resulting in a large percentage of missions being aborted. One early decision taken was to restrict our area of operations, including hospital transfers, to 50 nautical miles from the centre of London. With the Dauphin this represents a response time of 20 minutes. To be caught 200 miles away from London on a transfer when a disaster of the Clapham Junction rail crash proportions occurred would indeed be embarrassing. With the arrival of our first registrar doctor in September 1989, the full potential of HEMS was finally realised. With the expertise of our medical crew, the sophistication of the medical equipment carried, a rapid response time, and subsequent transfer of victims to the correct specialist hospital for their injuries, lives could now be saved.

From the RLH the aircraft can reach any part of the M25 within 12 minutes of call out. All our tasking comes through the London Ambulance Service Control Centre in Waterloo where a Special Incident Desk (SID) is manned by one our paramedics who monitors all calls of a serious nature. A dedicated phone link exists between LAS Control and the HEMS Operations Room at the RLH. On receipt of a 'scramble' call it takes 2 minutes to get the aircraft airborne with a computer print out of all details necessary of the accident site for the aircraft's navigation system together with the nearest hospitals and their specialities.

Turning to our area of operations. As can be imagined with major airfields such as Heathrow, Gatwick, Stansted, Luton and City all in close proximity it is a complex Air Traffic Control environment requiring careful monitoring to ensure safety. Despite this congestion G-HEMS has been allocated a priority callsign 'MEDEVAC' with a special transponder code both of which can only be used when responding to primary accidents. We are then afforded the utmost priority, operating under radar cover the whole time. Further complications arise in the fact that a great deal of our flying takes place over London itself, the largest built up area in the UK. It was decided from the outset that two pilots were essential for this area, because of the cockpit workload, to give the greatest margin of safety. To respond to accidents and land within London requires certain permissions from the Civil Aviation Authority to operate outside the normal Rules of the Air. That we have gained these is a measure of the experience and professionalism of the pilots that have been chosen for HEMS. London is a 'greener' city than most people imagine and yet it is the captain's decision to choose the best and safest site to the accident without endangering persons and property. This decision has to be taken quickly knowing that lives are at stake. Out of a total of 7500 missions we were forced to abandon only 14 missions because of the lack of a suitable site to land near an accident.

Once on the ground the pilots remain with the aircraft to provide security, additional communications link and to carry further medical equipment to the accident scene when requested. Communications are a vital part of EMS

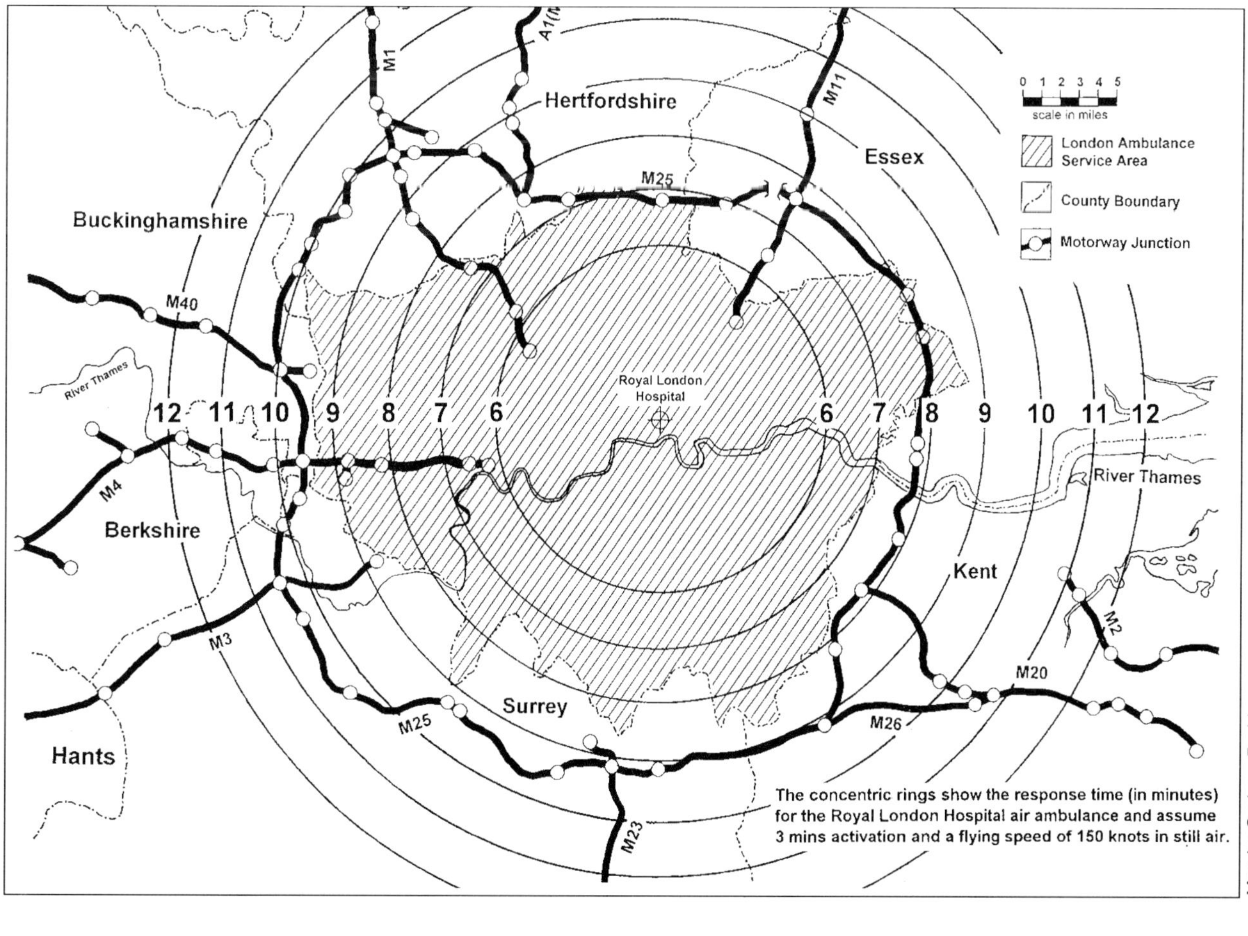

Map by Graham Budden

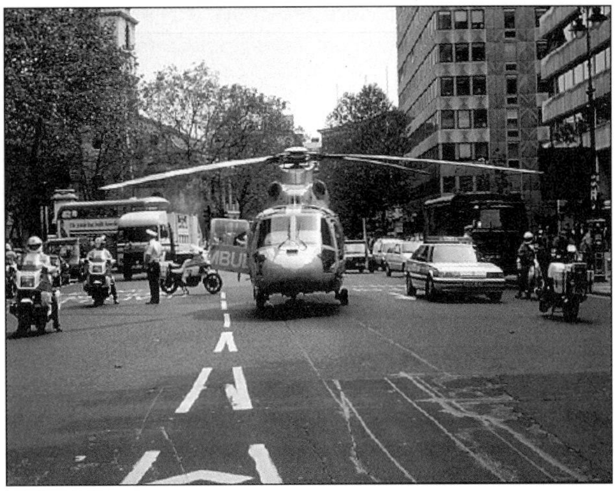

Photo: Mark Landon

operations. The aircraft now has the ability to talk not only with Air Traffic Control and the LAS Control on Aeronautical VHF radios but also with all emergency services on VHF FM/AM radios. We can also talk to the police forces at the accident site which is a distinct advantage as the police are usually the first on the scene. Communication with the police provides essential safety inputs for the aircraft and the general public, particularly during the landing phase. In addition to the aircraft radios the pilots and the medical team each have a hand-portable radio and a mobile telephone which allows communication between each other and the LAS Control Centre also allowing the doctor to contact the receiving hospital to give full details of the victim's injuries. In October 1991 the aircraft was fitted with a Skyshout system which allows the crew to use a public address from the air and warn people on the ground of our arrival where this is considered essential for the public's safety.

The decision to carry a patient from the accident to a hospital lies with the doctor. Basically if transportation by the helicopter is in the best interests of the patient then either the RLH or the nearest specialist hospital is prepared. If the patient could just as easily go by road ambulance then that will release the helicopter to be available for the next serious accident. Within the South East Counties we now have authorised landing sites at 75 hospitals. As hospitals were built before the advent of helicopters not all the sites are ideally situated and quite a number require a further short ambulance drive to the hospital. This is where the RLH comes into its own. Not only is it centrally placed within London, but being a multidisciplinary trauma unit, it can deal with the majority of trauma cases and with the dedicated trauma lift from the helipad, patients can be in the resuscitation room within two minutes of landing.

As with all aircraft operations the weather plays an important part. Fog, low cloud, poor visibility and icing are the *bete noire* of all aviators. Some of these weather phenomena are the cause of many serious accidents. We operate to rigid weather minima in the best interests of safety; we are not in the business of taking risks.

The Future

Looking to the future, there are two major areas for progress. Most important must be the adoption of a coordinated nationwide system, government funded, and administered by a central body for a uniform policy. West Germany, before unification, had such a system with 35 EMS helicopters giving almost complete coverage of the country. Not all the aircraft are government funded but the administration is managed by ADAC, their equivalent of our AA. The Germans have 26 years experience of EMS helicopters behind them which has honed the system to a razor edge operation in every respect. It is not advocated that every helicopter has to be manned to the same level as HEMS. In more rural and remote districts of the country an air ambulance manned by advanced trained paramedics could be a solution. However, the ideal solution is to have a doctor on board every helicopter to deal with the most serious trauma cases. Tied in with this nationwide coverage should be the formation of regional trauma centres which can deal with multiple injury cases. For those of us who have been involved from the beginning of HEMS and have witnessed the living proof of people who otherwise would have died without the intervention of a medical helicopter, it is a matter of great urgency that this nation acts quickly – too many unnecessary lives are being lost.

The second area for progress is night flying. It is already possible to transfer patients between airfields and hospital sites that have approved lighting and dimensions. However to respond to accidents in a primary role at night presents a number of problems, particularly in built up areas. Equipment such as Night Sun which gives much improved lighting is a necessity and Forward Looking Infra Red (FLIR) could be an advantage in some cases but cannot guarantee to pick out all dangerous obstructions. Night Vision Goggles could also be used in rural areas. They are however completely useless in the urban environment where the street and building lighting would destroy their effectiveness. Annoyance to the general public in the small hours is yet another consideration. Helicopter noise levels is a sensitive subject during normal daylight hours. Nevertheless, coverage of motorway accidents at night would provide a useful service. The extension of the service into night operations would mean extra expense with additional pilots and operations staff being required. At the moment HEMS does have clearance to complete a mission which starts in daylight hours and goes on into night time because the Royal London Hospital helipad is fully equipped and cleared for night operations.

Captain Alan Rock has been chief pilot for HEMS since 1988. He has done 18 years in the Royal Navy as a helicopter pilot, retiring with the rank of Lieutenant Commander. This was followed by 10 years working in North Sea oil and gas industries as a pilot. His total flying hours are 9,500.

DAILY EXPRESS INVOLVEMENT (1988-96)

Andrew Cameron

'There is nothing more difficult to take in hand, more perilous to conduct than to take a lead in the introduction of a new order of things, because the innovation has for enemies all those who have done well under the old conditions and lukewarm defenders in those who may do well under the new'. Niccolo Machiavelli,The Prince ,1513.

This quote in many ways says it all about the establishment and operation of HEMS. Frankly, without *Express Newspapers*, it would probably not have happened so perhaps newspapers do have their uses after all. The fourth estate can be a powerful ally when harnessed to a cause.

Express Newspapers bought the helicopter and paid full operational costs for three years, costing the not inconsiderable sum of £4 million or more. The contents of this volume tell it as it is – as it has become – a crucial arm of the Emergency Services.

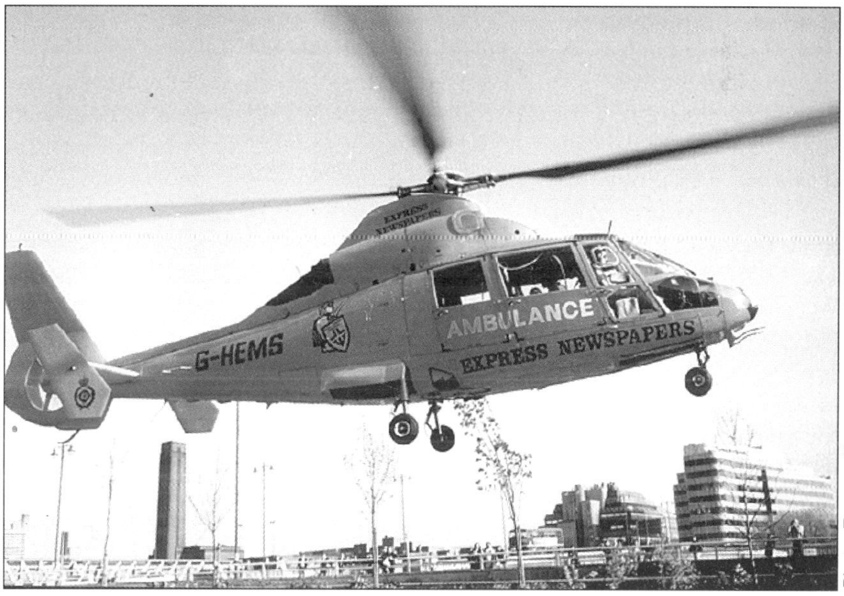

Photo: Express Newspapers

The helicopter on the Thames Embankment with the Daily Express building in the background

It started with a casual conversation between Richard Earlam, a surgeon, and Lord Stevens of Ludgate, chairman of *Express Newspapers*. Little was known in the UK about HEMS services by the media, industry or the public at large concerning its life-saving benefits not only in rural areas but also in suburban districts and city centres. Ever increasing volumes of road traffic and distances from Accident and Emergency departments do and will continue to make early and vital medical intervention for serious cases more and more difficult. The ability to deliver the patient rapidly to a suitable hospital following competent intervention on site to stabilise the patient is critical for avoiding death or long term disability with its financial dependence on the State. Lord Stevens was impressed with what he heard and rapidly spoke to me as the then Managing Director of *Express Newspapers*. What could we do? Could we cost such a service? What did helicopters cost? Dozens of questions arose. However all could be overcome with care and expertise. The involvement of the Department of Health was sought early because it was critical that they came to the party. After all, the money invested by *Express* would need to be at least matched by the Department for the construction of a helipad at the Royal London Hos-pital, the establishment of trauma beds and the operational costs attached to these developments which would include firemen, nurses, doctors and a burden of administration. What resulted has to be considered a first class example of cooperation between public and private sectors.

My dedication must be to Richard Earlam and Alastair Wilson, who have suffered sticks, stones and medical missiles in the cause of the establishment and running of these services. But they have never been shaken in their commitment.

Mr Andrew Cameron was Managing Director at Express Newspapers PLC (1986-96)

THE FIRST 1000 PATIENTS ADMITTED TO THE ROYAL LONDON HOSPITAL *VIA* HEMS

Clive Kirk

At 20 minutes past 2.00 on the afternoon of 30 August 1990 HEMS received a call to go to an elderly lady who had been knocked down by a car. She became the first patient to be admitted by HEMS to its base hospital the Royal London Hospital (RLH). At 2.08 on the afternoon of 9 March 1995 the helicopter landed on the roof of RLH with the thousandth such patient; in this case a 23 year old female motorcycle pillion passenger who had fallen off the machine at around 100 mph. Between these two events HEMS had flown 4750 missions and around 4000 patients had been treated by the HEMS doctors and paramedics.

The 1000 patients taken to RLH represents a cross section of the serious trauma occurring in London with the exception of burns. Patients with severe burns are taken direct to a burns unit. What follows is a description of the 1000 patients taken to RLH.

Age and Gender of Patients

(Table 1) As is usual in trauma series the males greatly outnumber the females. This is true of all age groups except the elderly. Trauma predominately affects the younger age groups with 75% of patients being under 50 and 17% under 16 years of age.

Causes of Injury

(Table 2) Road traffic accidents constitute the major part of the work load (53.9%) with over half involving pedestrians. Accidental falls are the next highest category, many occurring within the building and construction industry.

Table 1: Age and Gender

Males	725	mean age 34.6 years
Females	275	mean age 39.2 years
Age range	1-92 years	
Overall mean	35.8 years	
Interquartile range	20-49 years	
Under 16 years	170 patients	

Stabbing is by far the commonest assault technique resulting in admission to RLH. In addition to the 17 assault shootings there were two patients with gunshot wounds as a result of legal intervention.

Among the more uncommon injury mechanisms were a weight lifter injured as a result of over exertion and two young men who, in separate incidents, decided to commune with the lions of London Zoo with unfortunate but predictable results.

Injury Severity

Injury Severity Score:: We have used the Injury Severity Score (ISS) as a measure of the degree of injury suffered by the patients. The non-linear score ranges from 0 for the uninjured to 75 for the maximally injured. Patients in this series have covered the entire range. The normally accepted definition of serious injury is a score of 16. The median ISS of the series was 16 and the interquartile range was 5-29. Overall 528 patients had an ISS of 16 or more.

Revised Trauma Score: The on-scene impairment of physiology was estimated using the Revised Trauma Score (RTS) which combines encoded values for the systolic blood pressure, respiratory rate, and the Glasgow Coma Score (GCS). The normal (maximum) value is 7.84. Of the 1000 patients 519 had reduced RTS (38 had missing data).

Outcome

Of the 1000 patients 770 were discharged alive from RLH. Of these 530 went home and 240 were transferred to other hospitals for continuing treatment.

Table 3 shows the distribution of day of death of the 230 patients who died. Of these 156 (67.8%) died within a day of admission.

Workload on the Royal London Hospital

The impact of an additional 1000 patients on the base hospital is not inconsiderable. As a measure of this work load we looked at bed occupancy and operating theatre times.

Bed Occupancy: Table 4 shows the bed usage of the 856 patients who stayed at least one night on a ward. Of the

Table 2: Mechanisms of injury

Totals

Mechanism	Total
Transport	574
Falls	175
Assaults	112
Self harm	78
Struck by falling object	23
Machinery	15
Miscellaneous	23

Transport 574

RTA	**539**
Pedestrians	278
Drivers	121
M/c inc pillion	58
Veh. passengers	48
Cyclists	34
Railways	**13**
Horse riders	**12**
Aircraft	**6**
Water craft	**4**

Falls 175

From buildings	90
Scaffolding	28
Ladders	22
Stairs or steps	6
Others	29

Assaults 112

Stabbing	83
Hand guns	10
Shot guns	7
Hit with blunt object	8
Others	4

Self harm 78

Jumping from height	43
Jumping in front of trains or vehicles	21
Self stabbing	7
Hanging	3
Nail gun	2
Hand gun	1
Crashing car	1

Table 3: Distribution of deaths

Day of injury	126	Days 8-14	12
Next day	30	Days 15-30	7
Day 2	18	>30 days	7
Days 3-7	30		

remainder 126 died, 7 were transferred to other hospitals (6 for plastic surgery before that specialty was available at RLH and 1 for treatment of an acute psychiatric condition), 4 took self discharge and 7 were discharged home on the day of admission.

Operating Theatre time: In all there were 918 operations on 519 patients involving 2180 hours of operating time. This gives mean times for operations of 2 hours 22 minutes and per patient of 4 hours 12 minutes. One patient

Table 5: Surgical Operations

Involvement by Speciality

SPECIALITY	PATIENTS	OPERATIONS
Orthopaedic	257	401
General Surgery	214	264
Neurosurgery	159	196
Plastic Surgery	65	107
Maxillofacial	63	81
Cardiothoracic	24	28

Many of the 917 operations performed were multidisciplinary

underwent a total of 11 operations. Many of the operations were multidisciplinary and the involvement of the various surgical specialties is shown in Table 5.

Summary

In the 54 months between the first HEMS patient and the thousandth arriving at RLH the service has used the equivalent of 42 years of bed occupancy (10.4 years in high dependency beds) and the equivalent of three months continuous surgery. Over half the patients (530) went directly home from RLH, 240 were transferred to other hospitals and 230 died.

Clive Kirk is Data Manager for HEMS at the Royal London Hospital.

Table 4: Bed Occupancy

Total Patients = 856

ICU

Total admitted	160 (18.7%)
Total days	958 days
Mean stay	5.98 days
Range	1-58 days
(interquartile range)	1-8 days

Trauma Unit

Total admitted	514 (60.0%)
Total days	2800 days
Mean stay	5.45 days
Range	1-60 days
(interquartile range)	1-7 days

High Dependency Bed Days
630 patients required treatment in TU or ICU or both

Mean stay	5.97 days
Range	1-60 days
(interquartile range)	1-7 days

Total Ward Days

Total admitted	856
Total days	15320 days
Mean stay	17.9 days
Range	1-394 days
(interquartile range)	3-22 days

HEMS MISSIONS FROM THE RLH HELIPAD IN SIX YEARS

	A1	*A2*	*A3*	*A4*	*Total*	*B1*	*B2*	*Total*	*C1*	*C2*	*Total*	*D*	*Total*	*% Abort*
1990														
AUG	2	0	2	1	5	1	14	15	3	1	4	43	67	65
SEPT	3	0	2	1	6	0	4	4	13	2	15	44	69	63
OCT	7	1	1	1	10	3	11	14	18	4	22	60	106	56
NOV	1	0	2	0	3	0	1	1	5	1	6	12	22	54
DEC	7	0	0	0	7	0	3	3	11	2	13	26	49	53
(Totals 1990	**20**	**1**	**7**	**3**	**31**	**4**	**33**	**37**	**50**	**10**	**60**	**185**	**313**	**59)**
1991														
JAN	8	0	1	1	10	1	4	5	20	5	25	42	82	51
FEB	5	0	4	2	11	0	8	8	15	3	18	32	69	46
MAR	16	0	1	3	20	2	4	6	24	4	28	83	137	61
APR	17	2	3	12	34	1	4	5	30	5	35	56	130	43
MAY	14	2	9	16	41	1	3	4	19	12	31	36	112	32
JUNE	11	2	5	14	32	0	3	3	27	10	37	40	112	36
JULY	17	4	3	18	42	2	4	6	14	5	19	32	99	32
AUG	18	0	1	15	34	3	2	5	23	8	31	20	90	22
SEPT	18	2	9	12	41	2	6	8	19	5	24	23	96	24
OCT	8	1	2	3	14	1	2	3	10	4	14	4	35	11
NOV	13	1	2	11	27	0	6	6	16	5	21	14	68	21
DEC	15	0	0	8	23	1	0	1	13	6	19	11	54	20
(Totals 1991	**160**	**14**	**40**	**115**	**329**	**14**	**46**	**60**	**230**	**72**	**302**	**393**	**1084**	**36)**
1992														
JAN	4	2	1	7	14	0	2	2	9	8	17	23	56	41
FEB	10**	0	2	8	20	1	7	8	15	13	28	13	69	19
MAR	19	0	6	7	32	1	2	3	20	9	29	23	87	26
APR	10	2	8	6	26	2	2	4	16	8	24	37	91	41
MAY	17*	2	6	13	38	0	5	5	19	13	32	25	100	25
JUNE	15	1	6	3	25	0	6	6	29	10	39	27	97	28
JULY	15	1	5	6	27	0	6	6	18	6	24	44	101	44
AUG	17	1	8	11	37	1	8	9	19	9	28	26	100	26
SEPT	17	1	6	11	35	0	4	4	10	9	19	25	83	30
OCT	14	0	1	7	22	2	1	3	11	7	18	18	61	30
NOV	12	1	2	10	25	2	6	8	9	8	17	20	70	29
DEC	9	1	3	7	20	2	1	3	11	5	16	19	58	33
(Totals 1992	**159**	**12**	**54**	**96**	**321**	**11**	**50**	**61**	**186**	**105**	**291**	**300**	**973**	**31)**
1993														
JAN	8	0	6	16	30	0	2	2	16	6	22	14	68	21
FEB	8	0	1	7	16	1	0	1	10	8	18	26	61	43
MAR	14	0	12	21	47	0	2	2	15	4	19	26	94	28
APR	18	1	13	9	41	2	4	6	18	9	27	28	102	27
MAY	30	1	6	18	55	3	3	6	20	11	31	12	104	12
JUNE	26	0	7	20	53	0	3	3	13	4	17	16	89	18
JULY	27	2	8	18	55	0	5	5	18	5	23	19	102	19
AUG	24	1	9	7	41	1	5	6	23	8	31	14	92	15
SEPT	24	4	8	11	47	1	2	3	11	5	16	8	74	11
OCT	28*	0	9	10	47	0	3	3	16	3	19	18	87	21
NOV	23*	1	5	9	38	1	5	6	9	7	16	13	73	18
DEC	27**	0	3	11	41	1	1	2	8	9	17	25	85	29
(Totals 1993	**257**	**10**	**87**	**157**	**511**	**10**	**35**	**45**	**177**	**79**	**256**	**219**	**1031**	**21)**
1994														
JAN	25	1	2	13	41	2	0	2	18	9	27	27	97	28
FEB	27	1	9	11	48	1	4	5	17	7	24	21	98	21
MAR	30**	0	5	15	50	1	6	7	27	4	31	19	107	28
APR	12	2	11	18	43	0	5	5	12	7	19	25	92	28
MAY	30*	2	5	26	63	0	6	6	21	8	29	29	127	23
JUNE	24	2	4	15	45	1	2	3	25	11	36	34	118	29
JULY	26	5	12	15	58	1	2	3	22	12	34	31	126	25
AUG	22*	2	13	12	49	2	2	4	19	4	23	22	98	22
SEPT	31	2	8	15	56	0	1	1	18	7	25	24	100	23
OCT	29	0	4	23	56	2	3	5	20	8	28	9	98	9
NOV	26	1	6	6	39	0	0	0	27	7	34	12	85	14
DEC	22	1	5	1	29	1	1	2	24	8	32	16	79	20
(Totals 1994	**304**	**19**	**84**	**170**	**577**	**11**	**32**	**43**	**250**	**92**	**342**	**269**	**1231**	**22)**
1995														
JAN	5	0	6	4	15	0	3	3	22	7	29	16	63	25
FEB	29	3	7	2	41	0	3	3	25	5	30	18	92	20
MAR	27	2	4	9	42	1	2	3	41	10	51	20	116	17
APR	35**	6	5*	10	56	2	6	8	30	8	38	18	120	15
MAY	40*	4	6	12	62	1	7	8	37	6	43	17	130	13
JUN	31*	1	4	13	49	1	4	5	29	4	33	22	109	20
JUL	30*	4	7	13	54	1	2	3	28	11	39	11	107	10
AUG	20	2	4	13	39	0	5	5	18	10	28	15	87	17
SEP	23	2	1	13	39	0	2	2	20	5	25	22	88	25
OCT	15	3	2	13	33	0	3	3	12	5	17	12	65	18
NOV	16	3	3	21	43	1	2	3	26	1	27	12	85	14
DEC	12	1	7	11	31	0	2	2	10	3	13	15	61	25
(Totals	**283**	**31**	**56**	**134**	**504**	**7**	**41**	**48**	**298**	**75**	**373**	**198**	**1123**	**18)**
1996														
JAN	16	0	4	12	32	0	1	1	10	10	20	22	75	29
FEB	28	2	4	9	43	1	0	1	21	8	29	29	102	28
MAR	18	3*	11	18	50	1	2	3	28	12	40	28	121	23
APR	29	5	5	18	57	1	1	2	30	10	40	28	127	22
MAY	33	3	7	11	54	1	3	4	42	6	48	20	126	16
JUN	19	2	10	11	42	0	1	1	34	6	40	32	115	29
JUL	25*	4	11	18	58	0	4	4	39	8	47	19	128	15
(Totals 1996	**168**	**19**	**52**	**97**	**336**	**4**	**12**	**16**	**304**	**60**	**264**	**178**	**794**	**22)**
Grand totals for 6 years	**1351**	**106**	**380**	**772**	**2609**	**61**	**249**	**310**	**1395**	**493**	**1888**	**1742**	**6549**	**27**
	A1	*A2*	*A3*	*A4*	*Total*	*B1*	*B2*	*Total*	*C1*	*C2*	*Total*	*D*	*Total*	*% Abort*

A: Missions resulting in patients being taken from scene to hospital accompanied by HEMS doctor.
A1 = To RLH by air A2 = To RLH by road,
A3 = To other hospital by air, A4 = To other hospital by road

B: Transfers from one hospital to another accompanied by HEMS doctor
B1 = To RLH, B2 = To other hospitals.

C: Other missions completed
C1 = Ground assists, patient to hospital unaccompanied,
C2 = Ground assists, patient dead at scene.

D: Aborted missions

* 2 patients carried on single mission

SECTION 3: CONCEPTS OF A TRAUMA CARE SYSTEM

Introduction

Richard Earlam

The Helicopter Emergency Medical Service in London commenced properly after the raised helipad at the Royal London Hospital was completed in August 1990. Prior to that, many plans had to be completed which included preparatory work with the helicopter itself, training staff to fly it, practice over London and cooperating with the London Ambulance Service, the police, fire brigade and Civil Air Authority. About 1,000 flights over London were performed with the helicopter stationed at Biggin Hill and when these are added to the 6,500 sorties done from the helipad, the total figure becomes 7,500 flights up to August 1996. This preliminary work in a new field could not have been achieved without help and assistance from other centres of excellence and many experts from other countries. The most important of these were Dr Howard Champion, FRCS, from Washington DC in the USA, Gerhard Kugler and Erwin Stolpe from Munich. Ken Boffard, FRCS, from South Africa helped by staying with us, advising and writing a report in the early days. But the authors in all these sections are also important to us and their articles are subdivided into systems :

A. USA
B. United Kingdom
C. European
D. Formula One Grand Prix

This last article was written by our chairman Professor Sid Watkins, FRCS, Emeritus Professor of Neurosurgery at the Royal London Hospital, who is the doctor in charge of medical care at the various Formula One Grand Prix races throughout the world. So we have also had his accumulated experience of trauma care in different countries to hand. The treatment of trauma is not actually a competitive sport but the editor sees absolutely no reason why there should not be a competition to obtain the best possible treatment for the patients one has to look after. When there is actually only one HEMS in the UK and we are the last country in the European Community to have one, it becomes even clearer why we had to look abroad at other countries.

The experience of trauma care in the USA is huge and their best beats the world. The Shock Trauma Centre in Baltimore treats 700 cases of major trauma each year and patients are brought in by helicopter onto a helipad which can handle 5 helicopters simultaneously. It is extremely difficult to obtain any similar figures for the UK but the busiest hospital for trauma is Stoke-on-Trent which handles up to 200 major trauma cases each year whereas the RLH has 185. The Major Trauma Outcome Study (UK) has data from less than 30 centres, contributed voluntarily from the total of 250 hospitals in the UK, and there are no centrally collected data to give us a figure for major trauma cases coming to hospitals in the UK in spite of 15,000 people dying from trauma each year. So we have to go to America for data and experience. They founded their Major Trauma Outcome Study many years ago based on the measurement of anatomical injury (Abbreviated Injury Scale AIS) and patho-physiological response (Trauma Score TS and Revised Trauma Score RTS, combined to give an Injury Severity Score, ISS). We have copied. They started superb teaching courses based on the Advanced Life Support Course (ATLS) which sired all their sons, daughters and grandchildren. We have copied. They institutionalised their hospitals into Level I (the best), Level II and Level III standards for trauma care. We did not need to copy at this moment, but some hospitals, which are mainly University Hospitals, have all the specialties on site and are like Level I centres, others remain Level III like 'cottage hospitals'. This must never be used in a disparaging negative sense and whenever it has been used as a term, it should be compulsory to provide fast transport to a larger centre. So in this area we have not copied, but we have learnt. Last of all, but not finally because there is much more to learn, they have founded and still publish the very best journal in the world on trauma care, the *Journal of Trauma* started in 1961. Do not copy it, merely pay the subscription and read it.

All these sections describe their own system and it will be seen that many do not have associated helicopter transport when it is not necessary. Each country has its own system and the UK has many different systems developed over the years. The history of the Birmingham Accident Hospital, written by PS London, MBE, FRCS, is included because the question must be answered – why was this excellent early solution to trauma care not copied? All must combine with the Emergency Services which are described in more detail in the next Section 4. It is a philosophical problem whether trauma care systems should develop haphazardly or be centrally directed. It is for this reason, but also important because of their expertise, that the systems in Germany, France and Switzerland should be examined. The full integration for a centralist, collective

SECTION 3: CONCEPTS OF A TRAUMA CARE SYSTEM

nationwide solution, namely SAMU in France, is described by Professor Huguenard in the best summary I have ever seen. The article on the helicopter service in Luxembourg is included to show what a small country has achieved by voluntary contributions. It must bring up the question as to what central government and its collection of taxes is really there for if not to look after the people. Is it really the correct solution to ask the inhabitants to contribute to a charity for HEMS with their money left over after the government has first extracted its taxes and health care insurance? Read on...

No – This is not downtown Dallas. This is the City of London seen from above the helipad at the Royal London Hospital (bottom left)

Photograph by Simon Hazelgrove Photography, Aeromega Ltd, Stapleford Aerodrome, Stapleford Tawney, Essex RM4 1RL

EMS SYSTEMS, TRAUMA CENTRES AND TRAUMA SYSTEMS IN THE USA

Andy Newton, Peter Mahoney

1. Emergency Medical Service (EMS) Systems

EMS Systems have evolved to deal with all categories of emergency but, in the United States, there are many examples of special emphasis being placed on the needs of the trauma patient. Trauma is one of the most serious public health issues facing the USA. Each year 140,000 Americans are fatally injured and a further 80,000 suffer long term disability.[1] In the majority of cases trauma can be prevented.

The aim of an EMS system is to rapidly attend the patient, provide quality on scene care, and take the patient to the appropriate hospital. To use the words of Trunkey, *'get the right patient to the right hospital in the right amount of time'*.

Although this sounds relatively simple, a consideration of the stages involved highlights the areas where the system can fail. First, someone has to recognise the patient needs help and then call for help. Lack of telephones in a rural area or non-working telephones due to vandalism will delay this stage. The call, when received, has to be processed by an emergency operator and an appropriate response initiated by tasking a vehicle and crew (if available). This response may be an ambulance with a crew trained in basic life support, an ambulance with an advance life support trained crew or, as in the case of HEMS, a helicopter with a doctor and paramedic team. The ambulance has to find the patient (which can be difficult in bad weather and when street signs are unclear), give appropriate care and take the patient to hospital. Depending on local protocols this may be the nearest hospital or the hospital most appropriate to the patient's illness or injuries. The two are not necessarily the same.

Although producing an Emergency Medical Service to meet the needs of all patients sounds a straightforward concept in practice, there are many difficulties. The American Emergency Medical Services Act was one of the first structured attempts to identify the components of a basic infrastructure.

2. Components of an EMS System

In 1973 the US Congress passed the Emergency Medical Services Systems Act. This Act set out to encourage the development of comprehensive regional EMS systems throughout the country, and required that each funded system address 15 system components.[2,3]

The 15 essential EMS components are:-

1. *Manpower:* including paramedics, doctors, nurses and communications personnel.
2. *Training:* clinical training and continuing education for the above people.
3. *Communications:* including public access by a 'single access number' (such as 911 or 999) and links between the dispatch centre and the personnel and vehicles on the ground (or in the air!).
4. *Transportation:* ground, water and air vehicles to meet the transportation and EMS characteristics of the system area.
5. *Facilities:* such as emergency receiving rooms.
6. *Critical Care Units:* providing specialist care for burns, trauma , neonates and acute cardiac care.
7. *Public safety agencies:* police and others likely to be the first on scene at an incident to have appropriate training, equipment and communications to link in with the EMS system.
8. *Consumer participation:* public input into the systems' policies.
9. *Access to care:* all patients to have access whether or not they have the ability to pay.
10. *Patient transfer:* to specialist emergency centres, definitive care centres and rehabilitation.
11. *Coordinated patient record keeping:* to cover the patient from initial contact with the system in the pre-hospital phase through to discharge.
12. *Public information and education:* to explain to people how to access the system (very important if the universal access number has been changed or recently introduced).
13. *Review and evaluation:* of the quality of the services provided.
14. *Disaster planning:* to respond to mass casualties, natural disasters or national emergencies.
15. *Mutual aid:* agreements with neighbouring services.

Many factors led to the writing and passing of this Act. Among the most influential were a report by a 1966 National Academy of Science National Research Council (NAS-NRC) and comparisons with military EMS.

The military EMS system in place in Vietnam used trained medical and paramedical personnel, adequate communications systems and appropriate ground and air ambulance services.

The 1966 NAS-NRC report, *Accidental Death and Disability: The Neglected Disease of Modern Society*, documented the failure of the US health system to care for the injured patient. Inadequacies cited included lack of public instruction in first aid, lack of research into trauma and shock, and emergency departments understaffed with inexperienced personnel. Similar problems existed within the ambulance services.

The NAS-NRC report proposed recommendations for EMS development.

3. Trauma Centres

Hospitals managing trauma in the USA – Trauma Centres – are designated by 'Levels' according to the facilities offered and staff available.[4]

- Level III centres are capable of treating most trauma victims and stabilising critically ill patients until transfer to an appropriate higher level facility can be arranged.
- Level II centres can manage almost all critically ill patients, but may not offer all sub-specialities and usually do not perform teaching and research.
- Level I centres can manage all trauma patients, cope with mass casualties and conduct research.

'Level' designation is also influenced by the specialities and grades of staff resident on duty to receive patients. Examples for a Level I centre include:

- In house trauma surgeon and anaesthetist
- Optimal trauma patient care
- Adequate buildings, staff and equipment
- Trauma quality assurance process
- Trauma training programmes
- 600-1000 trauma patients per year
- Trauma public education
- Teaching programme
- Research

Guidelines and standards for designation of a centre is given in the EMS acts and by the American College of Surgeons Committee on Trauma.

4. Trauma Systems

A 'trauma system' provides regionalised trauma care. Eight essential characteristics of a trauma system have been identified by West,[5] in a 1987 survey of US systems. These are:

1. The presence of a lead agency with legal authority to designate trauma centres. 'Designation' of a hospital requires independent verification of the hospital's compliance with accepted standards and adherence to patient transport guidelines.
2. The use of a formal process for trauma centre designation.
3. The use of American College of Surgeons' standards for trauma centres.
4. The use of an out-of-area survey team for trauma centre designation
5. A limit to the number of designated trauma centres in a community, based on assessment of population need. (Failure to limit the number of designated trauma centres means that costs are duplicated and experience of the medical, nursing and paramedical personnel diluted.)
6. Application of written triage criteria allowing by-pass of non-trauma centre hospitals.
7. The presence of ongoing monitoring systems for trauma centres.
8. The state-wide availability of trauma centres (i.e the percentage of the area covered by trauma centres).

Bazzoli et al[6] felt these criteria have limitations in that they deal mainly with the characteristics and coordination of the trauma centres, but not other system activities. Further areas of importance in the 'system' are pre-hospital triage protocols, medical direction, interfacility transfer agreements and on-going system audit. Their study found that only five states could be considered to have complete trauma systems.

West,[5] set out a five-step strategy for developing a trauma system:

1. Obtain data to define the local trauma problem.
2. Develop a regional plan dealing with care from the pre-hospital phase through to rehabilitation based on standards set by the American College of Surgeons.
3. Identify barriers to change (usually economic, political and social such as staff not wishing to change working patterns).
4. Develop a management structure (such as a Department of Health) with the legal authority to designate centres and coordinate protocol developments.
5. Implement the plan, encouraging regional hospitals to participate. The latter could be assisted by appropriate legislation.

Summary and Conclusions

Trauma in the US has reached epidemic proportions and presents an enormous social and medical challenge.

Systems of trauma care work to save lives and reduce disability in severely injured casualties.[7]

Development of systems within the USA has been inconsistent; the 1973 EMS Act was not extended into the 1980s and some systems did not progress due to lack of funds. Trauma centres have closed, often due to financial difficulties. Causes have included not being reimbursed for care provided, and competition between centres for patients and available resources.

The recent availability of federal grant support has, however, renewed interest by state agencies in developing trauma systems. The 1990 Trauma Care Systems Planning and Development Act has awarded grants both to initiate development and refine present systems.[8]

Efforts must, however, be directed at preventing injury as well as treating injury when it occurs. Trauma prevention requires a combination of public education, legislation and efforts by manufacturers to improve the safety of their products. Although the injury toll can be reduced, it will not be eliminated completely. Avoidable injury has been regarded as the price society pays for access to motor vehicles, alcohol and, particularly in the USA, firearms.[9] Health care systems need to meet the challenge of dealing with trauma through improved communication, organisation and integration of pre-hospital and hospital care.

References

1. Model Trauma System Plan, US Department of Health and Human Services, Public Health Service, Health Resources and Services Administration. September 30 1992.
2. A Brief History of Emergency Medical Services. In: Fitch, JJ EMS Management: Beyond the Street, 1993. Jems Communications, Carlsbad,CA.
3. Mustalish AC, Post C. History. In: Kuehl AE (Ed). Prehospital Systems and Medical Oversight. Mosby Year Book, St Louis, 1994: 3-27.
4. Cicala RS, Murphy MT. Trauma Centres, Systems and Plans. In: Grande CM. Textbook of Trauma Anaesthesia and Critical Care. Mosby Year Book, St Louis, 1993: 56-70.
5. West JG, Williams MJ, Trunkey DD, Wolferth CC. Trauma Systems. Current status-Future Challenges. JAMA 1988; 259: 3597-3600.
6. Bazzoli GJ, Madura KJ, Cooper GF, Mackenzie EJ, Maier RV. Progress in the development of Trauma Systems in the United States. JAMA 1995; 273: 395-401.
7. Cooper GF, Ryan S, Ehrlich F. System Related Complications. In: Mattox KL (Ed). Complications of Trauma. Churchill Livingstone Inc, New York, 1994: 155-63.
8. Trunkey D. Trauma Systems. A model for Regionalised Care. JAMA 1995; 273: 421-2.
9. Nyhus LM (Ed). Problems in General Surgery; Social and Economic Problems in Trauma Care. Vol 7, No2. Lippincott. June 1990.

Mr Andy Newton, A&E Services, Stafford Ambulance Service.

Dr Peter Mahoney, Emeritus HEMS Registrar, Senior Registrar in Anaesthesia, Nottingham City Hospital.

THE BIRMINGHAM EXPERIMENT – WHAT HAPPENED?

P S London

In 1841 the initiative, drive and, when necessary, the financial support of William Sands Cox, bore fruit in the form of the Queen's Hospital in Birmingham, where he had seen the need greatly to improve the facilities for teaching medical students. One hundred years later, the initiative and drive of William Gissane, with the financial support of industrialists in Birmingham, set about establishing the Birmingham Accident Hospital and Rehabilitation Centre in the former Queen's Hospital which had been supplanted by Birmingham's new Queen Elizabeth Hospital. The principal purpose was to provide prompt and skilled care for the increasing number of casualties in the wartime factories of the city and thereby to return as many as possible of the victims to productive employment as quickly as possible.

Gissane grasped the opportunity to set up a comprehensive accident service for Birmingham as a whole that would seek to prevent, as well as to treat, all sorts of injuries and also their disabling consequences. To this end, he obtained the support of the University in teaching nurses, students and others as well as doctors, and of the Medical Research Council in research in the treatment of burns and in the cause and prevention of industrial injuries and their consequences. In later years, road accidents figured prominently in this and his colleagues', notably Dr JP Bull's research. After the war ended and staff could be increased to deal with the steadily increasing load of casualties that came from well beyond as well as within Birmingham, the hospital's organisation reached its final form. Apart from the Burns Unit, there were three surgical teams that dealt with injuries of all grades of severity and of all parts of the body – a truly general sort of surgery that was ungrudgingly supplemented when necessary by specialists from other hospitals and units in Birmingham.

Each of the three teams had two surgeons and an anaesthetist as well as junior staff. They took it in turn to treat all sorts of casualties attending during 24 hours (48 at weekends) and to follow them up thereafter. The system was based on Gissane's three principles which were:

- to separate the injured from the ill;
- to provide continuity of care, and
- to do this under close supervision by experience surgeons.

This meant that except for the few that it was necessary to transfer to special units, each patient remained under the care of the same team from the time of arrival (and sometimes even from the scene of the accident) at the hospital, through any necessary resuscitation, operations, in-patient and out-patient care. Any secondary treatment required could usually be provided by the same team.

In addition to the clinical staff, Dr S Sevitt provided a unique and comprehensive pathological service that he combined with research in a wide range of subjects. These included renal failure, thrombo-embolism, the blood supply of bone and healing of fractures as well as bacteriological and pathophysiological studies.

All the senior staff had whole-time contracts and their interests and activities were concentrated on the comprehensive care of injured persons. From 1950 onwards they spread their knowledge and skill by means of the courses provided by the Institute of Accident Surgery and by many publications. This concentration of interests, service and research quickly established the Accident Hospital's reputation to such an extent that colleagues from other hospitals in Birmingham ruefully reported that when they visited other countries the Accident Hospital seemed to be the only hospital in Birmingham that had been heard of.

Within the general service that they provided, individual members of the staff developed special interests and, in addition to those already mentioned, the names Ruscoe Clarke, Essex Lopresti, Mervyn Evans, Hicks, Jackson and Proctor became well known and were rewarded by civil honours as well as eponymous, Hunterian and other Lectureships in Britain and abroad. Gissane used to speak of the Birmingham Experiment as though to emphasise that what he had conceived and established should be regarded as a provisional pattern for what he believed should become a nationwide system of care of the injured. He did not live to see something like his vision accepted, at least on paper, but he was spared the bitterness of seeing his service gradually eroded and finally abandoned just over 50 years after he started his experiment. What went wrong?

Having spent more than 30 years in the service of a unique institution it would be all too easy to be critical and unrealistic about what happened to it but the following are facts. When the Accident Hospital began its work there were those in Birmingham that saw no need for a group of surgeons to take over some of the responsibilities that they saw as their own, even though they were delegated to junior staff. Fortunately, as already mentioned, there were others who gave generously of their time and skill when requested to do so.

Orthopaedic surgeons have played a large part in raising the standards of care of injured persons. The then Mr Robert Jones established a comprehensive emergency service for workmen injured during the building of the Manchester Ship Canal and later, during the Kaiser's war, brought a similar breadth of vision and organisational ability to the treatment, including rehabilitation, of wounded soldiers. The then Mr Harry Platt established a fracture service in Manchester in 1914. Messrs Watson-Jones and Osmond-Clarke gave the Royal Air Force an outstandingly successful rehabilitation service. LW Plewes recognised the role of industry in rehabilitation and JC Scott applied his wartime experience to the establishment of an exemplary accident service in Oxford.

In the circumstances it was not surprising that orthopaedic surgeons saw themselves as the right persons to be in charge of what were to change their names from Casualty to Accident and Emergency departments and, it was intended, to restrict their service to conditions that were beyond General Practitioners' abilities. Hardly had these changes taken place than the orthopaedic surgeons were dismayed to find that the departments under their care continued to receive large numbers of all sorts of mild and even trivial conditions that were in no sense orthopaedic; a change of name did nothing to realise Gissane's principle of separating the injured from the ill. The orthopaedic reaction was to press for what one distinguished surgeon described as 'a super GP in Casualty'. So came the new specialty of Casualty Consultants, with recognition and appropriate training programmes and career structure. Unfortunately from the point of view of surgeons wishing to devote themselves to the care of injured persons, orthopaedic surgeons did not see any need to press with comparable determination for the acceptance of accident surgery as a specialty. That might to some extent have been because the treatment of injuries of the locomotor system provides a large, but not the most vital, part of the work of accident surgeons, who could, in this respect, be regarded as unnecessary competitors. Also, medical political policy became opposed to the concept of special units that were not attached to the larger general hospitals. In addition, without a specialty with its own training programme and career structure it became increasingly difficult to find surgeons with the necessary skill and experience that would be willing to concentrate their attention on the comprehensive care of the injured and the Birmingham Accident Hospital and Rehabilitation Centre closed its doors little more than 50 years after it first provided its service. Moving to a 'trauma unit' in a general hospital had depressing consequences for both morale and the quality of service that could be offered.

In the light of all this, it might seem beyond all doubt that Gissane's 'Birmingham Experiment' had failed and, in a sense, it did. On the other hand, at least lip service has now been paid (if without credit to him) to Gissane's recommendation that what British surgeons ought to call major accident services rather than Level 1 Trauma Centres should be established nationwide.

If this leads ultimately to putting staff with the necessary interest, availability and goodwill at the service of injured persons as they were in Britain's first major accident service, Gissane's example will have been followed and the success of his experiment established.

PS London, MBE, FRCS, was Surgeon to the Birmingham Accident Hospital from 1954 to his retirement in 1987. He had been Registrar to Mr Ruscoe Clarke of the Burns Unit and then to Mr William Gissane from October 1950 to June 1952. He was Senior Surgeon from 1980 and Chairman of the Medical Staff Committees. Originally Secretary of the Institute of Accident Surgery, he ended up as Chairman of its Council.

WILLIAM GISSANE

P S London

William Gissane died in his sleep on 1st April 1981, the 40th anniversary of the establishment of the hospital that he did so much to make world famous.

He was born on 28th April 1898 in Sydney, the son of a prosperous tea merchant. At both school and university he distinguished himself at cricket, rugger and boxing. After a spell in the Royal Australian Artillery he went to Sydney University where he graduated in medicine in 1925. He had intended to become an architect but he yielded to his father's persuasion that medicine offered a better financial prospect. Nonetheless, his surgical planning and organisation showed the breadth of vision and attention to detail that would have served him well as an architect.

William Gissane 1898-1981

Shortly after graduating he came to Britain. He worked at St. Mark's and the Royal Devon and Exeter Hospitals and became FRCS in Edinburgh in 1927 and FRCS in England in 1932. Experience in Boehler's Allgemeine Unfallkrankenhaus in Vienna, as Surgeon Specialist to the London County Council and Surgeon in Charge of the Accident Unit at St James' Hospital, Balham and in the Fracture Service of Lewisham Hospital, prepared him well for his appointment in July 1941 as Clinical Director and Surgeon-in-Chief of the newly established Birmingham Accident Hospital. This experience enabled him to publish papers on intussusception, successful treatment of a stab wound of the heart, post-traumatic cerebrospinal rhinorrhoea and fractures. The pugnacity and determination of a boxer showed in the way in which Gissane went about the establishment of the hospital and its policy and directing the activity of his colleagues, but other sporting qualities showed in the way in which he went about creating a team of doctors, nurses, remedial therapists and others, both inside and outside the hospital. At the same time, he altered the buildings so as to improve the service that could be provided for injured persons.

Honours and distinctions included Vice-Presidency and Emeritus Fellowship of the British Orthopaedic Association, Honorary Membership of the British Association of Plastic Surgeons and the American Society of Automotive Engineers. Lectureships included the Joseph Henry in Occupational Medicine, the Robert Jones and the Alex Simpson-Smith and Ruscoe Clarke Memorial. In 1959 he visited Australia and New Zealand as Sir Arthur Sims Commonwealth travelling Professor and in 1973 the Worshipful Company of Carmen elected him Carman of the Year and presented him with a medal.

Gissane used to quote a Chinese proverb that included the recommendation 'if you plan for 100 years, plant men'. Gissane's choice of colleagues conformed with that recommendation but it was no fault of his that his plans were brought to nought after little more than half that time.

STOKE-ON-TRENT TRAUMA SYSTEM

Peter Oakley

The North Staffordshire Hospital is a 1300-bedded district general hospital situated in the North West Midlands with regional neurosurgical and cardiothoracic units and a postgraduate medical school. The emergency department is the third busiest in the UK, treating more than 105,000 patients per year. The Intensive Care Unit admits more than 600 patients per year with almost 25% of the bed days accounted for by trauma patients.

Since 1991, the hospital has been acting as a pilot trauma centre. It receives 220 severely-injured patients per year (Injury Severity Score > 15)[1] and over 1200 patients with serious injuries satisfying the Major Trauma Outcome Study (MTOS)[2] criteria. While less than in most North American cities, these numbers exceed those in the majority of British centres.

Since the start of the trial period, the trauma system has been evolving. Initially the trauma team call-out involved a junior representative from each surgical speciality. This resulted in too many doctors attending the patient simultaneously, many of whom were not needed or were too junior to make important decisions. The current 'nuclear' team soon developed. The immediate cardiorespiratory problems are addressed by the nuclear team, but other specialists are called in as soon as a specific problem is identified or suspected. From the outset the trauma team leader role has been assumed by a group of six consultants rather than junior staff. Until recently, the team leaders were resident 24 hours per day and when on duty treated medical and other surgical emergencies as well as cases of major trauma. As the local purchasers will no longer fund consultants to sleep in the hospital, the team leader is now non-resident but is still rapidly available owing to the use of ambulance service pagers. The team leader can be alerted from the scene of an accident via ambulance control, minimising any delay in trauma team preparation. Changing the resident status of the team leader has made little difference to the trauma team response.

In the first few years as a trauma centre, considerable effort has been put into immediate resuscitation in the emergency department. The approach to resuscitation closely follows that of the Advanced Trauma Life Support (ATLS) course with meticulous spinal precautions in all cases of severe blunt trauma.[3] Definitive airway care and early invasive monitoring are particularly emphasised in severe head injury. There is immediate preparation for vigorous fluid therapy but due recognition is given to the current trend towards low volume resuscitation and early resuscitative surgical intervention.

Essential additional equipment for the resuscitation room, such as robust portable patient monitors, high flow blood warmers and a portable diagnostic ultrasound machine, were obtained. Intensive care methods have been widely employed with the vast majority of major trauma patients receiving invasive arterial blood pressure monitoring prior to being transferred for CT scanning.

Until the junior staff had been sufficiently trained, the team leader remained 'hands on', but the need for a structured training programme to develop resuscitation skills in the junior staff has been increasingly recognised. ATLS courses are provided four times per year. In order to provide training for the entire system, the courses are shared with the surrounding hospitals. In addition, courses in Trauma Anaesthesia and Disaster Management have been been run regularly.

At the start of the pilot trauma system, the level of pre-hospital care was insufficient to allow pre-hospital triage and bypassing hospitals to be practised safely. There was no local paramedic training in Staffordshire at that time. Since then many developments have resulted in the ambulance service becoming one of the foremost services in the UK. Organisational changes introduced by the Chief Executive have included the appointment of a Medical Director who is also the Director of Operations. This was the second medical appointment of its type in the UK, but the first in which the director maintains hands-on clinical practice in pre-hospital care. The local Ambulance Service has been pioneering Pre-hospital Trauma Life Support[4] (PHTLS) training and was early to implement the comprehensive use of spine boards. In addition to their technical developments, the service has achieved the best response times in the country this year.

Although a close working relationship has always been present between the emergency department and the ICU, other aspects of in-patient care have recently received more attention. A surprising early omission from the centre was a High Dependency Unit (HDU). Within the last year, an HDU has been established and serves the trauma patients either as a safe step-down area following ICU care or for seriously injured patients not requiring full intensive care. The operating theatres run a trauma list daily and although a specific theatre is not reserved for major trauma, a vacant theatre can generally be arranged at very short notice.

No trauma system is complete without a comprehensive rehabilitation service. The two consultants in the Rehabilitation Hospital from the nearby Haywood Hospital and a Head-Injury Coordinator/Research Nurse provide the links between the acute trauma wards and longer term rehabilitation.

The role of the trauma team leader has largely been confined to immediate resuscitation and continuing coordination over the next few hours. The need for longer term continuity of care is recognised and one of the team leaders spends a session each week tracking the progress of all patients with Injury Severity Scores over 15. The data collected is stored in a specifically designed database and letters are sent to each senior clinician involved in the patient's care, including the referring team at another hospital. In addition, the emergency department, ICU and operating theatre nurses have confidential access to the reports to provide feedback. The reports include details of the patient's presentation, injuries (coded according to the Abbreviated Injury Scale) and other problems, operations and other procedures and progress. By subjecting the data collected to scrutiny by a senior clinician and making it available to all of the teams involved, accuracy is enhanced and clinicians have the opportunity to correct any errors in the coding of injuries. This approach contrasts with that frequently used in other hospitals, where a non-clinical audit clerk sifts though the clinical notes without clinical supervision to identify injuries.

In this age of organisational change and financial restraint, no trauma system can focus only on clinical issues. the North Staffordshire Hospital received pump-priming funds of £1m from the government for four years. With the formation of a Trauma Executive Committee to set organisational policy and control financial affairs, the Trust has been able to maintain full funding for the trauma centre through the contracting process.

The trauma centre was effectively launched in the summer of 1991 but was not fully staffed until 1992. An external study from the University of Sheffield examined the first two years of the trauma centre's development, finishing before many of the current developments were in place.[5] In order to assess the system's cost-effectiveness, the study aimed to identify a 33% improvement in the death rate, comparable to that found in the classic Orange County study in North America.[6] Given the preponderance of blunt trauma (98%) and the fact that 75% of major trauma deaths in North Staffordshire are due to critical head injury (Abbreviated Injury Scale code 5 or more)[7] or are in patients aged over 70 years, this was to be a difficult target to meet (Figure 1). The study identified trends towards improvement which were not statistically significant and the pilot scheme was declared as not cost-effective. The study itself was hampered by difficulties in data collection, which are acknowledged in the report. The data were collected by non-clinical researchers who sifted through clinical records in retrospect. Many of the records had by then been reduced to microfiche. The researchers were not trained in trauma scoring on the standard Major Trauma Outcome Study course and there was no intra-observer variability check and only one inter-observer check, performed towards the end of the study. The single inter-observer variability check showed 17% difference between the observers in ascribing patients as having an ISS over 15. Because of these uncertainties over data collection in what was effectively a snapshot at the start of the system, the Sheffield report should not be regarded as a final arbiter on trauma system development in the UK. Nevertheless the study provides a useful perspective on the development of trauma services and addresses many of the central issues which deserve recognition.

Since 1992, a detailed clinical audit of patients with major trauma has been carried out at the North Staffordshire Hospital. A single research worker liaises with senior clinicians to clarify injuries to achieve a high level of accuracy and consistency in injury scoring. The results of the audit extend to 1996, more than 2 years beyond the Sheffield report. The outcomes of patients have been compared with a similar audit performed by Keele University Trauma Research Group in 1989-90.[8] The results show an increase of 58% in the number of trauma patients admitted to the North Staffordshire Hospital since that time. The median ISS has increased from 21 to 25. The spectrum of injuries remains the same with road accidents and falls accounting for 84% of cases and head

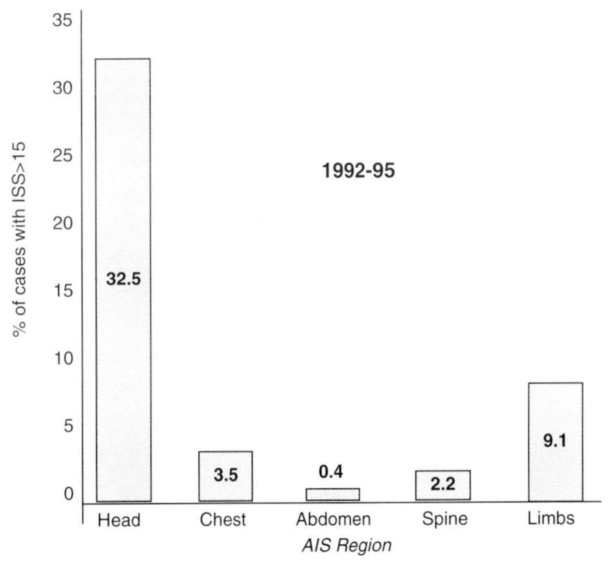

Figure 1:
Body regions with isolated injuries (ISS>15 and other regions AIS<2)

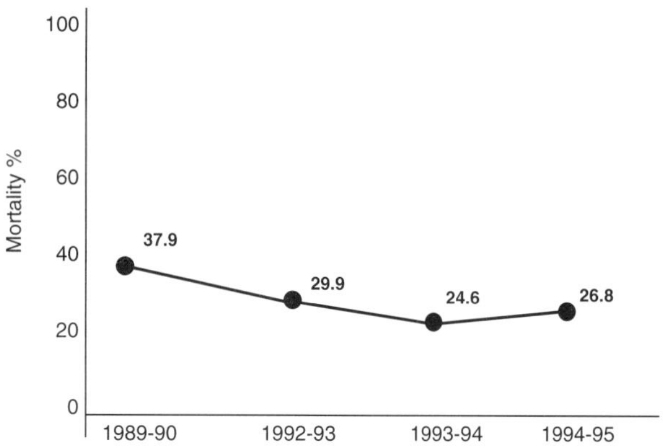

Figure 2:
Mortality in patients admitted with ISS>15

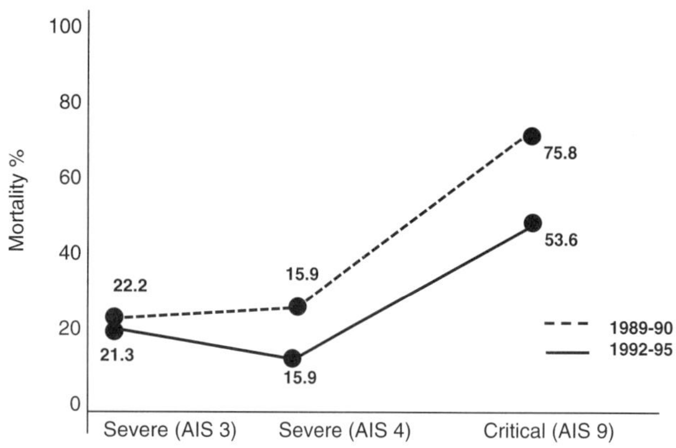

Figure 3:
Mortality in severe head injury (ISS>15)

injury being the predominant injury in over half of the patients. The mean length of stay in hospital has increased by 3.5 days and mean intensive care stay by just over 2 days, reflecting an increase in hospital costs. The overall mortality in patients with ISS over 15 has fallen from 38% in 1989-90 to 27% in 1994-95 (Figure 2). The mortality has decreased in patients aged over 70 years and in all decades from 10-89 years except in the 50-59 group. The mortality has decreased in severe life-threatening (AIS code 4) and critical (code 5) but not in severe non-life-threatening (code 3) head injury (Figure 3). Survivors of major trauma spend less time in hospital and the proportion of early deaths has decreased.

Crude mortality comparisons may be extended by using trauma 'dose-response curves', in which mortality is plotted against the probability of survival derived from TRISS analysis.[9] The probability of survival is determined from the Injury Severity Score (based on anatomical injury), the Revised Trauma Score (based on physiological derangement) and the patient's age, using logistic regression analysis.[10] It represents a combined anatomical and physiological 'dose' of trauma, while mortality represents the 'response'. The improvement in mortality in 1992-95 compared with 1989-90 is shown by a right shift of the dose-response curve. This is particularly evident in the lower probability of survival bands. A right shift is present in patients with and without critical head injury (AIS code 5 or more). An alternative graphical representation is based on the W statistic used in the TRISS method. W represents the number of excess survivors compared with the North American Major Trauma Outcome Study reference database. The W statistic in North Staffordshire falls below the North American norm in 5 out of 6 probability of survival bands when all patients with ISS over 15 are considered. This leaves no room for complacency although direct comparison is unreliable because of the different spectrum of trauma seen in North America. However when patients aged over 70 or with critical head injury are omitted (Figure 4), the W statistic then exceeds the North American norm in 5 out of 6 bands.

In summary, much has been learnt from the pilot trauma scheme. The infrastructure for an effective trauma system is now in place and steady improvements in mortality trends have been demonstrated. The early emphasis on establishing pre-hospital care and on improving initial resuscitation in the emergency department is now being followed by a focus on continuity of care and on integration of the system elements. Current audit of major trauma uses mortality as the main outcome measure. As most of the deaths are in patients who are elderly or who have a critical head injury, further significant improvements in mortality may be difficult to achieve. Future efforts must focus on assessing and reducing morbidity.

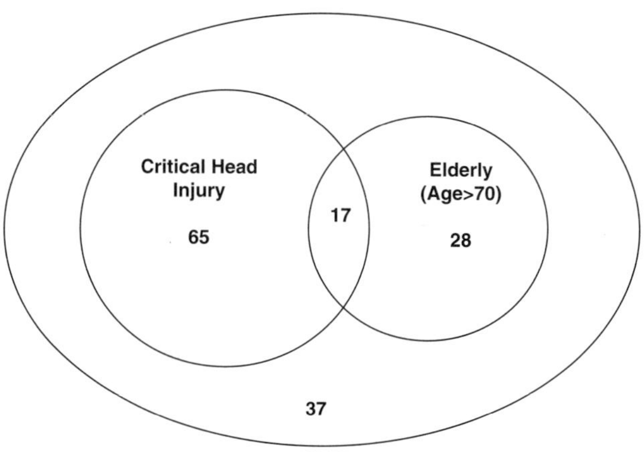

Figure 4:
A review of all deaths (147) between 1992-95 with an ISS>15. 82 deaths were associated with a critical head injury (AIS>4) and 45 were in patients over 70 years of age. 110 deaths (75%) either had a head injury or were aged over 70.

References

1. Baker SP, O'Neill B, Haddon W, Long WB. The Injury Severity Score - a method of describing patients with multiple injuries and evaluating emergency care. Journal of Trauma 1974:14;187-96.
2. Yates DW, Woodford M, Hollis S. Preliminary analysis of the care of injured patients in 33 British hospitals: the first report of the UK Major Trauma Outcome Study. British Medical Journal 1992:305;737-40.
3. Committee on Trauma, American College of Surgeons. Advanced Trauma Life Support. American College of Surgeons, Chicago 1993.
4. Pre-Hospital Trauma Life Support Committee of the National Association of Emergency Medical Technicians. Pre-Hospital Trauma Life Support. Mosby-Year Book, St. Louis 1994.
5. Nicholl JP, Turner J, Dixon S. The cost-effectiveness of the regional trauma system in the North West Midlands. University of Sheffield, 1996.
6. West JG, Cales RH, Gazzaniga AB. The impact of regionalization: the Orange County experience. Archives of Surgery 1983:118;740-44.
7. American Association for Automotive Medicine. The Abbreviated Injury Scale: 1990 revision. Des Plaines, Illinois 1990.
8. Keele University Trauma Research Group. An incidence study of trauma in the North Staffordshire Health District. December 1991.
9. Boyd CR, Tolson MA, Copes WS. Evaluating trauma care: the TRISS method. Journal of Trauma 1987:27;370-78.
10. Champion HR. A revision of the Trauma Score. Journal of Trauma 1989:29;623-29.

Dr Peter Oakley is a Consultant in anaesthesia and trauma at the North Staffordshire Hospital, Princes Road, Hartshill, Stoke-on-Trent, ST4 7LN and is a member of the Trauma Research Group which have recently published 'Trauma System Review (1992-95)', the most recent assessment of their successful results. The original illustrations are in this document.

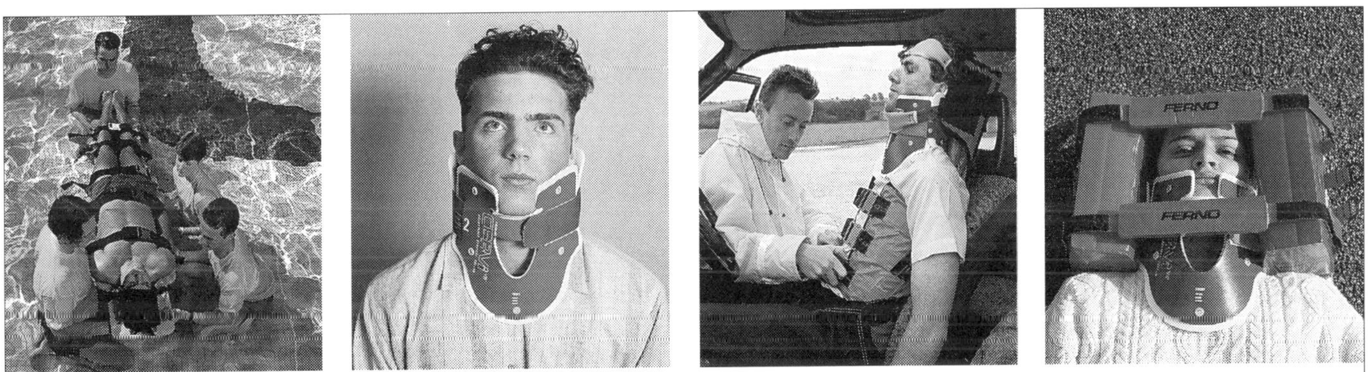

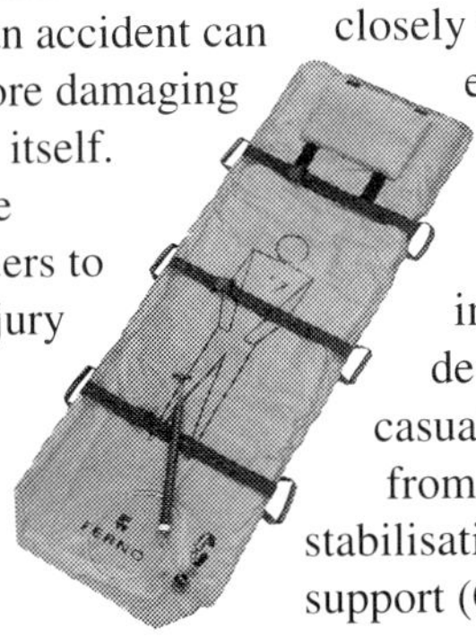

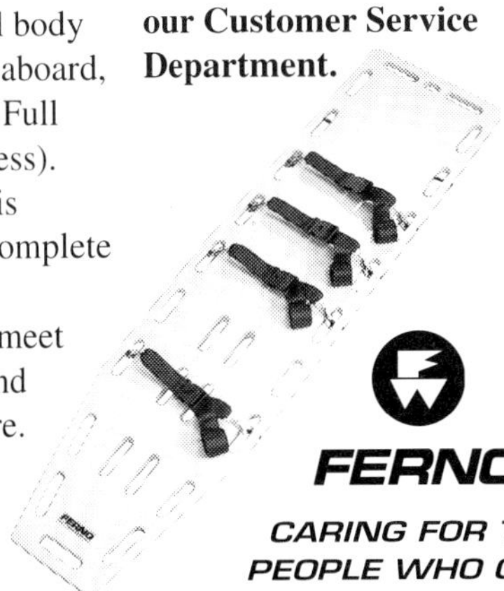

SEARCH AND RESCUE HELICOPTERS AND CIVIL AIR AMBULANCE UNITS

Graham Budden

The Royal Navy and the Royal Air Force have been undertaking helicopter Search and Rescue (SAR) operations around the UK since the mid 1950s. The overall size and deployment of their SAR helicopter force is determined by the requirement to provide cover for NATO military aviation in the event of war. In peacetime the force's primary responsibility is to provide SAR cover for military exercises and training flights, but since its earliest days the police and coastguards have requested SAR assistance at incidents involving civilians either lost or in difficulties in inaccessible places. The military helicopter crews were quick to recognise the value of assisting with such incidents – doing so was far more interesting than practising their skills using dummies and floating oil drums – and the military authorities have appreciated the public relations value of the civilian rescues.

Civilian incidents now account for more than 80% of the rescue missions flown by the military SAR helicopters and, although the units are located to cater for the military requirement, their deployment and operational readiness takes account of criteria agreed with civil authorities. Civilian SAR units have been integrated into the UK SAR network in the past. Currently there are four civilian SAR contracts, with Bristow helicopters based at Sumburgh since 1983, at Stornoway and Lee on Solent since 1987 and 1988 respectively, and at RNAS Portland since October 1995. The disposition of SAR units, particularly the proximity of Portland and Lee on Solent and the coverage provided around the South East coast of England, is subject to review during 1996.

There is a fundamental difference in concept between SAR helicopters and helicopter air ambulances. The SAR helicopter is specifically designed and equipped for flights in all weathers, with full instrument flying and high endurance capabilities, enabling them to carry out protracted searches in difficult weather conditions. On board radar provides a very effective means of locating objects at sea, as well as providing navigation information, and radio homing equipment allows the helicopter to locate emergency locator beacon transmissions. Night Vision Goggles (NVG) greatly improve the crew's search capability after dark and assist with overland navigation at night at low level.

Automated descent and hover systems allow SAR helicopters to make approaches to sea level in weather conditions which would preclude normal helicopter operations. The winch, fitted with a cable in excess of 200 feet in length, allows a winchman to be lowered to, or casualties to be lifted from, the sea or situations where the helicopter is unable to land, such as a small ship or mountainous terrain. Such rescue equipment is unlikely to be fitted to civilian air ambulances because the helicopters used in this role are simply not large enough and would not be able to carry the additional weight.

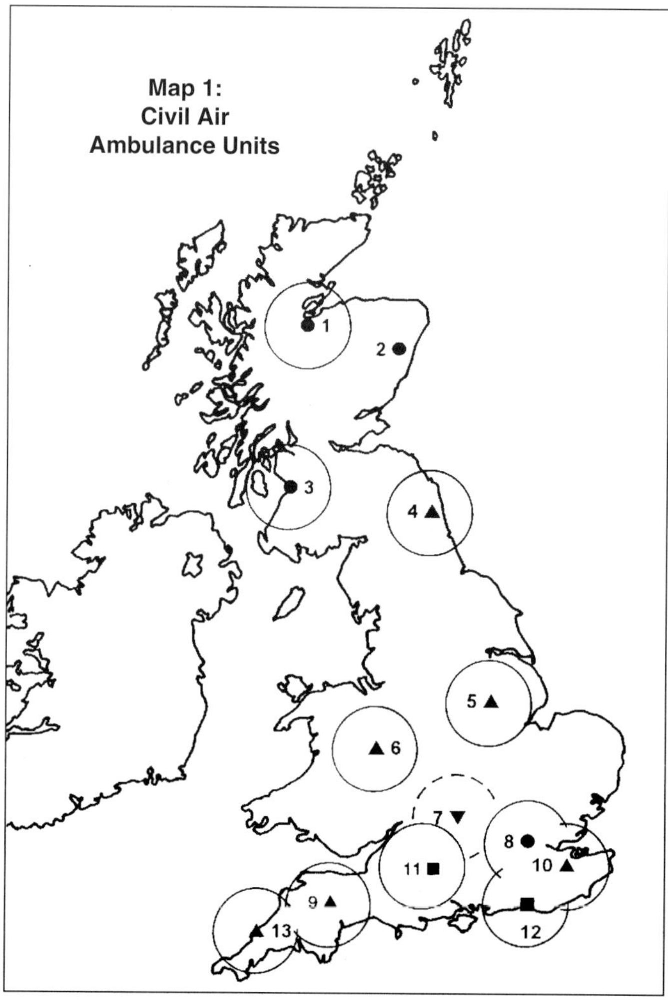

Map 1: Civil Air Ambulance Units

Map: Graham Budden

Table 1: Civil Air Ambulance Units

	Location	Tasking Authority	Aircraft Type	Hours of Operation[1]	Crew	Operator[2]
● 1	Inverness Airport	Scottish Ambulance	BO105	0830-1630 7 days	1 pilot, 2 paramedic	Bond
● 2	Aberdeen Airport	Scottish Ambulance	Beech B200 (Fixed Wing)	24 hours 7 days	2 pilots, 2 paramedics	Bond
● 3	Prestwick Airport	Scottish Ambulance	BO105	0830-1630 5 days a week	1 pilot, 2 paramedics	Bond
▲ 4	Blyth Heliport	Northumbria Ambulance	AS355F1	10 hr shift 7 days	1 pilot, 2 paramedics	MAS
▲ 5	RAF Waddington	Lincolnshire Ambulance	BO105	10 hr shift 7 days	1 pilot, 2 paramedics	MAS
▲ 6	RAF Cosford	West Midlands Ambulance	BO105	0800-1800 7 days	1 pilot, 2 paramedics	Bond
▼ 7	Oxford Projected start late 1996[3]	Oxfordshire Ambulance	BK117	Daylight hours 7 days	1 pilot, doctor, paramedic	HEMS Oxford
● 8	London	London Ambulance	SA365N	0800-1900 7 days	2 pilots, doctor, paramedic	HEMS London
▲ 9	Exeter Airport	West Country Ambulance	BO105	0930-1730 5 days a week	1 pilot, 2 paramedics	Bond
▲ 10	Rochester Airport	Kent Ambulance	AS355F1	8 hours 5 days a week	1 pilot, 2 paramedics	MAS
▲13	RAF St Mawgan	West Country Ambulance	BO105	0930-1730 7 days	1 pilot, 2 paramedics	Bond
■ 11	Devizes Police HQ	Wiltshire Constabulary	BO105	10 hr shift 7 days	1 pilot, 1 police observer, 1 paramedic	PAS
■ 12	Shoreham Airport	Sussex Police	BO105	2 x 8 hr shift 7 days	1 pilot, 1 police observer, 1 paramedic	PAS

▲ Service provided by the Ambulance Service funded by public donations

● Service provided by the Ambulance Service with Central Government funding

■ Service jointly funded by Police and Ambulance Service

1. Times are normal duty hours anticipated for 1996 and are subject to change.
2. HEMS = Helicopter Emergency Medical Service.
   MAS = Medical Aviation Service.
   PAS = Police Aviation Service.
3. The details of the projected Oxfordshire air ambulance are to be confirmed.

Radius of action shown = 50 km (See **Map 1**)

NB: Aberdeen does not have a radius circle on the map because it is a fixed wing (aeroplane) operation rather than a helicopter and is used primarily for longer range transfers

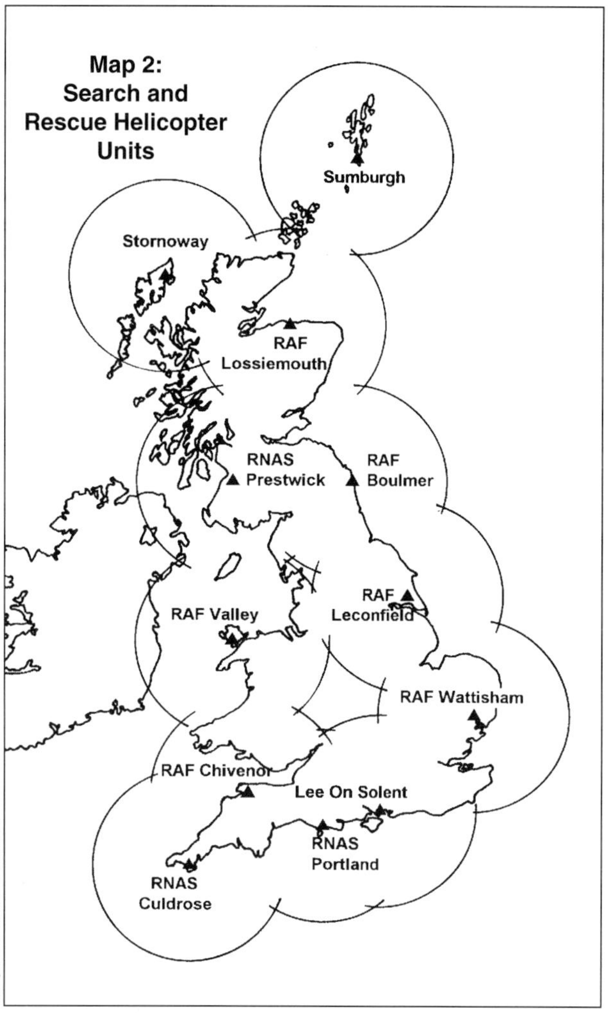

Map: Graham Budden

The helicopters typically used by air ambulance operations are smaller, lighter and more manoeuvrable, allowing them to operate into areas too small for a SAR helicopter, or where the strong downwash from the Sea King or the S61N rotors would cause a lot of damage. Most air ambulance helicopters normally carry just the one patient and can take a second, at a squeeze, if necessary. A SAR helicopter can accommodate more than 18 survivors.

SAR crewmen are trained in 'immediate and emergency care' to a level roughly equivalent to an ambulance service paramedic and the helicopters are equipped with a comprehensive medical kit and drugs pack. For missions which are known to involve serious medical injuries each SAR flight has arrangements to collect a doctor or a medical team from a nearby hospital.

Military SAR helicopters are tasked through the Aeronautical Rescue Co-ordination Centres (ARCC) at Plymouth and Kinloss. In 1997 these are due to combine into a single ARCC at Kinloss. The Civilian SAR units are tasked by the Coastguard, but the ARCC and Coastguard cooperate closely during major rescue operations.

Graham Budden is a HEMS pilot who was in the RAF for 10 years of which four were spent on Search and Rescue duties.

Table 2: Search and Rescue Helicopter Units

Location	Tasking Authority	Aircraft Type	Hours of Operation	Crew	Operator
Sumburgh	Coastguard	S61N	24hrs 7 days	2 pilots, 2 crewmen	Bristow Helicopters
Stornoway	Coastguard	S61N	24hrs 7 days	2 pilots, 2 crewmen	Bristow Helicopters
RAF Lossiemouth	ARCC	Sea King	24 hrs 7 days	2 pilots, 2 crewmen	Royal Air Force
RNAS Prestwick	ARCC	Sea King	24 hrs 7 days	2 pilots, 2 crewmen	Royal Navy
RAF Boulmer	ARCC	Sea King	24 hrs 7 days	2 pilots, 2 crewmen	Royal Air Force
RAF Leconfield	ARCC	Sea King	24 hrs 7 days	2 pilots, 2 crewmen	Royal Air Force
RAF Valley	ARCC	Sea King	24 hrs 7 days	2 pilots, 2 crewmen	Royal Air Force
RAF Wattisham	ARCC	Sea King	24 hrs 7 days	2 pilots, 2 crewmen	Royal Air Force
RAF Chivenor	ARCC	Sea King	24 hrs 7 days	2 pilots, 2 crewmen	Royal Air Force
Lee On Solent	Coastguard	S61N	24 hrs 7 days	2 pilots, 2 crewmen	Bristow Helicopters
RNAS Portland	Coastguard	S61N	0800-2000 7 days	2 pilots, 2 crewmen	Bristow Helicopters
RNAS Culdrose	ARCC	Sea King	24 hrs 7 days	2 pilots, 2 crewmen	Royal Navy

ARCC = Aeronautical Rescue Co-ordination Centre

Radius of action shown = 145 km (**Map 2**)

Radii represent the standard 1 hour daytime response quoted by the Ministry of Defence, consisting of 15 minutes standby and 45 minutes flying time at 105 knots for Sea Kings/S61Ns.

INTERHOSPITAL TRANSFERS BY HELICOPTER

Aubrey Bristow

Introduction

Helicopters have been used to support medical services from their earliest days at the end of the second world war. Initially their main use was the evacuation of casualties to base hospitals, and when civilian medical helicopter schemes began in Denver in the 1960s, they too were concerned with primary evacuations.

Since the early 1980s the pattern has changed and today over 60% of American transfers are secondary or inter-hospital. Some of this shift is due to the historically high accident rates in primary work as well as greater financial security, but the main reason has been a realisation of the need and benefit of this work. Not surprisingly, other countries have also changed their emphasis, whilst the UK has been at the forefront in having one of the original dedicated secondary schemes.

The Need for Interhospital Transfer

The vast majority of patients can be well managed in the hospital to which they initially present. A minority will need to be transferred to another hospital because the services or specialties they require are not available locally, yet most of these patients are well enough to travel by road especially if the distance is short.

Many ICU patients only need a short transfer, but this leaves a small number of critically ill patients who need to travel over 40 miles to another hospital. Each patient is unique; many will be trauma victims or patients who have undergone surgery and subsequently developed complications. Spinal injuries are another important group, as are burns patients. The common thread is that these are frequently young, productive members of society who must be transferred to give them the best chance of survival and the highest quality of life. In addition, there are children and premature babies who have such serious problems or who are so premature that they require a regional or supra-regional service, yet with this service may well lead a completely normal life.

Photo: author

Caring for critically ill patients is difficult enough on an intensive care unit. They are attached to numerous drug infusions to support the heart and kidneys, various pressures must be continually monitored and they are dependant on a ventilator for oxygen. To provide this level of care in the back of an ambulance, on the move and in the dark, is yet more dangerous.

The equipment to undertake these transfers is available but costs tens of thousands of pounds, so it is not surprising that audit after audit demonstrates that most hospitals do not have it. Many hospitals cannot provide senior doctors and nurses to leave the hospital for many hours, and the ambulance services have difficulty releasing ambulances from 999 calls. Not least, each year people are killed on the roads by emergency vehicles.

The Rationale for a Helicopter

The helicopter is merely an alternative form of transport, but it does make these difficult transfers easier to carry out. Travelling smoothly at two miles per minute, it is relatively easy to observe and care for a patient. A helicopter can cover a much larger area than a single ambulance, so it is more economical to purchase one set of intensive care equipment and provide dedicated doctors and nurses than to try to replicate this in each hospital. The helicopter is faster, reducing the time out of hospital, the at-risk time, but it also eliminates the danger to other road users from speeding ambulances.

Is it Beneficial?

Secondary transfers have been undertaken by helicopter in the UK for some five years. They can be flown night and day, and there are landing sites for all acute hospitals. The often quoted problem of bad weather only rarely produces problems, and clinical care in flight has been proved to be a practical proposition.

Secondary transfers are more fortunate than primary helicopter schemes in that it is easier to audit the benefits. A growing number of papers now exist which scientifically prove that secondary helicopter transfers save lives. In the UK, the 'Careflight' project has shown that the death rate in the more seriously ill patient is half that seen in patients transferred by a land ambulance, even when provided with the same level of staff and equipment. In part this is thought to be due to the lower accelerational and vibrational forces in the helicopter, since these forces are known to damage critically ill patients.

Benefits have also been shown for individual illnesses or injuries. The Swiss have demonstrated a reduction of up to a half in deaths amongst spinal injured patients by the use of helicopters, and the outcome after head injuries has been reduced in the USA.

The 'Careflight' project has also looked at alternative methods of transport. In 28%of their cases, no land ambulance could have provided adequate amounts of electricity or oxygen to allow the patient to be moved. In these cases the helicopter was not just a nice alternative but the only option. It must be emphasised that the quality of life for these survivors is good. Most of them return to work, playing a full and productive part in society.

Secondary helicopter systems may provide further benefits elsewhere. Releasing ambulances and medical staff to their main roles has financial benefits. NHS Trusts can build up centres for relatively rare conditions knowing that there is a capability to transfer patients to them. Nowhere is this more evident than in paediatrics, where there may only be a need for one or two centres for a particular condition.

Costs

Helicopters are not cheap, but their costs must be compared with the costs of managing patients on intensive care, itself an expensive exercise. A 24 hour dedicated secondary system will cost about £750,000 per annum, including medical staff and equipment. Because secondary transfers can be undertaken both night and day, one helicopter can easily transfer 350 long distance transfers per annum (the average distance is currently 128 miles), giving a cost of £2142 per patient.

Against this, an ICU bed costs £1000 to £1700 per day, on top of which will be the costs of further operations, x-ray and pathology as well as long term treatment and rehabilitation. Some papers have found the average ICU stay for these patients to be 43 days, others more, so that the cost of helicopter transfer is only 2% of an individual's care, and this ignores the cost of any alternative land ambulance transfer. There is no evidence that Trusts do not transfer patients to another Trust for intensive care

Careflight Air Ambulance (Stansted Airport) October 1989

when indicated, and if they can meet this commitment (which is open ended at the time of making it) there is no excuse that they cannot afford the additional cost of helicopter transfer, equivalent to one or two days' ICU charges. Indeed, it is estimated that the total cost for each Trust would be less than £15,000 per year.

It may well be that a well executed helicopter transfer can reduce the length and complexity of treatment, and there is good anecdotal evidence of poor transfers resulting in complications costing tens of thousands of pounds to remedy, but definitive evidence from patients with differing illnesses will take several years to collect.

The UK Today

In England and Wales there is only one dedicated secondary helicopter system, which serves the whole UK. Several of the primary helicopter systems do undertake secondary transfers, but this is far from ideal. The equipment and staff are quite different for the two types of flight, and one is back to scrounging staff and equipment from the hospital. These doctors and nurses may not be used to working in a helicopter, increasing risks for both themselves and their patient, and the helicopter is now removed from its intended primary role.

All medical helicopter systems are represented on the British Helicopter Medical Group, which meets regularly to exchange knowledge and set standards. This Group has laid down guidelines on when to use secondary helicopters. Minimum standards have been set for interhospital transfers by a working party representing the medical Royal Colleges and the Civil Aviation Authority, and recommended protocols for the use of helicopters have been published for purchasing authorities by the Royal College of Anaesthetists and the British Trauma Society. Despite this, managers continue to refuse or delay authorisation for helicopter transfers, sometimes with fatal results. Others use unequipped and inappropriate military or civilian charter helicopters, risking their own staff and patients in violation of national guidelines to save a few pounds.

The Way Forward

The most urgent requirement is for NHS Trusts to act upon the recommendations listed above. In particular, each Trust should appoint a consultant from a relevant specialty to be responsible for interhospital transfers of seriously ill patients. He or she will know where patients come from or go to locally, and can lay down criteria on when to use a land ambulance or helicopter.

For the minority of patients requiring helicopter transfer, guidelines must be set. Only dedicated secondary schemes should be used. If a patient meets the criteria, the doctor looking after him should be able to call on that scheme without further authority. This will prevent the current situation where such requests need multiple approvals, by which time the patient has either died or been transferred by road.

All transfers must be properly audited so that we can produce better and more accurate guidelines on which patients benefit and how they should be managed.

Finally, the ambulance authorities must become more efficient at assisting hospitals with long-term transfers. As experts in transportation they have an onus to advise hospitals on whether or not to use helicopters.

The Future

The need for secondary transfers by helicopter will never be large. Current estimates for both adults and children amount to some 550 transfers per annum, and this could be undertaken by two helicopters working together. There may be logic in bringing all helicopters, both primary and secondary, under a national structure, but the secondary schemes must work together to provide blanket coverage for the NHS.

The funding will come from individual Trusts using the helicopters to move their patients, but aircraft cannot be provided on empty promises. The main problem to date has been the lack of any Regional or Supra-regional Authority which has the funds to set up the service and to be subsequently reimbursed by the Trusts. Private capital has been singularly absent as it has throughout the NHS. Government must itself set up a body to take responsibility for secondary and perhaps primary helicopter schemes, similar to UK Transplant. It must underwrite the initial funds or broker others to do so, whilst in return those operating the schemes must provide on-going audit and act upon the results to ensure these resources are properly targeted.

This leaves one unique group of patients, those with head injuries, who, because of the need for urgent transfer immediately following admission, fall between primary and secondary in nature. Secondary head injury transfers for neurosurgical intervention or CT scanning may amount to some 1200 transfers per year. There can be no excuse for admitting patients with head injuries to hospitals without CT scanning, and ambulance services and Trusts must stop this dangerous practice which amounts to perhaps half the total.

Improvements in intensive care training and provision means that many serious head injuries can be managed separate from surgical provision, but some transfers will still exist, and a minority will benefit from helicopter support. A national umbrella organisation, as outlined above, could best coordinate the provision of urgent helicopter transfers, calling when available on the secondary aircraft. When these cannot respond, primary aircraft could be employed.

Clearly there would be a need for medical cover if the primary helicopter is staffed by paramedics, but this is no different from the requirement for land ambulance based transfer, and does not detract from the benefits detailed above. It may be that the umbrella organisation could help stimulate training in inter-hospital transport which will in turn improve the quality of non-helicopter transfers. Each primary helicopter would carry an additional equipment pack in the cargo hold for these patients.

In summary, secondary transfer of ICU patients by helicopter has been proved to save lives, returning people to the community. It must be available for the minority of patients who require it. Secondary transfers would, if guidelines were followed, be sensibly funded by individual Trusts for a minimal cost to each, and would make good economic sense in medical terms. A national organisation for all medical helicopters schemes, both primary and secondary, would facilitate this service, resolve many of the difficulties encountered in primary transfers and assist the head injured patient.

Dr Aubrey Bristow has been a Consultant Anaesthetist at St Bartholomew's Hospital since 1986. Amongst his special interests are the management of the head injured patient, neurosurgical intensive care and the difficult airway. Dr Bristow is the Medical Director of *Careflight*, a Barts project that transfers critically ill patients between hospitals worldwide.

AIR AMBULANCE OPERATIONS IN ENGLAND

Laurie Caple

The current position in England is that there are now five dedicated EMS air ambulances crewed by ambulance paramedic officers. They are located in: Northumbria, covering the five counties in the Northern region; West Midlands, covering five counties; Devon and Cornwall; and Kent. A new service in Lincolnshire is currently being trialled and is likely to be a permanent feature soon. In addition, there are two joint EMS/police operations, one covering Sussex and the other Wiltshire. Each of these machines is crewed by an ambulance paramedic officer and a police observer.

With the exception of Northumbria and Kent which both use the F1 Aerospatiale Twin Squirrel, the other operations use the stretched Bolkow DB105. Excluding Northumbria, all helicopters are leased and the costs of leasing and day to day running are met fully from sponsorship and continuous charitable fundraising. Northumbria exceptionally elected to purchase its helicopter outright through charitable support and maintains the charity for a future replacement. All operational running costs are met from Northumbria core contracts with its purchasers and extra-contractual referrals.

A common feature of all the English air ambulance operations is a 10 hour, seven-day week operation in daylight hours. Northumbria has CAA approval for night flying and provides an out-of-hours service for secondary transfers. Northumbria believes that its 1994/95 all-embracing operating costs of £805 per flying hour, confirms the value for money benefits of outright purchase. These costs equate to 630 missions. It is important to emphasise that the EMS/air ambulance, crewed by ambulance paramedic officers, is a different operation to the HEMS operation based at the Royal London Hospital. The air ambulance is simply an ambulance which flies. Its primary function and benefits are an emergency response to an incident in a remote location and/or transfer to a specialist centre where a lengthy road journey is the alternative. It follows that air ambulances are at their most effective in rural ambulance services, offering rapid response and transfer for patients and greater local availability of road ambulances in rural areas.

The secondary role of air ambulances is the transfer over long distances of suitable patients being transferred from one unit to another or discharged back to their home area. Their speed of travel benefits both the patient and the Ambulance Service, with the latter able to retain local road ambulances for emergency cover which otherwise might have been out of area, unavailable for a complete shift, or tour of duty.

An increasing role for the air ambulance is the rapid transfer of neonates to specialised ECMO units and special care facilities. There is work currently being trialled in Scotland and Northumbria to provide adequate power and support systems for specialised incubators conveyed in helicopters and satisfactory securing devices to meet CAA requirements. Other benefits of an air ambulance operation include providing strategic emergency cover over large areas at periods of peak demand, aerial reconnaissance in major incident situations and rapid transport of emergency medical supplies in multi-casualty incidents.

There is increasing evidence to suggest that the introduction of air ambulances has provided added value to maintaining and improving the standard of pre-hospital care. Selective tasking of missions, as a complementary measure to an existing robust road ambulance system, offers real life-saving potential, not just for the patient conveyed by air ambulance, but also the patient who has been responded to by a road ambulance which might not have otherwise been so readily available if the air ambulance was not in place.

Now that the existing schemes are well established, there is a need to determine good practice and consider a more strategic deployment nationwide of a unified air ambulance system which is linked to the development of Trauma Centres, but operated by the Ambulance Service. Health purchasers of ambulance services would do well to look beyond the initial high cost of air ambulances and analyse the overall benefits they offer which has long been recognised elsewhere in the world. An estimated 24 separate, but unified, air ambulance operations would adequately cover the United Kingdom.

Mr Laurie Caple is Chief Executive of the Ambulance Service NHS Trust, Interlink House, Scotswood Road, Newcastle upon Tyne NE4 7BJ.

PATIENT AIR TRANSPORT IN SCOTLAND: AN INTEGRATED SERVICE

Andrew Marsden

Scotland has had the benefit of air ambulances since 1933 when an Islay fisherman with a perforated stomach ulcer was airlifted to Glasgow in a Dragon Moth fixed wing aeroplane operated by Midland and Scottish Air Ferries. Over the years many hundreds of air evacuations of the sick and injured from the islands have been facilitated. In addition, Scotland obtained the first and only publicly funded rotary wing service in the United Kingdom.

In 1993 the responsibility for managing and integrating the various air ambulance assets in Scotland was passed to the Scottish Ambulance Service. An Air Desk was established to receive requests for missions and coordinate the transport arrangements. Based at Aberdeen, it can be accessed by doctors from anywhere in Scotland, phoning at local call rates.

The air assets available to the Service are as follows:

In **Inverness** and **Prestwick** there are dedicated stretched Bolkow 105 helicopters which, operating in HEMS (Helicopter Emergency Medical Service) mode, are under two minutes' notice to move during daylight hours and, under the command of local ambulance control centres, can respond to motor vehicle and other accidents as well as medical emergencies occurring in remote and otherwise inaccessible places. The Bolkows in the Scottish Ambulance Service livery, are equipped to the standard of a mobile intensive care unit with a specially designed medical bulkhead, enhanced oxygen supply and multifunction patient monitors. The aircraft are crewed by two paramedics who receive special training in aviation medical procedures as well as helicopter safety, fire fighting, ditching and dunking and survival at sea. In non-emergency mode the helicopters are able to assist in Medevacs from the Highlands and Inner Isles and specialist interhospital transfers. A dedicated transport incubator is available for this aircraft.

Dedicated fixed wing aircraft operate out of **Glasgow** and **Kirkwall** in the Orkney Islands in the form of Britten Norman Islanders, little craft ideally suited to short take offs and landings at the small island air strips. Again, there are specially trained air crew who provide escort facilities to the patient in transit. At **Aberdeen** there are two Beech 200 King Air turbo prop, pressurised aircraft, well-suited to

Photo:author

A Bolkow air ambulance in a 'hover'

the longer distance journeys involving high dependency and intensive care cases, for example, transport of patients from the north of Scotland to cardiac or liver transplant units further south.

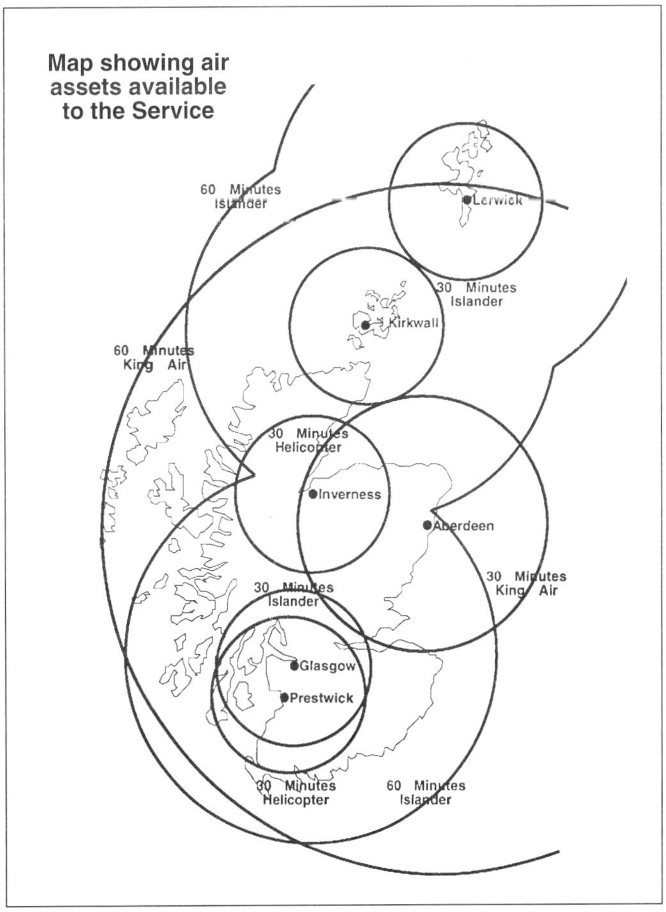

Map showing air assets available to the Service

Photo: author

The Super King Air showing 'air-ground' interface

One of the King Air aeroplanes is available for non-NHS work for assisted repatriation within the United Kingdom and Northern Europe.

The fixed wing air ambulances are each equipped with the LifePort Patient Loading Utility System (PLUS) which comprises a dedicated utility base containing a giant sized medical oxygen tank, an invertor unit for 12v, 24v and 240v power supply, vacuum and compressed air and a self-contained 'double-decker' Aerosled which provides a seamless interface with the standard trolley cots on land ambulances.

In addition to the dedicated aircraft there is the shared use of the inter-island Islander in **Shetland**, support from a 24 hour Super Puma helicopter in **Aberdeen,** and for night-time missions with all weather capability are the two Coastguard Sikorskys and the two MOD Sea Kings of the Search and Rescue Service from **Prestwick**, **Stornoway**, **Sumburgh** and **Lossiemouth**.

Since 1993 the Service has been arranging over 2,000 missions per year, 650 or so of these being emergency journeys. Planned journeys number over 400 with most of the 40 intensive or critical care journeys being in this cate-gory. The vast remainder are island airlifts where, in a very urgent case, the Service undertakes to deliver the patient to hospital in 6 hours or, in urgent cases, by the following morning (9 hours). 150 maternity cases are moved each year. About 30 to 50 cases per year utilise the larger Search and Rescue helicopters of the MOD or Coastguard Services.

The amalgamation of all the air assets in Scotland into one service has presented the public of Scotland with an unrivalled comprehensive service for air ambulance transportation. Opportunities have arisen for formal clinical audit, for on-line specialist help, coordinated intensive care retrieval services and nationwide planning of integrated care for trauma patients.

Andrew K Marsden, FRCSEd FFAEM DiplMRCSEd, is the Consultant Medical Director of the Scottish Ambulance Service NHS Trust, Edinburgh.

MAGPAS: THE CAMBRIDGE WAY WITH GP IMMEDIATE CARE

H M Sherriff

Bernard Shaw said: *'The reasonable man adapts himself to the world; the unreasonable man persists in trying to adapt the world to himself. Therefore all progress depends on the unreasonable man.'*

'They had to call a MAGPAS doctor!' 'A magpie?' 'No, MAGPAS – the flying doctor service'. That is how many of the local public in Cambridgeshire describe MAGPAS – the Mid Anglia GP Accident Service. It is strongly supported by the public in Cambridgeshire and the press frequently refer to it as the 'flying doctor service'. That does not mean they have aeroplanes or helicopters but is the dramatised way that the press and the public perceive prompt medical responses to emergency situations.

Twenty five years ago this year MAGPAS was founded, mainly by the initiative of local GPs, led by Neville Silverston in Bottisham and Derek Cracknell in Huntingdon. At that time there were three counties consisting of Cambridge, Huntingdonshire and the Soke of Peterborough. The constabulary covered all three counties and was known as the Mid Anglia Police, and to parallel the emergency services the Immediate Care scheme was called the Mid Anglia General Practitioner Accident Service. At the outset the scheme aims were to provide care and resuscitation to the injured.

In the 1950s and 1960s it was traditional for the doctor to be called out to road accidents by police. The founder members and others lived close to main trunk routes which had a notoriety for road traffic accidents. The trunk roads in those days were not dual carriageways. They consisted of three lane highways with regular 'jousting' in the middle lane with disastrous consequences from head on accidents. The situation was such that the ambulance service used to pre-position vehicles at Girton at 8.00 am every morning for the three to four times weekly head on accidents on the A604 between Cambridge and Huntingdon.

Historically the GP would turn up to such incidents, often late at night, wearing a mac over pyjamas or gardening clothes. The emergency bag was usually equipped for obstetric emergencies. The rural GP was used to being called out to sudden events with domiciliary obstetrics, but soon found that their equipment and protective clothing were grossly inadequate.

The father of Immediate Care, Ken Easton in Catterick, gave talks to local GP groups about his work which sparked local enthusiasm. It was recognised that the key to successful call out was communications and rapid responding to a call rather than rapid driving. The early fund raising was to establish good communications to bypass the GP's surgery telephone. This was usually engaged first thing in the morning and in the evening because of surgery commitments, so radios and pagers were purchased. This resulted in the Cambridge Medical Answering Service being formed with radio transmitters and links to aerials covering Peterborough, Huntingdon and Cambridge areas.

At the outset it was recognised that the assessment of calls by the emergency services and the public were based on the visual impact of the wrecks, but they did not take into account the pathophysiological damage to the human. It was agreed that MAGPAS would respond on a 'blanket' basis to all calls in rural areas with the exception of accidents in the cities of Peterborough and Cambridge, unless they had been assessed. The reason for that was the response times of the ambulance vehicles within the cities was in a matter of minutes, and not all city GPs were interested in or had joined MAGPAS.

In the early days the recruitment of doctors was probably due to considerable discounts on the Answering Service charges. Those that joined MAGPAS were given their equipment and pagers at no cost in return for their voluntary services.

For the first ten years or so the MAGPAS radio room was a small office in the Old Addenbrookes Hospital manned by volunteer operators all of whom were SRN trained and operated from 8.00 am to 23.00 hours, after which the police initiated the call out. Eventually the demand on the service was such that twenty four hour operators were employed.

MAGPAS now has a large control area on Cambridge with two to three operators at peak periods. Calls are received from the Ambulance Headquarters, which until recently was in Cambridge but is now based in Norwich as part of the East Anglian Ambulance NHS Trust. The ambulance controllers passed every reported injury accident call to the CMAS (Cambridge Medical Answering Service) operators. They call out an Immediate Care GP from a sophisticated call out list which lists every village and trunk road location. The list is up to five doctors for each site. It also includes their work and home availability based on a daily diary. Doctors can remove themselves from on or off call by a single telephone or radio call to base.

With the blanket call-out system in 40% of the calls a doctor arrives before the ambulance. Eighty per cent of the calls are covered on an unassessed basis. Paradoxically the areas of limited cover are often on the fringes of the county.

In the early years the Immediate Care doctor turned up and was expected to treat the victims. In other parts of the country the pre-hospital care had been supplied by hospital flying squads. Theoretically these units provided a team of doctors and nurses using consultant-led clinical management principles used in hospital. A disadvantage of these teams is that the most experienced doctor was often a registrar with less than six months experience before they moved on. Most of that was hospital based experience. This criticism could be levelled at HEMS doctors.

The arguments for using local GPs are theoretically sound. They live locally and know the local roads and terrain. Statistics show that 60-70% of traffic accidents (RTA) occurred within three to five miles of the patient's home. Therefore the local rural GP was probably their own doctor. On a day to day basis they know and relate to the ambulance crews, the other services, and the hospital staff. An unusual feature of my own involvement is the opportunity to follow up and review pre-hospital patients in my own hospital.

The clinical skills of an Immediate Care GP can be widely variable. There is no reason for a GP, whether new or experienced, to have appropriate clinical skills for the unique nature of pre-hospital work. After all this is nearly all trauma related.

Over the years the MAGPAS trainers recognised this, and the fact that a new doctor could not be left to muddle through until experienced. My own view is that certain 'experienced' doctors continue to make the same errors time after time. Now a senior doctor is called when a new recruit is responding, for an appropriate period, usually six months. Because of the GP's 'independent' clinical status peer review was difficult. The most significant advance in the United Kingdom was recognising that the trained doctor can improve standards, firstly with the introduction of ATLS (Advanced Trauma Life Support) followed by the Diploma in Immediate Medical Care, Pre-hospital Emergency Care (PHEC), and Pre-hospital Trauma Life Support (PHTLS). The quality of care using a properly trained experienced Immediate Care doctor moves this on to a different plateau.

Currently MAGPAS responds to 2,500 incidents each year. At present there are fifty three members of MAGPAS. Ninety five per cent of the calls are to traffic accidents, but house fires, industrial accidents, sporting events, and horse riding account for significant numbers of the remainder. There are about twelve accidents each year involving aircraft, gliders and other aviation activities. Within the fifty three members there are two RAF units participating and five hospital staff, mainly consultants.

I joined MAGPAS in 1976 while serving in the Royal Air Force, initially as a research project while I was seconded to Cambridge as a Senior Registrar. Currently I attend over 150 calls each year. As well as hospital doctors being members and participating in Immediate Care, the three Accident Departments in Cambridgeshire offer considerable direct and indirect support to MAGPAS. This was not always the case because in formative years GPs were regarded by the hospital establishment as 'interfering in our business'.

Various trauma reports have highlighted the hospital problem, mainly by unsupervised junior medical staff, so it probably was the GP's business, particularly when the patient was registered with that GP. When MAGPAS was set up doctors attending accidents caused some surprise and occasional friction with the Ambulance Service. It was seen by some ambulance staff as doctors trying to show up weaknesses in ambulance training. This rumbled on until about 1980 when GPs around Cambridge, mainly Dr John Scott and Dr Paul Silverston, and Dr Robin Glover in Peterborough, got together with ambulance crews and started voluntary training for Emergency Medical Technician qualifications. Peterborough had qualified paramedics long before the official NHS training commenced.

This proved to be a major breakthrough because doctors and ambulance staff understood their respective roles, and it was not a competition, but a desire to complement each other's roles that doctors attended accidents. Initially in rural areas the doctor was likely to be in attendance several minutes ahead of the Ambulance, or indeed the Police or Fire Service, to initiate the first life saving skill of air way protection. Within the records of twenty five years of MAGPAS work, at a rate of 2,500 calls each year, is a small but significant percentage where the patient's airway was restored. In reality this means a life saved, but never recorded as such.

To justify Immediate Care there is a continuing demand to prove and demonstrate life 'saved', whether the care is provided by paramedics, BASICS doctors or helicopter units. Current research is beginning to show that ten to 15% of pre-hospital deaths are preventable, in the same way that the 1988 Trauma Report demonstrated that 20% of those dying in hospital were preventable. One theme coming out of current work is that the preventable pre-hospital deaths are likely to be due to excessive time delays at the scene. Has HEMS looked at its preventable deaths? If they are significantly lower than those stated above then the concept of a helicopter and medical response is justified. I believe that is due to a time specific response. In the same way that the ATLS and Trauma centres talked of the 'Golden Hour' the pre-hospital workers coined the phrase 'The Platinum Ten Minutes' on Cambridge education courses.

With the advent of NHSTD (National Health Service Training Department) paramedic training some within the national ambulance hierarchy publicly stated that at last there was no need for doctors to be called out as complete patient care could be given by the NHS ambulance paramedic. Such arrogance!

The BASICS logo demonstrates that knowledge in medicine is never complete by the three quarter circle. In East Anglia the number of calls specifically requesting doctors went up after the introduction of the trained paramedic who recognised the more significant and often subtle physiological changes, as well as the need for practical procedures, not taught to paramedics. Personally I have rarely experienced difficulties with the men and women at the roadside. Perhaps that is because I have been involved in their final assessment after their paramedic training and hospital attachment.

However, a valid comment by the ambulance services was, and still is, if we are putting paramedics on the road at a certified standard what is the standard of the doctor turning out to such accidents? While BASICS and the Faculty of Pre-hospital Care in Edinburgh are still working on accreditation and Immediate Care standards the regular joint training with MAGPAS doctors, ambulance and fire personnel has taken place in Cambridge over the last two decades. While this aided the on-scene team work it did not solve the question of a proven standard for doctors.

In 1989 MAGPAS held a course for twenty six doctors with Dr John Scott as Course Director. The course had a series of lectures and practical skills and demonstrations. The decision to fund and hold the course in Churchill College, Cambridge came from the initiative of Dr Neville Silverston, a founder and Vice-Chairman of MAGPAS. In reality this was the pre-cursor of BASICS Education. Following this course Dr John Eaton of MEDICS (Mid Essex Doctors Immediate Care Scheme) produced his text book in Immediate Care, which became the first standard text.

In 1988 the Royal College of Surgeons in Edinburgh ran its first Diet of Diploma in Immediate Medical Care. The need for training people for Immediate Care standards was developed from the first course at Churchill College. As a result the five day Cambridge Immediate Care Course was introduced and runs twice a year at Madingley Hall with considerable and continuing support from MAGPAS, Addenbrookes' Hospital staff, and others. These courses were adopted as the premier BASICS Education course under John Scott's leadership. Those who take these courses have an 85% pass rate in the Diploma of Immediate Medical Care. After this course was set up and developed BASICS and the Edinburgh College set up the Pre-hospital Emergency Care course for doctors, paramedics and nurses, which covers trauma, medical emergencies, obstetric and paediatric problems in a three day theoretical, practical and assessment course.

At the same time Chris Maimaris, my colleague in Accident & Emergency at Cambridge, and Paul Silverston in MAGPAS, founded the Cambridge PHTLS courses and were trained by Professor Norman McSwain and others from a USA PHTLS faculty. As a result about 30% of MAGPAS doctors have either ATLS, PHTLS, PHEC, Provider or Instructor status, or have passed the Diploma in Immediate Medical Care. Several of the members have at least two qualifications. It can be reasonably stated that within East Anglia many Immediate Care doctors have accredited qualifications.

The clinical application of these skills is needed in about one in eight calls when doctors are called on an unassessed basis. The advantage of these calls with good radio communication is such that doctors on average spend twenty minutes per call. Additionally they have the resource to stand down an ambulance, or request additional ambulances or doctors.

When trouble strikes and there are multiple casualties or a difficult entrapment, two minds and two pairs of hands prove invaluable. Paul Silverston is in charge of the MAGPAS call-out system. He initiated MAGPAS' two doctor response to reported entrapments or incidents requiring two or more ambulances. Examples of this include an incident several years ago when on a wet Saturday there were three separate accidents within ten miles of each other resulting in nine fatalities and twelve injured. MAGPAS responded by sending at least three doctors to each of the incidents, most having just enough time to get into dry clothing and re-equip before the next call.

One of the most striking developments is early intubation, particularly for the serious head injury. The current MAGPAS Training Officer, Dr Jurgen Klein is an Anaesthetist. He has carried muscle relaxants for several years and has used them successfully in the difficult struggling head injury. In the Neurosurgical Unit at Addenbrookes Hospital we are beginning to see quite remarkable recoveries by early intubation, although much of this is unpublished at the present time. There is considerable thought being given to an advanced tier of training for Immediate Care doctors with intubation techniques used by MAGPAS doctors, rather than dependency on hospital anaesthetists, and rarely utilized mobile hospital teams. This of course was something pioneered by HEMS. One of the paradoxes is that superficially HEMS and GP Immediate Care appear diametrically opposed. However, they appear to be evolving to a common pathway which is predominantly care of the airway and breathing, and aids to circulation only if needs must. In a rural area support of the circulation is only needed when distance or entrapment determine this. The

University of Sheffield are running a trial with West Yorkshire and East Anglian Ambulance Trusts. MAGPAS doctors participate in this on a blind cross-over study to evaluate the effect of the minimal resuscitation concept.

The motivation for doctors to take up and remain with Immediate Care is obscure. Looking around at a MAGPAS or BASICS meeting the 'hardware' or vehicles are usually fast executive cars. As an aside they are all nearly new and well maintained. Nearly all the MAGPAS regulars have had police driving instruction, including Institute of Advanced Motoring sponsored courses. Is it the chance of fast driving that motivates the doctor? I think this is less so nowadays as this is considered anti-social by an increasing number. Is it an escape from the routine of medicine?

In the practice of Immediate Care there are moments of humour, such as the time a passing chest specialist offered to take over while I was applying a synthetic cast to a tibial fracture as an aid to speed up extrication. To moisten the cast I needed a small amount of water. This was brought in a two gallon bucket by a fire fighter! As the passing doctor tapped me on the shoulder to advise me of the next step I literally stepped into the bucket of water. 'Never mind doc', said the fire officer, 'I thought you needed to cool off'.

There are one or two 'black' memories which I rarely discuss except to very close friends, or others who have witnessed similar events. There are times of sorrow, but also a sense of achievement when the whole team sits down in a debrief of all the pre-hospital services and the hospital team to talk through and counsel staff. We are fortunate in Cambridge with the unique integration between the pre-hospital workers and the Accident & Emergency staff. My support comes from my consultant colleagues, Chris Maimaris and Sue Robinson, and the A&E nursing staff who I have worked with and known for many years.

Recently walking the rail track at a suicide I asked the ambulance crew and the police how they felt – 'we gave up being humans long ago', one replied. A quiet word to Ian Morris, the hospital chaplain, and a visit for coffee will provide help and support as needed.

I believe it is a deeper relationship in being a member of the emergency services with a special camaraderie that makes people participate in Immediate Care. The military know that there are only certain people you go to war with. Deep down I believe the Immediate Care doctor genuinely cares for the patients and has a belief in improving quality of the patient care as first proposed by Ken Easton.

I also believe there is a change in the new doctors coming into medicine. There is still recruitment into Immediate Care in spite of demand for shorter hours and GP cooperatives who provide a service only when they are on call. Being a member of an Immediate Care scheme is a unique experience which adds an extra dimension to working practice. On a personal level it has given me considerable insight into the mechanisms of injury and the ability to work out injury patterns as a consequence of this.

In my opening remarks I referred to Bernard Shaw and his view that only unreasonable people promote change. Perhaps there would be no Immediate Care whether it is GP based or helicopter based without these 'unreasonable people'. Perhaps because of unreasonable people pre-hospital care thrives in Cambridge.

'On doit des regards aux vivant; on ne doit aux morts que le verite' – 'We owe respect to the living, to the dead we owe only the truth' (Voltaire 1795).

H M Sherriff, MA, FRCS, FFAEM, Director of the Accident and Emergency Department, Addenbrookes Hospital NHS Trust, Hills Road, Cambridge CB2 2QQ

RAISED HELIPADS AT LONDON AND LEEDS

Nicholas Dorey

It is gratifying at the end of any engineering project to witness its successful commission into operational service. This was particularly so in the case of the elevated heliport at the Royal London Hospital, since its completion provided a permanent daytime base for the Helicopter Emergency Medical Service (HEMS) in the heart of London's East End.

By virtue of the fact that the facility was the first of its kind in the United Kingdom, little was known at the scheme stage as to precisely what was required for operational efficiency. Consultations were held with many parties to evolve the eventual design solution.

In planning the facility every effort was made to maximise the space available for the landing area, fire standby locations and accommodation zones. However, there were limits as to what could realistically be achieved in view of the restrictions imposed by the size of the existing building. We were fortunate that the Alexandra Wing at the Royal London Hospital was on the outskirts of the city with only one obstruction to flight operations, a boiler house chimney in close proximity. By raising the new structure to match the level of the upper roof it was possible to create a relatively free, obstacle clear zone. This was important since it meant that flight operations would not be impeded by winds originating from directions within what would be a banned sector.

It was also fortunate that the existing structure of the Alexandra Wing had sufficient residual strength within its vertical supports and foundations to accommodate increased loads. Detailed design assessments were undertaken to identify the critical structural elements and to establish precisely what additional loads could safely be supported and where.

The new imposed heliport structure had to be kept as lightweight as possible in order to maximise the load available to accommodate the aircraft. For this reason aluminium sections were employed to form the landing platform, access ramp and staircases. These in turn were supported on a steel grillage to ensure the resultant loads could be safely transmitted direct to the building's existing column heads.

From the detailed design assessment it was established that the maximum aircraft weight that could safely be accommodated was 5 tonnes (5000 Kg).

The twin engined Group A helicopter selected and purchased for the London EMS operation was an Aerospatiale SA365N Dauphin. This aircraft has a maximum take off weight (MTOW) of 4000 Kg. The limiting design load case therefore gives scope for the Trust to utilise the services of a more modern, quieter but slightly heavier aircraft in the future should one become available.

Three independent fire fighting systems were installed at the Royal London Heliport such that should one system fail, for whatever reason, there would still be adequate facilities to deal with an incident. The systems provide a rapid intervention capability for use by the trained fire crew. Before finally selecting the equipment to be installed, a special visit was arranged to the fire fighting school at RAF Manston for consultation and assessment purposes. With the equipment and quantity of principal and complimentary agents provided, there was, as a result, sufficient foam media to sustain independent fire-fighting operations for a period in excess of 20 minutes. Initially the regulatory authorities were of the opinion that the level of active fire protection provided was substantially more than the minimum required. However, subsequent opinion is that the level adopted set the standard for others to follow and current regulatory guidance notes confirm this.

In order to be able to transport the trauma patient from main roof level to the resuscitation unit at ground floor, a dedicated lift had to be added to the building. A conventional traction lift could not be employed since its high level motor room would have constituted a further obstruction to flight operations, resulting in yet more flight limitations. The height of the building precluded the use of a hydraulic lift, so the choice was limited to either a bottom drive traction or rack and pinion lift. Economy and ease of installation dictated the selection of the latter. This form of lift has a proven track record of reliability when properly maintained. The lift recall facility is guarded by a hands free security installation such that the lift remains in constant readiness for its dedicated role.

In view of budgetary constraints an in-house refuelling facility could not be included in the original construction contract. It was recognised, however, that a refuelling provision would provide operational advantages, but it was decided that this was something that would have to be added at a later date.

Introducing a new noise source into an existing urban environment will always evoke concerns within the local community. The London Heliport project was no exception. Whilst the residents acknowledged the merits of the service they were worried about a further source of noise nuisance. Sensibly, a policy of consultation rather than confrontation was followed. This gained the necessary planning consents and agreements, albeit to be reviewed after an initial three year trial period. That review has now taken place and a further three year extension has been granted. Experience at London has now shown that once the initial novelty wore off, the EMS helicopter operating from its elevated pad is rarely noticed in the local community.

Throughout the design and planning stages of the project, constant endeavours were made to ensure that the design was economical and did not compromise either operational or safety aspects. The final project cost for the heliport facility installed in 1989 was £1.2 million; not an excessive building cost by today's standards, but a significant sum nevertheless.

Following the initiation of heliport operations it was immediately apparent that far more people were congregating at roof level than had originally been anticipated. As learning progressed and the HEMS operation grew in both work load and stature, space at roof level became a premium. To alleviate the situation, accommodation modules were installed on a raised steel platform, over a designated area of main roof, to provide additional office, wash down and storage facilities.

The London Heliport project provided a unique learning curve for what is precisely involved in planning and constructing such a facility. Having done it once it is natural that one would wish to do it again, but this time starting with a blank sheet of paper so to speak. This opportunity, in essence, arose with the Leeds General Infirmary.

The United Leeds Teaching Hospital Trust had embarked on a major redevelopment programme, the first phase of which included the construction of a £42 million new wing. This, amongst other facilities, includes a new Accident and Emergency department, Intensive Care Unit and Neurosurgery Centre. The redevelopment programme was part of a rationalisation by the hospital to join all its acute services on one site. At some point in the future the hospital may well become a designated trauma centre for West Yorkshire.

With the Leeds General Infirmary, set to become one of the foremost Accident and Emergency centres in the North of England, the inclusion of a rooftop heliport facility to accept patients arriving by helicopter, or to base a Helicopter Emergency Medical Service, was considered an important feature. A preliminary scheme had been prepared which mirrored the form of construction employed at the Royal London, but it was rejected by the Trust due to financial constraints.

The appointment of European Helicopters as consultants was to undertake a feasibility study to report and advise on ways in which the original proposals could be improved and savings made.

The site for the new wing was ideally located, set on a hill overlooking the city centre. A mixed variety of municipal buildings surrounded the hospital campus, with the nearest residential properties located well away to the north west and south. Immediately adjacent to the north west of the site is a generating station complex. A large flue stack that arose from the roof of this building was demolished as part of the redevelopment programme. Two further chimneys were located at the northern boundary of the complex that were to remain and would constitute an obstruction to flight operations resulting in an operational limitation to helicopter operations.

The new helipad at Leeds

Photo: N Dorey

The planned new building, for which sub-structure site work was shortly to commence, was large indeed – seven storeys high in a reversed L plan configuration each leg of which was to be 110 metres long by 40 metres wide.

The new building, which would adjoin the modern Clarendon wing, was also to be linked to the existing Victorian hospital buildings. Part of the new building's reinforced concrete structure was required to span a tunnel over the Leeds inner ring road.

It has long been European Helicopters' view that, if included at an early design stage, a heliport should not greatly add to the cost of a hospital building whilst offering great service to the hospital and the public. In this case, examination of the original proposals for a helipad were found to be less than ideal for a number of reasons. Incorporation of the helipad was made towards the end of the design process and, instead of making it integral, was an additional structure. The original proposals would also have failed to meet internationally accepted aviation standards and by virtue of the obstructions present, be inefficient in operation.

The feasibility study concluded, however, that the many conflicting demands could be met and that a safe, effective and affordable helicopter facility could be included into the hospital redevelopment. The recommended solution was for the design team to make a reappraisal of the upper levels of the new hospital building to incorporate a clear, unobstructed level area of roof equipped with a variety of safety measures. It was acknowledged that this would cause extra design work at this stage but should result in a safe design, in better keeping with the environment and at a lower, more affordable, cost.

The study went on to illustrate a design proposal on a building block principle. Initially it was to provide the basic minimum facility which must be in place for any operation, together with additional elements that could be added either during build or at a later stage to upgrade the facility and make it capable of providing a full Helicopter Emergency Medical Service.

A study was submitted to the Trust for consideration and evaluation. Budget estimates were prepared for the various options, namely:

Landing facility day only
Landing facility day and night
Full HEMS

The price for the construction of the full HEMS package was estimated to be of the order of £600,000. The Trust decided to proceed with the construction of the heliport with basic facilities, but to allow for a full HEMS facility to be brought into operation at some later date.

Unfortunately, European Helicopters Limited involvement was after the building's initial design development had advanced to a stage whereby certain recommended changes could no longer be accommodated and a number of compromises had to be made.

In view of the size of the building space was not a problem. Sufficient room and more was available at roof level below the landing surface to provide full HEMS accommodation facilities should that option be exercised in the future.

One of the design features of the new building was the aluminium clad, steel framed, curved roofs that extend over the front portion of the two wings of the building. Local planners were keen that all items of plant should be concealed within these roof zones. Within these areas there was ample space to accommodate the tanks to supply the necessary fire fighting equipment.

The initial planning submission for the main building incorporated provision for the helicopter facility and the detailed physical design was negotiated and agreed with the local planning authority. At that stage, however, full details of the proposed use were not finalised. In order to avoid delay in the progress of the principal application the Council agreed to reserve final approval of the use of the helicopter facility to a separate application. This subsequent application to use the agreed facility was supported with information relating to the experience of the London HEMS operation.

Noise consultants were appointed by the Trust and Leeds City Council. Following a joint meeting a noise impact assessment report was prepared by the Trust's representative. This technical report identified the noise index measurement to be used, gave appropriate noise contour levels, together with typical and worst case scenarios. Further information was supplied on likely flight paths and landing and take off profiles on which these figures were based. As experienced in London, a local residents group was, understandably, concerned with certain aspects of the proposals and in particular with noise.

During the course of the planning negotiations, which were somewhat protracted, the operational Royal London Heliport provided unrivalled first hand experience. Visits were made by the Leeds planning officers, followed by a delegation of local Leeds residents. Finally, a group of Leeds City Councillors visited to gain first hand experience and permit them to determine the planning application.

Being a new build development, freedom existed for the LGI heliport structure to be designed to accommodate a selected imposed load and hence to choose a range of helicopter types. The most suitable types for the air ambulance role are multi-engined machines classified into the light or medium size category. Heavy helicopters, in excess of 5700 Kg, are rarely used since their size and weight will generally not only preclude their use on to the rooftop pad but also limit their access to an accident site. They are also very costly to buy and to operate.

At the time of our feasibility study the European Helicopter Industries EH101 helicopter was under development as a prototype. In size it is very similar to the Search and Rescue Sea King with a maximum take-off weight of 14,600 Kg. Fitted with three engines, it is much more capable following an engine failure than the more common two engine types, having lost proportionally much less of its available power. Accordingly it can be expected to have excellent performance to an elevated heliport of the size proposed for the LGI.

Although it is too large and expensive to be a dedicated air ambulance, it is expected to be taken into Navy and RAF service following purchase announcements by HM Government. It may eventually be used by the rescue services, replacing the Sea King in these duties. Following a major incident in the north of England involving multiple casualties it would likely be deployed. The ability to land on the elevated LGI heliport was considered to be a valuable asset and the structure has been designed to accommodate this aircraft. Unlike London where space constraints inhibited layout, the fire standby areas at Leeds are large with ample room to accommodate apparatus and equipment. The fire fighting system to be installed will be similar to that employed at London but with improvements and modifications to achieve greater efficiency at reduced cost.

With such a large plan area the new wing of the LGI contains a number of lift cores. Two traction lifts in the main central core complex were selected to serve the main roof level. It is not intended that they will be dedicated lifts but will have the facility to be switched from public use to an EMS mode. Once in its EMS mode the lift will remain secure and only respond to those people authorised to use it.

From knowledge of the London operation it was known that a dedicated refuelling facility would offer substantial advantages in terms of the availability of the helicopter and its operational flexibility, as well as reducing operational costs. Since the area of coverage in the Yorkshire region is more widely dispersed than in London, it is likely that the average length of sortie will be greater. Consequently, more fuel would be required and refuelling would be necessary after most missions. The problem will be aggravated in the summer when higher temperatures reduce the payload for safe single engine operation onto the rooftop. The directive issued to the Leeds design team was that they should make all necessary provisions for a refuelling facility to be easily accommodated at a later date, if not actually included in the initial build.

If a Helicopter Emergency Medical Service, similar to that operating in London, were to be set up and based at the LGI, the geographical area to be served would encompass West Yorkshire, North Yorkshire, Humberside and part of South Yorkshire, north of Sheffield. Contained within this operational zone would be the major trunk routes of the A1, M1, M62, M18 and M180 and a population of 3 million people.

The United Leeds Teaching Hospital Trust has not yet committed itself to what type of emergency helicopter service it will operate. However, learning from the pioneering work undertaken at the Royal London, the Leeds General Infirmary will have the most modern elevated heliport facilities in Europe at what is considered an affordable price. We wish them every success for the future.

Nick Dorey, Consultant working in association with European Helicopters. Associate, John Spelzini & Partners, Consulting Engineers.

CONCEPT OF THE AIR RESCUE SYSTEM IN GERMANY (ADAC)

Gerhard Kugler

The development of aeromedical services in the Federal Republic of Germany began on the initiative of the German Automobile Association (ADAC). ADAC was challenged by the tremendous increase of motor vehicle accidents. The first programme started on 2 November 1970.

Today, there is a dense network of 50 programmes in Germany. The following major features set the framework for a uniform standard:

- Day flight operation daily from 0700 hours (in winter sunrise) until sunset.
- Air rescue bases are usually located at hospitals.
- Infrastructure for flight operation (hangar, fuel facility, rooms for the crew) is established at the hospital base.
- In case of grounding due to maintenance a back up rescue helicopter for replacement must be available.
- Medical crew on each flight consists of a doctor and a medical attendant.
- Standardised medical equipment so that all kinds of emergencies can be handled.
- All rescue flights have to be dispatched by that Regional Rescue Control Centre (RCC) to which the helicopter base is attached.
- The RCC must be reached from public telephone by a uniform call-number (110 112 or 19222).
- Free of charge service to the patient and for the people who call the helicopter.

The entity of the aeromedical system in Germany is not commercially orientated. It is governed and controlled by the local authorities or the federal states. To make full use of the time advantage over ground vehicles, the mission radius of each helicopter base has been limited to 50-70 km. For primary missions, the flying time to the scene is approximately 8 minutes.

Since the philosophy of the airmed system is the rapid provision of patient care by a physician, patient transport on board an airmed helicopter is of secondary importance. After treatment by the flight doctor at the scene in more than a third of all missions the patient is handed over to ground ambulance for transport.

For reasons of saving lives, the helicopter must take off before the mission's urgency is confirmed and, in cases of

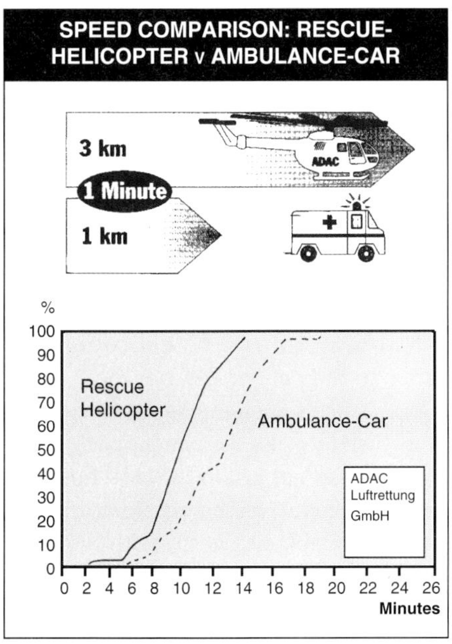

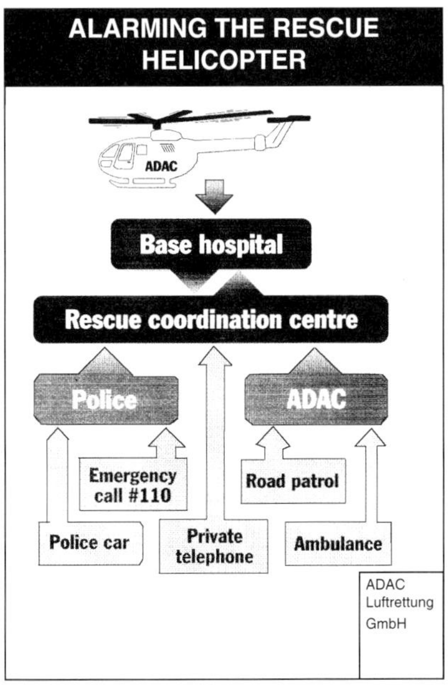

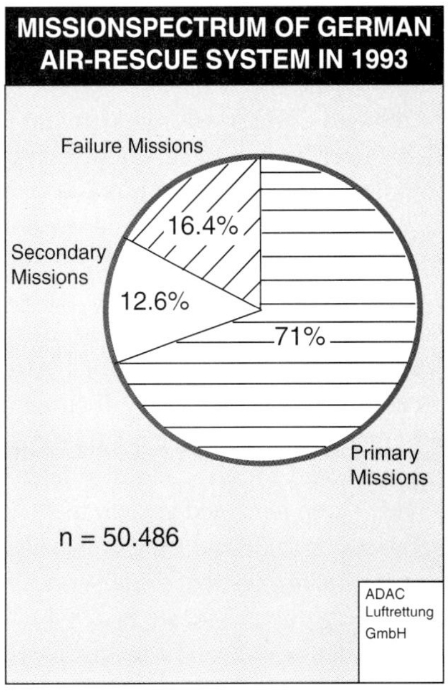

doubt, the decision is made in favour of the patient. To facilitate the task of the RCC-people in charge of decision making there are so called indication catalogues in use.

Since 1970 616,000 rescue flights have been flown in Germany. All 50 bases do some 50,000 missions per year. In the early years of operation, more than 75% of the missions involved road trauma victims. However, although the total figures for such flights have increased, their relative share has reduced markedly and is now only 31%. This development is obviously the result of the convincing success of the daily air rescue missions and has prompted a higher demand for this system even than for other kinds of emergencies.

In the initial period it was only when the German Automobile Club ADAC bore the cost of the flights that airmed helicopters could literally get off the ground. Meanwhile since 1974 Germany's EMS legislation has been assigned the obligation to the Social Health Care System that costs of the rescue service have to be paid. But due to the fact that the tariffs negotiated with the insurers do not cover the costs completely, ADAC contributes continuously from their own financial resources each year for its 16 owned rescue helicopters which are integrated in the network.

In 1994 the compensation paid by the health insurers for air rescue missions flown from all 50 bases amounted to 100 million DM. Compared with the overall costs of the rescue service, both on the ground and in the air, this sum is less than 4%.

From 1970 to 1994 the number of vehicles in Germany doubled from 18 Mio to 40 Mio whereas the number of road traffic fatalities dropped from 20,000 to 9,800. In 1994 fewer people died on the roads than in 1953.

Since airmed helicopters have contributed considerably to this development the role of the Airmed Services has become vital for our country.

'The best ambulance on earth is in the sky'

Professor Gerhard Kugler has been Head of ADAC Helicopter Service in Germany since 1970 and responsible for its organisation and development.

SECTION 3 C (i) b: CONCEPTS OF A TRAUMA CARE SYSTEM/EUROPEAN

THE FIRST AIR RESCUE SERVICE IN GERMANY: CHRISTOPH 1

Erwin Stolpe

At the end of the 1960s, the demand for a doctor directly at the scene of an accident in cases of life threatening complications came ever more frequently. However this was not the first occasion, because originally Professor Kuerschner had introduced his Klinomobil, a mobile operating theatre, with the purpose of delivering the maximum therapy possible actually at the site of injury which was not always feasible. Attempts to solve this problem were made by introducing the emergency doctor scheme (Notarzt) for land based services, at first in Frankfurt and Munich, and then later in thickly populated towns. There remained gaps in the overall cover especially in the countryside and these were solved only after legislation for a compulsory rescue service was introduced. An emergency doctor scheme evolved covering the whole of the population of West Germany, based on statutory laws.

At the same time as the emergency doctor land ambulance system (Notarztwagen) developed, the German automobile association (ADAC) took the initiative and founded the first civilian air rescue service in 1970 at the district general hospital of Harlaching, Munich. This was the foundation stone for the air rescue system in Germany.

The original idea had been to use the helicopter for transporting the doctor to the patient and not the patient to the hospital, but experience soon demonstrated that the helicopter must also be used to take the patient back to an adequate treatment centre and not just to the local hospital by land ambulance. In the countryside and along motorways it was no longer acceptable to put up with the long journey times needed for land ambulances to return to hospital. This principle still holds today even though the widespread emergency doctor ambulance network may reach an accident before the helicopter service. After first aid and stabilisation of the patient the journey back to a hospital must be as fast as possible. The normal circle of activity for a helicopter doing primary rescue has a 50km radius and a maximum time from call out to arrival at the patient of 12 minutes. Occasionally single flights might be longer but the return is always much shorter because there is no wasted time looking for an emergency landing place. Christoph 1, which is the name of the first helicopter service at Harlaching, flew 1733 sorties in 1995.

The general principle in Germany is to call out at the same time both the land based emergency doctor ambulance and the helicopter emergency medical service (Rettungstransporthubschraubers RTH) so that the patient can be treated by whoever arrives first. If the emergency call is vague and detailed information is lacking, the less severely injured patient can be looked after by the land based emergency doctor or, if necessary, the helicopter service can then be called. Additionally the land based Notarzt can give information about what further help is needed. Both rescue systems are called out by the same central control where there is a doctor and experienced personnel. In spite of this system there is an aborted mission rate of 20% for the helicopter service which cannot be reduced further.

In addition to this primary rescue there are secondary transport journeys from smaller hospitals to larger ones. Another specialised service is the emergency service which requires a winch. Christoph 1 is the only civilian helicopter with this facility which can rescue patients in the mountains or where there are no roads. This winch service was introduced in 1994 and, in conjunction with the mountain rescue services, we have done about 30 such rescues each year with a steadily increasing number.

The crew of the RTH in Munich comprises one pilot, a winch-operator/co-pilot, a rescue assistant and an emergency doctor. The rescue assistant (Rettungsassistent) has already had many years of service on a land based emergency ambulance and has a rota between land and air based systems. The emergency doctors are chosen from the 30 doctors in training at Harlaching and come from the specialties of surgery, medicine and anaesthetics. They must have the basic rescue doctor training, higher training of three years and a six month intensive care unit experience.

Christoph 1, with all this special training and staff, has flown more than 500,000 sorties since 1970. Throughout this time standards, techniques and instruments have improved as have our successful missions. The basic principles of the German air rescue system nowadays are:

1. Compulsory maintenance of a 12 minute maximum time to medical intervention from the time of call out both for land and air based rescue systems with a doctor.
2. All rescue helicopters to be stationed at the hospital and not at a local airport or service station.
3. Primary rescue helicopters must all be staffed by an emergency doctor and a rescue assistant.
4. Integration of both the land and air rescue systems through a common control room.
5. Rescue helicopters in their primary rescue role should be confined to flying only in daylight hours because of technical reasons and above all to maintain safety standards.

Dr Erwin Stolpe has been the leading doctor of the helicopter service Christoph I at Harlaching, Munich, ever since it started in 1970 under the aegis of the German automobile club (ADAC).

The map overleaf shows the Helicopter Centres for Air Rescue in Germany. *Acknowledgements*: Professor Gerhard Kugler.

Helicopter Centres for Air Rescue in Germany

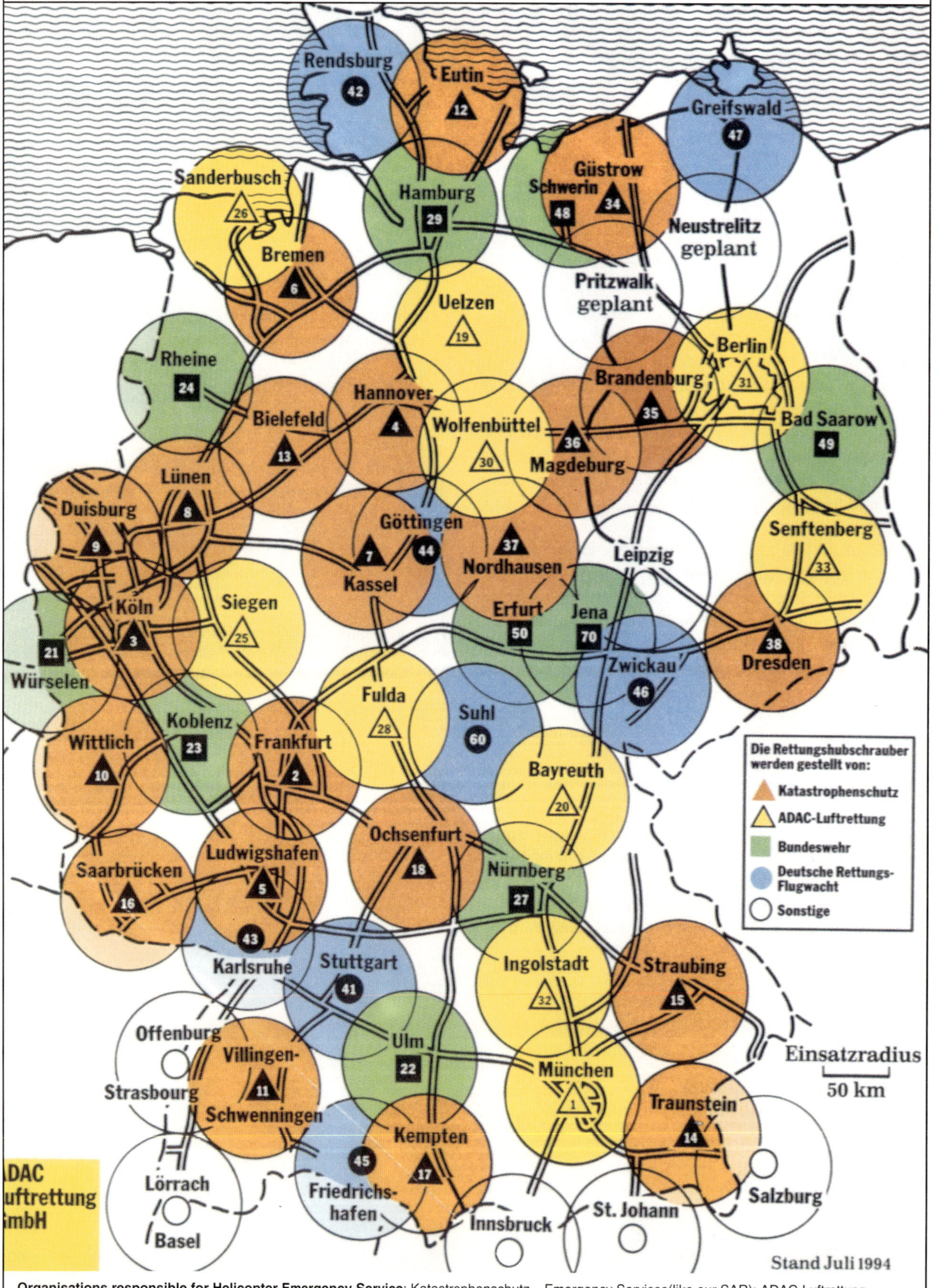

Organisations responsible for Helicopter Emergency Service: Katastrophenschutz – Emergency Services(like our SAR); ADAC-Luftrettung – Automobile Club Air Rescue; Bundeswehr – Armed Forces; DRF – charitable organisation; Sonstige – Others.
Also: Strasbourg – French; Basel – Swiss; Innsbruck, St Johann, Salzburg – Austrian.

SERVICES DE L'AIDE MEDICALE URGENTE EN FRANCE: SAMU

Pierre Huguenard

Introduction

The French emergency medical service, l'organisation de l'aide medicale urgente, has been running since 1972 and its principles were constituted by Act of Parliament on the 6th January 1986.

1. All citizens are equal when sick and especially in an emergency.
2. The coordination of emergency medical services is centred on specialised medical institutions called the Services de l'aide medicale urgente (SAMU) (Lareng, 1968).
3. SAMU provides a graded response based on triage. Major cases merit the intervention of a specialised medical team in rapid transport vehicles with resuscitation equipment at their disposal. Minor cases are usually managed by general practitioners (GPs) in group practice who also provide continuity of care. SAMU refers appropriate cases to these general medical practitioners.
4. All demands for emergency treatment must trigger a response.
5. Emergency medical care is provided free to patients. If the treatment is justified, the costs are reimbursed by the Department of Social Security.

Photo: author

Implementation

Since 1986 SAMU has been constituted as a hospital based service with its own management and specific budget providing a reception centre and control room (CRRA). There is a SAMU organisation in every county under the responsibility of the prefect who represents central government. Each SAMU covers a variable population and geographical area. In urban areas the average number of emergency calls is 6 per 100 inhabitants per year. In rural areas there are 4 per 100 inhabitants per year. A centre providing medical care dealing with around 6 calls per hour (about 60,000 per year) should cover a population of about a million. Actually there are about one hundred centres for a population of 55 million in France.

Each SAMU is equipped with a telecommunications network integrated with the other emergency services (Fire Brigade, Police, Ambulance), as well as public and private hospitals involved in acute medical care and GP organisations. Many radio frequencies allow communication with the intervention teams. The emergency telephone number for the public is 15 for SAMU, 16 for the police and 17 for the Fire Brigade. In the UK there is only one number 999 for all three emergency services and the telephone operator has to decide which one is relevant.

The personnel of SAMU includes radiotelephonists, control room doctors, medical auxiliaries (physician assistants), and administrators. The radiotelephonists are more skilled than hospital switch board operators, but paid the same (they should have higher status). They are called 'Permanencieres' and work, two or three at a time, for periods of six to eight hours. The SAMU of Val de Marne (SAMU 94) employ 17 radiotelephonists. Their role is to receive the calls, fill out forms, reassure callers, take clown the details (address, circumstances, seriousness of problem) and make sure return calls from control are possible. They also transmit the calls to the doctors, find available hospital services and keep contact with the intervention teams by radio.

The doctors are generally hospital doctors with a training in anaesthetics and ICU. They answer the calls put through to them by the radiotelephonists, give their opinion, choose the most suitable response, pass on certain calls to other emergency or health care services, activate and advise the intervention teams (detail the medical incident, find appropriate receiving hospital, arrange admission and organise transport, sort out medicolegal and other problems). These tasks are more difficult if there are multiple calls, numerous victims, over stretched hospital services, bad weather, multiply injured or complex medical problems and especially during catastrophes and major incidents.

They are known as 'medecins regulateurs' – control room doctors. In the main they have an honorary university position. Their salary is modest and night duty is badly paid. Recruitment of these doctors is therefore difficult. The low risk patients are put in the charge of other doctors also called 'regulateurs' but 'omnipraticien' (GP standard of training) who have less sophisticated resources and respond to 60% of calls. Minor cases are managed as GP home visits. They are tasked by the control GP (omnipraticien) and maintain radio contact with the SAMU headquarters.

The SAMU medical auxiliaries are anaesthetic or ICU nurses who assist the doctors.The administrators manage the budget, draw up rotas, make inventories of equipment and are responsible for putting information in the computer database.

Management of Major Cases

For major cases, intervention is provided by the Services Mobile D'Urgence et de Reanimation (SMUR). They are hospital based services led by a hospital doctor and administered by hospital managers. Their range of distance should allow intervention within an average of 10 minutes. But the 300 SMUR in France could not cover the whole population if they only used ground vehicles so helicopters are used to increase the range. 20 SAMU had full time use of a helicopter in 1994.The others 'borrow' aircraft and pilots from the military or police when required.

SMUR teams must be led by a doctor trained in airway management, assisted by a specialist nurse and a trainee. The team is completed by either a helicopter pilot or ambulance driver, often a holder of a first-aid certificate. The SMUR doctor is most often an anaesthetist, although sometimes a paediatrician or cardiologist accompanies special transfers. They receive on-call pay like the control room doctors; c'est a dire, trop peu.

Their role is to make a diagnosis as fast as possible with minimum means, to transmit a medical report to the control doctor, to ensure all emergency interventions (fluid resuscitation, intubation, ventilation, sedation, drainage, etc) are carried out rigorously according to protocol, continue careful monitoring during transport and maintain discipline within the team. This does not stop at the hospital door because care of the patient must be handed over to the staff actually in the hospital. Good emergency medical care starts at the scene, continues during transport without interruption until admission to hospital. Ideally, every hospital based SMUR should have a receiving room for emergencies where they can triage, assess, and resuscitate their emergency admissions as well as plan definitive management of the patient with direct access to operating theatres, radiology department or most often to the ICU. It is a difficult job, heavy with responsibility, not always appreciated, poorly paid and sometimes dangerous. The young doctors in SMUR practice hold out for no longer than two to three years.

SMUR Equipment

The SMUR teams carry two standardised colour coded cases: *blue* for respiratory support and *red* for circulatory resuscitation. The strong waterproof cases are found on the helicopters and in front-line resuscitation ambulances which also have stocks to replace used equipment. Additional equipment includes stretcher, suction, defibrillator, monitoring, ECG, oxygen saturation and capnography.

SMUR Transport

There are many types of aircraft suitable for adaptation to medical use: the old **Alouette III** – basic, strong, rustic, powerful, multi-purpose, for transporting a casualty and four attendants, not very fast (160km/h) and a little noisy with poor fuel consumption costing an inclusive hourly rate - 7000 FFr; the **Ecureuil** SA35OB – economic single engine, faster (250km/h), less noisy, more comfortable carrying one recumbent casualty and three attendants (4500 FFr/h); the **Dauphin** AS 365 N2, (in a superior category), twin engine, carries two casualties and four seated attendants at 250 km/h over a 1000km range (10,000 FFr/h); the **Puma** (SA 330) even more superior, very useful for a major incident because it carries six recumbent casualties (15000 FFr/h).

These French aircraft are currently used and have a single engine, except for the Dauphin and Puma. They are in the light helicopter category, less expensive, easily maintained, less cluttered, quieter, quicker take-off from a smaller landing site, with a single pilot, but carrying a team of three personnel, enough space for a stretcher to allow medical care and with a hold for equipment. They are ideal for primary interventions at the scene of an accident or close to a house.

European regulations have recently imposed twin engine aircraft for medivac flights over towns and for long distances including interhospital transfers. Although there is a choice of excellent machines, they are three tunes more expensive; the Dauphin as above, the Bell-Augusta A 109 G and aircraft from the Franco-German company Eurocopter like the BK 117 B2 or the new C 135 are all possibilities.

Four wheel drive light rapid response ground vehicle can compensate a little for the lack of a helicopter. Their advantage is that they can go out in all weathers, but they take longer. They can always reach terrain inaccessible to ambulances and without helicopter landing sites.

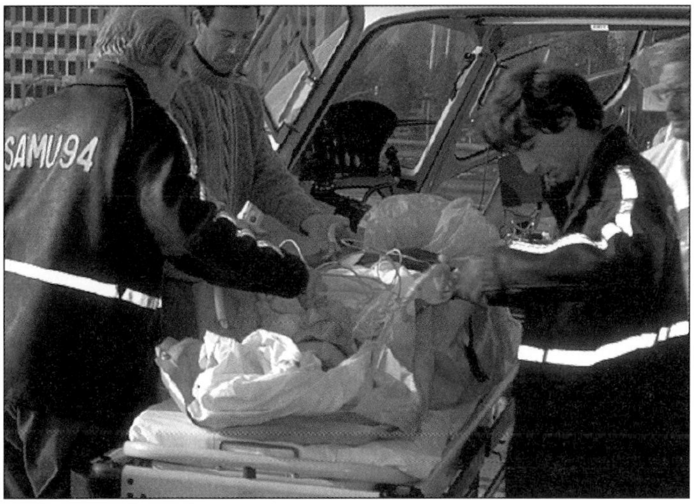

Photo: author

SAMU Offices and SMUR Facilities

Obligatory facilities for SAMU include a sound proof large room for the radiotelephonists and the communications equipment, a separate office for telephone exchange, computers, continuous multi-channel recorders and batteries, offices for the control room doctors, and the SAMU controller for serious cases next door to the GP control room doctors for less severe cases.

The premises depend on the degree of activity of the SMUR. Busy SMUR are attached directly to a SAMU which is ideally on the same site. They must have an authorised and well constructed helipad, a garage, staff facilities for pilots and drivers and on call rooms, a room for storing, preparing and cleaning equipment, a drugs cabinet, briefing or map room, secretarial facilities and optimally a receiving room for admission of patients.

Teaching and Public Relations

All personnel from telephonist to consultant are paid too little. As a result, the provision of medical and paramedical manpower is the biggest problem for SAMU. Through the use of undergraduate and postgraduate teaching, and courses aimed at non-university educated emergency specialists SAMU improves recruitment. Such teaching programmes must be based on current research.

SAMU doctors conduct epidemiological research as well as studies into the techniques and planning of medical emergencies. The SAMU must get the cooperation of the media to inform the public. Good communication with the public can avoid unjustified calls for medical assistance. Similarly it may prevent the impatience of those complaining of the delay in an ambulance leaving for hospital, when in fact the patient is already in the hands of the pre-hospital resuscitation team.

Interhospital Transfer

Interhospital transfer is not always medically justified. The indications must be considered by experienced personnel in the light of precise information about the state of the patient. The two most difficult problems are the transfer of a single patient over a very great distance and a flood of patients from a limited area after a major incident. The rapid organisation of a complicated journey, particularly to a foreign country (visas, customs, surplus baggage, money, telex and telephone communication, multiple seat reservations e.g three for the recumbent patient, and also one for the (doctor) presents difficulties. Aeroplanes such as the Lear Jet are more appropriate than helicopters for distances more than 300 km and will have to be specially chartered. For the duration of such long transfers medical teams will be unavailable for acute emergencies in their own region.

Major Incidents

During major incidents in France, the SAMU and SMUR doctors play an important role. At the permanent command post (usually found in the Prefecture) the chief SAMU doctor is director of emergency services and is responsible for major incident planning, advising the Prefect. An operational command post is set up near the incident where a senior SAMU doctor with knowledge of the major incident plan and the resources available act as medical incident officer.

At the scene of the major incident, the SMUR doctors who are trained for intervention in the field deliver the greatest service. They collaborate with the extrication teams, mine, cave and avalanche rescue, as well as nuclear accident intervention teams. They also lead and advise any volunteer aid workers, who may be well intentioned, but are more often a nuisance. SMUR teams also have a role in limiting panic at the scene. The job of the triage doctor is perhaps the most difficult and requires experienced SMUR staff. Their presence is indispensable for conducting triage at forward medical posts. The ultra-rapid classification takes three minutes per patient for three grades – extreme emergencies, potential emergencies and walking wounded or moribund (1st, 2nd, 3rd emergencies). This must be the meaning of *triage*, namely division into three. However, there is an alternative suggestion etymologically for the origin of this French word which may go back to the Napoleonic Wars and Baron Larrey, that it comes from *trier* meaning to sieve or sort out coffee beans from the dust.

Each patient is given an individual label to direct the emergency services. The SMUR doctors direct the stretcher bearers and accompany the injured. They ensure the evacuation of victims by a fleet of ambulances, medical trains, or air ambulance. These diverse functions cannot be improvised. Doctors trained in emergency medicine must receive supplementary training. Under the aegis of the University of Paris XII and with the help of the Army medical service, the SAMU 94 run two 80 hour courses per year on the management of major incidents for 'medicins de catastrophe'.

The Operation (Le Fonctionnement)

Emergency medical care is the principle mission of SAMU. The following is a description of a mission:

1. A call reaches a particular SAMU either directly from the public (20%), via a GP (30%), from the police (15%), the fire brigade (15%) or other sources.
2. The radiotelephonist notes the patient details, incident site and circumstances and transmits this information to the control room doctor who can activate a SMUR team by car, in resuscitation ambulance or by helicopter.
3. At a domiciliary attendance for a cardiac case as an example, resuscitation doctor, nurse and ambulance crew actively cooperate.
4. On public roads and building sites the police have an important role.
5. The patient is treated at the scene, then in the ambulance. The transporting doctor communicates by radio with the control doctor who arranges the hospital admission and reception of the ambulance or helicopter.
6. The patient is admitted to hospital. The role of SMUR is completed when the patient is handed over to a doctor at least of equal rank to the transport doctor.
7. On return to base, reports audit forms are completed before preparation for the next mission.

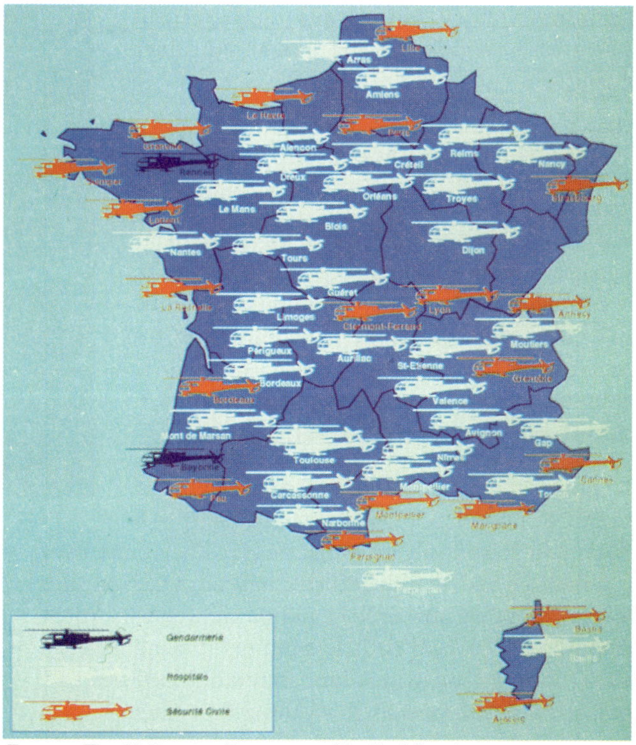

Map: Claude Wetzel

France: The Helicopter Emergency Medical Service

Conclusion

The French emergency medical system is ambitious. It aims to provide early diagnosis and medical care 'on scene' that continues without interruption until recovery. The objectives of this programme are clear, but the resources needed to achieve this are difficult to coordinate.

Firstly, it is almost impossible to find a sufficient number of young doctors competent to man the 300 SMUR, even when some of that number come from those doctors doing their National Service in army health service. Secondly, the cost of the system is high, requiring 3 to 4 million FFr per annum to fund a SAMU entirely from the public purse (subsidised by the state and private health insurance) and 900,000 FFr per annum for each SMUR paid directly or indirectly by the social security. There are about 100 SAMU and 300 SMUR in France.

Although the benefit of the system is expressed in human lives saved, it is almost impossible to form a cost analysis. The average cost of a premature death has been estimated at around one million FFr. Therefore one life per year saved covers the cost of one SMUR and two lives saved pays for one SAMU. Less than ten lives saved would be sufficient for example to justify the activity of SAMU 94 and its eight SMUR teams. The authorities and politicians have provided the system adequate funding, but have actually never accepted the idea that they themselves are getting good value for money. Fortunately, and most important, the SAMU has popular support.

Professor Pierre Huguenard is Emeritus Professor in the Faculty of Creteil, University of Paris, and has been closely involved with SAMU and French helicopter operations since their start.

This article has been translated from the original French by **Mike Machesney**, FRCS, Emeritus HEMS Registrar.

SWISS AIR RESCUE: REGA

Carlo Hoefliger

Historical Background

At first, no more than an idea, Swiss Air Rescue has its roots in mountain rescue. From the onset of mountain climbing until after the end of the Second World War, the only form of rescue for people in trouble in the mountains was by land, namely rescue teams organised by the Swiss Alpine Club. However, ever since the pioneering days of aviation, the need continually arose for assistance by air to cope with situations where overland rescue was rendered impossible due to snow, avalanche, ice or lack of time.

Landing in high mountainous areas to help people in need increasingly approached the realms of possibility during and after the Second World War with the appearance of aircraft with short landing capacity. In particular the 'Fieseler Storch' aircraft type used by the Swiss Air Force was capable of landing on runways of less than 100 metres in length to deliver supplies to mountain shooting sites. Nevertheless, using aircraft to rescue people remained no more than an idea at this stage.

Forced into Action

In November 1946 a Douglas DC-3 'Dakota' transport aircraft, belonging to the US Air Force, crashed in the Swiss Alps with eleven people on board. When, after long days of uncertainty as its whereabouts the aircraft was finally located at 3000 metres on the Gauli glacier overlooking Meiringen in the Bernese Oberland, the idea of rescue by air suddenly become reality.

Thanks to emergency radio signals the rescuers were certain that at least some of the crew must have survived the crash. Two military pilots, Viktor Hug and Pista Hitz, decided to put the idea into practice and, in a spectacular operation, succeeded in landing on the glacier. This marked the very first time in aviation history that an aircraft had landed on a glacier for the purpose of rescuing human beings. With their Fieseler Storch machines the pilots organised an airlift. In the course of several trips they evacuated first the injured then the unharmed crew members and passengers, thereby saving all eleven people from certain death. This pioneering feat marked the birth of mountain air rescue throughout the world.

SAR is Founded

In the civil sector, the Swiss rescue association – Schweizerische Lebensrettungsgesellschaft (SLRG) – decided at its meeting of delegates on 27 April 1952 to found Swiss Air Rescue (SAR) as a subsection of its organisation. Pioneers such as Fredy Wissel in Samedan and Hermann Geiger in Sion, who used aircraft that could land on glaciers, were increasingly called out on rescue missions on behalf of SAR. The helicopters of the time were not able to function well at high altitudes which meant that in alpine regions where the use of aircraft was impossible, another form of rescue was put into operation: by parachute. SAR rescue crews received parachute jumping training at the Royal Air Force base in Abingdon, England. The notion of people being rescued by parachutists was pursued into the early 1960s. In the course of countless exercises, the rescuers perfected their skill in landing near to the scene of the accident loaded with equipment and even carrying avalanche search dogs. Unfortunately very little is known about the actual rescue operations which took place at that time.

Photo: author

In 1960, Swiss Air Rescue broke away from SLRG and founded an association of its own headed by Dr Fritz Buhler. By now helicopter rescue was playing an increasingly important role in air rescue. The Hiller 306 and Bell 47G2 helicopter types, operated during the initial phases, were replaced by new models which were better able to cope with high altitudes.

The everyday costs of flying helicopters slowly began to exceed the resources of the SAR which was entirely run by volunteers. In 1966 after the Swiss government had rejected his application for support from public funds, Dr Fritz Buhler appealed to the Swiss people. To enable his work to continue he asked for individual financial contributions, offering free emergency air rescue in return for a donation of Sfr.20. This appeal met with an unexpected response and led to SAR's patronage system which has remained fundamentally unchanged to this day. This guaranteed the continued existence of Swiss Air Rescue.

Figure 1: Helicopter base locations in Switzerland

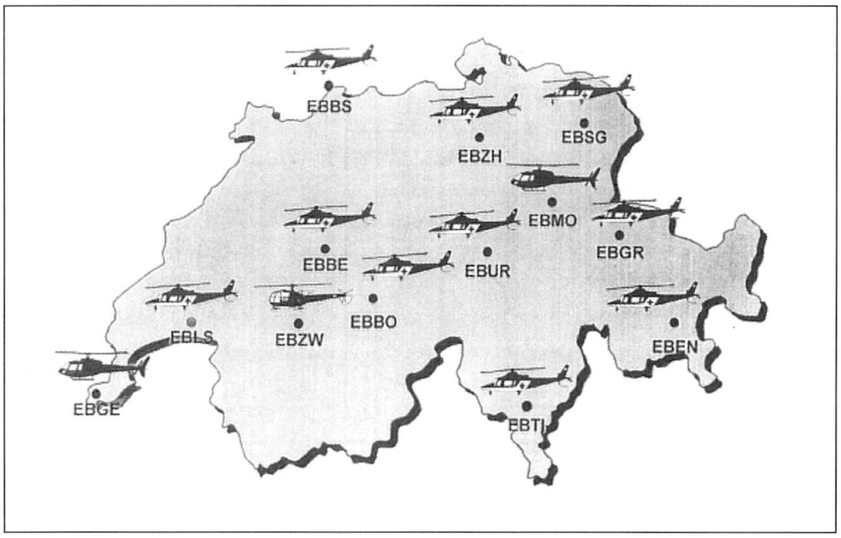

The Alouette III

In the meantime the helicopter had firmly established itself as a reliable means of mountain air rescue which was increasingly being put into operation by the Swiss Alpine Club in collaboration with Swiss Air Rescue. The introduction of the Alouette III in 1971 saw the real breakthrough of helicopter rescue in the mountains. The first helicopter of this type, the HB-XDF, was also the first machine to be entirely financed by voluntary donations. For many years, the Alouette III machines formed the backbone of REGA's 15-strong helicopter fleet.

Association to Foundation: REGA

As the association gradually broadened its scope of operations and took on increasingly important functions in the area of rescue, its legal form was no longer appropriate. In 1979 the Swiss Air Rescue Foundation (REGA) was founded. The SAR association assumed a supportive function in the rescue operations, training and PR work. Since 1982 REGA has been a corporate member of the Swiss Red Cross which, above all, facilitates the operation of repatriation flights from all corners of the globe.

Helicopter Base Locations and Stand-by Times

REGA has 11 helicopter bases located throughout Switzerland at its disposal. In addition there are two bases in Monis and Geneva which are operated by partner organisations (Figure 1). In the canton of Valais, air rescue is carried out by Air Glaciers in Sion and by Air Zermatt in Zermatt. Since 1995 REGA's entire fleet has comprised 15 helicopters of a single model – the Augusta A-109-K2, a new twin-engine rescue helicopter. The A-109-K2 can fly at a speed of up to 270 km/h which means that its fly-over time is reduced by around 30% in comparison with the Alouette III. All A-109-K2 machines are also equipped with a rescue winch.

The helicopter bases are distributed throughout Switzerland in such a way that any location can be reached within 10-15 minutes, depending on the helicopter type. REGA rescue helicopters do not undertake any commercial flights which means that they are on permanent stand-by 24 hours a day in order to be able to respond immediately to emergencies. During the day the helicopter is airborne within just 5 minutes of the alarm being raised and at night-time within a maximum of 20 minutes. Due to different requirements during the evening, the time until take-off at both the mountain and the lowland bases varies somewhat (Figure 2). The availability of the helicopters during the summer and the winter also varies depending on the prevailing conditions.

Raising the Alarm

Both the REGA head office and its operations centre are located in Zurich. The operations centre can be contacted around the clock on the emergency phone number (01/383 11 11). Anyone can call out a rescue helicopter without having to fear that he will be made responsible for the costs. In order to restrict the length of time between the alarm being raised and the helicopter arriving at the scene of the accident to a minimum, the operations centre needs to be provided with as exact details as possible.

The person raising the alarm should, wherever possible, provide the operations centre with the following information:

- What has happened? Where? When?
- Number of patients, type of injury/acute illness?
- Weather in the area where accident has taken place? (Visibility in km, is the horizon visible?)
- Obstacles near the site of the accident (cables, powerlines, etc.)?
- Landing possibilities? Rescue winch necessary?

A suitable landing place requires the following:

- obstacle-free area measuring 20 x 20 metres, with a flat area measuring 4 x 4 metres .
- possibility for obstacle-free landing and take-off, 50-100 metres from the site of the accident.
- no loose objects should be left lying around (clothes, blankets, etc).

Hand signals can indicate to a helicopter crew, particularly in mountainous regions, whether or not assistance is required. A person should never stand behind a helicopter when it is landing. Only once the rotor blade has come to a standstill you may approach the helicopter from head on, at the same time making eye contact with the pilot.

Hand signals to the rescue helicopter

For safety reasons, the following minimum visibility conditions are necessary:

Daytime: Horizontal visibility 300 m; vertical 50 m

Night-time: Horizontal visibility 2,500 m; vertical 300

Staff and Equipment

The rescue team comprises a pilot, a paramedic and either an emergency physician or a doctor specially trained in emergency medicine. At the lowland bases, these emergency physicians are provided by the anaesthetic department of the central hospitals. The services performed by these hospitals are paid for by REGA. At the mountain bases where, in addition to medical skills a sound knowledge of mountain rescue is required, REGA

Figure 2: Helicopter stand-by times

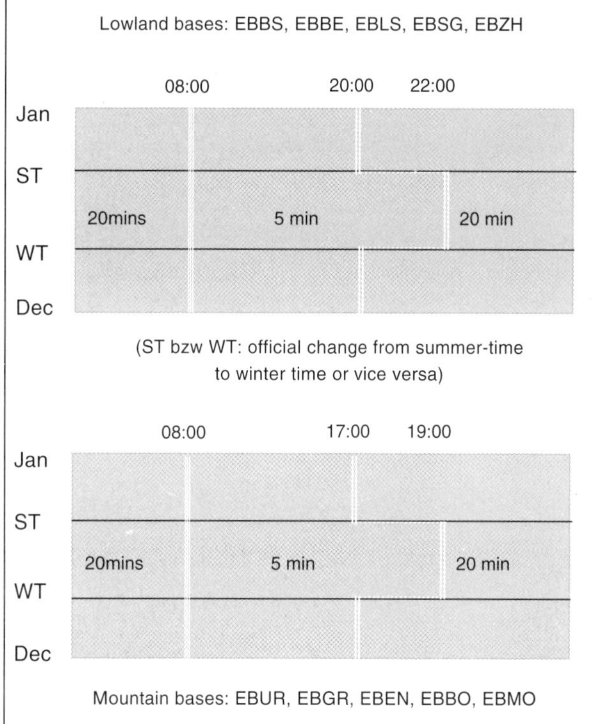

recruits its own emergency physicians. The physician decides to which of the local hospitals the patient should be taken depending on the severity of his wounds or illness. Deviations from this operational principle may occur as a result of adverse weather conditions or in the rare case of the relevant clinic not being able to accommodate the patient. All rescue helicopters are equipped with the necessary rescue apparatus and medications.

Types of Mission and Statistics

REGA flies around 7,000 missions a year, approximately 6,000 of which are carried out using helicopters. In mountainous regions REGA is above all called out to deal with mountain rescues, winter sport accidents, searches and evacuations. In the lowlands, the majority of the operations involve traffic accidents, followed by sports and occupational accidents and assistance with illness-related emergencies. In addition, around 2,000 flights are carried out to transfer emergency patients to main hospitals or specialised clinics. REGA is also responsible for transporting specialists, organs, blood, serum or special drugs and medications. Occasionally one of the three air ambulances which are stationed at Zurich-Kloten airport are used to transport patients within Switzerland.

The main objectives of air rescue are to transport professional medical staff and the necessary rescue equipment to the scene of an accident as rapidly as possible. In addition great importance is attached to rescuing the patient in a way that is as painless and as careful a manner as possible, making him transportable and flying him to the nearest suitable hospital. The air rescue

Photo: author

Augusta A-109-K2

services provided nowadays are, however, only possible in this form thanks to widespread sponsorship by the people of Switzerland.

Carlo Hoefliger is the Medical Director of REGA Medical Services, REGA Medical Department, Mainaustrasse 21, CH-8008 Zurich, Switzerland.

SECTION 3 C (iv): CONCEPTS OF A TRAUMA CARE SYSTEM /EUROPEAN

GARGANTUAN EFFORTS IN TINY LUXEMBOURG

Wendy Porz

Luxembourg Air Rescue operates in the smallest country within the European Union, but the efforts to get this vital, life-saving service off the ground and keep it running have been gargantuan.

Prior to 1988, when Luxembourg Air Rescue was founded, Luxembourg depended upon the air rescue services provided in the countries which border it, Germany, Belgium and France. A group of locals, including the man who would later become Luxembourg Air Rescue's president, Rene Closter, had witnessed countless emergency situations where the service provided wasn't good enough. Despite the proximity of its neighbours, it could sometimes take up to four hours for a helicopter from abroad to arrive in Luxembourg for a secondary run to transport a patient from one hospital to another.

Experienced in providing assistance in Luxembourg, the German air rescue service, the Deutsche Rettungsflugwacht (DRF), was called upon for help in setting up Luxembourg's own air rescue service. The DRF lent to the fledgling service one of their helicopters, a couple of its pilots, and its know-how. Without this the Luxembourg Air Rescue would never have flown its first mission.

While help came readily from abroad, Closter and his colleagues met with adversity on their home turf. In the Grand Duchy, a strategically located country which historically has had to struggle for its own independence, the national motto is '*We want to remain as we are*'. That attitude reflects an admirable determination to safeguard national identity and culture, but it can sometimes translate into a stubbornness not to change the status quo. For Closter, that was certainly the case when the founders of the Luxembourg Air Rescue appealed for local support. '*We had tremendous enemies,*' Closter said, '*among them some members of the regular rescue services.*' Although transporting patients by air is seven times less turbulent than transporting them by ground – an important consideration – as well as being obviously faster, some medical professionals and others in the Grand Duchy did not support the idea of operating a national air rescue service. In fact, says Closter, they downright opposed it.

The Luxembourg State does provide limited support by providing funding toward petrol costs, but it only provides the same amount per kilometre as it gives normal ambulances, whose expenses are considerably lower. Since 1992, the government has given Luxembourg Air Rescue an annual grant of nine million Luxembourgish francs; the services' expenses total over 80 million a year.

Crown Prince Henri of Luxembourg supports Luxembourg Air Rescue as its patron, and support also comes from donations made by various local organisations, including the Luxembourg branch of the Royal Air Forces Association. But unlike countries such as Germany, where the service is largely funded by the national automobile association, Luxembourg Air Rescue is almost entirely dependent upon membership fees for its survival.

Luxembourg Air Rescue has managed to convince nearly a quarter of the Luxembourg population of their need for the service and, equally important, the service's need for them. More than 61,000 members, a total of 22% of the country's inhabitants, keep Luxembourg Air Rescue viable by contributing 1,000 Luxembourgish francs (about US$ 30) per year for individual memberships or 2,000 Luxembourgish francs for family memberships.

This grassroots approach isn't the only thing that sets Luxembourg Air Rescue apart – the size of the country makes it possible to achieve goals unthinkable in other countries. Where else in the European Union, for example, could an air rescue service boast of its ability to reach anyone within its national borders within 16 minutes? In Luxembourg, with a total surface area of about 1,000 square miles, 70% of all Luxembourg Air Rescue runs are completed within 10 minutes.

At least once a day residents can see one of Luxembourg Air Rescue's two bright orange helicopters in action – a constant reminder of how vital this service is. Luxembourg Air Rescue runs an average of 460 missions a year, not counting the repatriation missions using DRF Leer jets. Running primary missions (transporting a patient from the scene of an emergency to a hospital) is the Christophe Lux, a twin-turbo BO 105 CBS, which Luxembourg Air Rescue owns. The Christophe Lux 11, a Ecureuil AS 350B, was added to the service in May 1995 to run secondary missions, transferring patients from one hospital to another both within the country and internationally.

Acquiring a second helicopter, which allows one helicopter to be permanently available for primary missions, had always been a priority for Luxembourg Air Rescue. Now, Closter and his team are working on meeting new goals. Initially they want to replace the Christophe Lux 11 with a helicopter owned by Luxembourg Air Rescue, preferably an EC 135 or a McDouglas Explorer and later, in order to operate more cost effectively, they would like to purchase the same type of aircraft to replace the original Christophe Lux.

With a staff of only three paid employees and a loyal group of 40 volunteers, Luxembourg Air Rescue has to continue making gargantuan efforts if it wants to reach those goals, but that is nothing new for this thriving organisation that has had to overcome so much adversity to enable it do its most important task of all – save lives.

For more information about Luxembourg Air Rescue, write to Luxembourg Air Rescue, 7 75a, rue de Cessange, L- 1321 Luxembourg, tel. (00 352) 48 90 06, fax. (00 352) 40 25 63.

Wendy Porz is a freelance journalist, editor of Luxembourg's only English Language newspaper.

AN APPLICATION OF EMS LESSONS: FORMULA ONE GRAND PRIX RACING

Sid Watkins

The essence of medical support for Grand Prix is rapid response. While in general terms in the treatment of trauma much has been written about the 'golden hour' in Formula One racing, the intervention is measured in minutes if not seconds. For example, in the recent spectacular accidents in 1994, the rapid intervention car containing myself and the Italian Consultant Anaesthetist,Dr Frederico Baccarini, reached the scene of Bafichello's crash as the marshals were turning the overturned race car the right way up. This was *fortunate* since the young Brazilian was unconscious with an obstructed airway. Prompt removal of his crash helmet, insertion of a Guedel airway, suction aspiration and an oxygen supply abolished his cyanosis. Fitting of a cervical collar and KED spinal splint in case of neck or spinal fracture allowed the safe removal from the car of the unconscious driver with his airway fully controlled and iv infusions in place. CT scan of the brain and neck in the circuit medical centre excluded intracranial haematoma and cervical vertebral fractures before the driver left by medical helicopter to go to the receiving hospital to recover from his concussion. He left the hospital for his home the next day.

In the case of Ratzenberger's accident the first doctor on the scene arrived in 15 seconds and at the Senna accident within 45 seconds. This rapidity of response with appropriate resuscitation equipment is achieved by the use of rapid medical intervention cars fully equipped and staffed to mandatory FIA standards. The number of cars required for each circuit which vary in length from 4 to 8 km is determined by the need for the cars to reach any point on the circuit within approximately 30 seconds. For example, at Imola which is 4.8 km in length and has a fast saloon car lap time of 3 minutes or less (Fl cars lap at 1.30 minutes or less) five medical intervention cars are placed at intervals around the circuit so each may reach the position of the next in 3 x 60 = 180 = 36 seconds. In addition, at various places on the circuit, doctors on foot are positioned at predictable points where experience has shown accidents are likely. The number of cars and standing doctors, therefore, will vary and at Monaco where the access to the circuit is difficult 3 intervention cars are supplemented by 100 standing doctors and paramedics!

At every circuit there are also two or three extrication teams depending on the length of the circuit consisting of a doctor as the leader and four or five marshals who have been trained in the management of spinal injuries by the use of cervical spinal, the KED body spinal splint and the 'bean bag' deformable mattress to protect the thoracic and lumbar spine. At each Grand Prix practice, extrications are made under the scrutiny of the FIA Medical Delegate using a current Formula One car to familiarise the teams with the cockpit and any special features of the individual cars. These teams are placed in Espace-type cars at strategic points to divide the circuit into two or three segments.

All the medical and spinal teams cars are under radio control from the Race Director and Chief Medical Officer in Race Control and are driven by experienced racing drivers who know the circuit. In the case of a major accident, as judged from race control, the practice or race will be stopped by the Race Director by red flag signals or red lights placed all around the track. On 'red flagging' an event all the medical intervention cars and the two or three spinal support teams leave their stations automati-

An example of the six maps showing the positions of emergency vehicles on the circuit

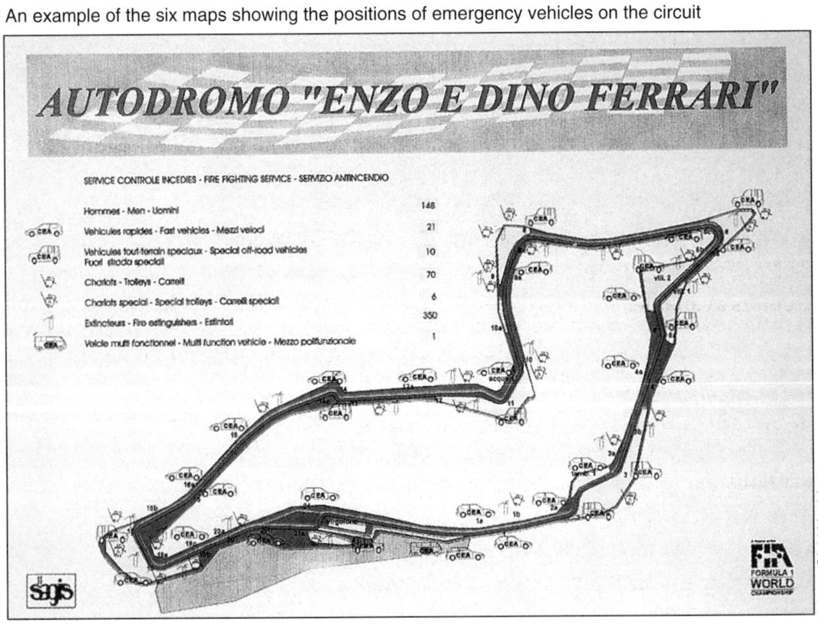

Map: Sid Watkins

cally to cover their segments of responsibility at full speed, ultimately all to reach the accident scene. Information about the site, nature or severity of the accident is sent from Race Control by radio. The modern Race Control receives its information not only by radio from the marshals posts and intervention cars, but from an array of TV cameras placed around the circuit feeding closed circuit surveillance to a team of observers and the Race Director in Race Control. Frequently there is TV cover also from the helicopters above the circuit to provide panoramic or specific views.

In the past the popular press often complained about the length of time the medical teams have taken to extricate a driver from a car mistakenly believing that the faster the better. As the resuscitation of the driver starts immediately in the car, provided there is no fire or immediate medical reason to remove the driver, care is taken to avoid exaggerating or producing additional injuries by hasty and uncoordinated attempts at speedy removal.

Ambulances again placed around the circuit at Imola (six in all) have only short distances to cover if called to the scene of the accident to take a patient to the medical centre. Occasionally one of the two medical helicopters, mandatory at all circuits, will be called to the accident to take a patient directly to the receiving hospital.

At the medical centres FIA regulations demand two fully equipped intensive resuscitation rooms with ventilation, suction, pressure infusion, full ECG and blood pressure monitoring, defibrillation etc, available to University Hospital or better standards. In addition adequate beds for observation and a burns facility with decontamination sprays or baths are mandatory. Diagnostic facilities include x-ray, ultrasound, blood gas analysis, sometimes mobile CT or MRI or both. The minimum consultant staff in the medical centre required are two consultant anaesthetists, consultant general and orthopaedic surgeon, a spinal surgeon (or neurosurgeon) and a burns specialist. These are supported by adequate nursing staff and the medical staff often exceed the requirement with radiologist, ophthalmic, ENT, and thoracic surgeons. Some centres have operating theatres that exceed in design, equipment and cleanliness most NHS hospitals. The medical centre is also the communication centre for the circuit medical and ambulance staff, the chief medical officer providing information and decisions from his post in Race Control. TV surveillance is also conducted to the medical centre and selection of the relevant view of the circuit is available.

All receiving hospitals for Grand Prix worldwide are inspected by the FIA medical delegate and high standards are required at the best University Medical Centre level both for the consultant and nursing staff and in terms of intensive care, operating theatre and diagnostic imaging facilities. Each hospital must have on site helicopter landing pads. Each hospital is required in writing to confirm its responsibility and readiness during all practice and race sessions with its spectrum of consultant specialists on call and available.

Prior to each practice or race the medical centres have to be operational with helicopter present one hour in advance for the centre to be inspected. All medical units around the circuit are then inspected by the FIA medical delegate and are operational 30 minutes before each start.

It has been said that the best place to be taken ill or have an accident is at a Grand Prix and clearly the level of medical cover provided is at the pinnacle of all sports and far exceeds motorway or road accident expectations. Nevertheless the immediate dispatch by helicopter or fast car (as practiced in Bologna) of medical trauma teams to an accident to resuscitate and retrieve the patient should not be beyond the wit or purse of British mankind. Those of us who have worked in trauma all of our lives can invoke memories of delays in reaching, managing and transporting patients by slow ambulance on congested or traffic blocked roads to hospitals ill equipped, poorly staffed and undermanned and already overwhelmed by routine clinical demands. Long delays in Accident & Emergency, on stretchers, and trolleys, in x-ray or CT, in a queue for surgical treatment in theatre, have regularly belied the lip service to ideal management in the 'golden hour'.

Cant and dogma practiced by unintelligent and inflexible members of the medical profession must be eradicated. False statistical comparisons made in totally different geographical situations by already prejudiced minds should be ignored. Britain and its services are years behind Europe in providing for the inevitable road and other accidents. Helicopter cover operating from trauma centres with trauma teams is required for the whole of the UK, not for only the M25 rim or isolated areas. Perhaps the Eurosceptics might concede that there is one good reason for joining Europe and that is the provision of European principles to medical retrieval and the protection of individual rights of British people and not only Europeans to survive.

One well known Professor of Surgery was surprised to be referred a patient who had experienced abdominal pains at a circuit in Japan with the diagnosis made and the ultrasound scans of the patients gall stones to prove it.

Sid Watkins is Emeritus Professor of Neurosurgery at the Royal London Hospital and was chairman of the Helicopter Committee from 1989–93. He has been in charge of Formula One medical care since 1978. His book, 'Life at the Limit' (1996) is published by Macmillan London (25 Ecclestone Place SW1), price £16.99. ISBN 0 333 657 748.

SECTION 4: EMERGENCY SERVICES IN LONDON

Introduction

Judith Fisher

London is a unique city within which to provide pre-hospital care. This is not only for all the usual reasons – traffic congestion, and a fifth of the population of England within its catchment area (approximately that area enclosed within the M25 motorway) during the working day – but also because of the vast numbers of mass gatherings including sporting events, exhibitions, concerts, state and civic ceremonies – all of which require medical cover at one level or another.

The recent high profile review of the service offered by the helicopter emergency medical system conducted by Deloitte Touche (at the request of the purchasers of health care for London) showed detractors of the service, who had felt we could offer better services based on some other emergency provision – be it motor cycle paramedics, flying squads, or further trauma centres, that HEMS was a cost effective service for trauma victims in London.

The helicopter is only part of a comprehensive pre-hospital care system (just as it is only part, albeit the highly visible and symbolic part, of the helicopter emergency medical system at the Royal London Hospital). The emergency system is run by the London Ambulance Service NHS Trust, divided into one central and three outer London areas. Emergency calls are dealt with centrally and average 2,000 calls per day. The sheer volume of calls means that the statutory service has to rely on the voluntary aid societies. For 25 years before the helicopter was available, members of the British Association for Immediate Care (Section 4 D) would provide medical support to the ambulance service at the road side and still provides valuable cover. The British Red Cross Society (Section 4 G) and members of St John (Section 4 E) provide nursing at home, medical, nursing and first aid cover, including the provision of ambulances at sporting events, major state functions and as back up to the daily ambulance provision. Although the major incident and communication control vehicles are frequently provided by the London Ambulance Service, many operations are totally covered by St John who provide doctors, nurses and first aiders, first aid posts and a stream of ambulances to such events as New Years Eve celebrations in Trafalgar Square and adjoining areas, the Lord Mayor's procession, pop concerts and many sporting events where the requirements of *The Green Guide to Safety at Sports Grounds* and the legislation introduced after Lord Justice Taylor's enquiry into the tragedy at the Hillsborough football stadium, stretch emergency resources to their limit.

The whole philosophy behind patient management is to get the right patient to the right hospital at the right time. In making decisions around this philosophy, skills wider than purely medical ones are required. London boasts a plethora of hospitals but each has its own strengths and weaknesses. Lord Tomlinson reviewed medical services in London at the start of this decade and found we had too many hospitals for our needs, and that much care could be moved into the community. However, the beds remaining needed to be served by staff experienced in the skills purported to be offered by such a hospital.

Major trauma forms a very small part of the overall medical emergency demand in our capital (about 5% of the 999 calls received at the London Ambulance Service control centre) and the helicopter staff need to be familiar with the services offered by each hospital. How often we hear that the patient was taken to a distant hospital when there was an A&E department only five minutes away. This is said in a pejorative manner but the answer should be 'Good, someone is thinking about where the patient will receive the most appropriate treatment by suitably trained staff'. Any patient taken to the nearest hospital may have to wait around for a trauma team to be called and then have to undergo prolonged land transportation to a facility suited to their surgical needs which may include cardiothoracic, burns, plastics or neurosurgical expertise.

At present the ambulance service takes the patient to the nearest hospital but it would be appropriate for the ambulanceman also to be encouraged to use a facility appropriate to the patient's needs, be they medical, surgical or minor injury. Within the service at present there is a move to target appropriate vehicles to specific conditions, with a system of well researched questions being put to the person requesting an ambulance, directed at assessing the priority and type of call, as well as offering the caller a chance to provide emergency first aid under telephone direction. The government has approved a change in ambulance response time from responding to all cases at 14 minutes to a response within eight minutes for life-threatening emergencies, estimated at saving around 3,000 victims of heart attacks each year. It would be timely to allow the appropriate hospital to be targeted too.

Implicit in the new ambulance response times is the assumption that a by-stander (usually a family member) will undertake emergency first aid and arrange for an ambulance to be called after passing a clear message to ambulance control. The Resuscitation Council (UK) has set standards for Basic Life Support along the lines of those recommended in the rest of Europe, the United States and other countries and the voluntary aid societies run regular courses. More and more hospitals are offering resuscitation training to relatives of patients who survive heart attacks. It is hoped that the general population in London will expand its cadre of volunteers proficient in basic life support so that the 'chain of survival' starting with the by-stander alerting the emergency services and initiating appropriate initial care through competent ambulance care as well as that from doctors and paramedic members of HEMS and BASICS (when necessary), to deliver a well resuscitated patient to hospital, will become the norm rather than the exception. A chain is as strong as its weakest link!

During a major incident, all these services work closely together and support the other statutory emergency services (Fire and Police) and voluntary agencies who, together with the Social Services, offer support (both emotional and physical) to both the victims and rescuers. The Women's Royal Voluntary Service provide food and shelter, Samaritans provide comfort and support to those weighed down by the tragedy of events and many smaller charities offer their services.

Photo: Mark Landon

LONDON AMBULANCE SERVICE NHS TRUST

John Pooley

Introduction

The London Ambulance Service NHS Trust (LAS) is responsible for the provision of all Accident and Emergency Ambulance/Paramedic Services within an area of some 610 square miles from the centre of London; in fact almost all of the area contained within the M25. As part of that service it is responsible for the tasking and Paramedical Manning of the Royal London Hospital's Helicopter Emergency Medical Service (HEMS). The paramedical manning element is coordinated by a full time LAS HEMS Liaison Manager. The tasking of the aircraft is carried out by staff manning a dedicated workstation (Special Incident Desk) within the LAS Central Ambulance Control (CAC).

Central Ambulance Control

In order to understand the magnitude of the problems faced by the LAS in the tasking of the aircraft, it is necessary to give a brief overview of the work of CAC. It is a newly opened, purpose designed and built emergency ambulance control room, situated at the London Ambulance Service Headquarters in Waterloo. This control room receives all the emergency calls originating in the London area via the British Telecom '999' system. At peak periods CAC will receive some 270 emergency calls per hour, equivalent to one call every 13 seconds. The call rate this year has shown a steady increase, and there is every sign of this continuing into the future. In addition to incoming 999 lines there are direct lines to all the other emergency/essential services in the London area. Control Assistants take all 999 calls, all of which are tape recorded with the facility for instant replay should a caller be disconnected or if any other difficulties occur.

At the initial inception of the HEMS scheme it proved difficult to task the aircraft appropriately as this was a totally new concept for the LAS and the lack of tight dispatch protocols in the early stages lead to a large number of aborted missions. However, as time has passed the LAS has worked closely with the Royal London Hospital to improve the service given. This has lead to the introduction of improvements such as the HEMS Desk in CAC and the use of HEMS paramedics in the tasking process. Initial improvements were seen as a result. Due to the continued wish to improve the scheme, further steps forward have been made with the introduction of a full time LAS HEMS Liaison Manager and the provision of a Special Incident Desk in CAC.

Special Incident Desk

As its title suggests, this workstation within CAC is dedicated to dealing with any incidents in our control area which may require special attention/services. One of these special services is the tasking of HEMS. The desk is manned throughout the 24 hour period. During HEMS flying hours it is also manned by a HEMS paramedic as part of their flying rota. This enables HEMS input to the interrogation of emergency calls leading to the appropriate tasking of the aircraft to incidents. The staff manning this desk are in direct radio contact with the

LAS Central Ambulance Control (CAC)

Photo: author

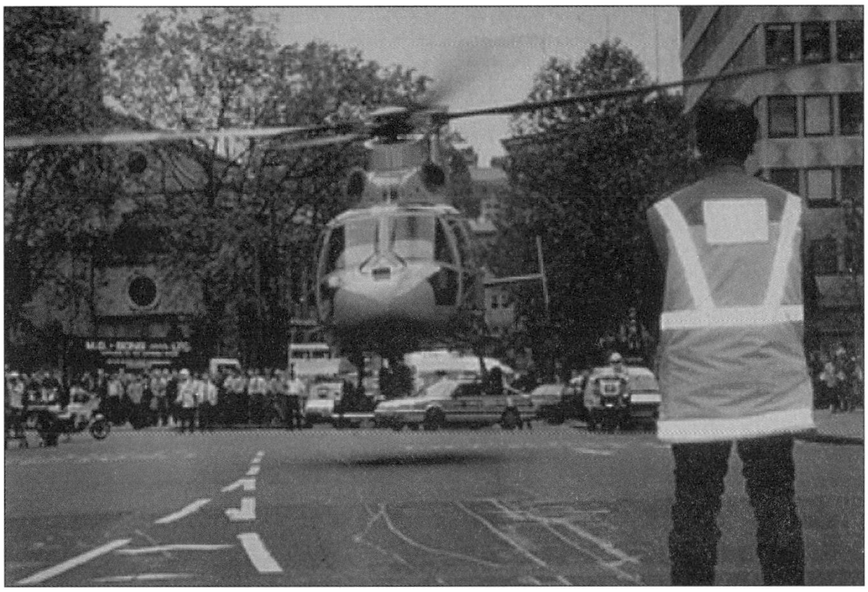
Photo: author

HEMS landing

aircraft via the airband radio and the doctor and paramedic via LAS radio frequencies.

Activation

As mentioned in the previous edition of this book the LAS had problems with the tasking of the aircraft due to the layout of the control room and training of ambulance control staff. The major shortfalls in the system have been overcome with the opening of the new control room and the dedicated hard work put in by the CAC training team.

All 999 calls are received by trained control staff. The information is directly inputted onto a computer screen. The computer system encompasses a Gazetteer which automatically logs the map reference and assists staff with street spellings. The information taken at present consists of location, problem and phone number. The call screens have been designed to have a standard layout so that a logical set of questions are asked of each caller. This will be of particular use in the future as the LAS is currently looking at priority dispatch systems. This will enable us to ask the same definitive medical questions of all callers so we can determine not only the nearest resource to the incident, but also the most appropriate to the patient's condition. Once the Control Assistant has finished entering the 999 call, the details are sent to the printer on the appropriate sector allocator's desk. Simultaneously a second copy of all calls is printed out on the Special Incident Desk. At this point the Control Assistant has the option to route the caller direct to the Special Incident Desk so that the HEMS paramedic can interrogate the caller direct and obtain extra information which will assist in the decision to launch the aircraft. Experience has shown that when a caller is rung back and it is explained that an ambulance is on the way but more information would be helpful, the vast majority of people are able and willing to give more specific information when carefully interrogated. This call back procedure has also led to the ability for paramedics to give first aid advice to the public whilst they are waiting for help to arrive. A new and useful addition to the new control room is the television monitor which is linked to the Metropolitan Police network of traffic cameras. These are placed on high buildings at major traffic black spots and allow CAC staff to view an incident, which may give early warning that an accident is of a serious nature or traffic conditions are such that it would be appropriate to dispatch HEMS.

Once the call is received at the Special Incident Desk the paramedic will either speak direct to the caller or, in the case of a disconnection, will ring back to ascertain the seriousness of the incident. If on receipt of the call the diagnosis leads the paramedic to consider that the aircraft will be required then they will pass a standby activation message plus a map reference to the helipad prior to ringing the caller back. This allows navigation information concerning the incident to be printed by the HEMS operations room computer. It also allows the pilots to prepare the aircraft for flight, thus saving valuable time if the call is confirmed. Depending on the result of the call back interrogation a confirmed message with any additional information is passed direct to the aircraft by radio or a cancelled message when the aircrew will stand down. If the result of the call back is that the information is inconclusive then CAC will wait for a report from the responding ground ambulance before activating. This has now become standard procedure as all ambulance crews are aware of the capabilities of HEMS and having worked along side it for some time view it as a part of the team to be used as and when required. The LAS has set up a working group to look at all aspects of the HEMS operation. This working group is presently involved in agreeing a set of aircraft dispatch protocols to try to ensure that the aircraft is only used in the most appropriate circumstances.

Immediately following a HEMS activation the Metropolitan Police are informed by CAC that HEMS is attending an incident, the details of which are passed. This cooperation plays a vital part in the team effort as quite often police officers have secured a landing site for the aircraft. If the landing site is some distance from the incident then police resources are often useful for transportation of the medical team to the patient.

Should any additional information be obtained regarding the incident whilst the aircraft is in flight the staff manning the Special Incident Desk can communicate directly with the aircrew via the airband radio.

Communications at the scene of an incident are an essential part of the emergency response to any incident. These are especially important when the HEMS team are rendering medical aid. The control and communications provided by the LAS permits the HEMS team using portable transceivers, to be telepatched via the radio system directly to any telephone number. This allows for example, direct communication from the scene of a serious road traffic accident to the emergency room of the Royal London Hospital, allowing vital patient information to be passed quickly and accurately between medical staff. It also allows medical personnel from other hospitals to be informed of a patient's condition, as it is becoming more and more frequent for patients to be ground escorted or flown to hospitals other than the Royal London.

LAS HEMS Liaison Manager

Following the re-organisation of the LAS into four divisions, the responsibility for the LAS side of the HEMS operation has been taken by the Central division. As part of the LAS's continuing support for the scheme, we have appointed a dedicated HEMS Liaison Manager. The role of this manager is to liaise on all matters between the LAS, the Royal London Hospital and HEMS. A major part of the role will be the promotion of the scheme in all areas including induction training of all LAS staff and the training of LAS paramedics on the HEMS course. The introduction of this post will ensure that the greatest possible support is offered to the HEMS scheme by the LAS.

Conclusion

Recently the HEMS Working Group has reported on the new dispatch protocols. These have been wholeheartedly accepted by the LAS, and can only serve to improve the service given to the public of London by the HEMS operation.

The ethos of the Special Incident Desk and the moulding of HEMS as an integral part of the overall LAS team has shown great improvements over recent months. The mission abort rate is currently at its lowest ever. With the introduction of more and more motorcycle/paramedic response units across the capital and great steps forward in the training of all of our front line staff, the LAS can be proud of the service it provides to the public of London. Improvements in emergency medical care in the capital is the goal of the LAS and we are committed to working towards this with all agencies providing services to the public in our area. HEMS continues to play its part in this mission.

John Pooley, LAS Divisional Training Manager, NHSTD Instructor and Paramedic.

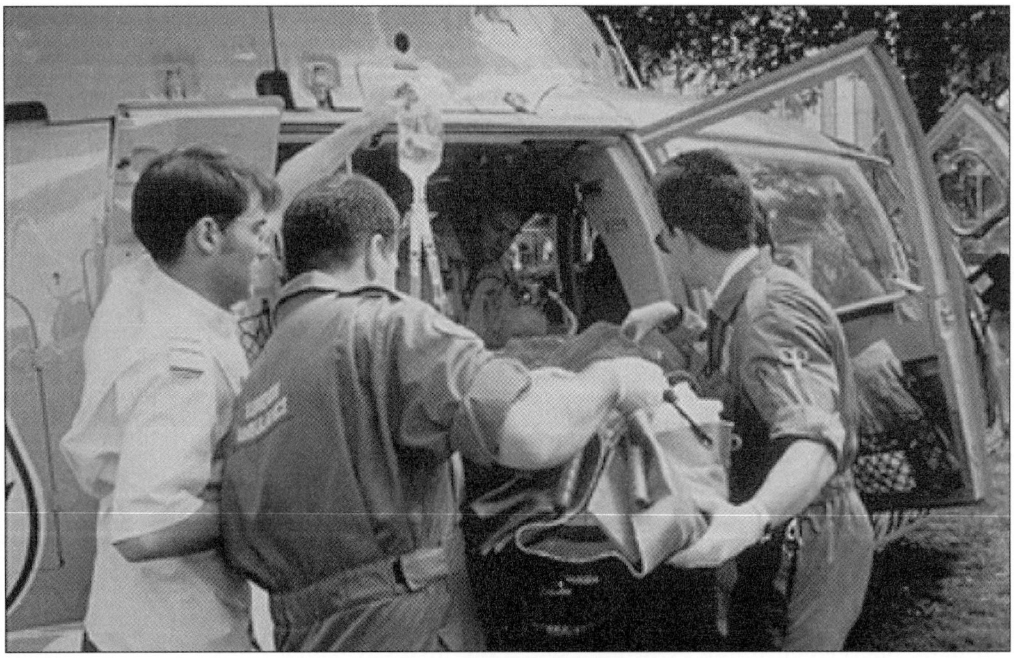

Photo: author

Loading a patient into the helicopter

THE METROPOLITAN POLICE SERVICE

Graham Collins

The Metropolitan Police is an integral part of the emergency services, working closely with the Ambulance Service, Fire Brigade and HEMS. We all work as a team with the same common aim – the preservation of life. To do this with the maximum efficiency we must all work as a team of which one of the most important aspects is *communication*.

The London Ambulance Service (LAS) who are responsible for the tasking of the air ambulance, have within the depths of their control room at Waterloo, a HEMS desk called 'Red Base'. Here you will find a HEMS paramedic who is responsible for vetting all incoming 999 ambulance calls and, from the sometimes limited information available, makes a decision to initiate the launch of the helicopter. Once this decision has been made a well-oiled machine of communication fires into life. Firstly Red Base will inform HEMS OPS which is situated within the helipad complex on top of the RLH in Whitechapel where the helicopter is kept during the day. Secondly, Red Base will inform the police at the Command and Control Complex (CCC) in New Scotland Yard. This serves two roles: a) police are aware of an incident not previously known about, and (b) officers on the street can be informed of the pending arrival of the helicopter. The days of a big yellow helicopter arriving unannounced on the roads are now happily a thing of the past. We, as police, are now aware of the impending arrival of the helicopter and, although occasionally time is not on our side, we are at least able to start securing the area and have transport available to collect the crew if a convenient landing site is not close by. The last thing we need is the medics having to run with all their equipment for any distance leaving them exhausted before they begin to deal with the casualties.

The system of communication between Red Base, the police CCC and officers on the street is simple, fast and very effective. Red Base call the police on a dedicated telephone line stating HEMS has been launched to an incident. The police operator will either link the message to one already being worked or creates a new Command and Dispatch (CAD) message. The computer will automatically know by the location given which police station covers the particular area. When all the relevant information is entered on the CAD, at the press of a button, the message will be routed simultaneously to the traffic control 'Oscar', the main area car radio channel, and the local police station control room where it can be transmitted to the local officers on their personal radios.

The system can also work in reverse. The police on scene can transmit over their personal radios to their control rooms further information. The CAD is updated and routed back to the CCC where the operator will pass the information to Red Base who can then inform the helicopter of any necessary updated information. This channel of communication is also very useful when the ambulance crews are for any reason away from their radios or vehicles, or are in a poor radio reception area so the police can be asked to summon HEMS on their behalf.

There is a facility for the officers on the ground to speak directly to the helicopter, but in reality this is seldom used. The usual method for the police to speak to either Red Base or the helicopter urgently on the radio is via a LAS radio installed in CCC at the traffic control supervisor's desk. Police can also monitor this radio during an incident to keep abreast of situations as they develop, enabling them to deploy their resources to the best effect.

After long discussion with the HEMS medical teams, guidelines have been drawn up whereby police officers at the scene of an incident can, through their respective control rooms, request the services of the helicopter. Although this is unusual there are instances where police are first on scene and those few minutes lost waiting for an ambulance to arrive and assess the situation may be seriously detrimental for the casualty. Therefore officers on scene will give all the relevant information that allows the Red Base operator to consider if the tasking of HEMS is appropriate. Those vital and valuable minutes saved could perhaps make the difference between life and death. Another advantage of police at the scene, knowing that HEMS has been tasked to their incident, is that they are able to reassure the casualties that it will only be a *few minutes* before medical assistance arrives. Unfortunately, at this present time, the police have no way of knowing how long it will be before an ambulance arrives on scene.

Once the helicopter has landed and the medical team are treating the patient(s), the police role becomes one of assisting wherever possible. We will, if necessary, guard the helicopter to prevent the souvenir hunters taking their mementos; these items are not only expensive to replace, but it makes the pilot's job so much harder trying to fly his machine with so many bits missing! We will help the medics by holding drips and carrying items. We can also travel to the local hospitals and collect further supplies and, if necessary, escort the ambulance to a hospital.

We will identify those casualties who are not so badly injured, comfort and support them and move them, if possible, away from the scene for their own safety, but this also enables the medics to work on the more seriously injured without the fear of upsetting relatives any further. We must also secure the scene, if necessary with the help of the Fire Brigade, so as to minimise the risk of further injury to anybody, and be aware of any evidence that may be of use in the subsequent field of investigation as to the cause of the incident. There is always in the back of every police officer's mind the possibility of criminal intent or action in all incidents, varying from perhaps tampering with the mechanics of a motor vehicle to attempted murder during a fight where a person has been stabbed.

The majority of people have never been close to a helicopter other than at a static display or an air show and are therefore totally unaware of the massive down draft caused by a helicopter during its landing or take off. We, as police, must move all on-lookers (rubber-neckers) back to a safe distance, also removing or securing any loose objects that may fly around. If the helicopter is landing on a dual carriageway we will try to stop the traffic in both directions; the reason for this is because motorists will watch the helicopter and promptly drive into one another.

After the helicopter has departed from the scene we must continue with our reporting and investigation of the incident. One of the roles where we are able to assist HEMS is to report on any damage that the helicopter has caused. There has been, in the past, the odd unscrupulous person who has tried to make a financial killing from someone else's suffering, but as all damage is now recorded at the time of the incident the police can help in assessing the amount of actual damage caused by the helicopter.

Continuity in the event of a possible fatality has been demanded by the coroner and if a casualty is airlifted to a hospital then police will attend and prolong the continuity from that point. The person who is airlifted to hospital may require guarding either because they may be able to help with further enquiries or for their own protection. It is not always possible to have a police officer accompany the casualty in the helicopter, but it has been agreed that if the police meet it on its arrival at hospital, this will fulfil the legal requirements.

All police vehicles are marked on their roof with three large black letters duplicated inside. This is for each vehicle to be identified individually so that instructions passed can be passed to the vehicle over the radio.

Graham Collins is a Metropolitan Police Traffic Patrol Officer with a private pilot's licence and is the HEMS Liaison Officer.

QUESTIONS ASKED AT THE SCENE:

1. Q. Why don't you take the patient straight to hospital when it is only a few minutes away?
   A. Because it may not be the most suitable hospital for the injuries of this particular casualty.
2. Q. It is my wife/husband/relative who is injured, can I accompany them in the helicopter?
   A. This is where we must seek advice from the pilots. If it is not possible then we may consider taking them by police car to the hospital.
3. Q. While the doctors are dealing with the injured can we go for a ride in the helicopter?
   A. No, the helicopter must be ready to take the patient at any time.
4. Q. Why does HEMS not fly at night when the police helicopter does?
   A. Because the police helicopter does not land at night. It is dangerous for a helicopter to land in the dark because the pilots can not see hazards like cables.
5. Q. Why do police cars have letters on their roof!
   A. So that the police helicopters can identify individual vehicles and give them directions. This can be of great benefit during a chase or searching for people.

VEHICLE ENTRAPMENT AND RESCUE: THE HEMS INTERACTIVE 'WORKSHOPS'

Len Watson

The HEMS interactive workshops grew out of a necessity to familiarise doctors and paramedics joining HEMS in the likely expectation of fire service performance of physical rescue at the roadside.

Vehicle accident entrapment rescue has evolved over the last ten years or so. Of course entrapments have been there for much longer, but modern philosophies, in terms of rescue, much less. It was in fact the removal of the chassis from the production car and built in progressive collapse in the form of crumple zones, that has increased the number of actual entrapments.

Coupled with the growing realisation that a casualty can be trapped by virtue of their injuries, rescue techniques have now established themselves as a basic science. The exponent of these new found skills – the firefighter – has for the most part been left to his own devices and subjected to the impracticalities of experiential learning.

In the mid 80s, I was busy collating the rescue techniques that appeared in my first book, and met with the uneasy realisation that it was impossible for me to mount a structured study that would corroborate best practice. I had to make do with consensus and common sense.

In 1990 I was approached to familiarise HEMS with the methods that were employed by the fire service in extrication rescue. Initially, I drew from the vast research material that I had assembled and gave an input that cross referenced the two disciplines of medical and physical rescue. This entailed a slide show of previous rescues followed by a demonstration drill.

A modular vehicle was clinically dissected and manufactured to aid both invasive care appreciation and highlight the main areas of physical rescue. The windscreen was removable, along with the roof structure. The centre post and rear door of the four-door saloon was also removable, effectively demonstrating side removal. The front floorpan of the car was cut and hinged which allowed the front of the vehicle to be tilted forward, effectively depicting the effects of dash relocation/'Dash Roll Up'. The steering wheel was removable and the seats adjustable.

The modular vehicle served its purpose for two years before falling apart. It allowed us to established a concise input, one which was to form the basis of workshops to come.

The HEMS structured study on 'Vehicle Entrapment Rescue and Pre-hospital Trauma Care' was completed in 1993 and established the guidelines for all future workshops to follow. 'Best practice' was no longer a matter of conjecture professed by the few. It had now been ratified in a retrospective study which analysed case histories to build a profile for practising in-vehicle Pre-hospital Advanced Life Support (PHALS) and injury friendly extrication. It also set performance parameters more in tune with the 'golden hour' concept. This was a very necessary deduction as growing trends were busy establishing the belief that once the casualty was stabilised the time clock stood still.

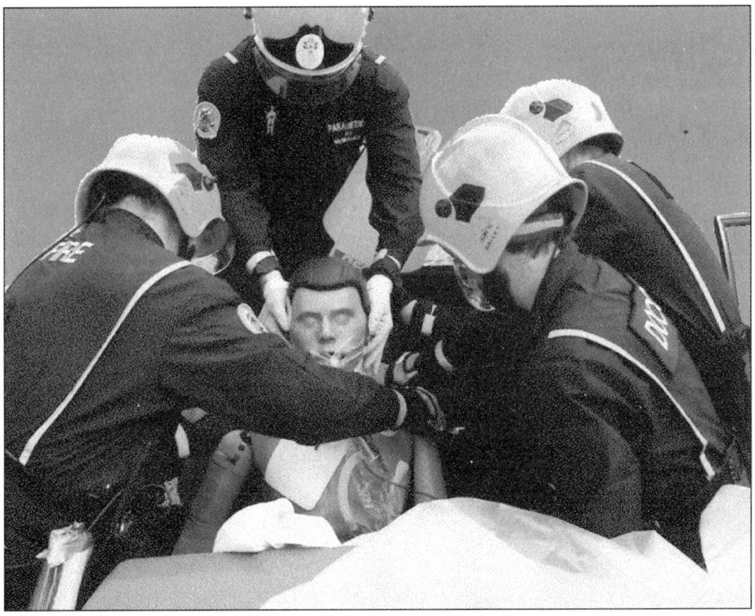

Photo: author

The workshops are now truly interactive with each discipline being expounded by the actual participants. Workshops are directed to a precise format to achieve specific objectives. Our goal is loose.

Aim

To offer an introduction and sufficient foundation for participants to meet a more rational operational approach at the more serious road traffic accident, where persons are trapped and have sustained life threatening injuries. Our objectives to meet this aim are somewhat more ambitious, with separate objectives for the two disciplines.

Objectives (1)

Medical personnel will have, or be able to:

- A greater understanding of the mechanisms of in-car accident injury – including the inference of airbags and seatbelt pre-tensioners.
- Perform the correct approach to in-vehicle casualty assessment.
- Equate to the three logic of rescue to cater for PHALS procedures.
- Control invasive procedures in line with physical rescue to cater for patient resuscitation, stabilisation, packaging and removal.

Objectives (2)

Fire Rescue personnel will have, or be able to:

- Implement the correct approach to an incident for majority scene assessment, control and vehicle stabilisation.
- Perform basic airway management alongside cervical spine manual immobilisation.
- Define and perform the three logic of rescue.
- Effectively perform physical rescue to cater realistically for patient resuscitation, stabilisation, packaging and removal, in four-door and two-door vehicles:-
    - Upright vehicle
    - Vehicle on its side
    - Vehicle on its roof

Placing a chest drain after side removal

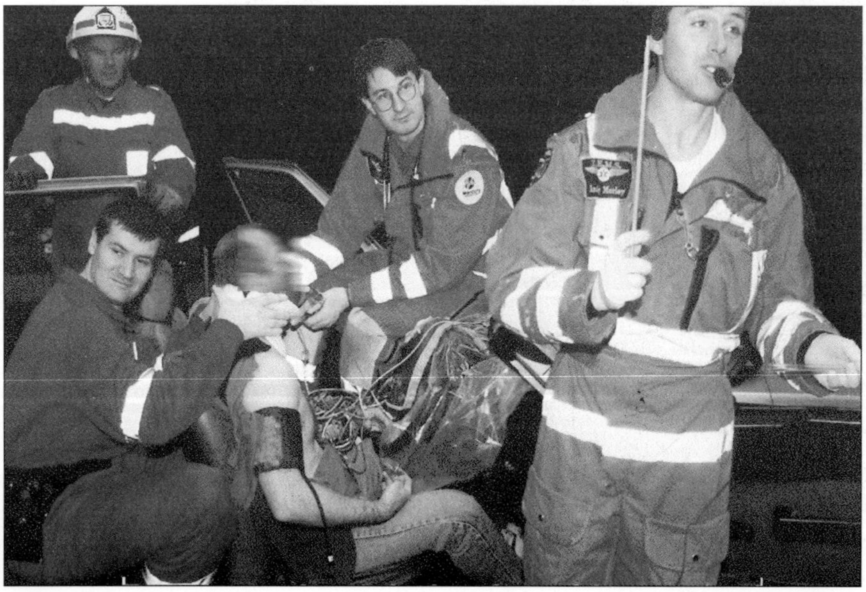

Photo: author

The Workshops Today

Four 'hands-on' workshops give an insight as to what can be realistically achieved at the roadside. Workshops include the majority situation of (1) head-on impact where the vehicle remains on road with the driver trapped. (2) vehicle on its side, and (3) vehicle on its roof with partial collapse in the roof pillars, with the driver pinned by the feet. In addition, a workshop has been built around the philosophy of 'Immediate Release' and the options open to the rescue team to achieve the casualty's release and speedy removal from the vehicle. 'Immediate Release' contains five different evolutions, including the practice of CPR management in-vehicle while working on the casualty's urgent release pending removal. Realistic rapid accessing, invasive intervention and controlled release is essentially what the workshops are all about.

You will appreciate that all participants are qualified people and these workshops are there to fine tune their existing skills to meet current expectations in extrication rescue. Session briefs to direct every element of the training event have been set out. Interactive participation, not only allows participants to experience the effects of certain elements of each other's role first hand, but also the benefit of the practitioner's advice and explanation of detail. Direction always promotes best practice, and the workshop Director ensures that events do not become side tracked with non-essential blurb.

Because realism has been built into the workshops, safety is paramount. The workshops are mounted with a Director, Assistant Director and at least one Safety Officer. Attention to detail starts with a mandatory safety briefing which continues throughout, sticking to established best practice procedures and safe application of power hydraulic rescue equipment (safe tool operation). Evolutions are standardised and all risk factors eliminated or controlled to an acceptable level. In terms of safety each risk element is debriefed and vehicle stability tested to prove confidence in the measure and give participants total acceptance for and credibility in the procedure.

What happens in the workshops is precise and will not deviate from one training event to another, unless structured analysis shows a better way forward. Although the workshops have been built around the HEMS structured study, workshop validation is continuous. Each doctor and paramedic is given a book of the contents of the input and is invited to offer their observations at the end of their stint on the unit. Additionally, participants are invited to revisit the workshops and give the benefit of their current experience and hindsight, and this proves very worthwhile to new participants.

Workshops are mainly held at fire stations. These have all the necessary ingredients to run the event, from amenities to suitable scrap vehicles and the necessary rescue equipment. In London, the last two years have seen it run at Southwark, the central training centre of the London Fire and Civil Defence Authority. The training event has been encompassed by the Skills Section and incorporated within the Fire Rescue Unit training for London's six heavy rescue vehicles. It has been well received and effectively completes the 'Heavy Rescue' module for vehicle entrapment rescue.

It has also been run on a seminar basis. A group of dedicated individuals have formed a team to enact the workshops in front of a participating audience. A studio with tiered seating was set up with a PA system and individual headsets to promote interactive exchange. The day's seminar is ambitious, but the workshops can be played by this dedicated group in approximately six hours. Judging by the feedback, the first one was a resounding success. Within this field of operation holds the key to the rapid expansion of this knowledge which hitherto has eluded rescue teams.

The Way Forward

Recently, displays were mounted to give a flavour of the way ahead. A corporate image was set and the team, 'Knights For Life', enacted new ideologies in rescue. The interactive rescue team of firefighter, doctor and paramedics will set a precedence in terms of ability and performance. Rescue evolutions generated by casualty requirements, necessitate a new and workable approach. The HEMS workshops have rationalised vehicle entrapment extrication training, and these displays show the implications and importance a proficient rescue team plays on such rescues. The displays they have set out show rescue, with basic and advanced life support, and coming of age at the roadside.

I would like to see the HEMS workshops expand and who knows, maybe a few seminars would help to see this philosophy spread. I certainly will work towards this goal as I am committed to this new found philosophy.

I firmly believe that interactive training is an essential requirement to gain proficiency and one to where audit will eventually lead the services.

Len Watson, 29 years a firefighter with the London Fire Service and currently an instructor in their special skills section, has made rescue his vocation in life. With three books on the subject, 'RTA Persons Trapped' (ISBN 0 951 6860 0 3), 'Advanced Vehicle Entrapment Rescue' (ISBN 0 951 6860 1 1) and 'How Will Supplementary Restraint Systems effect Rescue?' (ISBN 0 951 6860 3 8), Len is somewhat of an international figure in terms of physical rescue. Len is currently writing multi-media, competency based training material, available through resQmed, 9 Fifth Avenue, Bluebridge, Halstead CO9 2SZ.

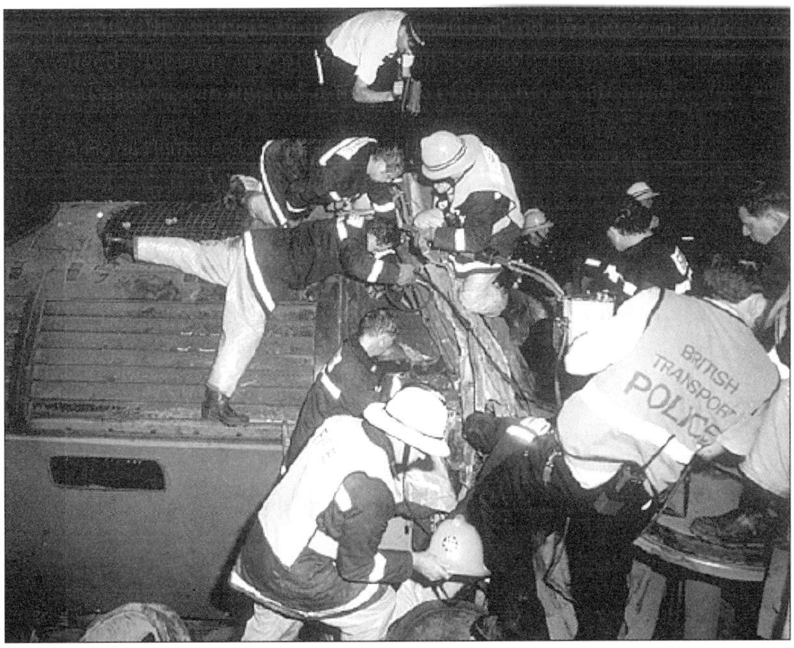

Photo: London Fire Brigade

At a major incident the expertise of all the emergency services may be required

THE BRITISH ASSOCIATION FOR IMMEDIATE CARE: BASICS

Judith Fisher

The wars of this century familiarised doctors with the fact that there were life-saving interventions that could be undertaken away from the bright lights of the hospital. In the 1950s road accidents were becoming a leading cause of death yet medical school training failed to equip doctors with the skills to deal with this carnage, and the ambulance service required of its members only a driving licence and a first aid certificate – not the sophisticated qualifications of today.

One young doctor in the RAF, Dr Ken Easton, having seen the mayhem on the A1 as it passed through Catterick where he was an RMO to the RAF depot, asked to apply his military medicine principles to this problem and was allowed to organise on site medical care for the victims of road traffic accidents. On leaving the service he became a general practitioner and established the first Immediate Care scheme, with the support of those colleagues who also became the driving force in forming a college of General Practice.

Death from road traffic accidents peaked in 1965 both here and in Germany where Professor Eberhard Goegler had demonstrated that he could reduce death from trauma by 20% within a 20 mile radius of his hospital through the provision of doctors responding promptly to accident victims, filling the 'therapeutic vacuum' between accident and hospital intervention. Dr Easton argued that the results obtained in Germany could be reproduced here through coordination of the ambulance service and teams of GPs in 'Immediate Care schemes and better Accident and Emergency departments'. His Immediate Care scheme was formally established in 1967 and others soon followed. One of the early ones, The Chingford and District Scheme became the North East Metropolitan Accident Unit and is now 'BASICS London'.

The schemes organised themselves into an association to promote pre-hospital care and pre-hospital care education in 1977 with the founding of the British Association for Immediate Care Schemes (later to drop the 'schemes'). Education in pre-hospital care was rarely provided in the undergraduate timetable but BASICS doctors did provide scattered informal input to some curricula. Pre-hospital care was needed for medical as well as surgical emergencies and the Resuscitation Council (UK) started as a sub-committee of BASICS. The Royal College of General Practitioners provided office accommodation for the association in its early days and has remained supportive of our aims. It was the first college to demand competence in resuscitation for its membership examination and which subsequently was required by other colleges.

In 1989 BASICS persuaded the Royal College of Surgeons of Edinburgh to establish a Diploma in Pre-hospital Medical Care which has been very successful and in January 1996, this college launched The Faculty of Pre-hospital Care, the first Royal College to launch a multidisciplinary faculty. This faculty will continue to promote education in pre-hospital care, including the management of major incidents. Membership will be open to doctors, members of the ambulance and voluntary rescue services and others with a special interest in pre-hospital care such as the fire service (who already have a medical rescue module designed by BASICS and the College in their training programme) and mountain rescue team members.

Many doctors who fly on the helicopter are members of BASICS and participate in educational activities as well as in the BASICS London scheme. It is appropriate that there is now a forum for other members of the team, reflecting the importance of teamwork, thanks to this innovation by the Royal College of Surgeons of Edinburgh.

Before London had a helicopter, road side assistance was given by BASICS London members who are available 24 hours a day. Today scheme members attend the majority of night time events requiring medical input and offer support and assistance to HEMS by day.

The scheme was established in the 1960s by two local general practitioners to serve the population of Chingford. As the scheme grew it served a wider population and in the 80s began to attract members from all over London. It provided medical cover to nearly all the major incidents in London since Moorgate, providing a valuable resource of doctors used to working in the often hostile outdoor environment, sparing hospital resources to deal with the victims arriving on their doorstep.

BASICS doctors are called out by the Central Ambulance Control. Their cars are equipped with sophisticated communications equipment, allowing them to monitor progress, and offer advice on their way to an incident scene. They carry a wide range of immediate care equipment to compliment that carried by the ambulance service All the members undertake the three day 'Medical Management of Major Incidents' course held annually at The Royal Postgraduate Medical School and undergo regular refresher training.

BASICS is committed to the improvement of patient care in the pre-hospital arena and looks forward to a long and rewarding association with the Helicopter Emergency Service.

SECTION 4 E: EMERGENCY SERVICES IN LONDON

THE MOST VENERABLE ORDER OF THE HOSPITAL OF ST JOHN OF JERUSALEM

Judith Fisher

This ancient order, often shortened to The Order of St John, was created in The Holy Land following the crusades of the 11th century, when monastic brothers established a hospital to care for the Knights of the Crusades. The tradition of caring spread world-wide and, despite some turbulent periods, is now providing a wide range of medical, nursing and ambulance aid. In England the order was founded in 1140 and the original home, The Priory at St John's Gate, Clerkenwell, is still in use as a headquarters, library and museum.

The British Order comprises three foundations, The St John Ambulance Association, The St John Ambulance Brigade and the Ophthalmic Hospital in Jerusalem. The Association was founded in 1877 to train the public in first aid and to establish and administer training courses. The Brigade, founded 10 years later, was to recruit a body of volunteers to be present at gatherings and to man the ambulances providing first aid cover. Now, members give over four million hours of their time annually, and this is increasing with the legislative requirements for cover at football stadia and similar gatherings following this good practice. The Order founded The Ophthalmic Hospital in Jerusalem in 1882 which treats all comers, regardless of race, colour or creed. For this work and the pioneering work in first aid to fill the gap in the community, Her Majesty Queen Victoria granted a Royal Charter in 1888 and the ruling monarch has been the Sovereign Head of the Order ever since.

The Brigade is organised on a county basis with two districts, one in Ireland and the other in London. Cover in our capital is provided by the Prince of Wales District. Many hospital staff, from students to consultants, offer their skills to this district in their spare time. Three of the senior doctors have been appointed Honorary Physicians to the Queen, while students find the work an excellent opportunity to augment their out-of-hospital and interpersonal skills (as well as frequently obtaining prime sites for state occasions or pop concerts). This brigade, in line with others, has developed Cadets and Badgers, providing young people, from 7 to 17 years, with an early taste of responsibility together with new skills and interests. One of my most rewarding activities is to judge the area cadet competition each year, where the enthusiasm and skill of the competitors is an inspiration to us all.

People of all ages provide a range of caring skills within their communities as well as support for overseas health promotion projects whilst the uniformed service provide cover at a wide range of mass gatherings, including state occasions, marathons, New Year's Eve celebrations and major sporting events. The black and white uniform has become a familiar sight at football matches, race tracks, motor sport and to those of us working in the Accident and Emergency department, providing much appreciated support to the hard pressed London Ambulance Service, without whom the latter could not survive. Next time you see an ambulance man or woman in St John uniform don't sneer – 'Oh, volunteers' – but remember these are well trained professional people giving up their own time to contribute to patient comfort and care. This end of the spectrum is equally important as the high profile helicopter service!

TRAINING DOCTORS FOR MAJOR INCIDENTS

Judith Fisher

Doctors on board the helicopter need to be prepared for their role in major incidents as do their colleagues within the hospital. Several training courses have been devised for the medical management of major incidents – one of the first has been run jointly by the Royal Postgraduate Medical School and the British Association for Immediate Care at the Hammersmith Postgraduate Centre since 1991. This is also suitable for other members of the medical team, both hospital and community, who are likely to be involved with major incidents including nursing and management staff. This course covers an overview of the medical aspects of major incidents: management, triage and documentation, specific aspects of casualty management under difficult circumstances, forensic implications and lessons learned from other major incidents. There is small group work and practical training sessions together with a short test. Emphasis is placed upon inter-service liaison, communication and co-operation. This is a well validated and evaluated course which I can recommend.

For those people who do not have time to spend three days, a slightly shorter course is run by BASICS for two days, with the deficit made up by pre- and post course work. More recently the academic department of Accident and Emergency Medicine at Manchester have been running a major incident course for doctors only. For colleagues who become more interested in specific aspects of major incidents, the Football Association run two one-day courses for Crowd Doctors and Major Incident Planning for Stadia. This follows the recommendations of Lord Justice Taylor in the Hillsborough Stadium Disaster Report.

Finally The Civil Emergency College at Easingwold runs a wide range of courses including those for the Voluntary Aids Society. Addresses for all courses are appended.

1. The Royal Postgraduate Medical School, Hammersmith Hospital, Ducane Road, London W12 ONN
2. The British Association for Immediate Care, 7 Blackhorse Lane, Ipswich, Suffolk IP1 2NF
3. Advanced Life Support Group, THEDOC Office, Trafford Road, Salford Quays, Manchester M5 2XB
4. Mr Alan Hodson, Director of Education, Football Association, Lilieshall National Sports Centre, Near Newport, Shropshire TF10 9AT.
5. The Emergency Planning College, The Hawkhills, Easingwold, York YO6 3EG

Dr Judith M Fisher, FRCP, Consultant in Primary Care, Accident & Emergency Department, Royal London Hospital. Past President of BASICS.

THE BRITISH RED CROSS SOCIETY

Sir Peter Beale

' The Red Cross is probably the best recognised emblem and the least understood organisation .'

This often quoted statement is a generalisation that nevertheless hides a good deal of truth. One only has to look at the television screen time to see the Red Cross emblem imprinted on vehicles, buildings and armbands in the context of some war, or conflict. There is a reasonable understanding of what the Red Cross stands for abroad; but it is in the United Kingdom, where there is puzzlement as to its significance and role.

'The British Red Cross gives skilled and impartial care to people in need and crisis in their homes and in the community, at home and abroad, in peace and war'. This was the Mission Statement issued by the British Red Cross Society in 1990 which not only reflects what has been practised since its foundation but encapsulates its philosophy to the present day.

Using this as a starting-point, it can easily be seen to embrace not only those harrowing scenes shown on our television screens, but also the everyday emergencies and crises seen in the United Kingdom. It is an all-encompassing concept, its very diversity contributing to the lack of understanding of what the Red Cross actually does. During 1995 a Focused National Strategy was devised, highlighting the key services that need to be provided by the Society so that outsiders will understand it better and those volunteers who provide the services do so with a greater sense of purpose and understanding. This understanding will be enhanced by having an historical perspective.

It was only in the 1850s culminating in the Crimean War that public attention was drawn to the dreadful conditions under which armies fought and casualties were cared for. The grossly inadequate medical arrangements were reported, amongst others, by WH Russell of *The Times*, who stimulated Florence Nightingale and further individuals to respond to the horrors of soldiers lying injured and ill on the battlefield in the Crimea. The Red Cross owes its foundation to Henry Dunant, a Swiss businessman who, in a similar fashion to Florence Nightingale, responded to the news of the battle of Solferino in Italy in 1859, by organising a band of volunteers to care for the sick and wounded. He published his findings in a book in 1862. Dunant and colleagues convened a conference in 1863 at which proposals were put forward to form volunteer aid societies at country level to assist the army medical services and founded what was to become the International Committee of the Red Cross (ICRC). The protective emblem of the red cross on a white background, which is the reverse of the Swiss flag, was chosen the following year. In 1876 Turkish soldiers mistook the Red Cross as a religious symbol and fired on it. As a result the ICRC was persuaded to let Islamic states use a red crescent to identify their medical services. This continued unofficially until 1929 when the revised Geneva Conventions conferred equal status on the Red Crescent, now used in some 25 Islamic countries. The Movement is now correctly termed the Red Cross and Red Crescent Movement.

Photo: author

Henry Dunant

After the First World War, great concern was felt over the natural disasters and potential disasters that were arising throughout the world. Although there was a relationship to the ICRC's aims, with the recognition of the need to care for disabled servicemen and their families and that local conflicts can never be totally separated from such natural disasters, the gap in the availability of Humanitarian Aid in peacetime became obvious to both the individual national societies and Geneva. So the Federation was formed - in fact it was called the League of Red Cross and Red Crescent Societies, and not until 1991 did it become known as the International Federation of the Red Cross and Red Crescent Societies. Basically it has three components:

- The International Committee of the Red Cross (ICRC) which operates in areas of armed conflict.
- Recognised National Societies, numbering 169 at the present time.
- The International Federation of Red Cross and Red Crescent Societies which assists the national societies in their development and at the same time uses its contacts to coordinate international relief disasters in non-conflict zones (peace-time disasters).

There were only 12 national societies who signed the first Geneva Convention in 1864, but steadily over the years other nations joined bringing the total up to the present 169. The UK joined in 1870. Considering the total number of nations is 234, the Movement can justly boast to be the world's largest humanitarian non-governmental organisation.

Red Cross Principles

The Red Cross Movement works under seven fundamental principles which are:

• *Humanity* • *Impartiality*	The purpose of the Red Cross/Red Crescent is to protect life and health and ensure respect for the human being. It is guided solely by individual need. It makes no distinction as to nationality, race, religious beliefs, class or political opinions.
• *Neutrality* • *Independence*	The Red Cross/Red Crescent does not take sides in political, racial, religious or ideological disputes. It is completely autonomous and independent from the Government in its country although subject, of course, to the laws of the land.
• *Universality* • *Unity* • *Voluntary Service*	Red Cross/Red Crescent members act of their own free will. All Red Cross/Red Crescent Societies are equal and support each other. There is only one Society in each country and it is open to all.

Under these guiding principles which are inviolate, the Red Cross has made its name and been respected throughout the world. It can enter areas where no-one else dares to tread. It is not regarded with suspicion like the military and yet its emblem is seen in the middle of dangerous military conflicts. The military themselves, the proud bearers being the Medical Services, are recognised as being non-combatant with broad humanitarian and health roles, and of course were amongst the first to carry the emblem after the formation of Red Cross Movement. All the nations signatory to the Geneva Conventions recognise the significance of the emblem as used by the military, and know that any violation of the Conventions is morally, ethically and legally wrong.

In the United Kingdom the British Red Cross Society is organised into a National Headquarters (NHQ) and some 86 branches which roughly correlate with the counties. At present (1996) there is a membership of 92,000 the vast majority being unpaid volunteers. The heart of the Red Cross lies in its volunteers. Young or old, these volunteers are central to the delivery of the Red Cross services and, indeed, governance of the Society. The Red Cross has the ability to complement the statutory services, sweeping up the bits and pieces and, with impartiality, integrity and great respect for individuals and their families, reduce the less definable and undesirable after effects arising from an incident. These volunteers are supported by a small nucleus of paid staff. The most senior body is the Council comprised of Trustees who include representative Branch Presidents. The Council dictates the policy for the Society, and is supported at NHQ by an administrative staff, headed by the Director General. NHQ has clearly demarcated divisions, two of which are responsible for International and UK matters respectively.

International Role

The United Kingdom has more Red Cross delegates and leaders of delegation working abroad than any other nation. They are sent to some of the many trouble spots of the world, for instance former Yugoslavia. Indeed by recent expansion of its activities, the British Red Cross has fast become one of the leading players in the entire Red Cross Movement. Delegates are sent in one of three ways, either under the auspices of ICRC, of the Federation, or as a result of their own initiative – in the proportion of 50%, 30% and 20% respectively. The mechanism for being called to work for the ICRC is that the Headquarters in Geneva telephones our International Division asking for specific delegates for a specific task. They are then sent under the command of the leader of a delegation appointed by the ICRC.

Finance is a continual problem for the Red Cross, because it is a Registered Charity and depends on donations and legacies for its income. Although this is true for its UK work, the International Division has significant contributions from the Overseas Development Administration Department of the Foreign Office and the European Union. However it is extremely careful not to compromise its non-political status, observing strongly the principles of Neutrality and Independence.

The UK Role

In the United Kingdom, the primary role is `emergency response'. This immediately distinguishes it from other services in that the services provided are time limited. Once the emergency is over, the service is handed over to other agencies on a more permanent basis.

First Aid training in progress

Emergency Response

The following categories apply to Red Cross work both in UK and overseas:

- The provision of local services in the UK which respond daily to individual emergency needs.
- The support of statutory services during major incidents in UK.
- Assistance to the medical services of the Armed Forces and National Health Service during national emergencies.
- Working as part of the International Red Cross and Red Crescent Movement during armed conflict and natural disasters overseas.
- Contributing to developmental projects that respond to the `silent emergencies' such as disease and hunger

We aim to improve the situation of those who are most vulnerable. This could apply solely to one person, or to groups of people during an emergency. In order to provide an emergency response of whatever size and with whatever resources it might involve, the Red Cross has to be prepared. This is achieved in two ways: by its day to day activities and by training.

The Focused National Strategy

During 1995, the opportunity was taken to define key areas on which the Red Cross should concentrate and which the public would readily understand. This led to the unoriginal title of `The Focused National Strategy'. Five key services have been defined which every Branch of the British Red Cross Society is expected to provide.

1. Health and Social Care

Under this heading lie four specific Services/Schemes:

- Home from Hospital
- Emergency Domiciliary Personal Care Service
- Domiciliary Respite Care
- Short-term Respite in Residential Homes

2. First Aid Duties

Perhaps this is the most widely recognised function of the Red Cross within UK. The uniformed volunteers have as their main aim the provision of First Aid. The Red Cross was responsible for First Aid cover at 38,687 events during 1994.

The other important facet to First Aid is training. I am afraid that the UK attaches less importance to First Aid than many of our 15 European neighbours although there has been encouragement from the recent legislation under `Health and Safety at Work'. Ignorance of First Aid costs lives and it is one of Red Cross' aims to combat this `crime' and bring awareness of First Aid into our homes and workplaces. During 1994, First Aid at Work was delivered to over 71,000 persons, and to the general public as well as First Aid members, another 66,000 persons, a total of over 137,000. Emergency Aid and Life Support training was also delivered to another 33,500..

3. Medical Loan

'Equipment to make life easier'. The Red Cross provides (within 24 hours of an emergency): wheelchairs, backrests, bath seats, commodes, bed pans and urinals, walking sticks and frames. Some 220,000 loans were made in 1994 from 903 loan depots

4. Transport and Escort

This service offers freedom and independence for people who cannot get about easily or use ordinary transport. By providing drivers with suitable vehicles – and escorts where needed – the Red Cross makes it possible for essential journeys to be made and trips that make life more pleasurable.

5. Message and Tracing Service

Within the British Red Cross, this is a unique service because it straddles the International and UK Divisions. Specifically mandated under the Geneva Conventions it strives to restore and maintain family ties, to reunite separated families and to register both prisoners of war and civilian internees in situations of armed conflict. There is no time limit to their enquiries, some cases dating back to World War II or even earlier; the only restriction on the organisation is that searches within the UK are not undertaken unless the case has originated abroad. The Salvation Army deals with UK to UK reunions. About 600-700 separate messages are handled every month within the British Red Cross and during 1994, 449 people were put back in touch with their families.

In addition to these services, other functions are taken on locally to cope with the needs of vulnerable individuals or vulnerable groups of individuals.

County Voluntary Aid Societies Emergency Committees (CVASECs)

Most counties sport Local Planning Committees and many of them also allow for the holding of County Voluntary Aid Societies Emergency Committees (abbreviated to County VASECS or CVASECs), which are chaired by the Voluntary Aid Services (VAS) – either the Red Cross or St John – and are composed of the Health Emergency Planning Officer (HEPO), the County Emergency Planning Officer (CEPO) and representatives from the Police, Ambulance, Health Services, the Military etc.

These CVASECs are the effective fora for calling together the voluntary organisations who could be needed in a local emergency; they help to arrange suitable training, especially in the form of joint exercises. In this way, the various organisations get to know each other and build up confidence and trust in each other's abilities and professionalism. The CVASECs were originally formed to plan for the anticipated return of casualties from abroad as the result of armed conflict,but there has been a change of emphasis whereby the CVASECs are now concentrating more on civil emergencies in an 'All Hazards' approach, coordinated centrally by the National Voluntary Aid Societies Emergency Committee (NVASEC) .

The Red Cross Role in UK Emergencies

The following groups of individuals might be affected in an emergency:

- Casualties (fatal, seriously or slightly injured)
- Survivors (involved but not injured)
- Evacuees (those needing to be led away and cared for from coaches, trains, buildings or areas)
- Relatives/Friends (at home, at work, at the scene, hospital or mortuary)
- Witnesses
- Those working for the Emergency Services
- Others responding to the incident

Some examples of what might be required because of an incident:

Information
Reassurance
Refreshments
Clothing
Blankets
First Aid and medication
Help with children/pets
Transport
Entertainment
Use of a telephone
Access to television/radio
Protection from the media
Protection from unwanted 'do-gooders'

The British Red Cross Society is capable of undertaking a range of pre-planned support functions within the following Centres:

- Survivor Reception Centres (for very slightly and uninjured survivors)
- Rest Centres (for evacuees)
- Friends and Relatives Reception Centres
- Feeding Centres (for all involved)

In addition, and because of their training they can take on other roles such as:

- Emotional support and reception duties in A&E
- Escorting, accompanying and transporting casualties, survivors, evacuees, relatives and friends
- Provision of healthcare support
- Provision of shelter, warmth and clothing
- First Aid at Casualty Clearing Point or First Aid Post
- Participation in an ambulance reserve
- International and national message and tracing services
- Distribution of European Union grants
- Operating a Disaster Appeal Scheme

These lists demonstrate clearly the breadth of help that the Red Cross can deliver. This must be known and appreciated by all and sundry and especially the Emergency Services. Procedures must exist for calling on their services – hence the CVASECs, Local Planning Committees, joint exercises and training, and there must be confidence in the abilities of British Red Cross Society personnel.

The Red Cross is there to help you. Members love to be asked, they want to be used and they need to be cherished.

Sir Peter Beale, Chief Medical Officer, British Red Cross, 9 Grosvenor Crescent, London SW1X 7EJ. He was formerly Major General in charge of all the medical services in the Armed Forces.

DISASTERS: LESSONS TO BE LEARNT

Wendy Neal

The concept of pre-hospital care has developed considerably in the last two decades and the practice of 'scoop and run' has, at least in most parts of Western Europe, been ousted by the more modern approach of 'stay and stabilise'. It might be presumed that the idea of sending a doctor to the scene of an incident evolved from increasing knowledge and interest in the field of accident and emergency medicine. The truth is rather different: the first immediate care specialists were active from the late 1700s. These qualified doctors, mainly general practitioners, were members of the Royal Humane Society (RHS) and dedicated to aiding accident victims and to discovering an effective means of resuscitation.

The RHS was founded in 1774 by Drs William Hawes and Thomas Colgan and was initially known as the 'Institution for Affording Immediate Relief to Persons Apparently Dead from Drowning'. The society depended on voluntary funding, but within a few years had set up more than 250 'Receiving Houses' close to lakes and rivers in London. These 'houses' were often little more than tents or rooms hired in public houses, but the more elaborate were purpose built mini-hospitals equipped with the most up-to-date resuscitation kit. London was divided into districts, each served by one or more of the 100-plus doctors recruited through advertising campaigns and willing to give immediate medical aid to those in need. 'Icemen', employed by the society guarded key lakes and canals and a network of 'runners', ensured doctors were notified of any accident where their help was required. RHS members had a keen interest in developing more effective techniques for resuscitation, and in the late 1770s produced guidelines outlining accepted methods. These included providing warmth; artificial respiration by mouth to mouth inflation with compression of the chest and abdomen; fumigation by the introduction of tobacco smoke into the rectum and colon; rubbing the body; stimulants, bleeding and inducement of vomiting. Mouth to mouth resuscitation was strongly advised against after 1812 because experts feared exhaled breath was poisonous. Drs Henry Silvester and Marshall Hall joined the ranks of the RHS in the mid 19th Century and devised resuscitation methods based on the premise that movement of the chest would induce inhalation. The methods were rarely successful.

A Royal Humane Society 'Receiving House'

The RHS's workload was sometimes heavy. As the *Illustrated Times* reported in January 1861:

'From the commencement of the frost, on the 17 of December last, to the present time, the total estimated number of skaters and sliders which have ventured on the ice in the various Royal parks and in Kensington Gardens is 170,000, of whom 160 have been immersed and rescued by the Icemen employed by this society (RHS) and then resuscitated by the excellent methods adopted by them; in addition to which nearly 600 persons have received surgical treatment at the hands of the medical officers of the society – some suffering from the most terrible burns, the result of firework torches ...other from every imaginable kind of broken bone, and the majority from sickening cuts generally of the forehead and eyebrows.'

The RHS dealt with a major incident in 1867, when ice on the ornamental lake in Regents Park shattered, throwing more than 200 merrymakers into the freezing 12 feet deep water. Resources were hopelessly over stretched. Survivors were taken to the Receiving House, in this case a tent, and RHS doctors from the surrounding districts were drafted in to help. Forty people, most of them young men, drowned but it was some days before all the bodies had been recovered. Following this disaster the lake was drained and its depth was reduced to three feet in an effort to ensure such a tragedy would never be repeated. Hundreds of people died on London lakes before this simple safety step was taken, but at least lessons of the Regents Park disaster were noted and acted upon. Very few disasters precipitated such effective action, and it is a general truth that disasters have a habit of repeating themselves through the centuries. In my book, *With Disastrous Consequences* (Hisarlik Press, 1992), I examined a wide variety of incidents that occurred between 1837 and the end of the First World War in 1918, and can conclude that lessons are rarely learned. Disasters captivate public interest for a brief and noisy period, and are almost invariably followed by public enquiries and promises that the same incident will never be repeated. The public outrage and the senseless loss of life and property is quickly forgotten. Haphazard and downright dangerous practices quickly creep back into everyday routine until that day, weeks, years or decades in the future when luck gives out and the whole sorry episode is repeated.

After the Clerkenwell bomb explosion

In 1887 Eyre Shaw, the chief of the Metropolitan Fire Brigade in London, was commissioned to investigate an Exeter theatre fire that killed 127 people, most of whom died in the rush for the poorly designed exits. In his report Shaw commented scathingly:

'The saddest part of this matter is that no lesson of any kind has been taught by the event, as everyone who had studied the subject either theoretically or practically knows beyond any possibility of a doubt what the whole action of the fire and the smoke would be under such circumstances; and, moreover, the lesson and warnings of recent years had prepared all concerned for the terrible catastrophe precisely as it actually occurred.'

Shaw had every right to feel anger. He had a strong interest in theatre safety and was convinced stringent legislation was needed to force proprietors to ensure adequate safety standards for their audiences. He led a vociferous campaign but despite his position and prestige – he moved in high society and was a close friend of the Prince of Wales – it was the end of the century before the legislative wheel began to turn with any real purpose. Even then the action was limited. The tragedy of Hillsborough, a public place of entertainment, revealed only too clearly that lessons that could have been learnt in the last century were ignored.

On a June afternoon in 1883, 183 young children were crushed to death as well-meaning organisers tried to hurry them from a Sunderland theatre by offering a prize at the exit. At Hillsborough in April 1989, 96 men, women and children were killed after doubtless well-intentioned officials hurried them into a football ground to watch the start of an important semi-final. In both instances the crowd was excited and expectant, and was in a rigidly confined space with inadequate exit facilities. In both cases the authorities were initially unaware of any problem, and continued to encourage the crowd to move even when those at the front were being trampled underfoot. The design of the theatre, like the design of the crowd pens at Hillsborough, was almost perfect for crushing large numbers of people. There was no escape for those unfortunate souls at the front of the melee. The Sunderland disaster, and scores more like it, should have taught lessons to prevent similar tragedies. They clearly didn't.

The sinking of the Marchioness in August 1989 was an almost exact replica of the sinking of the Metis in 1867 and the Princess Alice in 1878. The main difference between the three events is in the loss of life. When the Marchioness sank 51 died, when the Princess Alice went down about 640 lost their lives and with the Metis the loss was only four. Like the Marchioness, the Metis and Princess Alice were pleasure vessels and they sank in the Thames after colliding with ships many times their own size and weight. The similarities between the incidents are striking, but the similarities in the public's reaction and subsequent inquiries are perhaps even more interesting. In each case there was a public outcry that such a disaster could occur on the apparently benign Thames, an almost desperate search for a scapegoat and calls for improvements in river safety that would render further such tragedies impossible.

At the inquest into the deaths on the Metis – where the low death toll was due entirely to the fact the vessel was close to shore and was effectively beached by the force of the collision – the jurors commented:

'The investigation has brought to light the existence of a state of things on the river which no man in his senses can contemplate without a shudder. It appears there are no rules whatever to guide captains of vessels. All is left to the chapter of accidents – to the chance that vessels will somehow or other manage to pass one another without coming into collision.'

Rescuers search for survivors and bodies after the Regent's Park ice disaster

That was in 1867. Eleven years later the Princess Alice was in collision with the collier, the Bywell Castle, and went down in midstream with the loss of at least 640 passengers. Again, there were calls for improvements in navigational controls and a series of long-winded inquiries that failed to pinpoint the cause of the accident. There were also public demands for the prosecution of the Bywell Castle's captain, a man reputed to have a drink problem. The coroner's jury demanded improved regulation of river traffic, better life-saving facilities on passenger ships and more stringent standards for crewmen. These recommendations were echoed by the coroner's jury at the inquest into the deaths on board the Marchioness more than 100 years later.

Most of us have experienced the disruption and fear caused by IRA terrorist activities. The methods of the IRA mirror those of their predecessors in the Fenian movement which was active during the latter half of the 19th Century. The Fenians, like the IRA, aimed to cause maximum disruption with the minimum of effort. Their targets usually fell into two categories, prestigious public buildings such as the Houses of Parliament, Scotland Yard and the Tower of London and places such as railway stations where even small devices could cause chaos. The Fenians sometimes organised devices at different locations to ignite simultaneously. In February 1884, for example, bombs were planted in the cloakrooms of Victoria, Paddington, Charing Cross and Ludgate Hill stations. This tactic, designed to stretch emergency services beyond their limits, has also been copied by the IRA.

In 1867 the Fenians ignited the first terrorist bomb on mainland Britain. They aimed to release one of their activists in custody by blasting a small hole in the wall of the Clerkenwell House of Detention. Their knowledge of explosives was rudimentary, and they succeeded in blowing up the prison wall and demolishing the row of houses opposite, killing 13 civilians. Public opinion, which until that point had held some sympathy for the Fenians and their cause, turned so violently that to be Irish and in London was to be guilty. The Metropolitan police found themselves under intense pressure to catch the culprits quickly and within hours two men and a woman were in custody.

The trio was hauled before a coroner's jury and found guilty of murder. Less frantic and more meticulous investigation revealed, one of the three to be a police informer. The other two were equally innocent of anything but being in the wrong place at the wrong time, and were eventually acquitted. Six people appeared at the Old Bailey charged with the bombing. Evidence was scanty and ill prepared and was obviously the result of policemen so desperate to get a result they were throwing caution and routine to the winds. Five of the six were acquitted. The sixth became the last man in England to suffer a public hanging.

In recent years our police forces have experience similar pressures from a public understandably outraged by atrocities. People demand instant results and police are sometimes driven to cut corners. The fiasco of the Guildford Four and the Birmingham Six are as much a reflection of public attitudes as they are on the thoroughness and professionalism of the hard-pressed police.

These are just a few example of incidents and attitudes repeated over the centuries, space precludes the inclusion of more. The philosopher Santayana once commented that if we do not learn by our mistakes we are bound to relive them. That cannot be more true than in the field of disasters.

Further Reading

With Disastrous Consequences, London Disasters 1830-1917. Wendy Neal. Published by Hisarlik Press, 1992. ISBN 1 874312 001. Available from BASICS London, Eastwood Medical Centre, Eastwood Road, South Woodford, London E18 1BN.

Wendy Neal is a professional freelance writer and public relations consultant. She has a strong interest in the comparative study of historical disasters. She is studying for an MSc in Civil and Emergency Planning. Wendy has two teenage sons and lives in London.

AMBULANCE SERVICES – THE FUTURE

Tim Coats, Alastair Wilson

The Ambulance Service is changing from a simple patient transport system to become the first phase in the medical treatment of the acutely unwell or injured. The challenge for the future is to use developments in information technology to integrate the pre-hospital phase, so that a continuum of care is available from the patient's earliest contact with the Health Service. Features of the Ambulance Service of the future are likely to include:

Control Systems

Most '999' calls do not require an emergency (blue lights and siren) response. The control system will grade calls based on their level of medical priority. This enables control staff to target resources to the most urgent need.

An information link with the telecommunications companies will provide an exact location of the 999 caller on a land line and an approximate location of a mobile phone, allowing automatic cross checking of the location of the incident. Satellite tracking of ambulance service vehicles will allow the controller to see instantly the resources that are available for a particular incident. Gaps in ambulance cover will be recognised by the computer system and suggestions made for the most effective stationing of vehicles given the known distribution of emergencies at that time of day.

An integration of information in the ambulance control room with data from the computerised information systems of hospital Accident and Emergency departments, will allow the Ambulance Service to distribute patients in such a way that the workload of these departments is evened out. The number of patients waiting long times for accident and emergency treatment will therefore be reduced.

Medical involvement in the control room will be essential. To work as a dispatcher will require a higher qualification than a paramedic. Only the most experienced paramedics will be eligible to undertake the additional training to become a dispatcher and pay will reflect the additional responsibilities.

Communications

Voice communication is slow and inefficient. Future communication in the Ambulance Service will involve digital transfer of information to and from the ambulance's on-board computer. The information on screen in the control room will be transferred to a screen in the ambulance. The data and message transfer system will be controlled by a touch screen and will provide rapid dissemination of information between the ambulance, control room and hospital. Details of the call and the patient's condition (including data from monitoring systems) will be transmitted ahead to the receiving hospital at a touch of the screen. Radio communications will be reserved for communication on personal radios between the paramedic at the incident scene and the consultant in charge of the patient's care.

Emergency Response

Not all '999' calls require the same level of response. Only a minority (approximately 10%) represent medical emergencies.

The future Health Service will have a number of options in response to a '999' call. These will include transfer of the call to the patient's general practitioner, advising the patient to make their own way to hospital, a car for non-urgent transport, an ambulance for non-urgent transport, an emergency (blue lights and siren) ambulance response, the addition of a paramedic response unit (by car or motorcycle) or a medical (including pre-hospital doctor) response unit. A helicopter will be added to the system in situations where early medical intervention by a doctor is needed, to allow a few (and therefore well experienced) doctors to be available over a large area of the country and to transport the patient with time-critical injuries to the appropriate centre for definitive care. There will be a greater integration of the Ambulance and Fire Services both in control and operations, with medically trained fire fighters acting as 'first responders' to selected critical incidents.

A sophisticated control system, as described, will be in place to direct the appropriate response to each call to the emergency services.

Route Finding

Satellite tracking of all ambulance service vehicles will be standard. An electronic map book will be part of the on-board computer system in every Ambulance Service vehicle, which will automatically direct the vehicle to the incident. The vehicles position will be displayed along with the best route given the current traffic conditions. It will also give estimates of the running time to possible destination hospitals with the facilities available so that each patient can be taken to the correct hospital.

Medical Treatment

Pre-hospital medicine will be seen as a speciality closely associated, but separate from accident and emergency medicine. A consultant will be clinically responsible for each patient's pre-hospital management. The academic base of pre-hospital care will be formed by funding for medical research in this area to define the interventions that are best performed in each pre-hospital situation and which are best left to the in-hospital phase. Instant medical advice will be available to pre-hospital personnel from the pre-hospital specialist (based either in the ambulance control room or the Accident and Emergency department).

Training

The training for a paramedic is likely to be to degree level with a corresponding increase in the academic standards required. Pay will need to reflect the increased calibre of personnel.

Record Keeping

Pre-hospital and in-hospital records will be electronically joined so that the information recorded during the pre-hospital phase in the ambulance computer and data downloaded from the ambulance monitors will automatically form part of the electronic case notes. All medical records for a patient will therefore be kept together and the Ambulance Service will not need to keep a separate record system. This integration of outcomes with pre-hospital data will allow audit to include the pre-hospital phase.

An infrared data transfer system could be used for direct communication between the ambulance and hospital communication systems as soon as the ambulance arrives outside the Accident and Emergency department.

This system necessitates some acquisition of keyboard skills by ambulance service personnel, although touch screen operation and perhaps voice recognition systems would be used whenever possible.

Audit

The merger of pre-hospital and in-hospital record will allow pre-hospital care to be included in medical audit, which will then be able to examine all phases of treatment from the first contact with the Health Service. Establishment of an effective audit cycle will need close association between ambulance service staff and their local hospitals.

Performance Standards

The medicalisation of pre-hospital care will lead to performance standards based on the medical treatment of the patient, such as the proportion of patients resuscitated from cardiac arrest, rather than logistics, such as the time taken to arrive following a '999' call. Performance standards will cross both pre-hospital and in-hospital phases, so time to thrombolysis following a myocardial infarct will become a performance standard, measured from the first '999' call rather than the time of arrival in hospital. In a similar fashion, time from injury to evacuation of an intracranial haematoma will become a performance standard for a trauma system.

Conclusion

The Ambulance Service of the future will be based on the utilisation of information technology to integrate pre-hospital care into a continuum of treatment for the acutely ill or injured. The emergency part of the future service will be smaller than the current ambulance service, providing early advanced treatment to those who will benefit. A close relationship between the non-acute transport service and general practitioners, as well as public education will be essential to allow the emergency service to operate more efficiently in its new specialised function.

Tim Coats, Emeritus HEMS Registrar is Research Fellow in Neurosurgery and Senior Lecturer in the A&E department at the RLH.

Alastair Wilson, FRCS is Accident and Emergency Consultant at the RLH.

SECTION 5: ANATOMY OF A 'CALL OUT'

HEMS CALL OUT

Date:	01-04-1996	Time:	09:35:38
A-Z Ref:	30 MC 45	Grid:	TQ417882
AA Square No:	Cent 49	Control Zone:	Inside City's

Data to the accident from	Bearing	Distance
1. The London Hospital	052.6	5.2 Nm
2. BIG Freq 115.10	005.2	14.7 Nm
3. LAM Freq 115.60	227.3	5.9 Nm

Data from the accident to

1. The nearest hospital Whipps Cross (4.7.8.9.10.11.12.13) Tel 61 Sq No 48 Tel No 0181 539 5522	281.6	1.5 Nm
2. The nearest neuro hospital Oldchurch Romford (1.4.7.8.9.10.11) Tel 41 Sq No 50 Tel No 01708 746 090	096.1	5.0 Nm
3. The nearest burns hospital QM Roehampton (4.5.7.8.9.11.12.13) Tel 43/44 Sq No 75 Tel No 0181 789 6611	239.3	12.8 Nm
4. The nearest multi-disciplinary hospital Royal London (1.2.3.4.7.8.9.10.11.12.13) Tel 04 Sq No 57 Tel No 0171 377 7000	232.6	5.2 Nm

1. Neurosurgery
2. Cardiothoracic
3. Thoracic
4. Maxillofacial
5. Burns Unit
6. Paediatric surgery
7. Orthopaedic
8. General Surgery
9. ENT
10. Ophthalmology
11. Plastic Surgery
12. Urology
13. Obstetrics/Gynae

Good Luck

A typical computer print out giving details of a callout

THE ANATOMY OF A CALL OUT

Graham Budden, David Gurney, Mark Griffiths, Wendy Chalk, Jim Seager
Mark Landon, Richard Shuttleworth

The following incident is entirely fictitious, but the sequence of events is based on those typically encountered by the HEMS team.

0930 *Brian Smith has made the first of two serious misjudgements when he underestimates the time it will take him to get into London on the M11 on a typically busy Monday morning. He is now late for an important meeting. As he turns off the M11 he is distracted and glances down to retune his radio. When he looks up he realises that he has made another misjudgement – one that he will never be able to remember. Under heavy braking he loses control of his car and clips the kerb of the slip road.*

HEMS is available 365 days a year, from 0800 until 1900 or sunset, whichever comes first. Routine maintenance is carried out overnight, and a replacement aircraft is leased during the annual major service. The major cause of unavailability, however, is the weather, accounting for some 3 or 4 days each year. Fog, low cloud or falling snow will keep HEMS on the ground. High winds and rain, although unpleasant, will not usually prevent normal service.

The seven members of the duty crew of the Helicopter Emergency Medical Service (HEMS) have been in position and ready on the rooftop helipad above the Royal London Hospital (RLH) on the Whitechapel Road since 0800. The two pilots flew in with the helicopter from Denham airfield where it is parked in a hangar and maintained overnight. The doctor and paramedic and the 3 helipad crew, consisting of an operations officer and 2 firemen, will have been on the helipad for 30 minutes prior to the helicopter's arrival, to ensure that all the equipment is in place and ready for use as soon as it arrives.

0931 *The operator puts the first 999 call relating to a Road Traffic Accident (RTA) at the Redbridge roundabout through to the Central Ambulance Control (CAC) at the London Ambulance Service (LAS) headquarters at Waterloo.*

The operator tells the control room assistant (CA) the telephone number of the caller before connecting the call. The CA is trained to establish the details of where the incident is and what has happened and to do so within a maximum of 60 seconds entering the basic details of the call into the LAS computer system.

0932 *The details of the call are automatically printed out at the sector desk for the ambulance area in which the incident has occurred, and simultaneously at the special incident desk. The printout states: 'Redbridge Roundabout, North Circular Road. RTA Car overturned – query persons trapped.'*

As the printout arrives on the sector commander's desk an ambulance is tasked to attend the incident. A copy of all the 999 calls received by the LAS is printed out at the special incident desk. There the duty HEMS paramedic will select the calls, from the 2000 or more received each day, which might require additional assistance beyond the attendance of a regular ambulance.

As well as tasking the helicopter the HEMS desk controller is also responsible for tasking a number of Paramedic Rapid Response Units. These are mainly cars and solo motorbikes but the assets vary from area to area depending on local factors. The HEMS controller will also liaise with neighbouring ambulance services in the event of an incident outside of the LAS area.

0933 *While sorting through the latest output from the printer the HEMS paramedic comes across the details of the RTA. Deciding that this could be a job requiring additional medical skills he rings the caller back to try and get some further information.*

When ringing back, the paramedic will always initially reassure the caller that an ambulance is on its way. The paramedic then tries to ascertain more details regarding the incident. There is no specific procedure for this since the circumstances vary so much from one call to the next, but they will try to determine the 'mechanism of injury' and will ask questions such as: 'is the patient awake?; is the patient breathing/talking?; is the patient still trapped in the car?; can you see any other injuries?' Not all callers feel able to remain at the scene and the paramedic will often try to get more information from other sources, such as the police who can sometimes observe RTAs using their traffic cameras, and are often the first emergency service on scene at serious incidents.

Incidents which indicate that HEMS might be required include the following:

AMPUTATION	**BURN/SCALD**	**CRUSH INJURY**	**DROWNING**
ELECTROCUTION	**ENTRAPMENT**	**EXPLOSION**	**FALL FROM HEIGHT** (15-20 ft+)
FIRE (with people)	**HANGING**	**PERSON UNDER TRAIN** 'One Under'	
RTA (pedestrian, cyclist, motorcyclist, trapped)		**SHOOTING/STABBING** (particularly to upper body)	
SPECIFIC REQUEST (LAS crew, other emergency services, other ambulance control)			**TRAIN CRASH**

On many occasions it is not possible to make contact with the caller, for example if a public telephone is used and the caller has returned to the scene of the incident. If that is the case the paramedic must rely to a degree on intuition and experience and will often have little choice but to wait for an ambulance to arrive to confirm the details of the incident. In this example, as frequently happens with RTAs, the caller can provide little additional information because he called from a mobile telephone in his car and didn't stop. However, he is able to confirm that the car rolled through 360°during the course of the accident, and that there was no sign of any movement inside the car which had suffered substantial damage. As the paramedic puts the phone down he notices a number of other printouts, all referring to the same accident and reporting a very similar story. The circumstances point to a strong possibility that someone is seriously injured.

0935 *The paramedic in CAC decides to task HEMS and calls the helipad operations desk using the speed-dial system. The telephone is answered within three rings. 'Hello HEMS I've got a go for you. Three Zero Mike Charlie page forty five. Redbridge roundabout, junction north circular road and A12. RTA. Car overturned – query persons trapped. Origin of 31, to you at 35.' The ops officer reads back the details as he finishes writing and puts the phone down.*

When the red telephone in the helipad operations room rings a series of high pitched buzzers positioned around the helipad ensure that all the duty crew know that they are being called out and the sound triggers a flurry of action. The two firecrew are often the first to move since they must be in position on the helipad to provide fire cover for the aircraft captain who goes directly up to the helicopter and starts the engines. G-HEMS is left prepared for flight and can be ready for take-off in just over one minute. Meanwhile the medical team start donning their orange oversuits and they collect a bag of fluids from the warmer in the medical store before following up to the helicopter.

The co-pilot, however, goes straight to the operations room where the duty ops officer will be copying down the call details. The first information passed from CAC is the grid reference and page number to locate the incident in the *Geographers' A-Z Map of London*. This reference is immediately entered into a computer programme which, in only a few seconds, prints out navigation information and details of the nearest hospitals to the incident. During this procedure the co-pilot will be checking the location of the incident and making sure that he can identify it before leaving the ops room. A few seconds spent confirming the location on the ground are worth many minutes in the air and once airborne the movement of the helicopter, and other tasks which require the co-pilot's attention, make it very difficult to search in the *A-Z*, and there isn't much time to identify the streets when crossing the ground at speeds of up to 200 mph. When the co-pilot has got all the details, and is happy with where he is going, he runs up the stairs to rendezvous with the rest of the crew and normally the helicopter lifts off from the helipad within two minutes of the telephone ringing.

After passing details to the helicopter crew the HEMS desk paramedic will notify the police that HEMS has been activated and confirm the incident location. As the co-pilot leaves the ops room the ops officer will also be on the telephone, but this time to Heathrow air traffic control, forewarning them that the helicopter is about to scramble from the helipad. If the incident is thought to involve serious burns the ops officer will also ring the nearest specialist burns unit and confirm whether they are able to accept the casualty if required, and can usually pass the reply to the medical team before they arrive on scene.

0937 *The helicopter air ambulance, having received air traffic control clearance using the callsign Medevac, lifts off from the rooftop helipad and sets course on the heading of 053 degrees magnetic indicated by the pilot's navigation instruments. The co-pilot reports to CAC (radio callsign Red Base) 'Red Base, Mike Sierra's airborne estimating 3 to 4 minutes'.*

HEMS is classed as 'Category A' when it is on a primary mission using the callsign 'Medevac' and takes precedence over all other flights in the vicinity. However, common sense dictates that normal flying procedures are obeyed as much as possible. The hospital helipad is situated within the London Control Zone which is overseen by Heathrow air traffic control. Consequently, as soon as the aircraft is started, and the co-pilot has arrived with the navigation details, the captain will call air traffic control requesting permission to take-off. To avoid potentially dangerous misunderstandings caused by asking for clearance to obscure place names, all the emergency service helicopters operating in London request flight clearances using a system of squares based on the page numbers in the *Greater London Street Atlas*. The air traffic controllers have the page layout overlaid on their radar screen and are usually able to issue the clearance without delay. The pilot is advised of any other aircraft in the vicinity and a maximum height at which he may fly.

The co-pilot will call the HEMS desk on the radio as soon as the team is airborne and pass an ETA to the incident. From the helipad HEMS can reach any part of the M25 in just over 12 minutes. However, most callouts are well within that and the average flight time is around six minutes. The controller will pass on any additional information regarding the incident as it comes in to enable the medical team to prepare themselves. The HEMS crew has two means of communication with CAC. The primary one while airborne is a VHF air band frequency but this usually only works along 'line of sight' and becomes less useful on the ground. The aircraft is also equipped with a radio capable of communicating on the LAS VHF/FM net, enabling the crew to speak directly to ambulances on the ground. The LAS network has repeater stations all over the capital and works very well on the ground. The pilots and the medical team each have a hand held radio for this system and it becomes the primary method of communication when the team has landed.

The computer print-out produced on the helipad has two sets of bearing and distances relating the incident to aeronautical radio beacons. The captain will enter one of these in the aircraft's RNAV equipment while the co-pilot is strapping in. This results in an arrow on the captain's flight instruments pointing towards the incident and is accurate to within half a nautical mile. This gives the pilots a double check on the navigation. The co-pilot will initially navigate to the incident using local landmarks, reverting to using a *London A-Z* during the last couple of miles.

Factors considered by the pilots when selecting a landing site include:

1. **Proximity** to incident and accessibility
2. **Size** (min 2 x rotor diameter) and **Shape**
3. **Surface** (firm and dust/gravel free) and **Slope** (max. 10° to close down)
4. **Surroundings** (Trees, pylons, telephone wires, cables, lamp posts, awnings, signs, open windows/doors, etc)
5. **People** (How many, age, how close)

0941 *HEMS reports overhead.*

Having positively identified the scene of the accident the captain has to select a safe landing site. There are many factors to consider and no two sites are the same. On occasions various criteria may conflict. For example, the closest landing site may not be the most accessible or may be rejected as unsafe.

While circling overhead the incident the pilots will assess the options available to them and before descending into a site will make sure that the medical team have noted the route that they must take to reach the incident once they leave the helicopter.

Although speed is of the essence when attending a medical emergency, the environment in which HEMS operates means that the pilots must always consider the safety of the aircraft and the general public paramount. The most commonly used landing sites are playing fields, parks, school playgrounds (though never if children are present) and car parks. The helicopter will only land on the road if the traffic is being controlled by the police, and on motorways and dual carriageways the traffic flow must be stopped on both sides during landing and take-off. In residential areas where the streets are too narrow to land, road junctions often offer the best opportunity and are usually free of overhead wires.

Although the area in which HEMS operates includes a large proportion of congested and built-up area, finding a safe and suitable landing site is not as often a problem as might be expected. During a survey carried out over a period of 2 years, and covering some 2,200 missions, the medical team were asked to record the distance they had to travel from the helicopter to the incident. Perhaps surprisingly, the figures show that 74% of the time HEMS lands within 200m and 40% of the time it lands within 50m of the incident.

The complete findings of the survey are as follows:

Distance	No.	%
<50m	882	40
<100m	419	19
<200m	322	15
<500m	235	11
>500m	116	5
Not recorded	233	10
TOTAL	2,207	100

When landing on a particularly busy road (for example Oxford Circus in central London) the captain may elect to drop the medical team and then reposition the helicopter to an alternative site to close down – returning later, if required, to pick up the team and casualty.

The helicopter is equipped with a 'Skyshout' system enabling the pilots to speak to people on the ground through an external loudspeaker system. Experience has shown, however, that speech can be difficult to understand and that a two-tone siren and wailer facility on the system is more effective in clearing the public from a landing site.

0942 *HEMS lands and the co-pilot reports to CAC. 'Red Base, Mike Sierra is on the ground with Alpha. Medic One will be on scene in 30 seconds'.*

The co-pilot reports to CAC using a code to indicate the helicopter's proximity to the incident. 'Alpha' indicates that they are within sight and easy reach of the incident, 'Bravo' would mean out of sight but only a short distance away, and 'Charlie' indicates out of sight and the team either require transport or will have a long run to reach the scene.

The medical team leave the aircraft as soon as they have the captain's permission. Once the rotors have stopped the pilots will ensure that the aircraft is secure. The sight and sound of a helicopter landing in a built-up area is generally a great attraction for people in the vicinity and the pilots will sometimes request police assistance to keep the public away from the aircraft. The pilots are in communication with LAS, HEMS Ops and the medical team by both hand-held radio and mobile telephone. At least one of the pilots will always remain with the helicopter to ensure its safety, and answer a torrent of questions from the inquisitive public.

0943 *The helicopter paramedic calls CAC 'Red Base, Medic One is on scene'*

The medical team's arrival on scene can provoke any number of responses ranging from relief that qualified assistance has arrived, from people whose basic first aid training hasn't prepared them to handle a serious and complex medical crisis, to occasional hostility, possibly from an ambulance crew who didn't ask for HEMS' attendance and interprets the team's arrival as implying that they cannot cope with the situation. At this stage a fine balance must be achieved between diplomacy and assessing the resources on scene and the immediate requirements of the casualty. Some cases which HEMS attends do not require urgent intervention by the doctor and consequently the team must be careful not to alienate emergency service personnel by adopting an aggressive and interventionist attitude. It falls to the doctor and HEMS paramedic to coordinate the resources available in the best interests of the casualty, and experience has shown – as in most situations – that this can only be achieved efficiently by maintaining the cooperation of all those involved.

At this stage the doctor will also be deciding his level of involvement with the patient, and this will depend on the injuries sustained. The three options available are:

1. If the patient's injuries are relatively minor, or can be treated by the local hospital without intervention by the HEMS team, they can be sent to the local casualty unit in a road ambulance.
2. If a local hospital is able to treat the patient's injuries but the doctor has administered drugs on scene, or if there is any concern that the patient's condition may deteriorate while en route, the team will accompany the patient to hospital by road.
3 If the patient's injuries require specialist skills or equipment (for example a brain scan or a burns unit) which are not available locally, they can be airlifted direct to a hospital capable of handling the injuries sustained.

The helicopter can land at some 40 hospitals within the LAS area, although some hospitals do not have a helicopter landing site within their grounds, and an ambulance must be arranged to meet the team and transport them to the casualty unit. This process can take a significant amount of time. On the other hand, it is sometimes quicker to load the patient into an ambulance and run them into the local hospital on 'blues and twos' (blue lights and two-tone horns). The triage decision is covered further in the following chapter.

In the event of a multi-casualty incident, triage decisions can be very difficult and the doctor and paramedic must work together to ensure that they have identified all the casualties and allocated priorities correctly.

0945 *Medic One passes a medical report to Red Base. 'Red Base Medic One. We have a middle-aged male trapped inside his vehicle, unconscious with a head injury and possible pneumothorax. LFB are on scene. Further report to follow.'*

In a case involving a trapped casualty the doctor will liaise very closely with the Fire Brigade – in this example the London Fire Brigade (LFB) – to confirm the priorities of the extrication. The HEMS doctors all attend an extrication training day with the LFB so that they are aware of what equipment is available, the techniques that can be adopted, and the risks involved.

0958 *The pilots pass a report to CAC. 'Red Base, Mike Sierra. The patient is now out of the car and Medic One is commencing a secondary survey. It looks like a carry back to the London but we'll confirm that shortly.'*

The medical team is often very busy working with a seriously injured casualty and on those occasions the pilots will often lend a hand by positioning equipment, liaising with the other emergency services and reporting on the radio or telephone to ensure that CAC and the helipad crew are aware of what is happening on scene. Communication plays a crucial part in the successful operation of HEMS, ensuring that each element of the team knows what the others are doing can become difficult if the helicopter is not able to land within easy reach of the incident scene, and the team's mobile telephones are crucial to the team's efficiency.

Frequently the triage decision for a casualty is not made until they are removed to a position of safety and a more thorough clinical survey can be carried out. If the helicopter is being used to move the patient the decision must be relayed to HEMS operations as soon as possible in order that preparations can be made to receive the team.

1004 *Medic One gives a final report to CAC. 'Red Base, Medic One. We have an approximately 40 year old male now out of the car. He's been anaesthetised and intubated. He has a head injury and right haemo-pneumothorax with chest drain in place. A litre and a half of blood has been drained. This will be a carry back to the London and we are loading the patient now.'*

By this stage one of the pilots will have brought the vacumattress and suction unit to the casualty. The vacumattress is a rubber mattress filled with small plastic balls. When the patient has been loaded onto it the air can be sucked out and it goes rigid. This not only immobilises the casualty, thereby acting as a splint on any injuries, but also acts as a stretcher and allows them to be easily lifted into, and secured within, the aircraft.

1008 *Casualty is secured inside the helicopter.*

To comply with Civil Aviation Authority regulations the patient is loaded in the vacumattress and secured to the helicopter's Helidyne stretcher by three seat straps. In the event of a multi-casualty incident one of the seats in the rear of the aircraft can be quickly removed and placed in the luggage compartment. A second patient can then be placed on the floor on the port side of the aircraft on a stretcher and secured to floor mounting points.

The process of placing the patient into the helicopter is very straightforward and takes no more time than loading into an ambulance. The only medical equipment permanently fixed in the aircraft is an oxygen supply and a ventilator. These will be prepared for use by one of the pilots as the patient arrives and simply checked by the doctor as the casualty is transferred from the systems used on scene.

1010 *HEMS takes off from the accident scene.*

Prior to starting engines for take-off the pilots will have cleared people well away from the immediate vicinity of the helicopter – though the public can be extremely reticent to accept well intentioned advice.

Lifting from an incident with a patient on board the helicopter retains the callsign 'Medevac' and its associated priority status. Returning from an incident without a patient the captain will revert to the aircraft registration callsign G-HEMS (Golf-Hotel-Echo-Mike-Sierra) and follow normal air traffic control procedures.

Under normal circumstances the patient is not placed on the aircraft until they are in a stable condition. However, during the transit the medical team have complete access to the patient, and they can carry out medical procedures in the aircraft if necessary, though the movement of the helicopter can make precise interventions very difficult. If required the pilots can isolate the medical team's intercom to allow them to talk without conflicting with incoming radio messages.

1014 *HEMS lands on the roof of the RLH.*

As the helicopter approaches to land on the roof of the Royal London Hospital the operations officer telephones down to the casualty department to instigate the trauma call which summons the team of specialists to the resuscitation room to receive the casualty. The fire crew will have already collected a bed from the department and positioned it on the ramp leading to the helipad. Due to the large number of expected helicopter movements and the helipad's raised location, on the roof of a hospital in the middle of a heavily congested area, the Civil Aviation Authority require that at least two qualified airport fire fighters are on duty whenever HEMS is operational. Apart from their fire fighting duties they are also responsible for controlling access to, and safety on, the helideck and act as ground support for the aircrew. When the helicopter returns from a mission they assist with unloading and transporting the casualty off the deck, and then remove any debris from the cabin and make ready the equipment for the next call out.

Fire fighting equipment on the helipad consists of three independent systems, each capable of extinguishing a major conflagration in its own right:

1. 1800 litres of pre-mixed AFFF delivered through either, or both of, two stations, north and south of the landing area.
2. Rising main pressure water supply with 250 litres of 6% foam concentrate delivered through separate hoses from stations to the north, south and east of the deck.
3. 2 x 50 kg mobile Halon extinguishers.

Once out of the helicopter the medical team wheel the casualty down the ramp leading from the helipad and into the trauma lift. HEMS has its own lift, with access limited by an electronic tag system, running direct from the rooftop to the ground floor, where the accident

PAGEONECOMMUNICATIONS

ADVERTISEMENT FEATURE

SAVING LIVES BY STAYING IN TOUCH

PageOne Communications Limited is providing vital life-saving contact between doctors, paramedics and operations staff on the Helicopter Emergency Service (HEMS) team, based at the Royal London Hospital, Whitechapel; and the many other hospitals where accident and emergency victims are air-lifted for treatment.

Stan Sech is Chief Executive Officer of PageOne Communications Limited, formed recently by the £60m acquisition of Mercury Paging. He explains the PageOne role: "The HEMS helicopter is scrambled from its rooftop helipad at the Royal London Hospital to all manner of often life threatening incidents throughout Greater London. We have provided advanced technology PageOne Message Pagers which are carried by all doctors and paramedics on duty. This enables detailed messages about emergencies to be received by the team as well as alerting team members required for any specific incident."

Colin Adey, a London Ambulance Service paramedic on the HEMS team checks messages on his PageOne Advisor pager

Messages to the HEMS team are sent by telephoning the PageOne bureau. The HEMS operations officer dictates messages which are transmitted via satellite and displayed on the pager's large screen within seconds. Messages can then be held in the pager memory for future reference.

"In addition to the pagers," says Sech, "we have also provided mobile phones which which are used primarily at the incident site. Once HEMS doctors have given initial emergency treatment - which may be as complex as open heart surgery – every second counts in getting the patient to a hospital with the necessary facilities to maintain the treatment. The mobile phones are used to contact the nearest suitable hospital, brief staff on the incident and arrange for the patient to be admitted."

Already HEMS deals with over 1000 calls per year and has saved more than 50 lives. Speed is of the essence and the helicopter is normally airborne within 2 minutes of an alert.

Dr Gareth Davies, a senior doctor with HEMS, says that while the team is invariably called out to high profile incidents such as the Bishopsgate bombing, it is the multitude of daily accidents and violent attacks where their skills in trauma treatment are constantly required. "In one week alone our tally of calls included two stabbings, two suicide attempts, one fire victim, one person who fell under a train and another who fell into a canal," said Davies. "We had four road traffic accidents, including one in which the victim was a pregnant woman, plus a football accident and a man who fell off a ladder. Ladders are lethal," he added.

On many occasions victims are transported directly back to the Royal London Hospital where HEMS has a specially developed trauma treatment facility and can often provide the most effective treatment.

Alastair Wilson, the Accident and Emergency Consultant at the Royal London Hospital, is in charge of the HEMS unit. "We have the specialist skills and equipment to deal with most emergencies here," says Wilson. "We also monitor the progress of all HEMS patients whether they are being treated here or at another hospital. By comparing our results with those achieved for similar patients using conventional A&E methods we have identified many cases of lives being saved through HEMS and a much improved recovery rate for those victims we can treat quickly."

Full details are available from: PAGEONE COMMUNICATIONS LIMITED
2 Brentside Executive Centre, Great West Road, Brentford, Middlesex, TW89DS, FreeCall: 0500 505 505.

and emergency department is located. The lift takes 45 seconds to reach the ground floor and, as well as oxygen, it is equipped with a supply of medical equipment in case the lift malfunctions or the casualty's condition unexpectedly deteriorates.

1017 *The casualty arrives in the Resus room in the Accident and Emergency department.*

On arrival in the resuscitation room the doctor hands th casualty over to the waiting trauma team and briefs them on the circumstances of the incident, actions taken and any drugs/medication administered. The trauma team which takes over the patient's treatment is made up of a number of specialist doctors and nurses with specific training and experience of handling multiply injured casualties. The resuscitation room at the Royal London Hospital has five patient cubicles with a mobile x-ray unit and the equipment to carry out emergency operations if required. The HEMS team's direct involvement with the patient ends at that point and they are available for a further mission with the helicopter. However, they will

The Public's Top Ten Favourite Questions

1. **What is happening, is this an exercise?** No, it is not an exercise. We usually also say that we do not know what is happening – simply because we try to give as little information as we can without misleading people, since a relative or close friend of the casualty may be within earshot, and the information that we have might be incorrect.

2. **How fast, high, fuel, etc?** The helicopter has a maximum speed, at sea level, of 200 mph, though our normal cruise speed is about 175-180 mph. We usually fly at 1500 feet over London. The aircraft can carry 915 kgs of fuel, which would give the helicopter a maximum range of 400 miles, but our normal fuel load around London is around 400 kgs, which gives the team just over 1 hour's flying time.

3 **How long did it take you to get here?** Depends where 'here' is, of course, but HEMS can reach anywhere inside the M25 motorway within 12 minutes of taking off from the Royal London Hospital. Add 2 minutes to be activated and perhaps a minute or two to choose a suitable landing site and the answer is virtually always under 15 minutes from the call out and usually less than 10 minutes.

4. **What do those two pipes at the front do, mister?** The two pipes in question are the 'Pitot Tubes' (pronounced Pee-Toe). They stick out from the front of the aircraft and children often think they are guns. In fact they measure the dynamic air pressure and provide the pilots with an indication of the helicoptor's speed through the air.

5. **How many people do you carry?** The standard crew is two pilots (captain and co-pilot), a doctor and a paramedic. The team will sometimes be accompanied by another doctor or paramedic undergoing training. The helicopter can carry two patients on stretchers.

6. **What area do you cover?** Because HEMS is tasked by the LAS its main area of coverage is the LAS area, which is, roughly speaking, the area inside the M25 London orbital motorway. However, the limit is indistinct as 999 calls made on the borders of Ambulance control areas may be fed through to the neighbouring area's control room. The helicopter is available to the neighbouring areas at no charge, although the further the team have to travel the longer they will take to arrive and the beneficial effect of their attendance may reduce accordingly.

7. **How long does it take to become a pilot?** It takes about one year to become a professional co-pilot and then about 5 years to Captain. But, as any of the HEMS pilots will tell you, you never stop learning!

8. **How much does it cost?** On average, the helicopter service costs about £700 per mission.

9. **Can you land anywhere?** The Civil Aviation Authority has granted HEMS a special clearance to land whenever the captain thinks it is safe to do so, but only when flying on a mission tasked by the Ambulance Service and where someone's life is believed to be in danger.

10. **What happens if you get another call now?** The medical team's priority is to deal with the patient they are with. On weekdays, and often at weekends, a second doctor is available at the hospital. If time and circumstances allow the helicopter can return to the helipad and collect the second team (callsign 'Medic 2' on the radio) and take them to the second incident. HEMS has been known to have three medical teams active simultaneously, but that is unusual.

usually spend 5-10 minutes completing their notes and recovering equipment before returning upstairs.

Once back on the helipad the team must ensure that the paperwork is brought up to date. Every mission flown by the helicopter is entered in a computer database which records the details and timings of the incident. The medical team input their findings and interventions and then file their original on-scene notes, along with any Polaroid photographs and print-outs from monitoring equipment, for future reference. The doctors are frequently summoned to appear in court on cases dealing with incidents attended by the helicopter – either the coroners court to ascertain cause of death or the crown court if a prosecution is involved – and these records will form the basis of their evidence. If a patient is carried back to the RLH in preference to a local hospital the doctors send them a fax outlining the details of the incident and explaining the triage decision.

No further formal record is kept by the HEMS team for patients taken elsewhere, but for patients who are brought back to the RLH the medical information is updated as the patient progresses through the hospital system.

1030 *Brian Smith has already left the resuscitation room on his way to have a brain scan. The operating theatre is being prepared with two teams of surgeons to operate on his chest and head injuries. The HEMS medical team has just arrived back on the helipad and switched the kettle on.*

The team is called out, on average, 3 or 4 times each day, but every day is different and unpredictable, so a cup of tea is often the top priority – the next call could come through at any minute.

Photo: John Pooley

Attending a HEMS callout

SECTION 6: ON SCENE MEDICAL CARE

Introduction

Tim Coats

Pre-hospital treatment is the first link in the chain of survival following injury. The pre-hospital part of the Royal London HEMS trauma system has the highest public profile, but occupies only a few critical minutes of the many months that may elapse between injury and recovery. The overall aims of treatment in the pre-hospital phase are the performance of critical (immediately life-saving) interventions followed by transport, still continuing resuscitation, to a trauma centre that is able to provide early definitive care. The combination of early critical interventions and early definitive care lies at the heart of the HEMS London trauma system.

These seemingly straight forward objectives are complex to put into practice. Efficient treatment during the pre-hospital phase requires the coordination of the various emergency services, maintenance of the safety of both the casualty and rescuers, urgent assessment and treatment of a complex medical problem, and triage to an appropriate trauma centre. This is not a situation in which a doctor will perform well without specific training and experience.

A helicopter does not provide medical treatment, being simply a method of transport. The crucial factor in treatment is the skill, equipment, decision making and triage ability of the medical team. The aircraft enables the match of a scarce resource (the experienced pre-hospital doctor and multi-specialist centre) with a rare event (major injury). The use of a helicopter is the most rapid and cost-effective way of achieving this match.

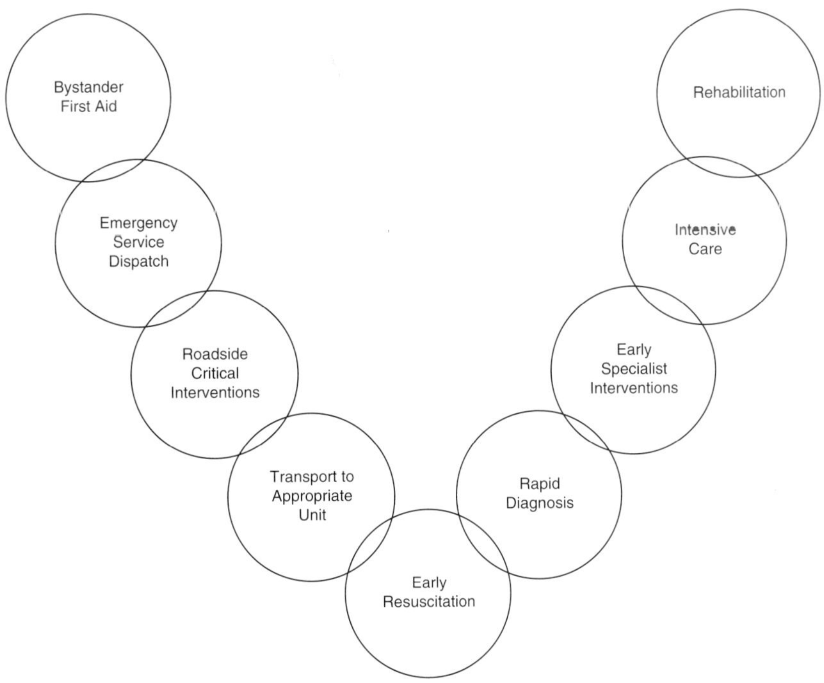

THE LIFE SAVING CHAIN
(Rettungskette in German)

DISPATCH PROTOCOLS

Jill Williams

The effectiveness of any emergency service is dependent on accurate tasking. It has become apparent that dispatch protocols cannot be transferred from one service to another but must be adapted to local need. What works effectively in Seattle does not meet the needs of London.

The original dispatch protocols for the Helicopter Emergency Medical Service (HEMS) were based on a wide range of data in discussion with the Department of Health, County Ambulance Services, LAS and the London A&E Consultants Group. HEMS paramedics are rostered to work on the special incident desk in the LAS Control Room and dispatch is largely dependent on their experience. It is extremely difficult to develop protocols that are sufFiciently sensitive to select the 0.2% of all 999 calls that HEMS was established to attend. The abort rate of 25%, is comparable with anywhere in the world, which suggests that the paramedics are using their experience well.

Until recently the LAS control room was paper driven, which made it difficult to audit the effectiveness of dispatch and even more difficult to audit the number of missed calls. The newly opened modernised control room should help to solve these problems.

As a result of a purchasers' review of the HEMS system, new, more detailed dispatch protocols were written jointly by representatives from HEMS, LAS and Inner London Health Authorities. These protocols have been in place since June 1996.

It became apparent that as the dispatch protocols affected a number of disciplines they had to be written in sections to meet the needs of the various parties. Therefore, there is a protocol for call takers, the special incident desk, the sectors, the ambulance crews and the HEMS medical team.

Criteria have been developed for immediate dispatch of the aircraft based on mechanism of injury, as follows:

- One under (train)
- Fall from more than two floors
- RTA occupant ejected (thrown from vehicle)
- All shootings (except air rifle)
- Stabbings (from neck to groin)
- Hangings
- Drownings
- Traumatic amputations (above wrist or ankle)
- Requests from emergency services (Fire, Police, Ambulance)

The other category of calls are those which are transferred to the paramedic on the special incident desk for further interrogation based on the mechanism of injury:

- Road traffic accidents
- Burns/scalds
- Electrocution
- Industrial accidents
- Fire/inhalation
- Persons trapped
- Assault – unconscious

It is planned to audit the dispatch of the helicopter against these agreed criteria to regularly review and alter the protocol if it is shown that medical intervention is routinely not required for some of the selected mechanisms of injury. This audit alone will not establish the effectiveness of medical intervention until there is a collaborative database on patient outcome from each and every hospital that receives a HEMS patient.

It is hoped that these protocols will begin to establish a tasking system within LAS which will enable them to send an appropriate response to a given situation. This should help to facilitate the use of special resources and to dispatch them to an incident where they can make a positive contribution to patient outcome. These special resources include motorcycle paramedics, rapid response units, HEMS or a BASICS doctor. A great deal of work and cooperation will be required to evaluate the effectiveness and use of these resources.

Jill Williams is Manager of A&E/HEMS at the Royal London Hospital, Whitechapel.

EXAMPLES OF STANDARD OPERATING PROCEDURES (SOP)

Tim Coats

SOP 9: Confirmation of Death At Scene

9.1 If a patient is obviously dead and no resuscitation has been attempted the doctor can only confirm death but not certify. Under these circumstances the body is technically Coroner's property and should not be moved until the police are happy that this should go ahead. They arrange transport to the appropriate mortuary.

9.2 If a patient undergoes an attempted resuscitation and has been 'interfered with' medically a number of rules apply:

a) no lines or tubes are removed.
b) nature of medical intervention is recorded and made available for the Coroner, together with the fact and time of death.
c) documentation on a 'Coroner's Information' form is sent with the body to facilitate procedures at the hospital/mortuary.
d) it is usually best for the HEMS registrar to stop the resuscitation and pronounce life extinct but not to 'certify' the patient, so that the ambulance crew can follow their usual local procedure (which varies in different areas). Be sure to note the time, at which you pronounced Patient Life Extinct (PLE), and make sure the documentation is comprehensive as there will inevitably be a police statement to fill out.

9.3 If a patient is carried from A to B and dies en-route or at the receiving hospital the usual rules apply and it is dealt with by the receiving area's Coroner. In practice if a patient deteriorates during flight it is almost always appropriate to continue resuscitation into the emergency room.

9.4 If the body is in a public place the ambulance service has a duty to remove it, but this will only take place after consultation with the senior police officer at the scene.

9.5 If there are relatives in the vicinity who cannot be led away when the decision has been made to stop resuscitation, it is kinder for them if cardiopulmonary resuscitation (CPR) is continued up to the time the casualty is put into the ambulance (this arises most often when the casualty is a child). Resuscitation is then stopped on the way to hospital. The relatives can then be talked to in a more controlled environment.

9.6 If the body is being taken to a hospital without the HEMS crew accompanying it, but the relatives are also going to that hospital, then it is prudent to ring the hospital to let them know that the relatives are unaware that life has been pronounced extinct.

9.7 It has been suggested that in the case of paediatric fatalities lines and tubes should be removed so that the parents will be spared further distress on viewing the body. Pathologists differ in their views on this and at present the advice must be to leave all lines and tubes in situ but to cover them with dressings and cut the tubes flush with the skin or mouth where appropriate.

SOP 18: Clothing

Germa suits

18.1 These are made of orange Nomex. They are fire resistant, but permeable to water and chemicals. They conform to British Standard visibility requirements. These suits can and should be cleaned on a regular basis in the stores room. Membership of Mensa is not required to understand the washing instructions, just remember not to boilwash the suit as it will damage the reflective properties of the suit and, no doubt, shrink it. Take the knee pads out of the suit before washing as these shrink whatever the temperature.

Waterproofs

18.2 The Germa suits are not at all waterproof so in the wet, wear one of the ambulance service plastic overcoats (these are orange and hanging up in the stores room). These are not fire resistant.

Footwear

18.3 Boots with ankle support and steel toe caps should be worn. Remember that these will not be proof against chemicals, so avoid stepping in any pools of liquid. We are presently trying to get these provided free of charge by the LAS but at the time off writing we are still required to provide our own footwear. (Camden Market seems to be a good place to buy.)

Gloves

18.4 You must wear plastic surgical gloves on scene. Put them on in the aircraft on the way to the incident.

They will not protect you against sharp objects so if you are in a high risk environment, e.g RTA with lots of broken glass and jagged edges, wear outer gloves, such as gardening gloves until you have to perform anything more delicate. We hope to provide gloves of the type that London Fire Brigade use for this purpose.

Eye protection

18.5 You should wear eye protection on scene. This is especially important when involved with firecrews who are cutting metal or glass. There are plastic goggles on the aircraft and ideally you should have a pair of safety glasses in a pocket of your suit.

Head Protection

18.6 Helmets are provided on the aircraft. They should be taken to all scenes as you cannot really tell ahead of time whether you will need them or not. It is vital that they are worn at one unders, on building sites, where there is a lot of unrestrained glass and during extrications from vehicles.

Torches

18.7 There are torches in the fluid bag. These can be opened and worn around the head. They should not be forgotten especially when going under trains.

Ordering suits

18.8 We currently order our suits from Paraid as they are the sole importers of this type of suit, At present Mark Landon (pilot) coordinates this. It is vital that new doctors to the service are measured for their suits well before their starting date as there is a big time delay between ordering and delivery.

Name badges

18.9 A name badge (available from Mark Landon) with your name embroidered on it needs to be sewn onto your suit. All personnel (including observers) must wear the appropriate identification or tabards when on scene.

SOP 27: Controlled Drugs

27.1 The controlled drugs used by HEMS are morphine and fentanyl. These drugs are controlled under Schedule 2 of the 'Abuse of Drugs Act' and the HEMS registrars have a legal responsibility to ensure that the drugs on the helipad can be accounted for and are secure.

Storage

27.2 Morphine and fentanyl must be kept double locked in the store room. This means that they are placed in the small compartment in the top drug cupboard, this is then locked and then the main door to the top drug cupboard is locked. The key should be returned to the Doctors Office where it remains hanging on the notice board.

Controlled drugs not locked

27.3 Each drugs pack contains five ampoules of morphine and one ampoule of fentanyl. There is also an ampoule of fentanyl in each fluid pack and remember there is a complete supplementary drugs pack in the blue Thomas Pack in the boot of the aircraft (with a further five morphine and one fentanyl). Thus the total number of controlled drugs which is not locked away is:

27.4 Morphine – 25 ampoules (five in each Thomas Pack and five in the Supplementary Pack). Fentanyl – seven ampoules (one in each Thomas Pack, one in the Supplementary Pack and one in each of the Fluid Bags – there are two fluid bags) The HEMS registrars must keep account of these.

Restocking bags after use

27.5 When a controlled drug has been used on scene the bag will be restocked from the supply in the store room. The 'Controlled Drugs Register' must be completed at the same time. This register is a legal document and is kept on the shelf above the controlled drug cupboard.

Filling in the register

27.6 Each box of drugs has a serial number printed on the white pharmacy label. This number corresponds to a numbered page in the register. If you are going to restock a bag with a drug from a particular box then open the corresponding page in the register.

27.7 The figure in the 'balance' column should tally with the number of ampoules in the box. You must fill in the page as the columns indicate. If you do not know the name of the patient to whom you have given the drug try to write something that may help identify him at a later stage e.g 'male RTA head injury' (this coupled with the date and time will help).

27.8 The signature must be signed by the doctor who gave the drug and witnessed by the paramedic. It is recognised that the paramedic has not always actually witnessed the administration of the drug and so if he/she is not happy to sign then the doctor should sign twice. If the ampoules are being issued to restock expired drugs in the major incident drug packs – 'issued to Major Incident Packs' should be written in place of a patient's name.

27.9 Once the number of ampoules removed has been subtracted from the previous balance the new balance should equal the number remaining in the box. If there are no ampoules remaining and the new balance is zero then put a line through that page and tear off the top right hand corner of the page as indicated.

27.10 It is vital that the balance figure is correct and corresponds with the number in stock. If this figure does not tally then double check that you have not made a mistake and that no other doctor has forgotten to fill in the register correctly. If the figures still are not correct then you must assume that there are some missing/lost/stolen and follow the procedure set out below.

Lost/missing controlled drugs

27.11 Make a note in the register of the date and time that it was decided that there were drugs missing (this can be written on the page corresponding to the serial number of the missing drugs). Inform pharmacy – currently the pharmacist who deals with HEMS (February 1996) is on Bleep . . .

27.12 There is a form which has to be filled out in these cases. This is a 'Risk Management Clinical Incident' form and is available from the administrator at main reception in the Accident and Emergency department.

Ordering controlled drugs

27.13 A pharmacy technician checks the stock level of all the drugs and iv fluids on a weekly basis and may note that we need more controlled drugs. In this case he/she should ask one of the doctors to fill out an 'order for Controlled Drugs' form and take it to pharmacy. If you feel that we are running low then fill out the form (which is attached to each page of the register) and send it to pharmacy.

Receiving controlled drugs

27.14 When they are delivered a HEMS registrar must fill in the top section of the corresponding numbered page in the register with: the drug name (e.g morphine); form (injection); strength and size (e.g 10mg in 1ml); sign and date it and state the number of ampoules received.

Destroying controlled drugs

27.15 If an ampoule is broken then discard it in the sharps bin and record the fact that it has been 'wasted' in the appropriate page in the register and have it witnessed by a paramedic or doctor.

Tim Coats, Emeritus HEMS Registrar, is Research Fellow in Neurosurgery and Senior Lecturer in Accident and Emergency at the RLH.

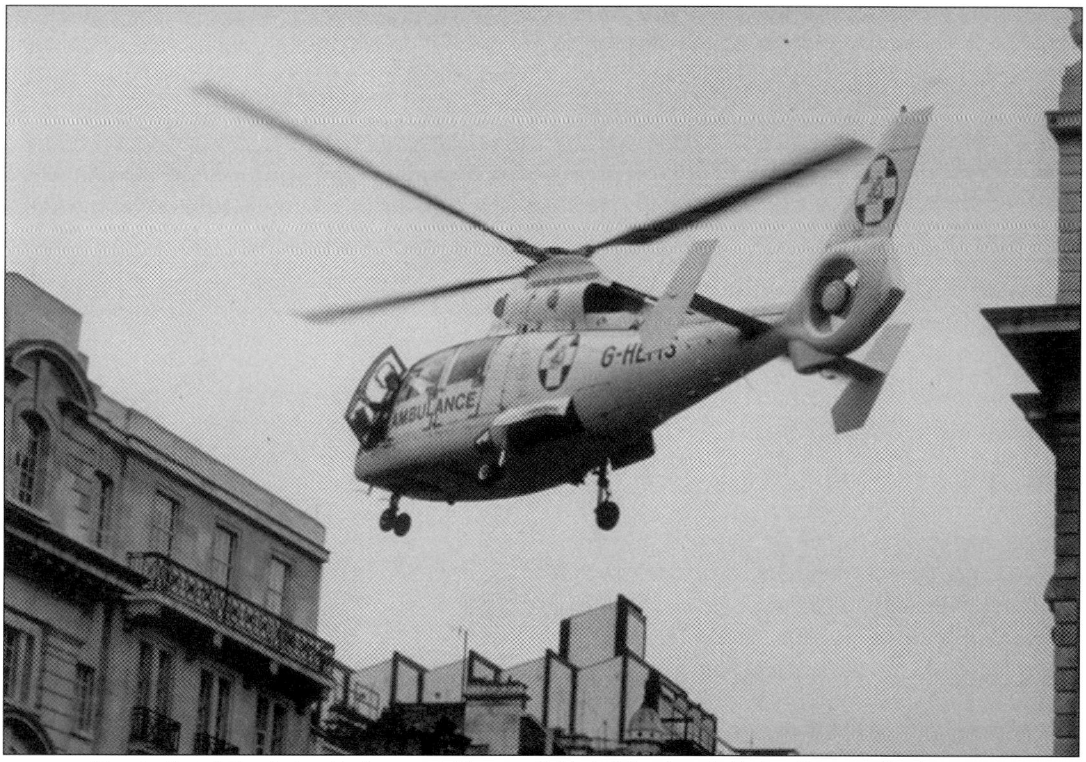

Photo: Mark Landon

No – he is not about about to jump out. The co-pilot is helping the pilot to land in a confined space.

CASE HISTORIES 1 : A LIGHT AIRCRAFT CRASH

Ronan Fenton

HEMS was called to a light aircraft crash. Two adult males were involved and one was reported dead on scene.

Initial Findings

The aircraft had undergone massive destruction. The patient was lying on his back still attached to part of the seat outside the aircraft. There were five other doctors, an ambulance and a fire crew already on scene and active resuscitation was in progress.

Primary survey revealed:

Airway	The patient's airway was patent and his oxygen saturation registered at 91%.
Breathing	The respiratory rate was 25 breaths/minute with good air entry audible in both lungs.
Circulation	The pulse rate was 140 beats/minute and the blood pressure was 156/128 mmHg.
Disability	The patient had a GCS of 15.
Exposure	The patient was very cold and peripherally shut down.

Suspected Injuries

Bilateral fractured femurs and fractured pelvis. There was poor circulation to the right foot and the patient had multiple facial and scalp lacerations.

Action Taken

Most of the critical interventions had already been carried out by the team on site before HEMS arrived. A cervical collar was on the patient and he was breathing oxygen. Two large bore intravenous cannulae were in place and fluid resuscitation was in progress. Analgesia had been provided with 10 mg of diamorphine. A pelvic splint was placed on the patient and the patient was transferred on a long spinal board. Midazolam 5 mg was given intravenously during extrication. In total 2500 ml of colloid and 1000ml of crystalloid were administered.

Triage

The patient was transferred by helicopter to a multi-disciplinary unit.

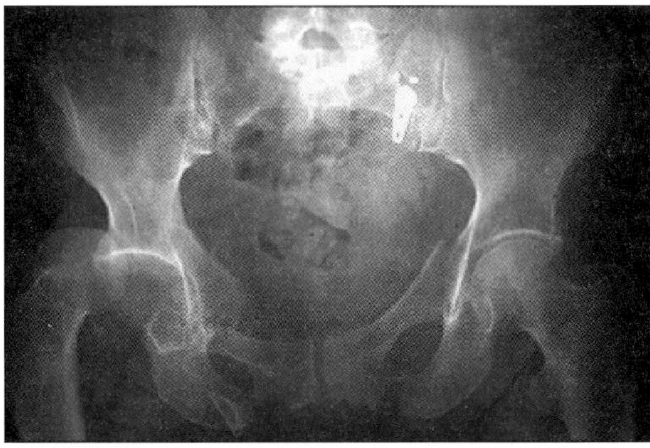

Photo: author

Timings

Incident	16.12
LAS informed	16.32
HEMS activated	16.33
HEMS on scene	16.48
Resuscitation room	17.34

Resuscitation Findings

The patient's pelvis was severely damaged (the right sacroiliac joint was disrupted and the right hip was dislocated). He had, in addition, a fractured left ankle and femur and a fractured left radius. There were extensive head and lower limb lacerations. The patient had suffered massive blood loss. The circulation to both left forearm and left leg was compromised.

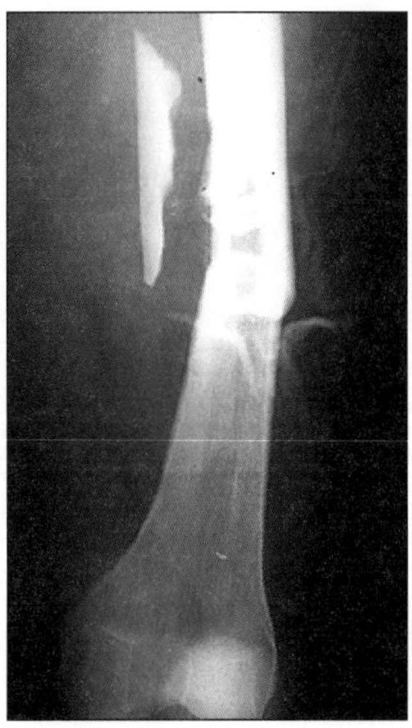

Photo: author

Action Taken

The patient remained in the resuscitation room for one hour and fourteen minutes and during this time he was transfused with 8 units of blood, 1500 ml of colloid and 2000 ml of crystalloid. He was then transferred to the operating theatre where he underwent combined orthopaedic and plastic surgery for a total of nine hours.

Outcome

This man spent 9 days on the Intensive Care Unit and a further 21 days recovering on the ward. He required counselling for post traumatic stress disorder and regular physiotherapy while on the ward. He was discharged from the hospital 32 days after admission. Apart from an area of numbness around two toes on the left leg he had recovered well from his life threatening injuries.

Discussion

This case demonstrates a number of important principles of trauma care. The safety of the emergency personnel must always be considered. In this case there was the danger of fire from aviation fuel at the incident site. The fire service was on hand to ensure that this risk was eliminated and no member of the emergency team approached the casualty until it was safe to do so.

The provision of early resuscitation in the field was vital considering the injuries sustained. The risk of hypovolaemic shock in this patient was very high. The fluid resuscitation at the scene together with the application of a pelvic splint may have maintained an adequate blood pressure until definitive treatment was available at the resuscitation room. All the necessary steps had been performed before HEMS' arrival and the final extrication and transfer of the casualty was done with the appreciation of possible spinal injury being present. The receiving hospital had been advised to have blood ready and so warm blood and fluids were immediately to hand in the resuscitation room.

The 'Early Hospital Phase' of this patient's treatment involved a lengthy resuscitation period before transfer to theatre and subsequently to the Intensive Care Unit for 9 days. The 'Late Hospital Phase' involved many days recovering on the wards and requiring skilled nursing, physiotherapy and counselling services. Much of this rehabilitation phase was carried on after the patient was discharged home. It is the combination of all these resources that leads to optimum success and outcome for the patient.

Ronan Fenton, Emeritus HEMS Registrar is a Senior Registrar in Anaesthetics.

PRE-HOSPITAL PHYSIOLOGICAL MONITORING OF HEMS PATIENTS

Andrew Morley

Where a patient's physiological variables are likely to change significantly and rapidly, those variables need to be continuously monitored. This is a central principle in the hospital management of patients on intensive care units or undergoing anaesthesia. It applies equally to the initial management of serious injury. Early detection and correction of physiological changes in trauma patients may improve morbidity and mortality.

For HEMS, the most basic 'monitor' of all is the attending doctor. He or she will be able to see cyanosis, to feel that there is no cardiac output, or to hear the unilateral absence of breath sounds well before monitoring equipment is applied and its first readings displayed. The doctor will also be able to judge, to a certain extent, whether information subsequently obtained from the monitor is reliable. Many factors combine in the pre-hospital environment to make equipment malfunction relatively common.

Several companies produce monitors for the care of critically ill patients in transit. Desirable qualities in a monitor of this sort include accuracy, multimodality, long battery life, lightweight and ease of carriage. Ideally, it should be compatible with equipment in receiving hospitals and possess a printer or downloading facility. Servicing arrangements and cost should also be taken into account.

The additional needs of HEMS are that, on scene, a monitor should be dependable in adverse environmental conditions and easily operable by attendant paramedical staff. Furthermore, equipment for use on board aircraft must have Civil Aviation Authority (CAA) approval specific to the type and model of the aircraft in which it is to be used. Testing by a CAA approved organisation is required to exclude any potential hazard to the aircraft in flight (e.g electrical interference, fire, explosion).

HEMS uses the Propaq 106EL (*Protocol Systems Inc, Beaverton, Oregon*). It measures 16.3 cm x 20.5cm x 16.8 cm and weighs 3.8 kg. It has a minimum battery life of four hours and has electrocardiogram (ECG), non-invasive blood pressure (NIBP), oxygen saturation (SPO_2), end-tidal CO_2 ($PE'CO_2$) and temperature facilities. Full monitoring is applied to the patient during the initial assessment and remains in place during ground escorts or HEMS transport, until care is handed over at the receiving hospital.

Electrocardiography

The ECG provides essential information in HEMS patients. The presence of coordinated electrical activity in the absence of cardiac output constitutes electromechanical dissociation. Possible causes in trauma patients include hypovolaemia, tension pneumothorax and cardiac tamponade, all of which are reversible. Myocardial contusion may be indicated by arrhythmias or ST segment changes. On scene, rain or blood on the chest wall may interfere with electrode adhesion. Mechanical and electrical interference on the ECG trace is also a common problem.

Non-invasive Blood Pressure

Automated NIBP monitoring of HEMS patients allows the doctor and paramedic to attend to more urgent clinical problems. Frequent measurement helps in the early detection of both hypotension (usually secondary to hypovolaemia) and hypertension, which may occur during laryngoscopy or when intracranial pressure is raised. However, in the trapped patient, access to limbs for cuff application may be difficult. In addition, patient movement, or vibration from extrication tools or the aircraft, may prevent successful readings.

Temperature

HEMS patients are often injured outdoors. Furthermore, removal of clothing is usually required to assess and treat the injuries. This increases the risk of hypothermia, the degree of which is known to be related to mortality in trauma patients. We attempt to prevent hypothermia by using warmed intravenous fluids, reflective insulation blankets and by heating the cabin in flight. Patient core temperature is measured using an aural probe.

Oxygen Saturation

Hypoxia is common in trauma patients. If it is progressive and untreated, death will ensue. It has been recognised as a major extracranial variable influencing outcome in severely head injured patients. Intra-thoracic causes include lung contusion, flail chest and pneumothorax. In unconscious patients, or those with craniofacial injuries, airway obstruction may be responsible. Pulse oximetry enables the early detection of hypoxia and may determine whether the HEMS doctor anaesthetises the patient and intubates the trachea on scene. These manoeuvres themselves carry the risk of hypoxia.

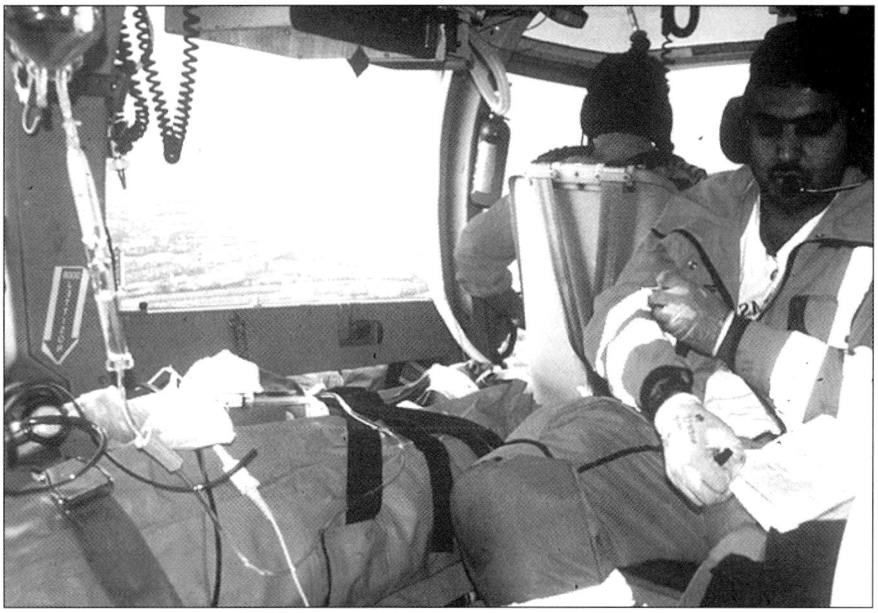

All equipment must be portable and capable of withstanding a hostile environment in pre-hospital trauma care

Oximeter function may be affected by environmental factors. On scene and in the helicopter, probe displacement is common. Where this is complete, no reading is obtained. With partial displacement, however, the displayed oxygen saturation may be incorrect. If erroneously high, the figure may reassure the attending doctor inappropriately. Intermittent oximeter malfunction during HEMS transport is a persistent problem. A German air rescue service recently found that its inflight oximetric readings were subject to interference 25% of the time. This proportion was greatly reduced using ECG synchronisation, which is a feature of the Propaq 106EL.

Patient factors too can influence oximeter function. Readings from finger probes may be unobtainable where the skin is coated in oil or bitumen. HEMS burns patients sometimes have high blood levels of carboxyhaemoglobin which cause overestimation of fractional oxygen saturation by pulse oximetry. In trauma patients blood loss may lead to anaemia which in turn increases pulse oximeter error at low saturations. Blood loss also causes peripheral vasoconstriction, a frequent cause of oximeter failure. In the last case, nose, ear or forehead probes may be useful, though formal studies have not shown them to perform any better than finger probes.

End Tidal Carbon Dioxide

The $PE'CO_2$ of patients intubated by HEMS doctors is measured using the in-line analyser supplied by Propaq. The resulting waveform is displayed on the monitor.

Capnography is the most reliable method to confirm endotracheal intubation, which is often hindered on scene by lack of access to the patient. Accidental oesophageal intubation is probably more common in these circumstances and may be difficult to detect by auscultation of the chest, especially with noisy extrication equipment nearby. Though a capnographic waveform is a good indicator of correct tube placement, it is important to remember that carbon dioxide (CO_2) can arise from the stomach. This may occur after prolonged bag and mask ventilation or where the patient has recently been drinking beer. Once the endotracheal tube is in place and ventilation commenced, repeated patient transfer increases the risk of circuit disconnection. In these circumstances, capnography is a useful indicator of circuit integrity.

As well as assisting in the detection of mechanical problems, capnography provides information about some aspects of the patient's physiological condition. If cardiac output ceases, there is no pulmonary blood flow to deliver CO_2 to the alveoli and the capnographic trace will disappear. On the other hand, raised $PE'CO_2$ readings are taken to reflect raised arterial CO_2 partial pressures ($PaCO_2$), though the validity of this assumption in severely traumatised patients is in doubt. A high $PaCO_2$ causes cerebral vasodilation, exacerbating the consequences of primary brain injury. Using $PE'CO_2$ as a guide, HEMS doctors follow standard practice in hyperventilating head injured patients in the acute phase.

In conclusion, monitors provide essential information which influences clinical decisions taken by the HEMS doctor. Some modern monitors are well suited to the pre-hospital environment, but their limitations must always be borne in mind. It is hoped that future design modifications will overcome some of the monitoring problems HEMS has encountered.

Dr Andrew Morley, Emeritus HEMS Registrar, is presently a lecturer in Anaesthetics at the Prince of Wales Hospital, Shatin, Hong Kong.

CASE HISTORIES 2 : A BAD FALL

Ronan Fenton

HEMS was called to attend an incident in which a 30 year old male had fallen 30 feet from a window onto a concrete path.

Initial Findings

The patient was lying on his side wearing a cervical collar.

Primary Survey revealed:

Airway	The airway was patent and the patient's oxygen saturation registered at 99%.
Breathing	The respiratory rate was 16 breaths/minute and good air entry was audible in both lungs.
Circulation	The pulse rate was 105 beats/minute and the blood pressure was 170/120 mmHg.
Disability	The patient had a GCS of 15 and was moving all four limbs.
Exposure	The patient was on his side on the path in the street.

Suspected Injuries

Fractured left knee and ankle. Facial lacerations.

Action Taken

Oxygen was administered via a face mask with reservoir bag and two large bore intravenous cannulae were sited. The patient was positioned on a spinal board in preparation for transfer to the nearest Accident and Emergency department accompanied by the doctor.

Prior to transfer the patient's condition deteriorated. He became confused and he fitted. In view of these changes a decision was made to anaesthetise the patient and to transfer by air to a multidisciplinary unit. The patient was anaesthetised using etomidate 10 mg. Intubation was facilitated using suxamethonium 100 mg and fentanyl 0.5 mg. Anaesthesia was maintained using increments of propofol and pancuronium. 50 g of mannitol were administered in an effort to further decrease cerebral oedema.

Triage

In view of the deterioration in neurological status the patient was airlifted to a multidisciplinary unit.

Timings

Incident	16.00
LAS informed	16.19
HEMS activated	16.23
HEMS on scene	16.31
Resuscitation room	17.08

Resuscitation Findings

There were bilateral fractured ankles and the left knee was also fractured.

The x-ray of the cervical spine demonstrated an unstable fracture of the sixth and seventh cervical vertebrae. The patient went from the resuscitation room to the CT scanner and was found to have a right subdural haematoma and an intracerebral haemhorrage with midline shift and obliteration of the right lateral ventricle.

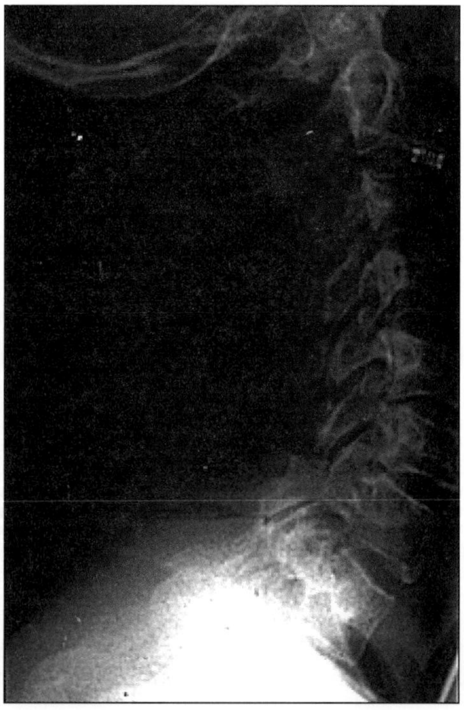

Photo: author

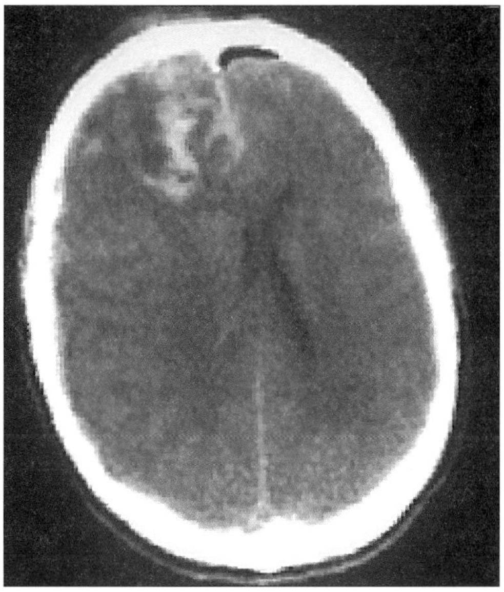

Photo: author

Action Taken

The patient underwent emergency evacuation of the subdural haematoma and had his lower limb fractures reduced at the same time. He was then transferred to ICU where ventilation and sedation were continued. Over the following days further surgery was performed to stabilise the neck fractures.

Outcome

This patient spent a further 26 days on ICU and this was followed by 30 days on the ward. He was discharged home having recovered full motor and sensory function with a moderate degree of intellectual impairment.

Discussion

The mechanism of injury in this case raised the suspicion of possible major injury. Falling 30 feet onto a concrete path generates a high kinetic energy of impact.

Initially the patient seemed quite stable, but at all times was treated as if there was a spinal injury. A cervical collar was placed on the patient by the ambulance crew and he was positioned on a long spinal board.

The case also demonstrates the need for constant reviewing of clinical signs and action in response to any changes that occur. The triage decision was changed in line with a change in the patient's condition on scene. This patient was talking sensibly initially despite his severe head injury but then became confused and fitted. Such rapid deterioration required prompt action to prevent secondary brain damage occurring.

The 'pre-hospital' phase of Trauma Care systems may seem the most dramatic part and often receives the most publicity. It is however only a part of an entire system and is the phase which takes the least time. This case demonstrates very well the time and manpower implications of achieving a good functional result in trauma care. This patient spent 37 minutes in the care of the HEMS team during which a number of critical interventions took place. This was followed by a further 56 days in the 'in-hospital' phase. During this time he was cared for by the intensive care team, neurosurgeons, orthopaedic surgeons, had three operations – all of which were critical in terms of achieving independent ability. Constant physiotherapy was provided together with counselling and rehabilitation which were carried on into the 'post-hospital' phase when the patient was discharged.

Ronan Fenton, Emeritus HEMS Registrar is a Senior Registrar in Anaesthesia.

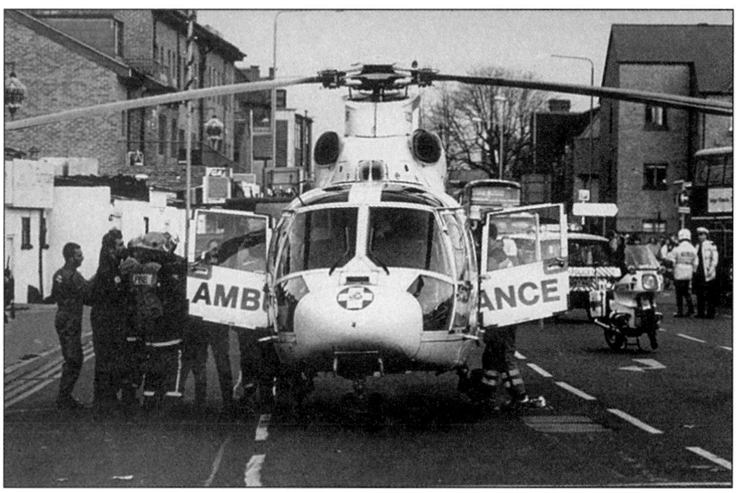

Photo: Mark Landon

When the police have cleared a site, the flying ambulance can land in a street or at a crossroads

PRE-HOSPITAL ANALGESIA AND ANAESTHESIA

Phil Hadjimichael, Tim Coats

PRE-HOSPITAL ANALGESIA

As in many areas of acute pain provision, pre-hospital analgesia is often poorly managed. This may be due to the lack of priority given to pain relief in an emergency situation, a lack of equipment, a lack of skill, or the worry that adequate analgesia will both cloud diagnosis and hinder the further management of head, chest and abdominal injuries. In many cases of severe injury, analgesia is probably best obtained as part of a balanced anaesthetic technique and as part of resuscitation. In patients with less critical injuries adequate analgesia may ease both casualty extrication and transport, as well as producing a calmer relaxed patient who can be readily assessed.

In the field, analgesia is more an approach than a simple set of drugs. Being involved in an accident is a very frightening experience which may lower the 'pain threshold'. In the pre-hospital management of the trauma victim, reassurance and psychological support may be more important than an armamentorium of powerful medications. Similarly, physical methods such as splintage of broken bones and the application of dressings (particularly to burns), can usefully ease pain. There has been no randomised controlled trial to show that pain is actually relieved by these techniques, nevertheless it is felt to be of value by numerous anecdotal accounts.

Pharmacologically there are three principal methods available to the doctor at the incident scene – inhalational analgesia, intravenous agents and local techniques. The most important issue in choosing between them is personal familiarity with both the technique of administration and the drug. The middle of the night, in the rain, upside down under a car attending to a screaming casualty is neither the time nor the place to do anything for the first time. Whenever powerful treatment is used the patient should be adequately monitored, have intravenous access and, if there is a specific antagonist, it should be available.

Inhalation Analgesia

By far the commonest pre-hospital analgesic drug in use is Entonox (50/50 mixture of nitrous oxide and oxygen) given via a demand valve. Most, if not all, emergency ambulances in the UK now carry this following its initial introduction over 20 years ago.

Because the delivery of the gas is demand driven, it depends on the patient maintaining a tight seal with the mask or mouthpiece. As such it is inherently a very safe technique with few side effects, the commonest being nausea and light-headedness. However, in the case of severe pain, it is difficult to master the coordination necessary to gain much benefit from it. Supplemental analgesia (usually in the form of opioids) is often needed upon arrival at hospital. Few studies have found more than 50% of patients gaining 'substantially' from this form of analgesia, although over 90% received at least some benefit. Nitrous oxide's tendency to diffuse into air containing spaces renders it potentially dangerous in decompression sickness and undrained pneumothoraces.

There are practical difficulties due to the bulkiness of the apparatus, and the fact that this mixture of gases is a vapour with the nitrous oxide condensing in the bottom of the cylinder at temperatures below -7°C.

Intravenous Agents

There are a number of intravenous agents which can be given in the field to alleviate pain. This route is preferred because of its predictability of effect and rapidity of action. This is particularly true in the cold, shocked patient where the intramuscular route carries the risk of a slow, delayed onset, with the drug often only entering the central circulation following resuscitation of the hypotensive casualty; an effect recently seen in the Falklands conflict.

With all the commonly used agents the Galenic principle applies: 'the correct dose is enough'. All must be titrated in small aliquots to the desired clinical effect.

Opioids

The opiate drugs, and morphine in particular, remain the gold standard of analgesia in the field. Morphine in aliquots of 2.5-5mg to a total of 10-20mg for an adult is the usual dose range. Diamorphine (in 2.5mg aliquots) and pethidine (in 25mg aliquots) will produce the same effect. Major side effects are respiratory depression and hypotension. The antidote naloxone should be available as well as oxygen and intravenous fluids. Nausea and vomiting is the commonest side effect and an antiemetic is frequently given concurrently (e.g cyclizine 50mg, prochlorperazine 12.5mg, or metoclopramide 10mg).

Whilst there is no doubt that opiates are effective, there are significant administrative problems in their routine pre-hospital use. As controlled drugs they have to be accounted for, stored and prescribed within strict guidelines. Their attraction as a drug of abuse with the attendant risk of theft, may expose civilian paramedical staff to the risk of violence.

Nalbuphine

Partial agonists, and particularly nalbuphine, are seen by many as providing a better alternative to morphine – supposedly as effective, but with fewer side effects and not a 'controlled drug' with all the attendant administrative problems. When given in a dose between 10-20mg for an adult it is as effective as 10mg of morphine. It has a similar depressant effect on respiratory drive and shows all the other opiate related side effects, though possibly less often. A major drawback is a 'ceiling phenomenom' that blocks the analgesic effect of any further doses of opioids, but not their side effects.

Ketamine

Of the non-opioid analgesics, ketamine has been the most widely used worldwide. Given in aliquots of 10 20mg to adults, it offers many advantages. Its analgesia is additative to that of opioids and, with increasing dosage, can be used to provide analgesia, sedation and finally full anaesthesia (at approximately 2mg/kg iv).

Compared to other anaesthetic agents it tends to least affect the airway reflexes, respiratory drive and cardiovascular system. There is still some risk of aspiration and hypoxia, though at analgesic doses this is minimal and necessitates monitoring only. The main drawback is of an abreaction on emergence. This problem is rarely appreciated in the field as it occurs following arrival at the receiving hospital. Ketamine should be avoided in head injuries as it can cause a further rise in the intracranial pressure, an effect which is only prevented by prior intubation of the trachea and hyperventilation of the lungs.

Local techniques

Unfortunately, local techniques are of limited value in pre-hospital care. The absolute inability to maintain sterility, a moving patient, poor visibility, and the need to evacuate rapidly from the scene, serve to render all but the most basic, rapid, reliable techniques to be of any practicable value in the field.

Useful blocks are: (1) Femoral nerve block for a fractured femur. This requires little skill and can be performed quickly (it is used by French firemen to good effect). (2) Intercostal nerve blocks for rib fractures or the insertion of intercostal drains for pneumothoraces. These may make a marked difference to a patient's depth of breathing and oxygenation. (3) Infiltration of the skin allows for venous cutdowns or surgical airways. More sophisticated and time consuming techniques are best left until arrival at hospital.

PRE-HOSPITAL ANAESTHESIA

Historically there are records of medical attention close to or even on a battlefield, dating back to the Ancient Chinese. An organised system of resuscitation, triage, treatment and evacuation of casualties started during the time of Napoleon. Following the need for surgery, came the need for anaesthesia. During the American Civil War (shortly after the birth of the speciality) field anaesthesia was first widely practised. Military anaesthesia has since progressed to achieve a position of marked sophistication with specific techniques, practices, equipment and training. Peacetime field anaesthesia has its roots in this warlike past.

The most important recent alteration in pre-hospital management is that anaesthesia in the field is performed to aid resuscitation rather than to facilitate surgery. The pre-hospital anaesthetist must overcome the triad of a hostile (even dangerous) environment, a sick, unstable patient in need of immediate resuscitation, and the physical isolation from a familiar 'safe' hospital milieu. This represents an interesting anaesthetic challenge for some, and a nightmare for others!

Indications for Pre-hospital Anaesthesia

The decision to induce anaesthesia as part of the resuscitative process rests with the degree of physiological derangement rather than any specific anatomical diagnosis. These are:

- *Airway:* Loss of or threat to the airway necessitating the placement of an endotracheal tube. For example, craniofacial trauma and burns involving the airway.
- *Oxygenation:* Inability to maintain oxygenation despite high inspired oxygen by mask. For example, lung contusion and multiple trauma.
- *Ventilation:* Inadequate lung ventilation requiring IPPV assistance. For example, multiple rib fractures with a flail segment.
- *Intracranial Pressure:* A need to control a raised intracranial pressure. For example head injuries with a reduced or falling conscious level (Glasgow Coma Score <12).

Aims of Pre-hospital Anaesthesia

The role of a pre-anaesthesia is to make these resuscitative procedures possible by producing the 'triad of anaesthesia': lack of awareness, analgesia and muscle relaxation.

This use of an anaesthesia, as opposed to muscle relaxation alone, is not universal. Some emergency services (mostly in the USA) intubate the trachea with muscle relaxation alone, arguing that in the hypotensive individual any drug induced vasodilatation is dangerous. Furthermore they suggest that hypovolaemia tends to preclude awareness of events. This is not so. In a follow-up study, spontaneous recall was very common in patients supposedly too shocked to allow the administration of any concomitant sedative during intubation. Unless the patient is pulseless, use of an anaesthetic is mandatory if endotracheal intubation is to be attempted.

Cervical Spine Control

One of the many effects of ATLS training has been to highlight awareness of cervical spine injuries. This issue seems to take up more space in most reviews of trauma anaesthesia than any other. Concern about the cervical spine is an insufficient reason for failing to adequately secure the airway when appropriate. In patients with unstable cervical spine injuries, emergency orotracheal intubation with cervical spine control is a safe procedure which does not worsen neurological status. The only drawback is that the methods of cervical spine control, whether the four man 'Baltimore technique' or simply keeping the rigid collar in place, tend to make the intubation more difficult. The regular use of a boogie has resolved this problem and in trained hands the failed intubation rate in the field is the same as that seen in the resuscitation room or theatre (i.e 1%).

In the field, with limited personnel, simply leaving a fitted rigid collar in place is a minimum requirement, with the addition of manual stabilisation being ideal.

Intubation

There is little difference amongst the various routes of intubation in effect on the cervical spine. The choice between techniques lies in ease and success rate. Essentially there are four techniques available. Blind nasal intubation, blind oral intubation, orotracheal intubation and pharmacologically-assisted orotracheal intubation (that is with a muscle relaxant and/or an anaesthetic).

Blind nasal intubation is a skill few in the UK have mastered. Even in the USA, where it remains popular, failed intubation rates are consistently between 5% and 20%. Similar failure rates are also found with unassisted orotracheal intubation. In some series of blind or unassisted intubation in the field, up to 20% of patients had to be given a surgical airway at scene: a procedure not without its complications.

In comparison, pharmacologically-assisted orotracheal intubation by a skilled doctor has a failure rate of about 1%, very similar to that found in the hospital environment. The difference in failed intubation rate is felt by some to be responsible for the improved survival of patients when attended by an appropriately trained doctor.

Comparison of failure rates for intubation between paramedics and doctors is difficult as a paramedic will not be able to safely achieve endotracheal intubation unless the patient no longer has laryngeal reflexes. This means that paramedics are unable to treat most patients with significant head injuries adequately.

Technique

Pre-hospital anaesthesia is always performed in a patient who may have a full stomach and is therefore at risk of aspiration. There is little choice, other than to perform a 'rapid sequence induction'. Other methods such as fibreoptic or awake intubation are simply inappropriate for the circumstances. The rapid sequence technique is designed to minimise the time between final loss of consciousness and the laryngeal protective reflexes, and securing the airway with an endotracheal tube.

It consists of preparation with pre-oxygenation, stabilising the cervical spine, laying out and checking all equipment, establishing a running intravenous line, with suction to hand, full monitoring on and a trained assistant ready. A precalculated dose of an induction agent and a rapidly acting muscle relaxant (namely suxamethonium 1.5-2mg/kg) given as a bolus and cricoid pressure applied upon loss of consciousness. Laryngoscopy and orotracheal intubation with a cuffed tube (over a boogie if necessary) is performed following cessation of respiration. The cuff is then inflated and the endotracheal tube position is checked. Only when correct position is confirmed is the cricoid pressure released.

This is a very safe, routine and basic anaesthetic practice, which is precisely the reason for choosing such a technique. Many anaesthetic registrars could do this in their sleep (and some possibly have!). This degree of familiarity is very important when under conditions of extreme stress in an unfamiliar environment.

Patients requiring pre-hospital anaesthesia can be classified into two broad groups:

1. Head Injuries

Following diffuse brain injury, 80% of disability is due to secondary brain injury, caused by hypotension and hypoxia, which may be preventable. Once the damage is done it cannot be reversed by molecular biology, expensive neuroprotective agents or extra neurosurgical ICU beds. At present the only way to minimise disability is to intensively treat the causes of secondary brain injury as early as possible. This means optimising oxygenation, preventing hypercarbia, controlling rises in the intracranial pressure, and maintaining an adequate cerebral perfusion pressure. In short, an emergency neuro-anaesthetic at the roadside.

All patients with a Glasgow Coma Score (GCS) below 9, or 12 and decreasing, should be anaesthetised and intubated. The absence of a cough or gag reflex is not predicted by a lower GCS, so in order to prevent surges in the intracranial pressure following laryngoscopy and intubation they should all receive both an induction agent and suxamethonium for intubation. The choice of induction agent is between etomidate and propofol. Both come ready to administer in ampoules and have appropriate effects on the cerebral circulation. Etomidate is probably to be preferred because of its greater cardio-stability. Thiopentone needs to be mixed with water and is therefore time-consuming to use, and ketamine has an adverse effect on the intracranial pressure which may already be critical.

2. Multiple trauma

In patients with blunt polytrauma, time to first medical attention, whether this is at the roadside or at hospital, is important. There are no emergency life-saving procedures for blunt trauma which cannot be equally well performed at scene. This is particularly true of the induction of anaesthesia and muscle relaxation in order to intubate the trachea and secure the compromised airway. This and the drainage of tension pneumothoraces are urgent procedures which should be performed immediately.

Multiply injured patients often have cardio-respiratory instability. This affects the choice of induction agent. World-wide there is most experience with ketamine. This has proved itself to be a remarkably safe agent even in inexperienced hands in a variety of hostile circumstances. The commonest side effect is of an unpleasant emergence phenomena.

Etomidate is also useful because of its cardiovascular stability. It has a more acceptable effect on the cerebral blood flow and intracranial pressure, which makes it the agent of choice in head injury. The often stated effect on steroid metabolism has yet to be shown responsible for an adverse clinical outcome after a single induction dose of this agent. Propofol is an alternative choice in these circumstances. While it has been used both in the UK and abroad, even in skilled hands it will produce a 20% drop in blood pressure within 2 minutes. The necessity to infuse large volumes of crystalloid in order to control this has of itself been recently shown to adversely affect outcome.

Equipment and Monitoring

Clearly if the anaesthetic is to be of the same standard as that provided in a hospital, so must the equipment and monitoring. It also has to be light and easily portable. The aim is to bring the hospital to the patient. Suitable equipment is widely available from any anaesthetic room.

Maintenance of Anaesthesia

Having intubated the trachea and instituted positive pressure ventilation with 100% oxygen, the next problem is how to maintain anaesthesia and sufficient muscle relaxation to allow continued resuscitation. Pancuronium (0.1-0.2 mg/kg) is a suitable muscle relaxant, which has the added advantage that it does not have to be reconstituted.

Maintenance of anaesthesia is only needed for a short period of time (especially with helicopter transport), during this time the patient must be easily and safely carried and moved. Both ambulances and helicopters are small enclosed spaces in which gaseous pollution and lack of scavenging would pose problems. A total intravenous anaesthetic technique (TIVA) is therefore required, and can be provided in a number of ways. The use of propofol either by infusion or intermittent bolus is the most widely known. Alternative drugs are midazolam, ketamine or even both in a fixed combination (a technique currently favoured by the Armed Forces).

Skill Maintenance

Severe injury is fortunately uncommon in Britain. Any pre-hospital care provider will therefore see relatively few patients. On average a paramedic in London will treat only one casualty with multiple injuries per year. There is obviously a problem with skill maintenance and anaesthesia will therefore never be performed by paramedics. Without a mechanism for concentrating experience, such as the HEMS helicopter, no doctor involved in pre-hospital care would gain sufficient exposure to maintain a high level of skill. In a six month attachment, a HEMS registrar would expect to perform 20 pre-hospital anaesthetics. The rotation to Intensive Care (25% of the HEMS attachment) is also helpful in ensuring maintenance at a high level of skill.

Conclusion

Anaesthesia at the scene of an accident remains a rare event. The HEMS service, for example, performs this procedure only about 150 times a year. It is an anaesthetic with its own unusual problems and the challenge is to carry this out to the same standards of safety and success as would be expected in the hospital environment.

Phil Hadjimichael, Emeritus HEMS Registrar, Senior Registrar in Anaesthetics.

Tim Coats, Emeritus HEMS Registrar, Research Fellow in Neurosurgery and Senior Lecturer in Accident and Emergency at the RLH.

CASE HISTORIES 3 : THE CYCLIST

Ronan Fenton

HEMS was called to a road traffic accident involving a cyclist and a lorry. The lorry had turned on its side following the collision.

Photo: author

Initial Findings

The cyclist was lying on his right hand side with both legs flexed and was complaining of severe pain. He was separated from the lorry by a crash barrier. The lorry was on its side having completely flattened the bicycle. The cyclist had been wearing a cycle helmet.

Primary survey revealed:

Airway	The airway was patent and the patient had an oxygen saturation of 100%.
Breathing	Respiratory rate was 15 breaths/minute with equal air entry in both lungs.
Circulation	Pulse rate was 80 beats/minute and the blood pressure was 170/70 mmHg.
Disability	The patient had a GCS of 15.
Exposure	The casualty was not trapped but was in great pain on movement of his legs.

Suspected injuries

It appeared that the cyclist had sustained multiple fractures to both legs (fractured left femur, tibia and fibula, fractured right tibia and fibula.)

Action Taken

Oxygen was administered via a mask with reservoir bag and a cervical collar was fitted. Two large bore intravenous cannulae were sited and fluid resuscitation was commenced. In total 1000ml of colloid was administered. The patient was in great pain and had to be moved onto an orthopaedic scoop stretcher. Analgesia in the form of morphine 20mg and ketamine in increments of 10mg up to 70 mg was required to facilitate this.

Triage

In view of the mechanism of injury and destruction of the bicycle, the patient was airlifted to a multidisciplinary centre.

Timings:

Incident	12.05
LAS informed	12.08
HEMS activated	12.20
HEMS on scene	12.25
Resuscitation room	13.20

Resuscitation Findings

Bilateral fractured tibia and fibula.

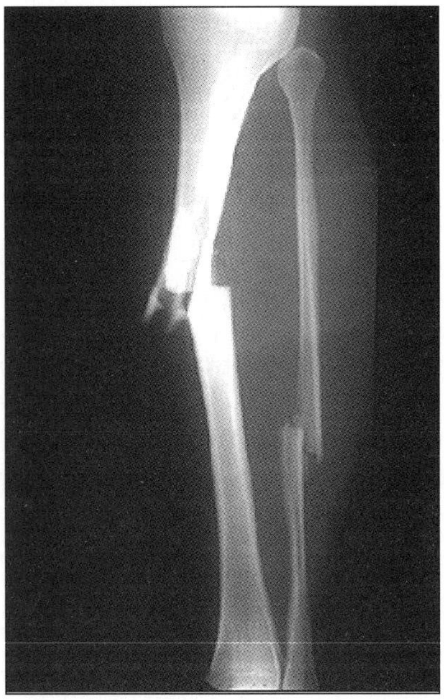

Photo: author

Action Taken

The patient underwent bilateral internal fixation of tibia and recovered on the ward.

Outcome

The patient was discharged home 8 days after admission.

Discussion

Initial reading of the timings of this case give the impression of a long delay in activating HEMS. This emphasises the difficulty involved in tasking the service accurately. The HEMS paramedic who activates the system screens every emergency call that is received by London Ambulance Centre during HEMS operational hours. This can total over 1500 calls per day. The information given in these calls is usually very brief and not always a true reflection of what has happened. It is important not to activate the system on inappropriate calls and much skill and experience is needed to task the system correctly. If there is doubt about a call the paramedic will often attempt to get in touch with the person who made the emergency call for further information. In many cases it is not possible to reach the caller and it may be appropriate to wait for a medical report from the ambulance crew on scene before activating HEMS.

The case also demonstrates the need for giving analgesia in the field. This is particularly important when a patient with fractures needs to be moved or a fracture needs to be manipulated and a splint applied. Morphine tends not to act fast enough in the acute situation. Ketamine in sub-anaesthetic doses titrated to effect has been found to be very useful in these situations as this case demonstrates. It also has the benefit of relative safety from respiratory and cardiovascular depression although the addition of a benzoidiazepine is often of benefit in reducing the incidence of hallucinations associated with its use.

Ronan Fenton, Emeritus HEMS Registrar, is a Senior Registrar in Anaesthesia

Photo: author

Ronan Fenton on active service

ENTRAPMENT AND RELEASE

Tim Coats

About 5% of the patients treated by the HEMS system suffer some form of entrapment. This is an important group because of the additional difficulties in medical management that are imposed by continuing hazards to the rescuer, difficult access for assessment and intervention due to confined space, continuing pressure on injured parts, and the removal of 'scoop and run' as a treatment option.

This is a situation in which the untrained doctor is unlikely to perform well. The incident scene gives rise to a sensory overload that is produced by multiple flashing lights, high noise levels from generators and cutting equipment, the strong smell of petrol and hot oil, the emotional impact of risk to the medical team, and the immediacy of contact with the mechanism of injury. This is an alien environment to the average hospital doctor or general practitioner, and not one in which they will be able to perform the high standard of intensive medical treatment which is to be given.

There is an absolute requirement for coordination between the medical and physical aspects of rescue. This requires the fire service to understand the assessment and interventions that the medical team is performing, and requires the medical team to understand how the fire crews are achieving the physical release of the casualty. The only way to obtain this co-ordination is by training together. The HEMS medical teams regularly take part in 'Extrication Days' held at the London Fire and Rescue Service (LFB) Training School at Southwark. These training sessions involve presentations by both HEMS and the LFB, with practical demonstrations of techniques and an exercise involving simulated casualties and cars retrieved from a scrapyard. In this way the priorities of each group and the terminology (and slang!) used can be exchanged so that understanding and communication are encouraged. The participation of Accident and Emergency trainees and other medical, ambulance service and nursing staff with an interest in pre-hospital care is encouraged. This type of training is expensive but absolutely essential.

Safety

An organisation which allows its employees into a potentially dangerous situation without adequate equipment or training is not fulfiling its obligations to their health and safety.

It is vital that the correct equipment is worn by all involved in an extrication. The HEMS medical team wear safety boots, a brightly coloured, tough, fire-resistant suit, a helmet on which 'Medical Team' is clearly marked, with eye protection and surgical gloves. An additional pair of heavy duty gloves for clambering through sharp wreckage is useful. All personnel should be up to date with tetanus and hepatitis immunisations.

A medical team assisting with an extrication must know the hazards of the environment and how to maintain their own safety. This can only be achieved by training. For example the medical team must know that the residue of explosive from a discharged air-bag may react on contact with water, either in sweat or when washing hands after an incident. The potential hazards are too many to mention here – the HEMS doctors undergo a four week training programme before being allowed into the field.

Extrication

The type of extrication required is variable, depending on the exact nature of the entrapment and the nature of the casualty's condition. If circumstances allow, the best approach is Rapid Access by the Fire Service to allow Initial Stabilisation by the medical team followed by Controlled Release by the Fire Service followed, in turn, by Casualty Movement supervised by the medical team, with Further Treatment and assessment before Triage and Transport. Medical and physical rescue are therefore coordinated, each team moving back at the appropriate time to allow access to others.

Rapid Access

After making the incident scene safe the fire service remove sufficient metal or debris to allow the medical team access to the casualty. For example, this would typically involve the removal of a car roof. This first phase has to be achieved rapidly, as the casualty may require critical interventions. Access through a window should be achieved in less than 10 seconds. A good extrication team will completely remove a car roof in 60 seconds.

Initial Stabilisation

Once access to the casualty has been established the medical team performs a Primary Survey and Critical Interventions as required, attaching sufficient monitoring equipment so that the condition can be continuously evaluated throughout the next phase. Interventions such as oro-tracheal intubation or a surgical airway are possible whatever the position of the patient.

If no abnormality is found during the Primary Survey the minimum intervention performed is cervical spine stabilisation, high flow oxygen, intravenous access, monitoring (pulse rate, ECG, oxygen saturation and blood pressure) and consideration of analgesia. The HEMS medical team uses a Propaq™106 monitor which is small yet robust and reliable in this environment. After the Initial Stabilisation has been performed the medical team move back so that the Fire Service has greater access to the area around the casualty. One person (either from medical team or fire service) should stay near to the casualty to provide continuing reassurance and explanation.

Controlled Release

The initial stabilisation buys time to carry out a controlled removal of the casualty. The techniques of this process are a complex specialist area that requires an experienced and trained team for most efficient performance. A number of powerful cutting tools and rams may be required. These have dangers for the casualty if they slip or if metal twists as it moves. Both extrication and medical teams must be aware of these hazards.

Controlled Movement and Further Treatment

Removing a casualty from the wreckage without causing further harm may be a challenge. Casualty handling may involve personnel from all emergency services, but the team should be lead by a member of the ambulance service or a doctor. Once the casualty has been released a further medical assessment can take place to decide if any further interventions are required before the casualty is transported. At this stage a triage decision can be made about the most appropriate hospital to treat the patient's injuries.

Immediate Release

If the casualty is in a critical condition that cannot be stabilised during the Primary Survey the chances of survival are very low. In these desperate circumstances where the casualty is dying and it is not possible to reverse this process in-situ, an immediate removal of the casualty into a position where they can be more easily treated is appropriate. It is inevitable that gentle handling and maintenance of spinal stabilisation will not be possible. This is a rare event and should only be performed when the casualty will die if a controlled release is attempted.

Crush Injury

A particular problem is posed by patients that are trapped with a continuing crush injury. Such injuries to the upper body are invariably fatal due to respiratory compromise, so patients seen by a pre-hospital medical team will usually have a heavy weight crushing the lower body. A typical example would be the collapse of a stack of metal sheeting or building collapse with the casualty buried under rubble or debris from the waist down.

The problem in these patients is that extrication invariably takes a long time as heavy lifting equipment is required. The casualty may be conscious with a stable cardiovascular system throughout the rescue, yet when the weight is finally removed they are likely to suffer a dramatic, probably fatal, cardiovascular collapse.

This can only be avoided if multiple large bore intravenous access is established early with a generous fluid replacement, such that intubation may be required due to pulmonary oedema. A MAST suit should be laid out on a long spinal board next to the casualty with a scoop stretcher and lifting teams prepared and instructed. The cardiovascular collapse must be anticipated and fast fluid infusion given before the weight is removed. Immediately the casualty is free the scoop stretcher must be used to lift him/her into the MAST suit which is immediately inflated. In this way everything possible is done to minimise the effect of cardiovascular collapse. This situation is certainly beyond the skills and training of both paramedics and most doctors. Only a specialist team such as that provided by HEMS is likely to obtain a good result.

Summary

The trapped casualty produces a complex problem that requires good coordination between physical and medical rescue. This can only be achieved by a training program that integrates the activity of the Fire and Rescue Services and medical teams.

Tim Coats, Emeritus HEMS Registrar, is Research Fellow in Neurosurgery and Senior Lecturer in Accident and Emergency at the RLH.

CASE HISTORIES 4 : UNDER A TRAIN

Ronan Fenton

HEMS was called to attend an incident in which a 50 year old male had fallen under a subway train.

Initial Findings

The incident had occurred in an underground station. On arrival of HEMS there were members of the fire service, ambulance service, underground police, underground management and underground rescue personnel already on the platform. The casualty was under the train, four carriages from the front. It was ascertained that the traction current had been discharged and that circuit breaking devices had been placed in front of and behind the train. Accompanied by the HEMS paramedic, the doctor went under the train to assess the casualty.

Primary survey revealed:

Airway	The airway was obstructed and required support. Oxygen saturation was unobtainable.
Breathing	Respiratory rate was 6 breaths/minute. There was poor air entry bilaterally.
Circulation	The pulse rate was 128 beats/minute. The systolic blood pressure was 150mmHg. Diastolic value was unobtainable.
Disability	The patient had a GCS of 3. His right pupil was dilated and unresponsive to light.
Exposure	The patient was lying on his right side under the train in the pit between the running rails. His right leg was partially amputated and was bent under his chin.

Photo: author

Suspected Injuries

Head injury, scalp lacerations, bilateral fractured ribs, fractured pelvis, bilateral compound femoral fractures, partial amputation of the right leg and significant blood loss.

Action Taken

The airway was supported manually while oxygen was administered and a cervical collar fitted. The patient's legs were straightened and he then was rolled onto his back.

Two large bore intravenous lines (14 gauge) were established and fluid resuscitation was commenced. The patient was anaesthetised using etomidate and the trachea intubated after muscle relaxation was achieved with suxamethonium. Hyperventilation was commenced. Anaesthesia was maintained from then on using bolus doses of propofol and pancuronium.

Due to the haemodynamic instability of the patient it was necessary for the doctor and paramedic to remain with the patient while the traction current was restored and the train moved forward. During this time the patient received mannitol 50g and two litres of colloid solution intravenously. After the train was moved off and the traction current had once again been discharged, a pelvic splint was applied and the patient placed on a scoop stretcher and removed from the pit.

Triage

The patient was airlifted to a multidisciplinary hospital.

Timings

Incident	11.50
LAS informed	11.51
HEMS activated	11.52
HEMS on scene	11.59
Resuscitation room	13.02

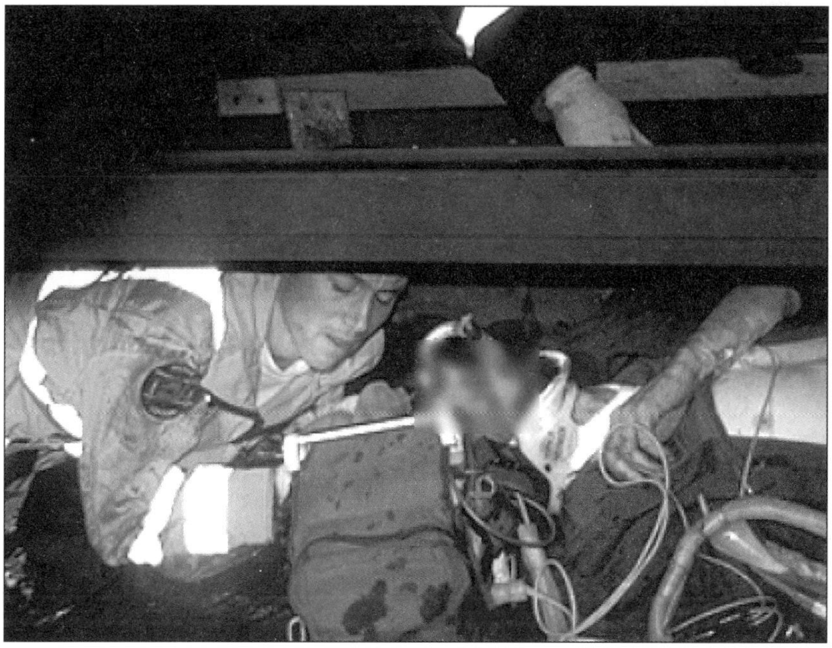

Photo: author

Resuscitation Findings

Fractured vault of skull, cervical spine fracture, bilateral fractured ribs, bilateral femoral fractures, intra-abdominal bleeding.

Action Taken

The patient had two chest drains inserted and was transfused a total of 9000 ml of colloid and 25 units of blood. He was transferred to the operating theatre for emergency laparotomy which demonstrated lacerations to the liver and duodenum.

Outcome

The patient died on the operating table.

Discussion

Patients under trains pose immense problems for the emergency services. The train driver is often affected and may need access to counselling. The casualty is underground and trapped. There is danger from the live tracks (630 volts DC) to both the casualty and rescue services. The casualty is usually severely injured and requires aggressive resuscitation in a very small space with poor lighting. Communication equipment may not function adequately underground and noise can interfere with relaying verbal messages from under the train to staff on the platform. In view of the presence of many members of the emergency services it is vital that control of the situation is achieved rapidly and diplomatically. Clear instructions should be given to appropriate personnel so that the goals of the team can be achieved.

While treatment and extrication of casualties in these circumstances cannot be rushed, the implications of unnecessary delay must be taken into account. If another train is stopped in a tunnel due to the accident for over half an hour the underground personnel may have to evacuate the passengers and walk them along the tracks to the nearest station.

It can be seen that organisation of the many emergency services on site is crucial and a knowledge of the safety precautions required in this environment is vital.

In this case it took an hour to extricate the patient and to transfer him to the resuscitation room. This is quite good considering the difficulties involved. The patient's position meant that he had to be rolled onto his back to gain access to the airway which was not ideal, but necessary given the situation.

Ideally when a train is rolled off a patient all unnecessary personnel leave the patient and remain on the platform. If the patient is anaesthetised, ventilated and stable we tend to leave the patient during this procedure for our own safety. In this case, it was not possible and the crew remained with the patient.

Restoring traction current to the rails and moving a train can take up to seven minutes. This is a long time to lie face down in a pool of dirty water knowing that there is a current of 640 volts between the rails on either side of you and that a couple of tons of machinery is moving a foot over your head!

Once the train has been moved it is vital that clear signals are given to indicate that the current has once again been discharged and that there are circuit breaking devices on the tracks in front of and behind the casualty and rescue team. It is only then that the casualty can be safely moved to the platform for further evaluation and transportation. The problems of extrication do not end at this point. Carrying a patient safely up a series of escalators (some of which are not working) takes team work and a lot of effort from an already tired crew.

Ronan Fenton, Emeritus HEMS Registrar is a Senior Registrar in Anaesthesia.

CONFINED SPACE AND SPECIAL RESCUE TRAINING

Peter Faulding

During recent years there have been a number of major incidents involving collapsed structures and confined space rescue. Rescuing casualties from confined spaces and structural collapse is a problem many members of the emergency services face. Physical restraints, a lack of natural light, abnormal temperatures, and difficulties in manoeuvring in extreme confines place an immense physiological load on human beings. When an incident occurs, the lives of fire-fighters and medical teams are often put at risk due to too little or no training in this very specialised field.

By using small, specialised teams trained and equipped to work in these environments, a victim's chance of survival is dramatically increased, while the risk of the medical teams becoming casualties themselves is greatly reduced.

Deaths involving confined spaces are on the increase. These areas include ventilation ducts, deep wells and shafts, water supply ring mains, trenches, tanks, sewers and collapsed structures. 50-60% of deaths in confined spaces are to would-be rescuers.

In late 1991 I was asked to structure a training course for all HEMS doctors and flight paramedics. Before any training commences participants are screened for their suitability to work in these unfriendly environments. A simple problem, such as a light going out in an extreme confined space, can bring on a panic attack that can lead to injury or death to the rescuer and casualty alike.

Training involves confidence building exercises using 400 metres of confined pipes and vertical shafts varying in diameter. A disused firestone mine is used for collapsed structure simulation and sump rescue techniques. Training begins with safety procedures, hazard identification, both physical and atmospheric; this includes the use of personal monitoring devices. These devices are used for pre-entry checks to establish whether the atmosphere is breathable and clear of gases such as hydrogen sulphide (toxic), methane (explosive), as well as oxygen deficiency or enrichment.

Other hazards include the risk of electrocution, drowning, chemical and biohazards. Moulds, mildew, spores and other bacteria found in sewage treatment can cause serious health problems. These areas must be highlighted.

Breathing apparatus familiarisation training is given. This covers a variety of respiratory protection devices and includes full working self-contained breathing apparatus sets (SCBA), compressed air escape sets and chemically generated oxygen sets. Escape sets have an advantage when used in conjunction with atmospheric monitoring. There is no bulk to carry allowing the wearer to enter extremely confined spaces that otherwise would not be possible with a full set of breathing apparatus, whilst still having access to respiratory protection if a monitor should detect gas.

When the safety procedures are complete the participant is put down a manhole in the ground that leads into an horizontal 18 inch pipe which runs for 200 metres and has no natural light. The individual must crawl the whole length of the pipe on his front feeling the way in total darkness amongst spiders and other creepy crawlies. This exercise is designed to build the individual's confidence and helps him to realise the physical and mental demands that confined space operations place upon the individual.

The next stage covers treatment and removal of the casualty from horizontal confined spaces. Basic knots are taught and the use of pulleys and lines for improvised hauling systems. Identification of anchorage points and the importance of protecting the lines over sharp edges is emphasised. The casualty is placed into the pipe at 50 metres. The scenario is then given; the primary survey that normally is fairly straightforward becomes an ordeal for the medical teams and access to the head and neck is

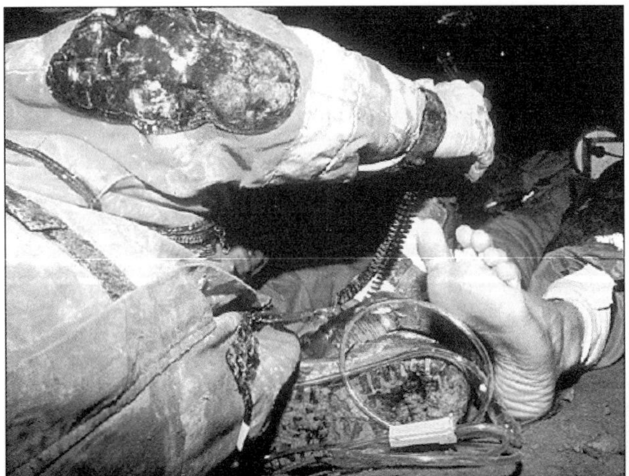

Photo: author

near impossible. The team must be able to improvise in this hostile environment to treat and extricate the casualty. Other problems include i.v access. Cutdowns are practised, pressure infusers are used to allow adequate infusion while carrying out other tasks. The casualty is then placed on a drag type full body stretcher and hauled from the pipe using lines and devices to grip the wet muddy rope.

Vertical confined space entry is another area that presents problems. Incidents involving deep wells and shafts are on the increase, with erosion taking its toll on outdated sewers and water supply systems. An 18 metre vertical steel lined shaft is used for training purposes. Candidates must ascend and descend the shaft three times wearing full breathing apparatus for a total of 108 metres. The use of full body harnesses and basic line work are taught. This allows the team to access the deep confined wells using single rope techniques (SRT), where no ladders or climbing rings are available

Vertical hauling techniques are taught using a quadpod system with a winch. This allows casualty removal from vertical wells. Collapsed structure familiarisation is taught using a network of disused mine workings and includes many natural roof collapses that I have excavated and shored up to represent a collapsed structure. Demonstration of debris removal using sledges, search mirrors and endoscopic cameras can locate trapped victims. This equipment is also used for training police forensic and search teams.

Casualty treatment is also practised in this area. This again proves to be very demanding in a cold wet environment with no natural light. In the final exercise the casualty must be located using search techniques taught on the course. Once the casualty is located they must be stabilised and extricated. They are then faced with removing the casualty through chest-deep ice cold water under low roofs. Finally the casualty is lifted 18 metres to the surface.

Though incidents of this type are rare, medical teams must be prepared for the worst. All the planning for major

Photo: author

Photo:author

incidents that can occur will not prepare us for a major structural collapse.

In August/September 1990, I was flown to the Kreka mine disaster in the former Yugoslavia, six kilometres outside Tuzla. On August Bank Holiday a huge explosion ripped through the lignite mine burying 180 miners. Many were killed in the initial explosion, and many were buried alive. The lower workings were full of methane gas and carbon monoxide. Bodies were buried 200 metres below the surface. The conveyor system that would normally be used for bringing the coal to the surface, and transporting the miners to the lower levels was completely destroyed in the massive explosion. The rescue effort was hampered due to hundreds of metres of twisted conveyor system.

It took over one hour on foot to reach the working faces where the miners were buried under tonnes of coal. Digging through the coal proved to be very hazardous, not knowing if a further collapse would occur. After two weeks I returned home. We managed to recover 156 bodies in total while another 24 still lie buried in the now flooded workings.

This could have been the scene in the heart of London if a massive explosion like that of the Bishopsgate bombing happened again. No training will prepare us for a disaster of that scale, but with the correct training and correct equipment the rescue will be less hazardous. This will boost morale amongst other rescue team members knowing that specialist skills are available.

The confined space training, provided by the author, proved to be invaluable. For HEMS doctors on the move after the six month tour they may find themselves being part of a mobile medical team at another hospital anywhere in the world, mobilised to major incidents from earthquakes to terrorist bombs. One day it could be your life in their hands!

Peter Faulding is Managing Director of the company, Specialist Rescue International, which provides training and operational services world-wide in extreme confined space and search and rescue. Address: PO Box 266, Redhill, RH1 1GA.

PRE-HOSPITAL MANAGEMENT OF BURN INJURY: THE HEMS EXPERIENCE

Michael Machesney

Burns are a severe form of trauma and a major cause of morbidity and mortality. In the United Kingdom about 10,000 people are admitted to hospital each year for the treatment of burn injury. More than half that number are children. The most common mechanism of injury is scalding. Thermal burns from fires cause the most severe injuries and are more common than electrical or chemical burns. In the three year period from March 1993, HEMS attended 145 burn patients comprising approximately 5% of the total number of missions. 65% (94) of these patients were conveyed by air directly to the nearest burns unit, the remaining 35% were taken by land ambulance to the nearest accident and emergency department.

The pre-hospital management of burn injury commences with the HEMS paramedic at the London Ambulance Control. HEMS is activated for paediatric burns >10% of body surface area (BSA), adult burns >15% BSA, smoke inhalation and burns with multiple injuries. Burns to face, hands, feet and genitalia may also initiate a response. The paramedic on duty often telephones the caller or ambulance crew and obtains further history and clearer description of the injury.

On arrival at the scene, the HEMS team report to the most senior Fire Brigade officer who is responsible for the safety of all personnel at fires, chemical spillages and road traffic accidents. It is essential that the burn victim is removed from the source of injury in a controlled manner while ensuring the safety of the rescuers. Burning clothes should be removed or extinguished and chemical burns should be copiously irrigated with water to stop the burning process.

Interventions at the scene may be life saving. The principles are the same as the initial management of any trauma case. The first priorities are the airway and maintenance of ventilation with protection of the cervical spine if there is the suspicion of neck injury. High flow oxygen is administered by reservoir mask while assessing for airway burns and signs of inhalational injury. Endotracheal intubation is indicated in cases of acute upper airway oedema, severe inhalation injury and burns with associated significant head, neck or chest trauma. 25% of burn patients carried by HEMS to burns or trauma centres have been anaesthetised, intubated and ventilated.

The second priority is maintenance of the circulating volume. At least one large bore cannula must be secured in an adequate vein; if necessary it may be sited through burnt skin. Fluid requirements are calculated proportional to the estimated burn surface area and the patient's weight. The choice of fluid regimen is as controversial in London as anywhere in the UK. In the USA, the Consensus (modified Parkland) formula is recommended by the American Burn Association, the ATLS and Advanced Burn Life Support (ABLS). In the UK, Hartmann's solution may be used in the place of Ringer's Lactate. Many burn units in London still use the Muir and Barclay (Mount Vernon) formula to estimate fluid requirements for colloid resuscitation with human albumin solution (HAS). HAS is not carried on the helicopter, but gelatin based plasma substitutes are available. The choice of fluid is made less critical by the short transfer times by helicopter, an adequate volume must be given. Similarly there is not time to place urinary catheters. The peripheral circulation must be assessed in circumferential limb burns, but escharotomy at the scene is not indicated. Pain relief is an essential component of burns treatment; all analgesia and sedation is given by the intravenous route.

Bed availability at the nearest burns unit is checked by the duty HEMS Operations personnel. The referral is made by the HEMS doctor to the burns unit registrar confirming the details of injuries, treatment and transfer. For cases with multiple injuries where the burn constitutes the least risk to life, the patient should be transferred to the nearest trauma centre. The HEMS role is completed when the patient is handed over to the doctors of the receiving hospital and a copy of the HEMS records is entered in the notes.

The ABLS provider course was set up with the American Burn Association in 1987 and a pre-hospital ABLS course in 1991. There is now a fully qualified instructor and ten instructor candidates in the UK. The first ABLS provider courses in the UK will be run under the auspices of the British Burn Association in October 1996. At a later date pre-hospital ABLS courses will be set up.

Michael Machesney, FRCS, Emeritus HEMS Registrar, is currently reading for a Medical Doctorate on hypertrophic scar formation. Institute of Plastic Surgery, Mount Vernon Hospital, Northwood, Middlesex HA6 2RN.

PAEDIATRIC TRAUMA: THE HEMS EXPERIENCE

Gurdip Singh Samra

Trauma has surpassed infectious disease as the leading cause of childhood death and disability in the developed world.

In the UK, three children die each day and approximately 10 000 are permanently disabled as a result of trauma each year. After the age of one year accidents are the leading cause of childhood death in this country, and in 1992 caused 767 deaths in children under the age of 15 years. Between the ages of 5-14 injury causes seven times as many deaths as leukaemia in this country.

Preventative measures have led to a significant improvement with a 50% reduction in death rate, in the under 15 year olds, from 12 per 100,000 in 1976 to 6 per 100,000 in 1991. The Health of the Nation document sets a further target reduction of 33% by the year 2005.

Fifty one percent of fatal accidents in children under the age of 15 are caused by road traffic accidents with the next largest category being fire (15%). The causes of fatal accidents in children in 1992 are shown in Chart 1.

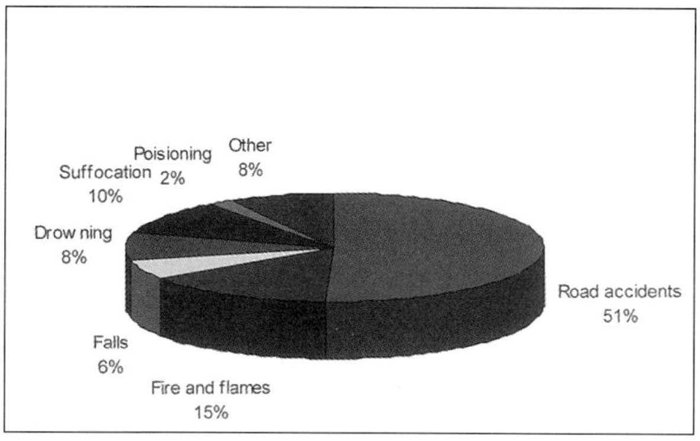

Chart 1: Causes of fatal accidents in children in 1992

The Helicopter Emergency Medical Service (HEMS) is appropriately equipped to deal with children of all ages who have been injured as a result of accidents. Rapid resuscitation and stabilisation is performed prior to direct transfer to the most appropriate hospital.

During the five year period beginning of April 1991 to the end of March 1996 HEMS attended 736 patients under the age of 16 years, representing 14% of the total patients attended during this time.

The cause of accident is shown in Chart 2. This differs significantly from the national figures in the number of children attended with injuries as a result of falls.

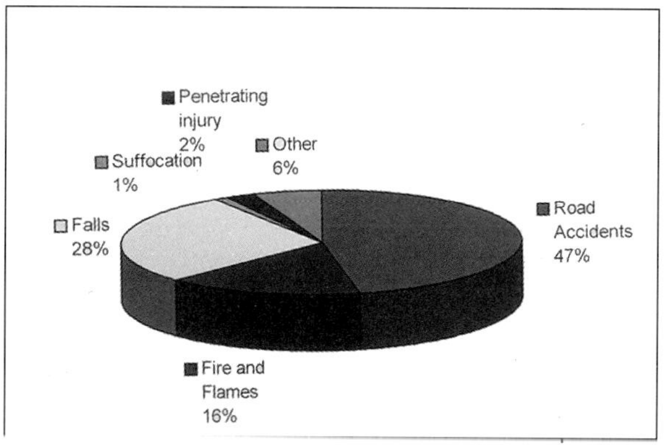

Chart 2: Mechanism of injury in HEMS patients (Age <16).

The triage and method of transport is shown in Chart 3.

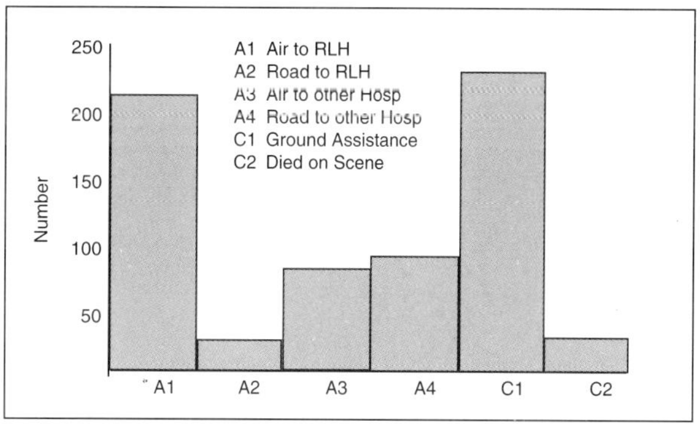

Chart 3: Triage of HEMS paediatric patients

The majority (71%) of patients flown to another hospital were for burns injury. The commonest procedure performed on scene, beyond the administration of oxygen and application of a stiff neck collar, was the insertion of intravenous access and this was performed in 32% of the children attended. Endotracheal intubation was performed in 16% of cases.

The mean age of the children attended was 7.8 years with a median value of 8 years, the youngest child attended was only three days old and the male to female ratio was 2.3:1.

231 children under the age of 16 were triaged to the RLH representing approximately one child per week. Of these children 76 (33%) were six years or younger.

Chart 4 shows the age and sex distribution of the patients triaged to the RLH. The mean and median of this group was nine years.

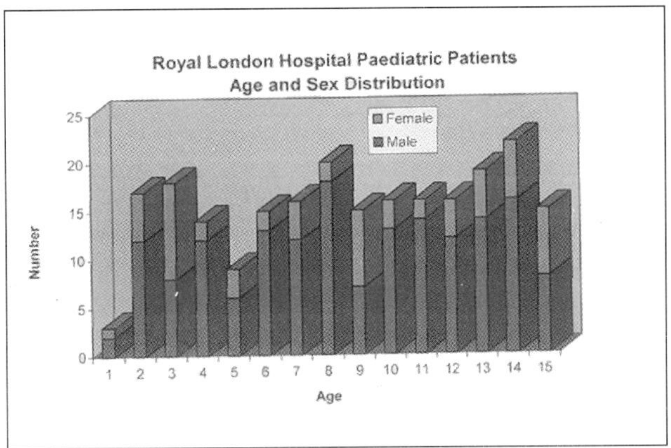

Chart 4: Age and sex distribution of RLH paediatric patients.

Chart 5 shows the age and Injury Severity Score (ISS) distribution for those children brought back to the RLH. The median ISS is 9 (range 0-75). 34% of the children had an injury severity score greater than or equal to 16. 141 (61%) of the children had injuries in the head and neck region and this was the commonest reason for triage to the RLH. 87 (38%) of children had a single region injury and of these half were in the head and neck region. Only five cases involved penetrating wounds.

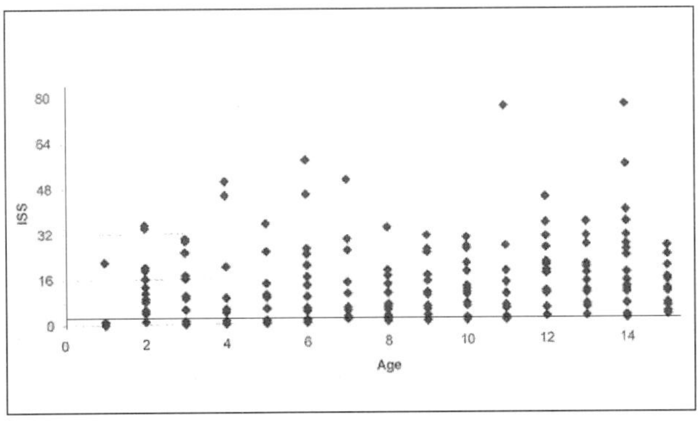

Chart 5: Age vs Injury Severity Score

The injury distribution pattern of the paediatric patients brought to the RLH is shown in Chart 6. There are two distinct body region injury peaks involving the head and the limbs.

Most, 194 (85%), of the children were discharged home from the RLH, 17 (7%) were discharged to another hospital and 18 (8%) died at the RLH.

204 patients (89%) of the blunt trauma group had complete data to allow TRISS methodology and probability of survival (UK) calculations. The median RTS was 7.11 (range 0-7.84), median ISS 9 (range 0-75) and a mean probability of survival of 90%. 191 (94%) of these patients survived to discharge and 13 (6%) died. The predicted death rate in this group was 21 giving an excess of 8 survivors in this group.

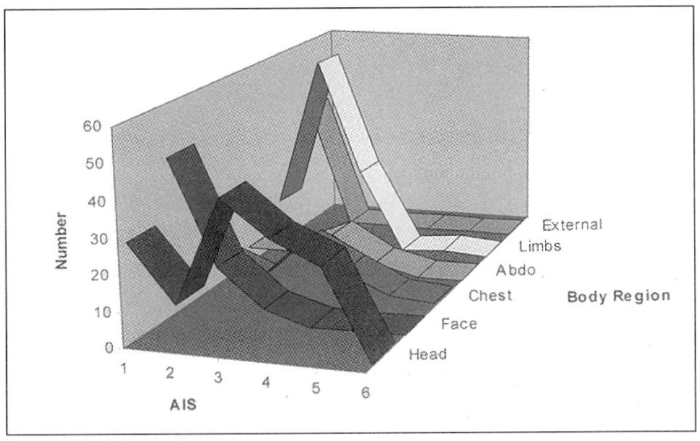

Chart 6: Paediatric trauma patients injury distribution

Discussion

Greater London has a population of 6.6 million of which 20% are aged less than 15 years. With an accident fatality rate of 7 per 100 000 this represents approximately 90 accident related fatalities per annum in Greater London. A study in the Metropolitan region of Merseyside quantified the prevalence of severe injury (ISS >16) of 12 per 100 000. In Greater London this translates to approximately 160 children per annum if these children were evenly distributed between the currently available Accident and Emergency departments each department would receive four children per year. Therefore regionalisation of paediatric trauma is necessary in London to allow accumulation of expertise. Since the injured child may often present to the local Accident and Emergency department the subsequent management of these children within regional units will require the use of specialist trauma transfer teams.

Even with the use of a dedicated trauma helicopter the RLH receives approximately four trauma patients under the age of 16 years per month and only one per month under the age of six years, so the paediatric patients form a relatively small part of the total trauma workload. There is therefore a need within the system for the further development of a paediatric trauma team.

The physical, physiological, pathological and psychological differences between the child and adult trauma patient means that special expertise is required in the management of these patients and only by concentration of resources and experience in specialist centres can the future management of the multiply injured child be improved.

Dr Gurdip Singh Samra, Emeritus HEMS Registrar, is a Consultant Anaesthetist at the RLH.

'THE PATIENT WHO TALKED AND DIED'

Richard Fairhurst

The nightmare scenario for trauma care is the patient who has been brought to the hospital alert and talking and who subsequently dies.

Mr X was a 24 year old motorcycle rider. He was travelling at about 30mph and passing a double deck bus which was stationary. The bus pulled out to the right and the motorcycle struck the offside of the bus a glancing blow at 30mph. *Mr X* was ejected over the handlebars, slid along the road and came to rest in the gutter. He did not hit anything besides the road surface and there was no loss of consciousness.

The paramedics arrived in six minutes. There were no lacerations and no obvious bone injuries. He was slightly tachycardic. He was treated with a semi-rigid collar, manual C-spine immobilisation and high percentage oxygenation.

He arrived in the A&E department some eight minutes later with no prior warning: pulse 105, respiratory rate 24, oxygen saturation 91% on oxygen. He was talking and well-oriented, complaining of pain in his shoulders, worse on the right than the left.

A trauma call was instituted.

Primary survey revealed:

Airway:	open and not compromised
Breathing:	rate 28; oxygen saturation 89%; left chest hyper-resonant with faint breath sounds; right chest upper zone hyper-resonant, lower zone dull
Circulation:	pulse 115; blood pressure 100/70.

Action:

100% oxygen; two wide bore cannulae inserted with rapid colloid infusion; x-ray C-spine – no abnormalities; chest – fractured fibs 3, 4, 5 on the right posteriorly, fractured fibs 4, 5 on the left posteriorly, large left pneumothorax, right haemo-pneumothorax mediastinum and cardiac outline normal; pelvis – no abnormality.

Action:

Left chest drain inserted with rapid drainage of a large volume of air; right chest drain inserted with rapid drainage of some air and 1500ml of blood.

Action:

Type specific transfusion. Cardiothoracic opinion: there was some debate with the cardiothoracic surgeon who was in the resuscitation room over the treatment for this 'massive haemothorax'. It was decided to treat the patient conservatively, to organise a CT scan and transfer to ICU.

Secondary survey:

No further injuries detected.

CT scan with contrast:

Fractured ribs as before, left lung fully expanded, right persistent small pneumothorax, small haemothorax, no cardiac or mediastinal abnormalities demonstrated.

On admission to ICU:

Pulse 90; respiratory rate 21; blood pressure 115/65; passing urine 50ml/hr; conscious, alert and talking.

Two hours later there was a sudden drainage of 2000 ml of blood from the right chest drain. *Mr X* was resuscitated and taken to theatre by a consultant cardiothoracic surgeon. The heart was exposed by sternal split. The patient suffered a cardiac arrest. Internal massage was performed, but it proved impossible to repair a large laceration to the right atrium and the patient died.

Reflections

What went wrong? What did we do wrong? What could we have done better?

Autopsy confirmed the known clinical findings and nothing else was found. The team was highly self critical and a formal review meeting was held. A literature search showed that isolated rupture of the right atrium is very rare in blunt trauma. The only sizeable series of cases reported was for penetrating trauma. Right 5th thoracotomy does not give access for repair. Sternal split gives access, but the repair is technically difficult and the perioperative mortality is more than 90%.

For weeks the hospital debated the treatment before eventually accepting that with the present state of knowledge some trauma victims die in spite of our best efforts. I reminded myself of a lecture by a very wise GP entitled '25 years of disturbed nights'. These were not when he got out of bed for emergencies, but the time which he spent awake after returning to his bed criticising his own actions. We must not cease to be critical, but we must learn to accept that some injuries are fatal in spite of our best efforts.

Dr Richard J Fairhurst, FFAEM, DIMC.RCS(Ed), Consultant in Accident and Emergency Medicine, Chorley and South Ribble NHS Trust, Publications and Public Relations Committee Faculty of Pre-hospital Care Member.

EDITORIAL COMMENT

A similar situation occurs at the roadside before transport to hospital when the patient, comforted by relatives, looks as though he has recovered from the original accident or head injury and actually continues a conversation with them. He then deteriorates before their eyes and passes away. In general terms this is the 'patient who talked and died' described originally by Professor Bryan Jennett, Professor of Neurosurgery at Glasgow, who was one of the originators of the Glasgow Coma Scale and the Glasgow Outcome Score. The description was used by him in a neurological sense to emphasise that patients with head injury and haemorrhage inside the skull can worsen before your eyes in the minutes and hours after an accident and therefore they must be assessed in hospital and have the brain decompressed as an emergency if there is a blood clot.

The same situation, however, applies to other victims of accidents who deteriorate rapidly within minutes before your very eyes with no external evidence of blood loss. It was for this reason that I asked Richard Fairhurst to describe one such case of a 'patient who had talked and died', but did not have a head injury. This emphasises that *internal* blood loss into the body cavities can cause death and when it is in the chest, abdomen, head or soft tissues of the limbs it is not clearly visible, but must be suspected and diagnosed in hospital.

It leaves the question that always must be answered – was the death of a 'patient who talked and died'[1] unavoidable? This does not imply they can all be saved.

Glasgow Coma Scale (GCS)[2]

15-3 higher the better lower the worse

Based on E (eye opening)
M (best motor response)
V (best verbal response)

Glasgow Outcome Score (GOS)[3]

Division into five categories:

1. Death due to primary brain damage
2. Persistent vegetative state.
3. Severe disability – conscious but disabled
4. Moderate disability – disabled but independent
5. Good recovery – resumption of normal life.

References

1. Riley PL, Adams JH, Graham DI, Jennett B. Patients with head injury who talk and die. Lancet 2: 375-7, 1975
2. Teasdale G, Jennett B. Assessment of coma and impaired consciousness. A practical scale. Lancet 2: 81-3, 1974
3. Jennett B, Bond M. Assessment of outcome after severe brain damage, a practical scale. Lancet 1: 480-4, 1975

CASE HISTORIES 5 : MULTIPLE TRAUMA IN A MOTORCYCLIST

Ronan Fenton

Photo: author

HEMS was called to an RTA in which a motor cyclist had collided with a truck.

Initial Findings

The patient had collided with the side of a minibus and veered across a three-lane roadway to collide with the rear wheels of an articulated lorry. The estimated speed of impact was 30 mph and the **patient had initially walked from the collision, removed his helmet and righted his motorcycle**. On arrival of the ambulance crew a cervical collar was fitted, oxygen administered and intra-venous access was obtained. When HEMS arrived on scene the patient was on a stretcher in the rear of the ambulance.

Primary Survey revealed:

Airway	A Guidel airway was in place and the patient's oxygen saturation was 85%. There was facial and oral bleeding from wounds received.
Breathing	Respiratory rate was 20 breaths/minute and there was good air entry in each lung.
Circulation	The pulse rate was 162 beats/minute and the blood pressure was 129/90 mmHg.
Disability	The patient had a GCS of 4 and his right pupil was dilated and fixed.
Exposure	The patient was cold and had been transferred to the back of the ambulance.

Suspected Injuries

Head injury, maxillofacial fractures, pelvic fracture.

Action Taken

The patient was anaesthetised using etomide and intubated using suxamethonium. Fentanyl was also given prior to intubation. Extra intravenous access was established and a pelvic splint was applied to decrease further blood loss. Fluid resuscitation was continued using 500 ml of crystalloid and 1500 ml of colloid. The patient was removed from the ambulance and placed on a 'vacu-mat' for transport. Anaesthesia was maintained using intermittent doses of propofol and the patient was airlifted to a multidisciplinary unit. He remained haemodynamically unstable during transfer.

Triage

A multidisciplinary unit was judged to be the most appropriate facility for the patient. On arrival the patient had a pulse rate of 121 beats/minute, a blood pressure of 193/150 mmHg and an oxygen saturation of 100%. He was in need of aggressive fluid resuscitation.

Timings

Incident	13.15
LAS informed	13.28
HEMS activated	13.37
HEMS on scene	13.44
Resuscitation room	14.20

Resuscitation Findings

The patient remained in the resuscitation room for 30 minutes where a further 1500 ml of colloid, 500 ml of crystalloid and 7 units of blood were required to maintain a cardiac output. Diagnostic peritoneal lavage was positive.

Action Taken

An urgent laparotomy was performed in theatre. The main findings were a lacerated lobe of liver which was free in the abdomen and a torn inferior vena cava.

Outcome

Theatre intervention continued for 1.5 hours when the patient succumbed to his injuries due to massive blood loss.

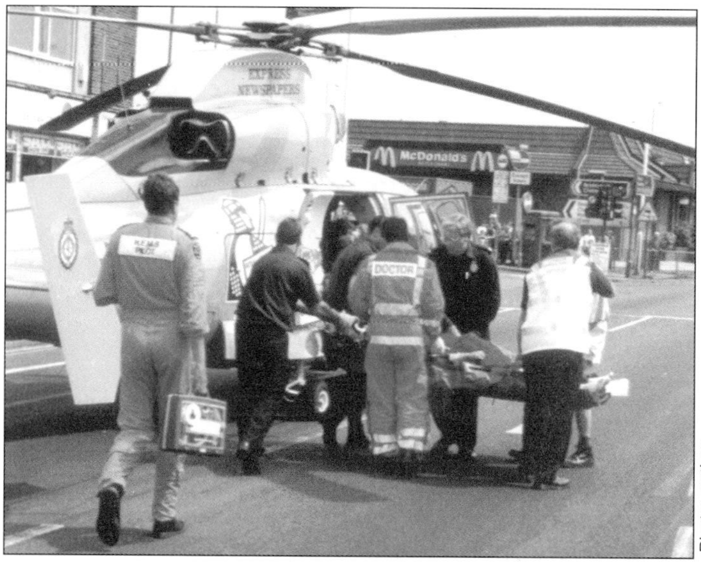

Photo: author

Discussion

This patient initially 'Walked and Talked' after the accident and even managed to remove his own helmet and place his bike in an upright position. The mechanism of injury and the extensive skid marks visible at the scene indicated a high energy impact. In retrospect the truck must have rolled over the patient despite the fact that witnesses did not report this, nor were there any tyre marks visible on the patient. The rapid deterioration in the patient's condition signified active life threatening blood loss and the application of a pelvic splint and administration of intravenous fluids was aimed at attempting to counter this. The patient required urgent assessment and surgical intervention.

The timings of the incident indicate that the time of impact to active resuscitation was twenty nine minutes while the time to theatre intervention was ninety five minutes. These timings would offer as favourable an outcome as is possible given the resources available.

Ronan Fenton, Emeritus HEMS Registrar is a Senior Registrar in Anaesthesia.

Photo: G Collins

Sometimes the team are allowed to go home

SECTION 7: IN HOSPITAL TREATMENT

Photo: A Wilson

The Royal London Hospital, Whitechapel

THE EMERGENCY ROOM (1990)

Alastair Wilson

Introduction

The 'crash room' as an eponym for the 'resuscitation room' is accurate in its evocation of clinical chaos, noise, movement and failure. As technology and clinical techniques evolved to provide the clinician with a veritable armamentarium of equipment and complex treatments, the design of the place and the way it should be operated did not keep pace.

While the housewife designed her logical kitchen, with ergonomically positioned ovens, grills and worktops, allowing her maximum efficiency with minimum movement, the resuscitating clinician presided over a hotch potch of poorly or even dangerously positioned equipment, demanding the maximum of unnecessary movement and effort.

At no other phase of trauma, cardiac or acute emergency care, are the 'place', with its correctly positioned equipment, and 'people', with the most sensible 'organisation', so important.

Of course, not all emergencies require the full attention of a trauma or cardiac arrest team but the resuscitation room has tended to be reserved for such events. Nevertheless many emergencies, if they were to be placed in the resuscitation room prior to the downward spiral of the disease process, would benefit enormously

Designing the Facility

Plans were made for a five bay emergency room which was to be placed close to the A&E department front door. All seriously ill patients would be brought to this room rather than to an A&E cubicle. The room had to be fully equipped for all types of resuscitation, though its philosophy of use required that any patient who would benefit from its facilities, should be treated within. This meant that the requirement for maximum resuscitative intervention was not the sole pre-requisite for entry to the room, allowing considerably more benefit to be derived from its costly and complex equipment.

Anaesthetic equipment had to be fitted alongside x-ray screens with wide worktops beneath to carry monitors and defibrillators. Lead dividers, with shelves containing strictly limited numbers of invasive surgical packs, were placed between the bays and strenuous efforts were made to keep kit off the floor and to enable as much diagnosis as possible to be achieved within the confines of the room.

The correct 'place' required the correct 'people' and this meant strict role definition for all team members. Clinicians had to be persuaded that not only were ACLS and ATLS guidelines desirable but that they must be applied by a well rehearsed team in an ordered, disciplined manner at speed and without duplication. Staff needed to be trained and practised to ensure that they knew exactly which tasks were expected of them and could complete them quickly so that they were away from their normal duties for as short a time as possible.

The organisation of the trauma team is dealt with in Section 7B; this contains details about the emergency room and all its equipment. It is called the emergency room rather than the resuscitation room to emphasise the change in criteria for admittance and it is always open, never closed. Medical, paediatric, orthopaedic and other surgical emergencies are dealt with. The advent of the emergency room has changed pre-conceptions that emergencies should progress slowly through the A&E system until they arrive in the hospital bed where diagnosis and treatment commence, and the patient sees the consultant for the first time (maybe waiting a week for this honour). Now, the hospital bed is for recovery and rehabilitation. The emergency phase occurs in the emergency room where the relevant staff and equipment are at hand. The consultant sees the patient there and resuscitation, diagnosis and stabilisation proceed in an orderly and speedy way. The patient moves straight to theatre, then on to the intensive care unit or trauma unit and finally to an acute bed on the general wards. Disability assessment and rehabilitation commence immediately after all these emergency events.

Overall Concept

Since multiply injured patients arrive unexpectedly, unannounced and frequently with other emergencies at the same time, it was agreed that a minimum of five bays would be required. These were to be positioned next to the A&E department front door in a spacious room – each bay separated from the next by a mobile, radio-opaque, dividing screen. The St George's Hospital resuscitation room has the best design that we could find and acted as the basis for all our plans. We acknowledge all their staff's help with gratitude.

In principle it was reasoned that floor space should be kept free for feet; floor 'mounted' equipment should be elevated to ceiling, walls or dividing screens. Within the bounds of this restriction all equipment for all forms of resuscitation had to be available and at hand without confusion and clutter. Locking it away for safety in cupboards was not considered to be an option though it looks neater on inspection.

Equipment

Much equipment was chosen because it was light, portable and could be placed on a trolley. It was therefore ideal for use in the emergency room as well as for accompanying the patient to CT scanning, theatres or ICU. The Propaq model 104 with non-invasive and invasive BP, ECG and twin temperature monitoring was ideal, with a small enough screen to avoid a lengthy multiple monitor scan. Oximetry and capnography with a similar screen to the Propaq is available on the Oxycap 4700. Defribillation was provided in three trauma bays by Physio-Control LifePak 9s and in the two cardiac bays by LifePak 8s; in all other respects each bay is exactly the same as the next. An additional bay is equipped for paediatric use and has a Resuscitaire. Two portable LifePak 10s with optional transcutaneous pacing are available for transporting the patient about the hospital. A blood gas analyser is mounted separately on a bench top for use in the emergency room. A four inch vacuum tube is available for sending specimens to the main haematology and biochemistry laboratory which speeds up the process and saves a porter. The tube system is large enough to transport blood packs from the transfusion laboratory directly to the emergency room. Each bay has its own separate trolley. The trolley is the C version of the Beta trolley distributed by Siemens and designed for use with the Siemens Mobilette XT. It can be lowered for loading and efficient cardiac massage. The back can be elevated to a right angle which facilitates erect chest x-rays and the C shape enables the use of the image intensifier. The trolley plinth is fully translucent, has strong side walls, a hydraulic elevation system, 'central' braking and telescopic drip stands which do not trap fingers.

Ceiling Mounted X-ray Equipment

In accordance with the general principle that both doctors and equipment should come to the seriously ill patient, rather than vice versa it was deemed absolutely essential that x-ray equipment should be placed in the actual emergency room and dedicated for use there. The usual response would be to have a 'portable' machine either standing in the corner taking up valuable space or colliding with clinicians assembled about the patient. This did not agree with another of our essential principles, namely that floors were for standing on and not placing equipment on. A ceiling mounted x-ray system was chosen to comply with the three main requirements:

a) it should be in the emergency room
b) it should never be moved out (mobile units are always elsewhere)
c) it should not be on the floor taking up space.

The only system that met our standards was the Siemens Mobilette. It had the additional facility of moving longitudinally on a ceiling mounted rail so that one unit reached all bays. Another added advantage was that the operating console is a hand held controller. Such a system also avoided the necessity for a console occupying yet more space. Obviously lead aprons have to be worn and the screens between the bays are lead lined for protection.

To complete this most efficient radiography organisation, an automated daylight processor (DUPONT) was placed within the emergency room. This automatically swallows the cassettes, processes the films in 90 seconds, delivers them dry and reloads the cassette ready for immediate reuse. Such an automated system is almost as important as the Siemens Mobilette because it enables a lone radiographer to move on to take the next film.

The Siemens Mobilette

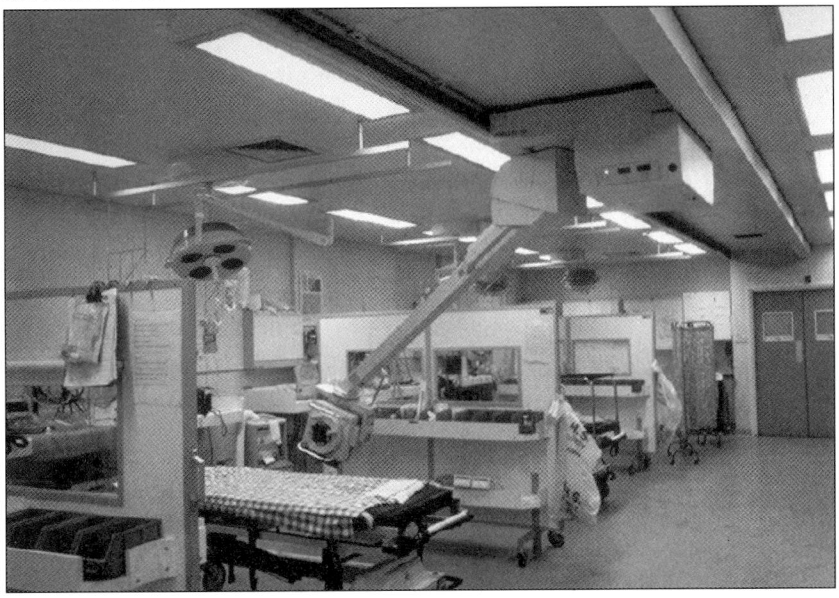

Photo: Ian Berle

Clinical Procedures

Members of any team attending the room are required to know where procedure packs are to be found. They are stored, together with clothes cutters, sharps boxes, povidone iodine, blood tubes, syringes, i.v cannulae and arterial gas samplers in racks on the radio-opaque screens between each of the bays.

An admission documentation pack is kept at the head of each bay with pre-numbered A&E/trauma cards, cross-match, haematology and toxicology request forms and blood bottles.

The acceptance of a predetermined number only system rather than naming prevents frantic labelling, confusion and delay because frequently the relevant name and address of the patient are unknown, but identification at an early stage is essential for radiology and cross matching blood.

All packs are kept with the appropriate extras, firmly attached to them e.g thoracic drainage set with the Sherwood type thoracic drain, hand needle, water for the underwater seal, local anaesthetic and an extra scalpel, otherwise they can never be found in a hurry. Intravenous fluids are kept in a warm cabinet at 40ºC.

Anaesthetic Equipment

At the head of each bay is a flat laboratory work surface with pre-cut endotracheal tubes, intubation equipment, CVP lines, cervical collars, sand bags and syringes, all kept under green drapes. Wall mounted oxygen, air at twice atmospheric pressure, nitrous oxide, suction and gaseous extraction service and the Boyle King Arm assembly, with vapouriser are all available if required. CO_2 is still provided in bottle form under the laboratory top next to the gaseous extraction filter and the thoracic suction bottles. The portable Ventipac 2 with Newton or Penlon valve is used with a Bains circuit.

Other Ceiling mounted Equipment

The ceiling above each bay provides filtered ventilation at operating theatre specification. Lighting is from a Hanaulux operating light controlled by a light handle. More novel are two curtain rails suspended by two chains each with four hooks upon which are hung pressure infusers and bags of prepared i.v solutions. The BP cuffs, tubes and wires are looped over these hooks allowing a clear area at the head of the patient under which the anaesthetist can operate. The essential principle was that the standards should be similar to or better than an anaesthetic room in theatre.

The anaesthetic equipment gives the anaesthetist facilities for urgent major surgery to proceed (lateral thoracotomy or median sternotomy) as well as simple anaesthetic or ventilatory procedures. Wall mounted high pressure air supplies the Stryker saw if required and suction is available not only for the anaesthetist but also the surgeon.

Summary

This is the Royal London Hospital's attempt at an ergonomically designed emergency room which, though not perfect, no longer demands previous rugby scrummage experience. It has changed the role of the emergency room considerably and this is now an area to be kept open and available at all times. Clinicians are familiar with its equipment, layout and team discipline. Even orthopaedic fracture reductions under GA somehow 'happen' here. Those patients who were likely to succumb secretly are spotted early and this is perhaps reflected in the statistics for cardiac arrest in the last quarter of 1990 when 36% left the emergency room alive and 25% were discharged home. This 'never knowingly under-utilised room' is not the resuscitation room of the past so the name has been changed to the 'emergency room' (British – not American). It is available for all patients including medical emergencies and is not just for use by trauma or patients brought in by helicopter.

Acknowledgements

The Wolfson Foundation and the Department of Health who provided the funds.
Mansell – who built the emergency room – as always on time.
Councillor Mrs J Ludlow, Mayor of Tower Hamlets who opened the Emergency Room on 28th November 1990.

Mr Alastair Wilson, FRCS, has been an A&E Consultant at the Royal London Hospital for over 10 years. His experience and enthusiasm were the prime motive power for establishing this new emergency room in 1990.

HOSPITAL TRAUMA TEAM ORGANISATION

Alastair Wilson, Tim Coats

Injury outcome, when set against a matrix of time and expert intervention, is a lottery, resulting in random death, gross disability or full recovery. When pre-hospital delays are minimal and early medical intervention expert, it is a disgrace if optimal patient outcome is ruined by a poor hospital trauma team.

Introduction

Injured patients expend the majority of Trunkey's 'Golden hour' in the pre-hospital phase, leaving no time for polite discussion about clinical management after reaching hospital. The minimal acceptable hospital response is the instant presence of a well-ordered team, trained in all aspects of patient resuscitation. This should lead into a seamless continuum of care, be it specialist intervention or intensive therapy. No gaps should appear as bolshy surgeons are disturbed from their contented laparoscopes or as neurosurgeons are scrambled from weekly outings to *Tesco*. All the team must be available when required. Only this can secure an optimal outcome.

Trauma victims suffer multi-system disease, so it is axiomatic that hospitals receiving trauma should provide multidisciplinary care by the most experienced individuals in the specialty required. The team design will vary from site to site, depending on the flavour of hospital commitment. Some will use cascade systems based on A&E assessment and basic resuscitation – specialties only being called when required. Some will utilise a mainly surgical response and others will let anaesthetists take the lead. At the Royal London Hospital, a system has evolved over the last 10 years which is based on a logical extension of the principles of Advanced Trauma Life Support (ATLS).

ATLS

ATLS philosophy has become the universal blueprint for early trauma management. Designed for a single operative working in sub-optimal conditions during the first hour after injury, it was never intended to be a formula for total trauma care in a multidisciplinary centre. At the Royal London Hospital, the management process was continuously reviewed while the guiding principles were respected. The result is a multidisciplinary team activity where each member is given tasks to carry out simultaneously. The priorities remain, but tasks are performed in parallel rather than in sequence. This method of organisation radically reduces the time taken to complete the Secondary Survey. A 'Team Leader' is essential to coordinate and focus the actions of the team

The team are encouraged to wear protective clothing (including lead aprons), gloves and eye protection throughout the resuscitation. The lead aprons have the role of the wearer emblazoned on front and back so that each team member can be instantly identified. 'Silence' is the rule, though it is seldom 'golden'. Communications are directed to the Team Leader and not between members of the team. All team members are made aware of the hazards of infection and must have Hepatitis B immunity. Procedures for the safe disposal of contaminated sharps are endorsed.

Roles within the trauma team are assigned in the hospital trauma management protocol. There is no room for uncertainty or conflict about who performs which task Each individual's activity is summarised on 'action cards' which are shown in Figure 1. Using this system, it is possible for individuals to change roles for training purposes, provided the Team Leader is in agreement.

The Team Leader should be a doctor with experience of trauma management, and training in how to lead a trauma team. The leader does not have to be the most senior doctor but must be acknowledged to be in charge. If junior staff take on this role they should be strictly evaluated. The Team Leader should never become involved in 'hands on' patient management. This leads to a coned view of particular problems and an inevitable lack of overall control. The temptation for the Team Leader to become involved in practical procedures encourages the evolution of secondary team leaders and direction by committee.

The Team

A doctor is assigned to airway control. This is an obvious role for an anaesthetist assisted by a member of the paramedical anaesthetic staff (operating department assistant or anaesthetic nurse).

An experienced doctor (surgeon or A&E) is designated as 'Doctor 1' to do the bulk of the 'hands on' management of the patient following ATLS guidelines, including the Primary Survey, some critical interventions and the Secondary Survey. This doctor works with an experienced nurse (Nurse 1).

A more junior doctor (Doctor 2 or A&E doctor) is required to secure intravenous access, take arterial and venous blood samples and perform interventions, such as urinary catheterisation or more advanced interventions according to ability, as directed by the Team Leader. This doctor is paired with a nurse (Nurse 2), who is responsible for recording pulse, blood pressure and conscious levels at regular intervals.

A 'Scribe' – usually the neurosurgical senior house officer – documents the patient's condition and all actions taken by the team. The majority of trauma cases become the responsibility of the neurosurgeons and it seems sensible that the notes should begin in the correct handwriting. The 'hands on' staff are too busy to make notes, and records written from memory are inevitably rose tinted. A Trauma Sheet or booklet ensures appropriate and comprehensive documentation.

To these four pairs is added the medical imaging team. Initially two radiographers take routine cross table lateral and trauma oblique views of the cervical spine, then chest, pelvis and axial skeletal views. These are reviewed by a senior radiologist who is responsible for arranging subsequent imaging modalities (CT, angiography, etc).

The team therefore divides into five pairs of staff, with a hovering radiologist. Each occupies a different area of space around the patient. The anaesthetic pair work at the head of the patient, Doctor 1 with Nurse 1 work on the patient's right and Doctor 2 with Nurse 2 on the patient's left; the radiographers and radiologist squeeze into the gaps. The Team Leader and Scribe are strategically positioned a little way from the patient. This avoids the traditional scrummage, though space is tight.

Medical staff from many specialities may be called to assess the patient. All must be prepared to obey the instructions of the Team Leader who, in turn, must perform 'crowd control'. All remain at a distance until invited to approach and evaluate the patient with respect to their specialist area. The Team Leader takes advice

Figure 1: Action Cards for the Royal London Hospital Trauma Team

TEAM LEADER

1. Prior to patient arrival identify each member of the team and ensure that they are aware of their role.
2. Obtain history from ambulance crew/HEMS team.
3. 'Hands off' supervision of trauma team function, organise and coordinate.
4. Check proper examination carried out and observations recorded.
5. Summarise injuries and DOCUMENT THEM.
6. Keep reviewing the overall picture.
7. Decide on priorities for further investigation or treatment.
8. Speak to relatives.
9. Check medical notes are complete.

GENERAL RULES

1. Silence is golden.
2. Gloves, glasses and lead aprons must be worn.
3. Observers must be behind the scenes.
4. Only six people to have hands on at any one time.
5. Work simultaneously.
6. Timings — Phase 1: under 12 minutes; Phase 2: under 20 minutes
7. Know your role and the equipment.
8. Don't ignore the patient.
9. Consider HIV and your immunisation status.

DOCTOR ONE (Surgeon/A&E)

1. Complete Primary Survey, saying your findings aloud at each stage.
2. Carry out any critical interventions as required.
3. Secondary Survey – report findings to Team Leader and Scribe.
4. Carry out procedures as directed by the Team Leader.
5. Supervise log roll, check back and perform PR.
6. Carry out diagnostic peritoneal lavage as directed by Team Leader.
7. Check the record of the examination.

NURSE ONE

1. Prior to patient arrival phone laboratory and record any information available on the white board.
2. Collect warm fluid.
3. Cut patient's right sleeve and attach BP.
4. Work in a team with Doctor 1, assist with practical procedures.
5. Prepare equipment and sterile packs as needed.
6. Assist with log roll.
7. Prepare antibiotics, tet. tox. and other drugs as requested by the Team Leader.
8. Speak to relatives with Team Leader.
9. Complete the resuscitation room register.

from the specialists before prescribing the management plan for the patient. It is best if the most senior staff are involved at an early stage so that a coordinated and agreed plan evolves.

Summary

Audit is vital. The team is multidisciplinary, therefore audit should be performed in a multidisciplinary forum. The audit cycle must continuously analyse the process of care and modify protocols to improve efficiency. Video recording of resuscitation is useful, particularly for training junior members of staff.

The physical design and layout of equipment in the resuscitation room must fit with the modus operandi of the trauma team. Equipment likely to be required by each doctor/nurse pair is located near to their area of work, reducing unnecessary movement. An additional member of the nursing staff can be designated as 'Runner' to bring additional equipment, to take blood samples and to collect drugs and blood as required. A blood gas analyser within the resuscitation room, ceiling mounted x-ray equipment, on-site x-ray processing and a pneumatic tube system for specimens and blood for transfusion, all improve efficiency. Each makes little difference on its own, but together the effect may be large.

Medical staff used to autonomy may have difficulty in acting as 'small cog confined to its sprocket'. The resuscitation of the multiply injured patient is a team effort, and there is no room for prima donnas or independent cogs. A coordinated team acting in parallel is usually more effective than an independent individual, and always more effective than a 'committee' of medical staff, with their own, often conflicting, set of priorities.

The confusion and panic that surrounds an uncoordinated trauma resuscitation is distressing for medical and nursing staff. To be part of a well-led team, acting in a planned and purposeful way, reduces stress placed on staff and encourages pride in a job well done. Many trauma victims are bound to die. Even so, there is satisfaction in being part of an efficient team that has taken every opportunity to secure an optimal outcome. It is even more encouraging when the team sees success plucked from the jaws of defeat on a regular basis.

DOCTOR TWO (A&E SHO)

1. Prior to patient arrival fill in blood bottles and forms.
2. Cut clothing from left arm and chest.
3. Site two large bore infusions (14G, 16G or Arrow)
4. Take blood – venous (Hb, U&E, Sickle, X-match, toxicology, plain spare) and arterial (gases).
5. Assist with log roll.
6. Catheterise the patient (after PR).
7. Assist Doctor 1 (Surgeon) as required.

NURSE TWO

1. Cut clothing from left leg, do not remove splints.
2. Work with Doctor 2 (A&E SHO).
3. Assist with insertion and securing of venous access.
4. Run through warm fluid and connect infusions, fully open.
5. Run fluid through Level 1 blood warmer as directed by Team Leader.
6. Assist with log roll.
7. Set up trolley and assist with catheterisation.
8. Continue as directed by Nurse 1.

SCRIBE (Neurosurgical SHO)

1. Record documentation of history, pre-hospital events, intervention and observations.
2. Fill in all of the Trauma Sheet.
3. Record timings of events.
4. Document examination as spoken by Doctor 2.
5. Document observations at least every 5 minutes.
6. Perform neurosurgical assessment.
7. Telephone CT scanner or theatres as required.
8. Ensure Trauma Sheet photocopied for the in-hospital notes.

ANAESTHETIST AND ODA

1. Maintain airway and cervical spine control.
2. Intubate and ventilate as directed by the Team Leader.
3. Give respiratory rate to the Scribe.
4. If the patient is conscious talk, reassure and explain throughout the resuscitation.
5. Insert central or arterial lines as needed.
6. Check monitoring.
7. Assist Nurse 2 with Level 1 fluid warmer.

PLANNING AND THE ROYAL LONDON HOSPITAL EMERGENCY DEPARTMENT

Alastair Wilson, Ray Moss

For efficiency, effectiveness and economy, form must follow function and when function changes rapidly, as in the case of the A&E department, then the structures which accommodate it must evolve with similar rapidity. Since the A&E department of the Royal London Hospital was repaired and built on its existing site in the late 1970s and early 1980s, it has been at the forefront of evolution complicated frequently by ill-defined health policies. More recently with a total redesign within the existing shell carried out in the early 1990s and with a case-load that has grown to over 80,000 patients, it is already showing signs of being obsolete and inadequate in size. On this evidence, scanty as it is, a life-cycle of some 10 years is indicated.

Not only is the future service and planning strategy unclear, but there is no generally accepted view as to how an emergency department will operate in the future. Even as this article is being written, the King's Fund are suggesting that A&E departments of hospitals with less than 50,000 attendances a year should close. For the Royal London, this could mean an influx of patients from nearby Homerton in addition to a considerable paediatric load from Queen Elizabeth Hospital, Hackney (27,000/year). Given such flux and uncertainty in operational policy, the Project Team in general and the architect in particular, are in some considerable difficulty. What would Florence Nightingale (1820-1910) have made of such a state of affairs?

For Florence and her architect Alfred Waterhouse (1830-1905), there was no such thing as uncertainty. She was absolutely clear as to where she was going and equally certain that it was right. In spite of some hesitation in government circles the result was that the ground rules for hospital planning were set 150 years ago. The Victorians built hundreds of hospitals to the same pattern, both at home and abroad and these buildings set the 'design theory', more or less, for all the hospitals that have followed, including the Royal London. Indeed, so powerful is this 'design theory' that it shapes our ideas about new hospitals today even though the business has changed totally. A good example of this is the insistence on physical adjacency in spite of developments in information technology (IT) which should make it irrelevant.

In Florence's day before the arrival of centralised services and highly technical procedures, nothing much moved around inside hospitals. They were confident but static and people knew their place. As the new services came along, they were accommodated between the bed pavilions in the correct location to the patients served. The corridors (30% of the floor space) were also filled up. It is one of the 'tablets of stone' of hospital planning that department A is next to department B and so on, even though, over the years, hospitals as institutions have become prone to continuous change and IT has liberated people to the extent that they can both see and hear each other no matter the distance between them. Indeed, in the highly systematised approaches to hospital planning developed in the 1970s and 80s locating departments on the need for physical adjacency became possible automatically by using computer aided design methods.

However, so many other considerations have changed over time that these somewhat simplistic design methods are of dubious value now. Patient focused care, remote diagnosis and treatment and the development of 'day' and 'off-site' care have to be taken into account. These considerations impinge as much on the A&E department as on any other department. But in many cases these wider views are not accepted and the 'tablets of stone' referred to earlier are clouding the real issues. It is almost as if the boot had been put on the other foot since Florence's time. In her day, pressure for change was being resisted by people above, but nowadays even when those at the top profess to want change it is made well nigh impossible because of the Byzantine bureaucracy over which they preside.

It is well-known that there is an acute shortage of trained health facility planners available to advise Trusts over their long-term best interests. This can be seen in the opportunistic way in which many sites are used. Additionally the problem is compounded by the combined dogmas of Private Finance Initiative (PFI) and Compulsory Competitive Tendering (CCT). PFIs which, on the face of it, were originally a good idea have not been thought through. For instance, a 'level playing field' ensures that bright, innovative ideas are not put forward by competitors as they know that these have to be discussed by the client with all the other competitors. It is difficult to be clever and still win on price when one's ideas have been kicked about by everyone else, whether they have fully understood or not. In principle, if private involvement gets better hospitals built it will have been a

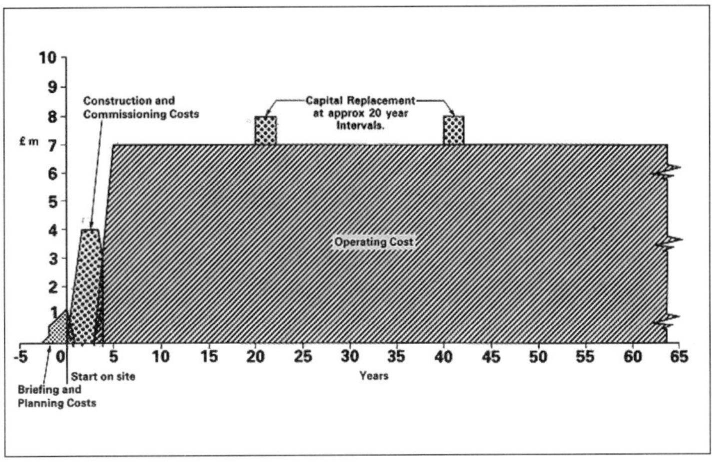

Model of the assessed cash flow pattern for the first phase of a nucleus hospital at 1982-83 prices.
Taken from Moss R. *Designing for reduced operating costs in the Health Care Estate*. Issue 56, Dept of Health, June 1985.

good idea but the private sector must be fully aware how much it costs to win jobs. All parties, Trusts included, must be well advised about a) whether the scheme is necessary at all, b) in line with modern thinking, c) not possible in any more effective way and d) most important of all is cost-effective to run. With hospitals gobbling up the equivalent of their capital costs in running costs every couple of years or so this last point cannot be over emphasised

Generally speaking, the consensus is that the acute part of new hospitals will be smaller, more flexible, more compact and more sophisticated that the previous monolithic District General Hospital, and than many of the less acute parts will be 'off-loaded' to more local accessible and possibly cheaper sites to comprise a 'federation' of buildings. Such a strategy will break up the previous institution called 'hospital' into smaller, more discreet and easily buildable parts which can be achieved within reasonable time-frames. In the present climate the trouble with huge institutions is that when they cost huge sums of money to build and even huger sums of money to run, one has to ask whether any developer in his right mind would want to put his money into it? Even if he does, who wants to live and work on a building site for the next 20 years? Satisfactory existing buildings should be adapted and re-used wherever possible (if it ain't broke, don't fix it).

So where does this leave the A&E department? Many fundamental questions require answering such as, what is the relationship between primary health care and A&E? Already there is a noticeable trend, inherited from the developing world which involves 'bypassing' the GP and going straight to hospital where things happen. Numerous journeys and waiting times, even though guaranteed by the Patient's Charter, are avoided thus speeding up diagnosis and treatment. Is this pressure from the bottom up? When the broad issues are agreed it seems clear that the A&E department will be located at the 'high-tech' unit.

Specific Comments for a New A&E Department

'Prevent penetration'

Patients should only penetrate the system as far as their disease severity dictates. The further into the hospital a patient reaches, the greater the cost. A patient seen, treated and discharged close to the front door is least intrusive. A patient who requires an x-ray after minimal examination, can be managed here then treated in 'minors'. The deeper the department is penetrated, the more likely the patient will be admitted and the more expensive the patient episode. Patients who require instant examination and investigation need to be held in A&E while results are accumulated and the decision to admit or discharge is made. A multiply injured patient who has to be admitted for surgery or intensive care will undergo speedy resuscitation and CT scanning in the department but this will only take 30-60 minutes.

'Beds are more expensive than CT'

Medical investigation in the emergency department must be done quickly on the fast axis. This means the use of 'near' patient testing and instant access to investigative equipment (in particular medical imaging). To admit a patient before investigations have been obtained is folly because expensive bed days will ensue while the same investigations are awaited by the patient lying on a ward.

'The fading foibles of fashion'

The Patient's Charter sets 'triage targets', which insist that all patients should be sorted into priorities in under five minutes. Triage requires an educated guess at diagnosis where conventional medicine demands a history, full medical examination and investigation before coming to conclusions. Not surprisingly, these imposed triage targets are fundamentally flawed, requiring excessive numbers of staff for their honest implementation, further staff to spot patients initially of low urgency who deteriorate and a large medico-legal department to pay-out when the triage guess is wrong. Unfortunately, before the death knell of these targets, facilities must continue to be provided to allow private conversation with nursing staff in the waiting area. At first glance, this appeared to be an insurmountable waste, but two triage rooms in the waiting area were linked to the computer and equipped as two minor examination cubicles for medical consultation. This has brought medicine into the midst of the waiting area next to the front door.

'Patients know what they want'

For years, a bizarre paternalist culture has pervaded the Health Service, based on 'only the GP can decide.' Patients object to this and use the A&E department as the most convenient alternative. If it hurts, then let it be seen immediately by someone who is not going to refer to outpatients, placement on waiting list guaranteed by the government to be less than one year long before the never-never operation and still more oscillations between hospital and GP. If it needs doing, it is probably best done straight away. This offends restrictive British convention, but pleases the punter. Facilities have now been provided for this type of health care delivery, so if money really is to follow where the patient has already gone, the fundholders must legitimise this flow and pay for it.

'Don't block the drains'

Beds are the present currency of hospital cost reduced to a frighteningly low number by successive managements who have indulged in an increasingly minimalist approach. This down-sizes (or euphemistically right-sizes) the number of beds until we are now in the position that hospital length of stay is so short that it is dangerous. Logically, hospital bed numbers relate to the diameter of a drain. As bed numbers reduce not only is the flow reduced, but the quality and substance of what needs to pass through the drain increases in severity, causing frequent blockages. A third factor in the drainage analogy is outflow into the community, who neither have the money nor the inclination to take patients home from acute beds. This leads to total outflow obstruction. The drain overflows in the A&E department in the form of long trolley waits, unwise early discharges and extra beds in wards and corridors.

All hospitals cater for variations in the flow of emergency attendances while competition between emergency and routine admissions is governed by agreed policies. No A&E department plan can provide adequate bed numbers or equitable admission for all patients so the problem must be transmitted to the wards where the beds ought to have been. Meanwhile, as the drain begins to overflow, senior presence in the emergency department calls attention to the problem, copes with increasingly complex medical workload, and ensures that patients are not left for unacceptable waits in corridors. The new design facilitates this function with on-call beds for senior doctors and more capacity for complex investigation.

'Measure the work done and not the size of the bust'

There is no absolute convention that hospitals have fixed bed numbers. But, our A&E department has been 'right-sized' for 100,000 patient attendances per year, on the assumption that in future the Department of Health will have to count sensible 'units of work', that reflect some sort of reality. This may yet prove to be one assumption too far. To improve efficiency, the old straight line layout of A&E cubicles has become a ring surrounding the supplies and staff bases reminiscient of covered wagons under attack. This reduces staff walking to supplies and increases visual sight lines. Fully operational since early 1996, this layout works well except that the 16 adult cubicles, 3 paediatric cubicles, 5 resuscitation trolleys and 6 spaces for 'minors', are already in full demand. Though well in excess of the Building Note and the official design guides produced by NHS Estates for such a department, this size is much more in line with modern requirements.

The principle of penetration is seen in the arrangement of areas in our plan. This holds good for all except the paediatric area, which has its own entrance and also access through the primary care unit or the orthopaedic department. A 28-bedded admissions ward is absolutely essential in the plan because this means that patients can be admitted throughout the evening and night without disturbing every ward in the hospital and allowing onward hospitalisation or discharge home next morning.

Mr Alastair Wilson FRCS is A&E Consultant at the Royal London Hospital and has been closely involved with all the different plans.

Professor Raymond Moss spent his professional life working in the NHS at Regional Department of Health and Academic levels. He is currently Chairman of Architects for Health, Visiting Professor at City University and a Health Facility Planning Consultant in private practice.

VALUE OF THE SPIRAL CT SCANNER IN THE A&E DEPARTMENT

Otto Chan, Mario Scolari

Trauma is the leading cause of death in patients under 40 years and the third commonest cause of death worldwide. The loss in number of life years is probably equivalent to ischaemic heart disease and malignancy together in the USA. Previous reviews suggest that up to 33% of trauma deaths in the USA and UK may be preventable. Therefore the management of these patients needs not only a multi-disciplinary approach but also properly equipped centres. The value of fast CT scanning cannot be understated in the management not only of polytraumatised patients but in a vast number of other conditions presenting through A&E.

There are also numerous other applications of CT which are not used in the UK, either because of the inconvenient siting of the CT scanner, long waiting times or lack of expertise. Simple applications, such as detection or location of foreign bodies, in particular when multiple fragments are involved (e.g bomb blast injuries) and detection of suspected peripheral limb injuries are impossible unless a CT scanner is conveniently sited with readily available access. Therefore, the Royal London Hospital made a conscious decision to place the new CT scanner in casualty. The new Somatom Plus 4A CT scanner provides an up-to-date top quality CT service for all routine body imaging, selected head imaging and in particular there is open access to all emergencies. The fast CT applications will not only dramatically reduce scanning times by up to 50 times (CT head from 10 minutes to 15 seconds, CT chest from 25 minutes to 30 seconds) but the siting of the CT scanner will also dramatically reduce transportation times from over one hour to under five minutes in potentially unstable patients. The combination of shorter scan times, siting of the CT scanner in the A&E department with open access to trauma patients, and greater trauma expertise means that severely injured patients will not have to wait too long for their critical injuries to be evaluated. The famous quote of 'patients are literally x-rayed to death' will no longer apply to the Royal London Hospital patients.

Technical Aspects of Spiral CT

Until recently most third generation scanners applied the stop and go principle. In this type of scanner, which utilises a cable take up assembly, minimal scan times are 2-3 seconds and minimal inter scan times are up to 10 seconds. This is related to the accelerating and decelerating large mass of the entire measuring system. In contrast, the introduction of a third generation CT scanner with a continuously rotating measuring system, the Somatom Plus, provided the technical basis for rapid uninterrupted data acquisition. Even in dynamic applications the continuously rotating measuring system offers zero interscan delays and opens up new horizons in Dynamic CT.

In 1987, a new trail was blazed in the field of CT by the Somatom Plus, the first scanner featuring continuous rotation which eventually set the cornerstone for all new CT applications. Two years later, volume scanning with Spiral CT was introduced as the unstoppable technical consequence of continuous rotation, thus making it possible to acquire a continuous volume through rotation of the tube and detector concurrent with horizontal travel of the patient table. In the course of time, Spiral CT has both established itself as a method of examining the abdominal region and opened up new possibilities. With the spiral and a table feed which could exceed the slice thickness, the scan times were short enough to enable a 'bolus chase' through a larger anatomical region. This breakthrough gave birth to CT angiography. However, due to various restrictions, it was still not possible to produce spiral images with an image quality equal to that of conventional scans in the neurological region. The new member of the Somatom Plus family, the Somatom Plus 4, has knocked down all such barriers.

This new CT scanner has been in operation at the Royal London Hospital since December 1995. Its flexibility and increased performance capabilities in comparison to earlier units open up new possibilities for clinical applications. These will be presented and discussed in the following text. One of the most eye-catching innovations of the Somatom Plus 4 is its exceptional user-friendliness based on its clear user guidance. The PC-like user interface makes the operation of this unit much easier to learn. The procedures for patient registration, examination planning, archiving and filming are executed automatically with a minimum of operator intervention, allowing more time for the staff to care for the patient during the examination. This holds especially true for colleagues and radiological assistants on night duty.

The Somatom Plus 4 makes it possible to create topograms with a total length of up to 1024mm. In contrast, the topograms produced by previous models were limited to a maximum length of 512 mm. At the same time, the current scan range is displayed on the monitor in real time and the topogram can be ended as soon as the desired volume has been attained, thus preventing unnecessary patient exposure to radiation.

Complex examination protocols with Spiral CT, including various examination parameters, can be realised with such a long topogram. Besides Spiral CT protocols with up to 80 rotations and three different rotation times for one full cycle (750 millisecs, 2 secs and 1.5 secs), a pitch of up to 2 and as many as 10 consecutive spirals can be realised without interspiral delays. At the same time, all the parameters for the individual spirals are freely selectable. The table position of 0.5 millisecs allows bed-trolleys and emergency patients to be more easily transferred. Furthermore this space allows an image intensifier to be introduced and combined interventional procedures using CT and image intensifier are possible, such as difficult biopsies and emergency angiographic procedures. The long topograms are also important for CT angiography, since they make it possible to examine an entire vascular province with only a single contrast medium injection.

The nuts and bolts of Spiral

Somatom Plus is a fast computer tomograph with continuous rotation of the whole measuring system. The energy transfer to the x-ray tube is facilitated by the use of high voltage slip rings. As a result of the Multifan principle, realised with state of the art Flying Focal Spot x-ray tube, over 2.5 million measurements are supplied for uninterrupted data acquisition.

The logical step, given the available technology, was to provide continuous data acquisition together with continuous increment of the table into the gantry aperture. Using the data acquired it is then possible to reconstruct CT images in any table position within the data volume. Modern spiral CT scanners not only need a high amount of technical innovation but must be ergonomically pleasing and patient friendly. The open design of the Somatom Plus is considered to be essential, reducing the likelihood of rejection from claustrophobic patients. The combination of large patient aperture with shallow scanning bore encourages the patient to relax during the examination and allows easy access for the medical staff to carry out a full range of clinical procedures without repositioning.

Many CT patients come to the department on beds and wheelchairs. One of the most important aspects of the design is the ease with which patients can get on and off the table. The ability to randomly position the table top at any height, even down to as low as 48 cm, helps the clinical staff transfer patients safely on and off the examination table, and this further reduces the likelihood of

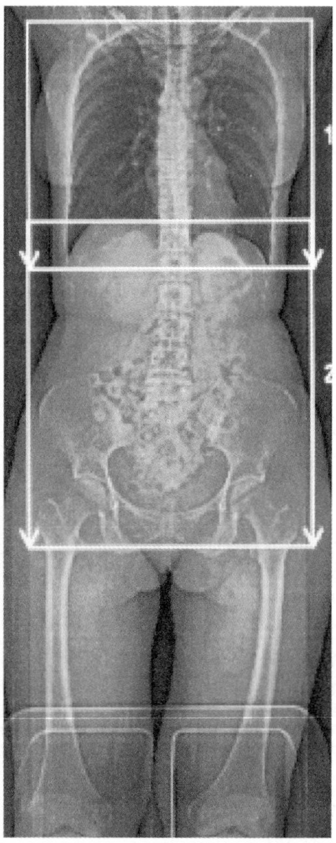

Figure 1: 104 mm topogram with two demarcated scanning images

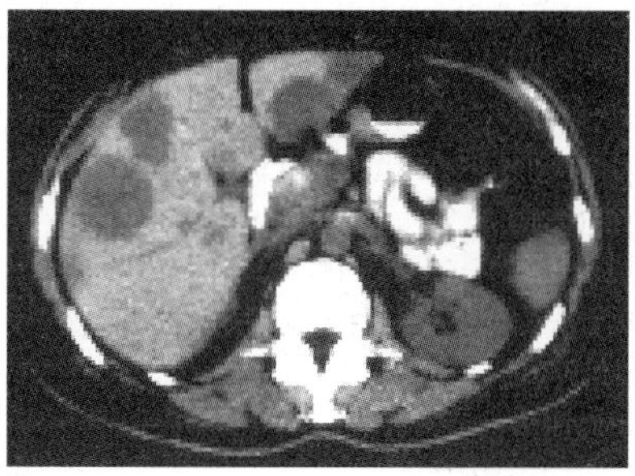

2a

Figure 2:
3-phase Spiral CT of the liver a = precontrast, b = arterial c= portal venous

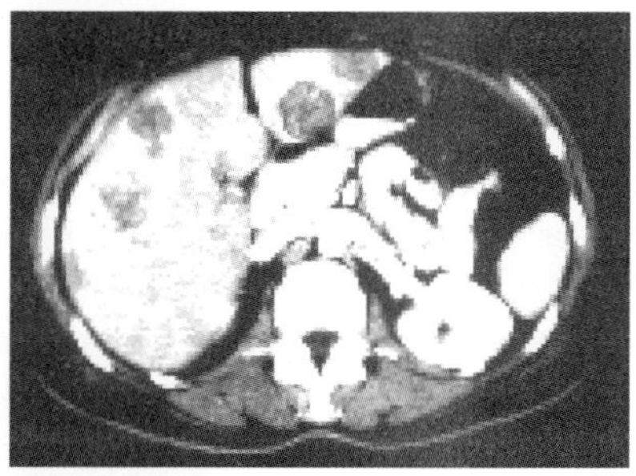

2b

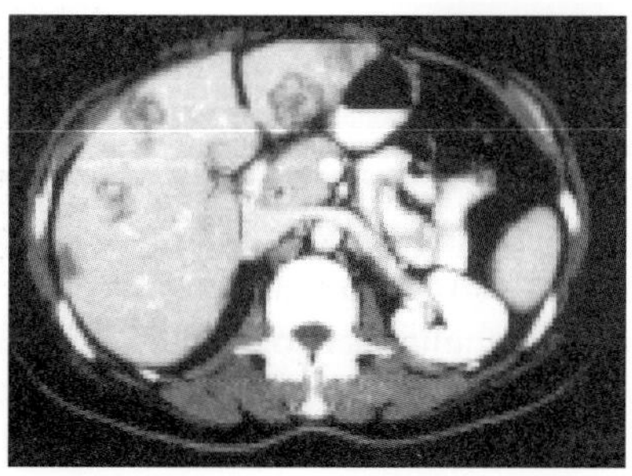

2c

staff sustaining a back injury. The Somatom Plus has a computer controlled table allowing incremental movements with sub millimetre accuracy up to patients weighing in excess of 32 stone. The gantry to table position of 500 cm, allows bed/trolley and emergency patients to be more easily transferred.

New Clinical Benefits of CT

Multiphase Spiral CT

One example of this technique is a three-phase study of the liver. This technique takes the arterial and portal venous vascular supply of the liver into account. Following a pre-contrast spiral scan of the liver, a contrast medium bolus is injected. Its duration is defined, based on the length of the region being examined and a predetermined flow rate. This increases the quality of the overall examination and guarantees a high probability of lesion detection. This part of the examination is especially important for the sensitive verification of focal lesions of the liver.

The multiphase technique can also prove advantageous in the thoracic region, in particular the pulmonary arterial phase, providing differentiation between tumours, tumour necrosis and atelectasis. Furthermore, vascular occlusions and infiltrations or compressions due to tumours can also be displayed in exact detail. Multiphase Spiral CT thus makes it possible to examine the perfusion phases of many different anatomical regions. Short breathing pauses can be inserted between the individual scans in cases where large volumes must be acquired. Only a single contrast bolus need be used for this purpose, thus enhancing both the sensitivity and the specificity of the examination.

Another possibility for displaying volume data is the shaded surface display (SSD) and maximum intensity projection (MIP). These techniques make it possible to image vessels and the outer surface of anatomical structures, providing good visualisation of selected structures for the clinician or surgeon.

The chief precondition for MIP and SSD displays is the clear segmentation of any surrounding or adjacent bone structures. However, through high contrast display of the vessels, decisive information can also be gained from single slices or multiplanar reconstructions without any need to perform elaborate segmentation procedures.

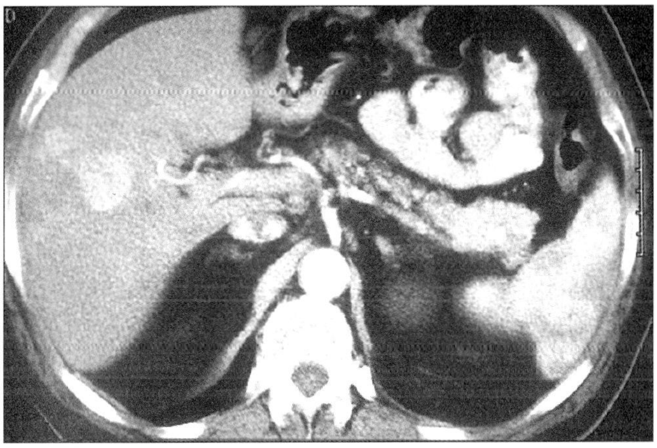

Photo: W Teh

Figure 3: Liver carcinoid, arterial phase

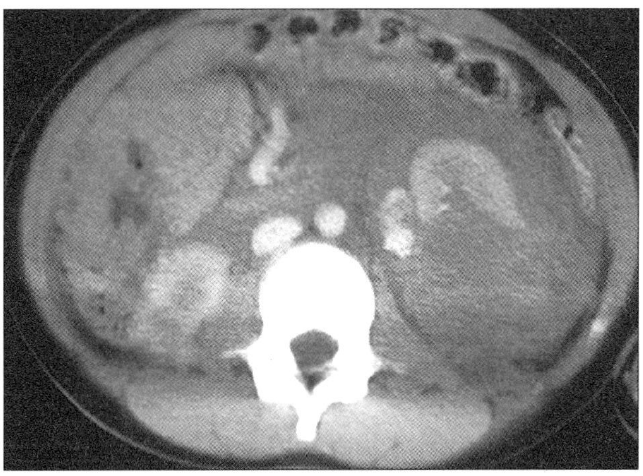

Photo: W Teh

Figure 5: Fractured left kidney

The intracerebral vessels can now easily be segmented and displayed with MIP or SSD. The shorter scan times of the Somatom Plus 4 now make it possible both to reduce the size of an more efficiently utilise the contrast medium bolus.

Spiral CT of the brain

With the new scanner, it will be possible to make use of the chief advantages of Spiral CT beyond the limitations of the single slice technique even for studies of the brain. The entire brain can thus be examined with a slice thickness of 3 mm in 26 seconds. The short scan time makes it possible to examine even uncooperative and unstable patients without movement artifacts almost without exception. Recently at the Royal London speed of scanning was put to good use scanning victims of the IRA attack on Canary Wharf in the East End of London producing vital diagnostic images within seconds.

Spiral CT of the spinal column

The degree of gantry tilt required for various different intervertebral disc segments can be planned for the examination in the topogram up to an angle of +/- 30°. Automatic execution of the examination of different disc segments, with gantry tilting from the control console, makes it possible to examine multiple intervertebral disc spaces via the thin slice technique.

The diagnosis of spinal stenosis requires the display of larger vertebral segments, since clinical examinations often do not allow for any clear allocation of segments. Due to the great amount of time involved, such examinations have been restricted to the domain of Magnetic Resonance Imaging until now. The new CT scanner makes it possible to acquire the entire lumbar spine including the sacro-iliac joints in a single pass within a few seconds. The acquisition of a volume data file using Spiral CT also offers two more diagnostically relevant possibilities. First of all, it enables high-quality secondary reconstructions of intervertebral disc spaces in paraxial and oblique slice orientation. Secondly, it allows the display of the corpus vertebrae in a sagittal or coronal slice orientation, thus making it possible to assess whether the front or the rear edge of a vertebral body is fractured and to what extent.

Spiral CT of the thorax

The upgraded performance spectrum of the Somatom Plus 4 offers additional clinical applications for examination of the thorax, and above all, of the heart. With a full rotation of 750 ms, a partial scan of only 500 millisecs is possible. This advantage is utilised to perform sequential scans in a single slice position, whereby the 500 millisecs partial scan is performed as a spiral.

Another major advantage of Spiral CT is the acquisition of a volume data file, thus enabling better display of anatomical detail through free selection of the reconstruction increment. With the new scanner, reconstruction increments in the submillimeter range are also possible, thus enabling scans of regions which require maximum resolution along the longitudinal body axis. The acquisition of volume data files also enable high quality secondary reconstructions with randomly oriented slice positions or even continuous MIP and SSD displays.

The shorter scan time makes it possible to utilise more efficiently a contrast medium bolus. In addition, the difficult setting of both an initial and a maintenance bolus, as is often required to maintain a satisfactory level of enhancement, can thus be omitted. At the same time, improved enhancement of the vessels and parenchyma is achieved along with a reduction in the contrast medium requirement (approximately 25%).

CT angiography

Angiography or the x-ray display of vascular structure, is one of the most time consuming but detailed examinations currently performed within a modern x-ray department.

With the Somatom Plus 4, the contrast medium bolus can be better utilised to display larger vascular regions such as the aortic arch, the abdominal aorta and vessels in the extremities. Using short cycle times of e.g 750 millisecs, the aorta can be examined from the aortic arch up to the bifurcation using only a single contrast medium bolus and 5 mm thick slices. This makes it possible to display the full course of a dissection.

The use of a 500 millisec scan with a cycle time of 1.9 seconds, performed in a single slice plane, supplies results comparable to those obtained using echocardiography with simultaneous display of the valves and the contrast medium dynamics. In the future, it will be possible to increase the precision of such indications through ECG triggering.

Improved image quality for less dose

The exceptional spiral image quality offered by the new scanner requires a comparison between the image quality obtained by conventional tomography and that obtained with Spiral CT. The possibility of examining a larger anatomical region fast with thin slices and a reasonable dose rate enhances the detail recognition. Comparison of an examination performed both with Sequential and Spiral CT techniques show that the difference between the two is negligible from a diagnostic standpoint but with an overall increase in image quality is obtained for lower doses and much shorter examination times. The previous limits of Spiral CT were chiefly caused by the x-ray tubes used. Due to the limited anode heat storage capacity, the tube power required for the spiral could not be generated for a sufficient period of time, thus resulting in spiral images which exhibited a high noise level. With the short duration of the spirals, larger anatomical regions could be examined only in conjunction with thicker slices, thus causing a loss of resolution along the longitudinal body axis. The longer tube cooling delays between two spirals prevented the performance of examinations such as three phase liver studies.

In CT diagnostics, the application of the Spiral CT technique has proved superior to sequential tomography in more ways than one. An entire anatomical volume can be examined in a single breathhold. This ensures complete and continuous examinations of, for example, the lung for the precise diagnosis of detailed pathology. The Somatom Plus 4 will allow routine use of spiral throughout the working day enabling up to 10 different anatomical regions to be scanned within a matter of seconds.

PACS

The very generous funding by the Trust for the new Spiral CT Scanner in the A&E department allowed the purchase of a mini PACS system, which allowed us to buy a small image store archiver, three workstations and an additional two VDUs. The images are digitally stored in the PACS system and can be retrieved within minutes at several different sites in the hospital even if hard copies are lost. A permanent record is therefore kept of all trauma patients for future evaluation and research purposes. The work stations have full capabilities for all forms of complex image processing including 2D and 3D reconstructions and CT angiography. Furthermore, review of the images on different window selections is possible and thus information can be obtained of the soft tissues, the lungs and the bony skeleton without the necessity for obtaining further imaging or provide hard copies. The PACS system is also capable in the future of having further imaging modalities linked into it, in particular other CT scanners, MRI or angiography. There are also capabilities for expanding this PACS system throughout the A&E department.

Acknowledgements

Siemens Medical Engineering, Siemens House, Oldbury, Bracknell RG12 8FZ.

Otto Chan is Consultant Radiologist at the RLH with a special interest in CT scanning.

Mario Scolari is CT Product Specialist at Siemens.

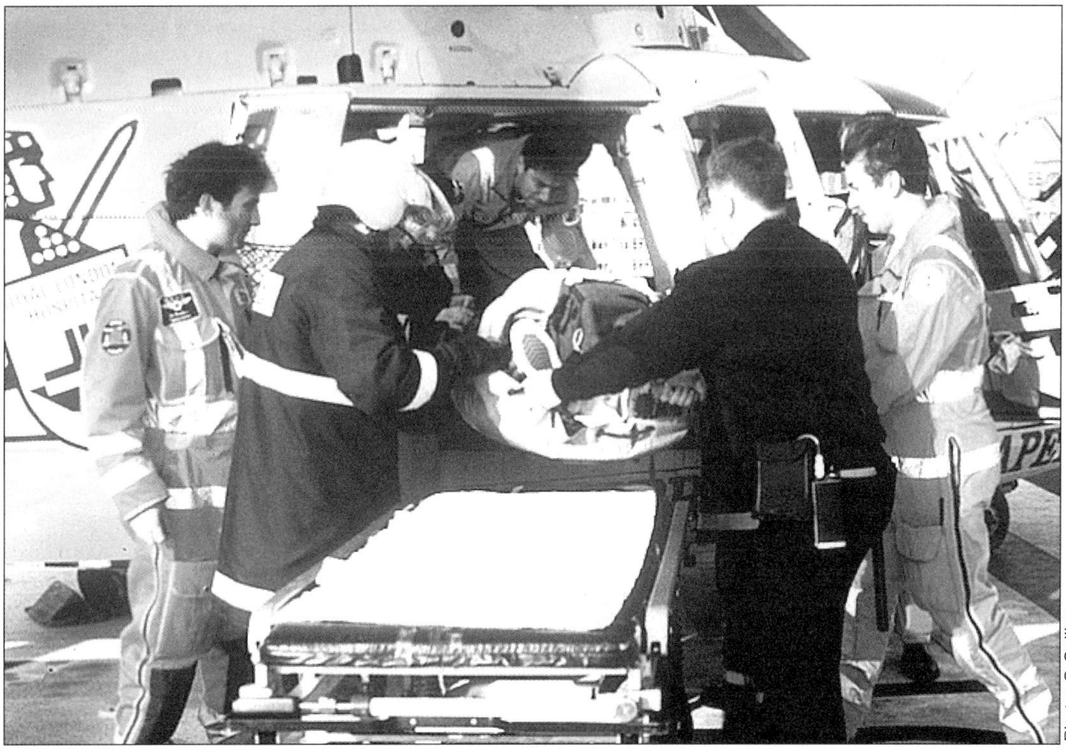

Photo: G Collins

Following transfer to the hospital helipad, the patient is unloaded

THE EMERGENCY THEATRE SERVICE

Helen Davis

Emergency surgery at the Royal London Hospital has always represented a significant percentage of operations performed. This rose from about 25% with the introduction of the Helicopter Emergency Service (HEMS) and currently represents in excess of 50% of total cases annually.

Siting of the Theatre

The siting of a trauma theatre is often the subject of debate. There are those who feel it should be situated within the Accident and Emergency department and those who would argue for it being part of the main theatre complex.

Financial and space restrictions dictated the siting of the trauma theatre at the Royal London Hospital. It is part of a five theatre suite, three floors above the A&E department, adjacent to the neurosurgical, cardiothoracic and orthopaedic theatres and on the same floor as Intensive Care and the Trauma Unit. This has proved to be an ideal location ensuring that the patient is treated appropriately by highly skilled staff with the best equipment available.

Theatre Utilisation

The aim was to provide a 24-hour theatre equipped to deal with multiple trauma patients. Built in 1899, the size and shape of the original trauma theatre did not lend itself to the accommodation of the amount of equipment required to treat patients in the 1990s .

In 1994, the Trust Board approved the business case to fund a programme for the major refurbishment of the theatre. The architects and project team worked closely with the theatre manager and staff to design a theatre layout most suitable for trauma patients.

Work started in April and took four months to complete with a total cost of £410,000. Figure 1 shows the new layout. The new theatre has proved a great success. In addition to a Laminar flow tent the theatre has a purpose built three-arm operating light and a range of multi-amp power and laser sockets to accommodate all modern equipment. The theatre also has a storeroom attached. Spacious and with natural light it is a pleasant environment to work in.

During the refurbishment work, provision of a dedicated trauma theatre was maintained through a rolling closure programme of scheduled operating lists.

Despite staffing shortages the theatre management and staff have shown a commitment to making the trauma theatre work. Audit figures show that approximately 80% of patients requiring surgery within one hour are accommodated within the department. Reasons for delay are commonly: patient not ready; i.e still in resuscitation or scanner or emergency priority. The success of HEMS has meant that there are frequently occasions where more than one theatre is required for trauma patients. Pressure of scheduled surgery does not allow for a second trauma theatre, however, the creation of a 'duty' theatre in the afternoons has reduced the pressure on staff and space. The requirement for second and subsequent theatres in the mornings sometimes results in the cancellation of elective surgery.

Figure 1: The new theatre

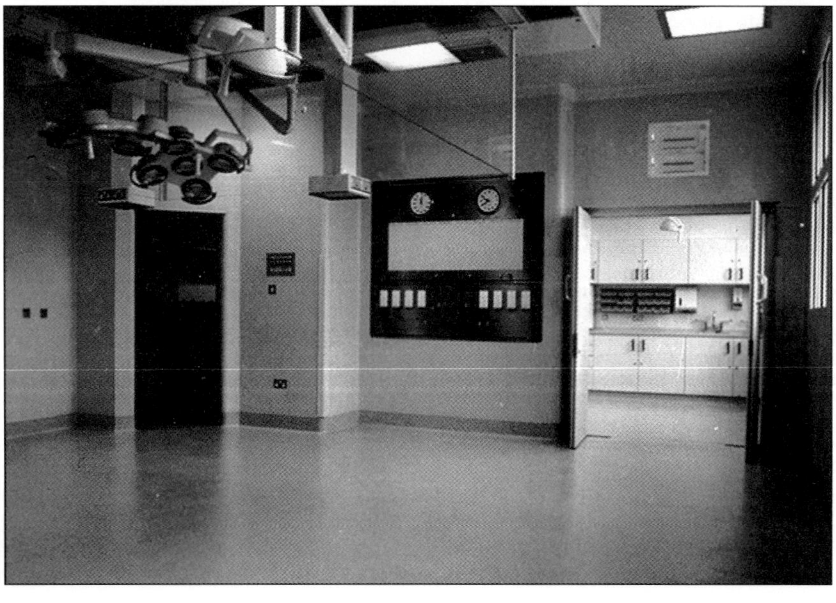

Photo: author

In 1995, the department implemented an audit of emergency

activity, the purpose of which was threefold:

1. To enable proper classification of surgical priority of patients, thus removing an element of the 'first come, first served' principle.
2. Improve communication between surgeons, anaesthetists and theatre staff.
3. Provide factual information to support a business case for funding to fully staff the trauma theatre.

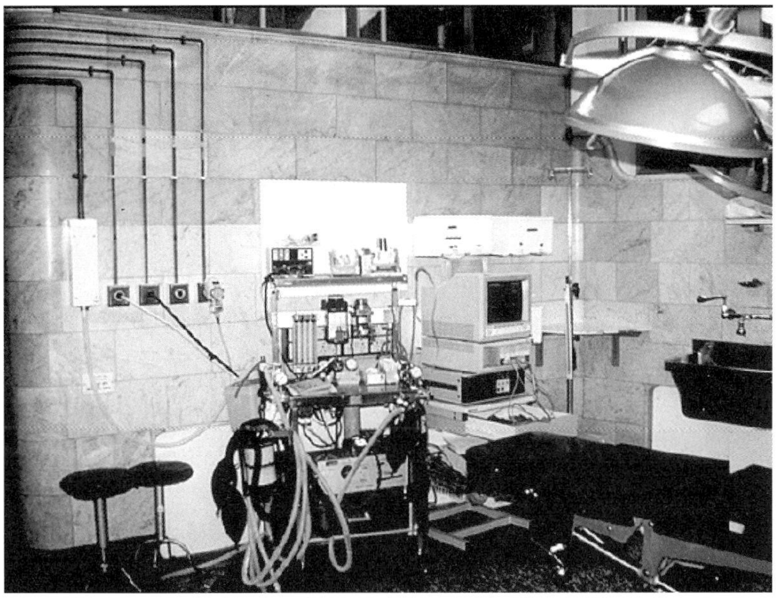

Figure 2: The old theatre with a fireplace hidden behind the marble.

Although the first year results are not available yet we have seen a definite improvement in the way the emergency theatre(s) are utilised. By offering four categories of urgency from urgent (within one hour) to ASAP (within 24 hours) we enable the surgeon to prioritise the surgery. The theatre staff have better information about patients requiring surgery and are able to plan the work more effectively thus reducing waiting times.

Staffing the Theatre

All patients undergoing surgery require the services of a team of skilled theatre personnel. This requirement is increased for emergency and trauma patients, where there is a need for the staff to be experienced in a number of specialities.

The HEMS project provides funding for a theatre team leader and anaesthetic assistants. The funding was initially used to appoint a senior sister with experience in trauma surgery. With her appointment came two main objectives:

1. To be available for all trauma patients during her span of duty.
2. To implement a training programme for other personnel with the aim of increasing the pool of staff competent to deal with multiple trauma patients.

The anaesthetic assistant plays a major part in the trauma team. Present in the resuscitation room, the assistant remains with the patient during scanning and x-ray and travels with the patient to theatre or the Intensive Care/Trauma Unit. The assistant is also the communicator with the theatres, alerting the theatre coordinator to the nature and complexity of the patient's injuries and expected time of arrival in theatre.

As a result of an ongoing training programme, there are now a large number of staff with experience in a range of specialities. These people are the pool from which staff are drawn for multiple trauma surgery.

In 1995, the Trust developed an in-house training course to encourage staff awareness to trauma surgery. To facilitate better working relationships with A&E, ICU and HEMS, the theatre management seconded a member of staff on to this course. It is envisaged that this member of staff and subsequent attendees will provide feedback and teaching to other members of staff.

In 1996 the Trust Board have approved a business case to fund the additional staff for the emergency theatre. The theatre management hope that by creating a dedicated team of staff for the theatre they will be able to form closer links with the staff in the A&E department with the aim of improving the communication and subsequently the service provided to the patient requiring surgery as a result of major trauma. Figure 2 is added to emphasise how far we have advanced since 1899.

Helen Davies is Theatre Manager for the Royal Hospitals NHS Trust, and together with Dr Tim Savege, Director of Anaesthetics, was closely involved in the planning of the new theatre.

A SIX YEAR PERSPECTIVE ON INTENSIVE CARE AT THE ROYAL LONDON HOSPITAL

Stuart Withington, Gillian Bradbury, David Goldhill

Six years have seen a great many changes within Intensive Care at the Royal London Hospital. During this time three hospitals have merged, the Royal London, St Bartholomew's and the London Chest Hospital. The A&E department at St Bartholomew's has closed, main cardiac services are no longer situated at the Royal London, all neurosurgery is now based at the Royal London and a specialist helicopter based trauma service has been developed.

The Helicopter Emergency Medical Service (HEMS) and the opening of the Trauma Unit in July 1990, were a radical departure from existing trauma services and, as such, have been subjected to constant evaluation and review. By 1993, the Trauma Unit had evolved into a four bed HDU/ICU, with facilities for monitoring 4 patients and ventilating two (usually head-injured) patients. Patients were being admitted in increasing numbers and with increasing severity of injury and the existing capabilities of both the ICU and Trauma Unit were being stretched.

Trauma Unit Staffing and Management

In response to this increased demand a number of changes were required. Firstly, the Trauma Unit establishment of 13 nursing staff was increased to 25 with an emphasis on intensive care training (ENB 100) and experience. Secondly, more equipment was purchased (ventilators, more sophisticated monitoring, and infusion devices) to allow a fuller range of intensive care modalities at each of the four beds. Patients who were haemo-dynamically unstable, requiring renal replacement therapy, or constant medical presence, continued to be cared for in the ICU.

By 1993, nurses working on the Trauma Unit were regularly attending trauma calls in the A&E department in order to learn about trauma resuscitation and to plan for new patient admissions. They were also attending the Advanced Trauma Life Support Course as observers. What was required, however, was a greater understanding of the spectrum of trauma care.

The report of the Royal College of Surgeons (1988) stressed that the care of the most severely injured left a lot to be desired. There was also general acceptance that trauma care should be extended from the point of accident to rehabilitation, identified by Trunkey (1985) as the poor relation of trauma care. With these considerations in mind, the Senior Nurse (HEMS) and the Link

Figure 1: Patient numbers and bed days

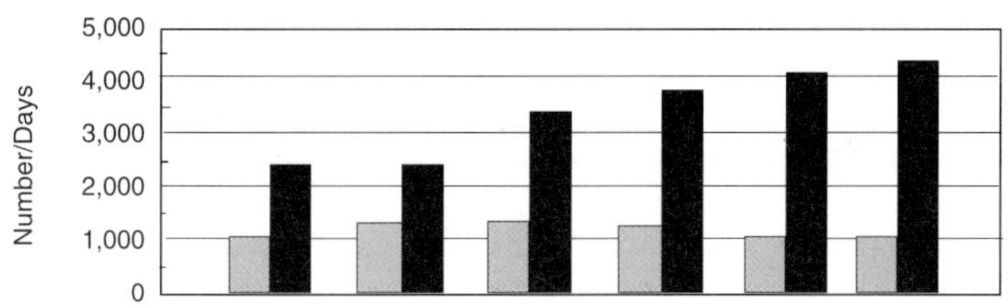

Year	1990	1991	1992	1993	1994	1995
Patient no.	975	1,082	1,345	1,314	1,039	997
Bed days	2,339	2,406	3,347	3,949	4,114	4,203

Figure 2

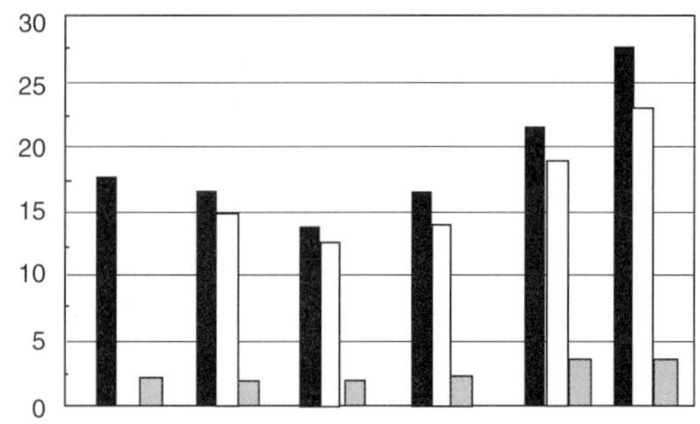

Year	1990	1991	1992	1993	1994	1995
Hospital Mortality %	18.4	16.1	13.5	16.1	20.9	27.1
Risk of Death % (Apache II)		15	12	14	19	23
Mean Stay (days)	2.4	2.2	2.4	3	3.9	4.2

Tutor from the College of Nursing and Midwifery, began collaboration on the development of a course in Trauma Nursing.

For doctors, nurses and paramedics there are the Advanced Trauma Life Support Course (ATLS), the Advanced Trauma Nursing Course (ATNC) and the Trauma Nurse Core Course (TNCC), all of which are aimed at the initial treatment and transfer of the injured patient. They do not, however, address subsequent care. What was required was a holistic, multidisciplinary approach to trauma, taking into account the requirements of individuals from 'the roadside to rehabilitation'. In addition, the larger issues of accident prevention, economics, health promotion, communication, and rehabilitation were to be addressed. In October 1995, the first group of students were admitted to the Trauma Care Course at City University (St Bartholomew's College of Nursing and Midwifery). This unique Level 3 course of two 12 week modules has been endorsed by the English National Board (ENB) as the A86, and is part of the BSc (Hons) Nursing Pathway within the ENB higher award and forms the clinical speciality branch. The result of this course will be the development of a growing number of Trauma Nurse Specialists whose expertise may be utilised in any phase of trauma care throughout the country.

Finally, in April 1995, the Anaesthetic Consultants of the Intensive Care Unit undertook the overall coordination of the critical care phase of Trauma Care. In December 1995, the Trauma Unit formally merged with the Intensive Care Unit. The nursing staffs were combined with the creation of eight nursing teams each led by a G Grade Sister/ Charge Nurse. The Trauma Unit nurses were divided among the eight teams, thus distributing their expertise. Evaluation of this merger is ongoing and issues arising out of this organisational change are constantly being addressed.

The future of trauma care provides many challenges for nurses, not the least of which is to develop their expertise and to make an impact not only on the quality of care given to those patients unfortunate enough to have been injured, but also on the prevention of accidents. The first group of nurses to complete the **Trauma Care Course** have identified a number of areas for attention: bicycle helmets, child restraint systems in cars, child road safety, pedestrian safety in the tourist population, and airbag safety issues. The next step is to make contact with the larger community and start the process of collaboration with the potential recipients of our care.

Figure 3: Trauma Admissions to Intensive Care

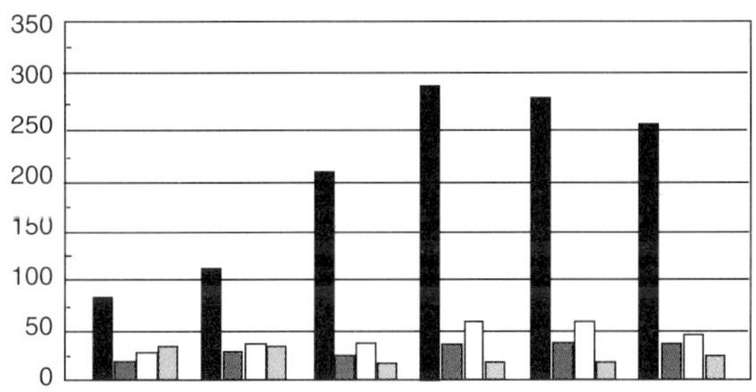

Year	1990	1991	1992	1993	1994	1995
■ Patient Number	85	106	211	295	284	262
■ ICU Deaths	19	31	26	37	42	36
□ Hospital Deaths	24	39	39	52	52	47
□ Hospital Mortality %	28.2	36.7	18.4	17.6	18.3	17.9

Figure 4: Isolated Head Injuries

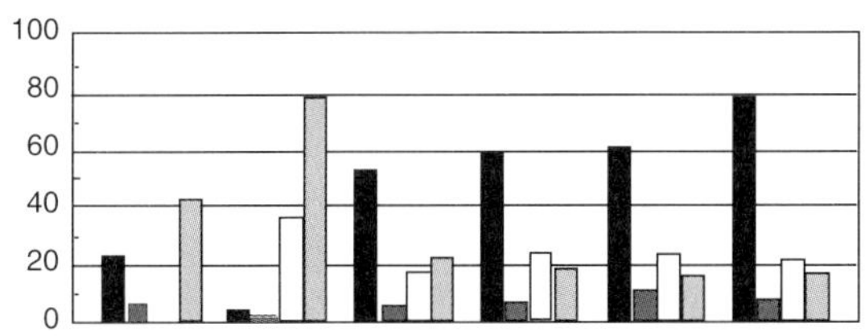

Year	1990	1991	1992	1993	1994	1995
■ Patient Number	21	5	53	60	62	80
■ ICU Stay (Days)	3	1.6	3.5	4	9.3	5.2
□ Risk of Death % (APACHE II)		35	18	21	23	21
□ Hospital Mortality %	42.8	80	22.6	20	17.7	18.7

Workload

All the figures shown represent data collected over a six year period for both ICU and Trauma Units.

As can be seen in Figure 1 there has been an increasing workload in terms of bed days provided, the large increase between 1991 and 1992 represents the opening of the Trauma Unit. Patient numbers reached a peak in 1992. Since then there have been several outbreaks of a new MRSA strain which has restricted admissions and routine post-surgical admissions (mainly cardiac surgery) have declined.

Patient Population

As the patient population has been changing, so has the APACHE II risk of death, hospital mortality and length of ICU stay. Compared to 1992 the ICU is treating fewer patients, they have a higher risk of death and mortality and are staying in Intensive Care for longer. These changes are illustrated in Figure 2.

The main explanation for the changing ICU pattern has been a reduction in the number of low risk post-surgical patients and an increase in the number of high risk emergency admissions. To a large extent this has been an increase in the volume of trauma victims being admitted This is shown in Figure 3.

Trauma Services

With the development of a specialist trauma service the number of trauma admissions has dramatically increased from less than 100 in 1990 to nearly 300 in 1993. Since this time the number of admissions has plateaued. This plateau partly reflects saturation of current Intensive Care resources and partly the relatively static level of major trauma throughout the capital.

Of note in these figures is the trend to improving hospital mortality with the introduction of a specialist trauma service.

This trend to improved overall survival rate for trauma victims is also echoed in the figures for isolated head injuries. This is shown in Figure 4.

Apart from 1991, where there is obviously incomplete data, some interesting trends can be seen. There has been a steady increase in the number of isolated head injuries being admitted to Intensive Care. The length of stay of these patients has been generally increasing possibly reflecting a more aggressive treatment policy. Along with these changes there has been an improvement in the standardised mortality ratio (Hospital Mortality/Risk of Death) as calculated by the APACHE II scoring system.

Summary

1. Intensive Care activity reflects general hospital activity and is heavily dependent on resource availability.
2. Changing patterns of care are needed to cope with changing patterns of patient referrals.
3. The establishment of a specialist trauma service relies heavily on the provision of adequate Intensive Care.
4. With increasing numbers of patients the quality of care as judged by hospital survival improves thus justifying the establishment of specialist trauma services.

Dr Stuart Withington is a Consultant Anaesthetist at the RLH and in charge of the ICU and Trauma Unit.

Sister Gillian Bradbury is Canadian and trained in the USA. After being in charge of the separate Trauma Unit, she is now head of the combined ICU and Trauma Unit.

Dr David Goldhill is a Consultant Anaesthetist at the RLH and Senior Lecturer on the Academic Unit with responsibilities for the ICU.

A Textbook of Intensive Care, edited by Dr Goldhill and Dr Withington will be published by Chapman Hall, London, in Autumn 1996. ISBN 0 412 601 303.

SECTION 8: ESSENTIAL DEPARTMENTS AT THE RLH

Introduction

Richard Earlam

In the introduction to Section 6 Tim Coats emphasises the importance of the Rettungskette or life-saving chain of events in pre-hospital care. The importance of each link in the chain and the fact that each and every link is vital otherwise the remainder of the broken chain is useless becomes the essence of this analogy. Similarly in-hospital treatment of a patient depends on many people rather than just one. Hospital treatment therefore requires a different analogy, so probably the best is that of an orchestra where each instrument player is important and an expert, but somebody has to start them off at the same time, hoping that they will also finish together at the end. The conductor is not necessarily the best musician, but he must respect the other's expertise and also earn respect. This is especially so with the urgent events of a Trauma Team resuscitation where priorities must be established by a conductor. The analogy of a football referee is of no use at all because colleagues take no notice of yellow or red cards. Therefore this section contains summaries from the essential departments and it is no mistake and not due to alphabetical correctness that Anaesthesia commences.

Some centres have developed with trauma surgeons who only specialise in all the aspects of trauma operations perhaps performing neurosurgery as well as orthopaedic and general surgery. However a policy decision was made early on to leave each specialist surgeon in charge of what he did best. The majority have a so called elective and an emergency component of their workload which splits 50:50 so this does not involve them in anything new. Multiple trauma can be single system, e.g head injury only, or multiple system but it is important to realise that a severely injured patient must have all systems examined before the designation of a single system injury can be diagnosed by exclusion. This requires a conductor – the generalist. When there are multiple injuries, simultaneous operations or procedures can be done together but priorities may have to be established. This requires a conductor, a referee or an impressario trained to place prima donnas on the stage for a Royal Variety Performance. We also have a policy that patients must, if possible, remain anonymous just like the surgeons and the best person to talk to the press should be anonymous who reads out a report to the press stumbling over the long words.

This section lists the essential departments with the exception of one vital group not given a separate heading here, but for all specialties nursing care is an integral and essential part of care. Simply expressed it must be emphasised that without nurses no doctor is of any use alone in hospital. Nurse training is described by Jill Williams in Section 10B, the emergency theatres by Helen Davis in Section 7E and the Intensive Care Unit in Section 7F by Gillian Bradbury and the anaesthetic consultants.

The form below is entitled the Trauma Patient Injury List and is used to integrate the different specialties. They are listed under the anatomical headings of the Abbreviated Injury Scale (AIS) which is then used to measure ISS. This form is used as a summary form in the emergency room which designates the consultant-in-charge of each of the different anatomical injuries all of whom have to be coordinated. With subsequent care on the ward the nurses can then obtain advice from each of these separate teams, each with a consultant-in-charge. If their teams visit the patient without writing in the notes that visit is called a social call of no nursing importance at all.

Trauma Patient Injury List

Name:
Number:
Date of Birth:
(or affix patient label)

Admitting General Surgeon:
Admission Date: Time:
Helicopter Patient: Yes/No
Cause of Injury:

Anatomical Region	Injury	Consultant
1. Head		Neurosurgery
2. Face		Maxillofacial
3. Neck		Neurosurgery or orthopaedic
4. Thorax		Thoracic or general surgery
5. Abdomen/ Pelvic Contents		General Surgery
6. Spine		Neurosurgery or orthopaedic
7. Upper limbs		Orthopaedic
8. Lower Limbs Bony pelvis		Orthopaedic, vascular general or plastic
9. External		Orthopaedic, general or plastic
Complications	Intubated and ventilated or Intensive Care Unit	Anaesthetics

THE ANAESTHETIC DEPARTMENT

Marie Healy, Peter Colvin

Introduction

The department of anaesthesia plays a major role in the management of all patients admitted to the Royal London Hospital (RLH) following significant trauma. HEMS has had a major impact on the nature and volume of clinical work undertaken by the department, and has presented us with an ideal opportunity to develop an efficient, well-trained, highly motivated, enthusiastic group of anaesthetic trainees and consultants to meet this challenge. Trauma, by its very nature, is unpredictable and therefore careful planning is needed to ensure that all patients receive optimum care to ensure the best possible outcome. This involves a multidisciplinary team approach where each person is familiar with their role and that of other team members to provide an organised, efficient response and avoid conflict. Senior personnel are required to deal with the diversity of complex clinical scenarios that may occur following blunt or penetrating trauma in adult or paediatric patients.

Twenty four hour cover by skilled anaesthetic personnel is immediately available for the initial resuscitation and stabilisation of all trauma patients admitted to the A&E department. The anaesthetist accompanies all patients who are intubated and ventilated and those with any evidence of airway, ventilatory or haemodynamic compromise to ensure their safe transfer for diagnostic radiology including CT and MRI scanning and angiography. In addition to the provision of anaesthesia the anaesthetist must continue to resuscitate and re-evaluate patients who require surgical intervention in the operating theatre. These patients may require the attention of different surgical teams simultaneously or in order of priority and many will need repeated anaesthetics for subsequent procedures. The clinical management of patients admitted to the intensive care unit (ICU) is under the direction of the anaesthetic department as is the acute pain relief team.

The Anaesthetic Department

The Anaesthetic Directorate of the Royal Hospitals Trust has 46 consultant anaesthetists, many of whom work between the different sites (the Royal London Hospital, St Bartholomew's Hospital, the London Chest Hospital and Queen Elizabeth Hospital for Children). The anaesthetic senior registrar and registrar rotations based at the Royal London and St Bartholomew's Hospitals were amalgamated to form the Royal Hospitals London School of Anaesthesia following the introduction of the Specialist Registrar (SpR) training grade in anaesthesia. The school has responsibility for training 90 SpRs in the North Thames East region. Twenty consultant anaesthetists, 8 senior registrars, 7 registrars (i.e 15 SpRs) and 8 senior house officers based at the RLH. Of the 11 theatres in the main theatre complex, two are designated for emergency work at any one time. This excludes the orthopaedic trauma theatre where eight lists are undertaken per week.

Organisation and Workload of the Anaesthetic Team

At the RLH the ICU registrar or senior registrar attends all trauma calls. An operating department assistant (ODA) also attends all calls to provide skilled technical support. A consultant anaesthetist, with a special interest in trauma, attends trauma calls on weekday afternoons to provide training, supervision and support. At other times consultant cover is provided either by the consultant anaesthetist on call for ICU or for emergency theatre. In 20% of cases a second anaesthetist is needed to manage unstable patients with multiple injuries or those with special needs such as paediatric patients. The anaesthetist and ODA remain with the patient until the patient is admitted to the operating theatre or ICU unless a decision is made, after consultation with the team leader, that anaesthetic support is no longer necessary.

In 1995 the anaesthetic department attended 320 HEMS and 80 non-HEMS calls. The average duration of anaesthetic input in the resuscitation room and diagnostic radiology was two hours per call prior to the introduction of the spiral CT scanner. Prolonged periods spent in isolated sites such as diagnostic radiology pose a particular hazard to patients in terms of adverse or critical incidents. The spiral CT scanner has significantly reduced this time and has the added advantage of being located in the A&E department.

Over 50 % of patients admitted via HEMS require surgery. The average time spent in the operating theatre is over four hours per patient who requires surgical intervention. This involves an average of over 500 hours of operating time per annum. Many of the patients require input from different surgical teams and have multiple operations.

The clinical management of patients admitted to the ICU at the RLH is directed by a team of six consultant anaesthetists. There are approximately 1000 admissions to our ICU per year although this figure is constantly changing due the rationalisation of services between different sites in our Trust. Approximately 25% of admissions aretrauma related and these admissions account for about 35% of the ICU bed occupancy.

Clinical Responsibilities of the Anaesthetic Team

(i) *Provision and maintenance of a secure airway with control of the cervical spine.*

Approximately 35% of HEMS admissions are already intubated and anaesthetised. Those who require urgent intubation are anaesthetised using a modified rapid sequence induction with manual in-line stabilisation of the cervical spine. In the trauma patient induction of anaesthesia and intubation may be particularly difficult in the presence of a full stomach, cervical spine immobilisation, anatomical distortion and haemorrhage from maxillofacial injuries, persistent hypoxaemia or haemodynamic instability. In less urgent situations, those with known unstable cervical spine injuries may be intubated awake with a fibre-optic bronchoscope using topical anaesthesia. Adequacy of oxygenation and ventilation must be continually reassessed. Advanced ventilatory techniques that may occasionally be required include independent and one lung ventilation.

(ii) *Assessment of the circulation and maintenance of haemodynamic stability*

Anaesthetists have particular expertise in resuscitating patients with shock due to the nature of their day to day work in intensive care and the operating theatre. They play a pivotal role in ensuring that diagnostic and therapeutic interventions are undertaken in a timely and systematic manner most appropriate to individual patient needs. This is particularly important in treating patients with multiple injuries from blunt trauma such as those with combined head and abdominal, chest, pelvic or long bone injuries. These patients may spend prolonged periods in surgery but will sometimes require numerous transfers for imaging and other interventions before transfer to ICU. Therefore the ICU must be taken to the patient.

Although acute haemorrhage is the most common cause of shock in trauma victims continued vigilance is required to detect occult or evolving injuries that may be contributing to the shock state. The anaesthetist is responsible for establishing arterial and central venous pressure monitoring, large bore central venous access, optimising fluid, blood and blood component transfusion and inotropic therapy, when indicated. The anaesthetist must continue to re-assess and monitor the response to therapeutic interventions and maintain haemodynamic, metabolic and haemostatic stability. Frequent blood gas, lactate, haematocrit and coagulation studies are required to assess tissue perfusion and haemostatic competence. Active measures must be undertaken to maintain core temperature >35°C. The management of massive transfusion is discussed in Section 8 J.

(iii) *Provision of analgesia and anaesthesia*

This must be tailored to take into account individual patient needs depending on the urgency, location, age, coexistent medical conditions, adequacy of resuscitation and the nature of the injuries sustained.

(iv) *Other*

When anaesthetised patients leave the resuscitation room the anaesthetist takes full responsibility for coordinating all aspects of patient care.

The anaesthetist is generally in an ideal position to ensure that communication with the patient is maintained, if the patient is not already intubated, and to take a full medical history.

In the resuscitation room department the neurosurgical SHO acts as a scribe and documents vital signs, interventions and results of baseline tests. This task is usually undertaken by the anaesthetist once the patient leaves the A&E department as it is vital that accurate records are kept for medicolegal purposes and audit. The anaesthetist is also responsible for ensuring that the spinal immobilisation is maintained at all times during resuscitation and transfer in patients who may have unstable injuries. All anaesthetic personnel are called when a major incident is declared. We regularly review the hospital major incident protocol so that staff are familiar with their roles when such an event occurs.

Developments in the Anaesthetics Directorate

In the department of anaesthesia there have been three new consultant appointments, with a special interest in trauma, over the last two years. One of these is a senior lecturer who has a particular interest in paediatric trauma and ICU. These consultants take responsibility for the education and supervision of trainees and ODAS, the organisation of trauma-related audit and research, the provision, updating and maintenance of resuscitation and monitoring equipment.

On 1st April 1995 the trauma unit was amalgamated with the ICU where the care of all patients is directed by the ICU consultant anaesthetist on call for the week. This has led to an increase in the number of potential ICU bed spaces from 13 to 17, and has facilitated closer links between the anaesthetic department and other specialists involved in trauma care.

A new senior ODA post has been created with a special interest in acute trauma and cardiac resuscitation. The senior ODA attends all trauma and cardiac arrest calls each morning and does a formal handover to their on-call colleague at 13.00hrs. This ODA checks each resuscitation bay in the A&E department every morning to ensure that the full range of stock for intubation, ventilation, invasive monitoring and high volume transfusion is immediately available for all age groups as required. Checks are also undertaken in the CT, MRI and angiography suites. This senior post was created to facilitate communication with other senior paramedical staff and to coordinate training of all ODAs attending the A&E department.

Training and Education

Advanced Trauma Life Support (ATLS) principles provide an ideal framework for the initial training of all staff involved in trauma care. We hold a minimum of 4 ATLS courses and one Advanced Trauma Nursing Course at the RLH each year. The majority of our consultant staff and specialist registrars have obtained ATLS certification and we have six ATLS instructors in our department. Each new registrar is encouraged to complete an ATLS course as soon as a place is available. Many of the senior ICU and A&E nursing staff and ODAs have completed ATLS observer courses.

The anaesthetics unit (Academic Department) convened our first national trauma and intensive care study day at the RLH in March 1996 and we hope to host similar meetings annually. The ICU nursing staff have organised annual national trauma nursing study days and annual paediatric trauma study days over the last two years.

The department of anaesthesia and intensive care hosts a multidisciplinary trauma meeting each week where individual cases are discussed and reviewed and trauma related topics are presented by anaesthetic and surgical colleagues.

The anaesthetic department provides training in resuscitation and pre-hospital anaesthesia for new non-anaesthetic HEMS registrars with limited experience in this area. In addition each HEMS registrar rotates to the ICU for six weeks during each six month post.

Recently two of the HEMS registrar posts have been formally linked with our School of Anaesthesia. The addition of these HEMS posts to our training programme compliments the training already available for our SpRs with a special interest in major trauma, resuscitation and intensive care.

Conclusion

The department of anaesthesia has evolved considerably, since HEMS began operations, to attempt to provide the best possible care for major trauma victims, We are closely involved in the pre-hospital phase, play an integral part in the resuscitation and definitive care and direct the intensive care management of all patients. Anaesthetists are therefore in an ideal position to ensure continuity of care for each patient and must be actively involved in coordinating the care provided by different surgical specialties.

Marie Healy is Consultant in Anaesthesia and Intensive at the Royal London Hospital.

Peter Colvin is the Clinical Director of Anaesthetic Services.

NUTS AND BOLTS – HEAD INJURY MANAGEMENT IN THE HEMS SYSTEM

Julia Harris, Tim Coats

Head injury is an important component of multiple injury and the commonest cause of in-hospital trauma death. Therefore, head injury management is a vital part of treatment within the HEMS system.

Of patients admitted to the Royal London Hospital 50% have a major head or spinal injury, so it is essential to have early neurosurgical involvement in patient assessment and treatment. The neurosurgical senior house officer is always a member of the trauma team at the Royal London Hospital. Their role is both to act as clerk for the trauma team and as the 'eyes and ears' of neurosurgery, obtaining senior neurosurgical opinion at an early stage.

The neurosurgical SHO obtains an accurate history of the incident from the HEMS crew whilst the trauma team begin the initial assessment of the patient, providing an ideal opportunity to clarify details – for example, the exact composition of the components of the Glasgow Coma Score recorded at the incident scene. During the resuscitation, the neurosurgical SHO documents the examination that is performed by the surgical registrar, and records the patient's observations, investigations performed, treatment given and subsequent progress. The neurosurgical SHO is also on hand to perform a comprehensive neurological assessment of the patient, or a rapid evaluation before induction if an emergency room anaesthetic is given.

If senior staff presence in the Accident and Emergency department is required, the neurosurgical SHO is able to alert the neurosurgical registrar at an early stage. Senior input at this phase may be vital, especially in making decisions about the priority of CT scanning or neurosurgery above other investigations and treatment that the multiply injured patient will require. A typical example is the casualty who is haemodynamically stable, has localising neurological signs, a negative abdominal ultrasound, but definite indications for a diagnostic peritoneal lavage (DPL). In this case it is appropriate for the patient to go immediately to the CT scanner rather than have a DPL performed in the resuscitation room. Definitive neurosurgical intervention can then take place in theatre, with the DPL being performed whilst the patient is on the table. Senior neurosurgical involvement is required at an early stage to assist with such decisions between conflicting priorities.

When a CT brain scan is performed the neurosurgical SHO will accompany the patient, ensuring the early detection of any changes in clinical status and continuing documentation. If it becomes apparent on the CT scan that the patient requires surgery, they can organise immediate transfer of the patient to the operating theatre.

The aim of the trauma team is to spend less than 40 minutes in the emergency room before transfer for scanning. CT scan included, it is expected that definitive neurosurgical intervention will be performed within 90 minutes of arrival at the hospital. It is well known that time from injury to operative intervention is a crucial factor in determining outcome after head injury.

HEMS is able to record physiological data from the time of arrival of the medical team at the incident scene, providing an opportunity to carry out research on the factors that may influence outcome following head injury. All patients are followed up and disability scoring performed at discharge, three months and one year following injury. The early involvement of the neurosurgical team has allowed participation in international trials for new therapies in head injury, particularly neuroprotective agents.

Most patients with severe head injury do not require neurosurgery (because most have diffuse injuries rather than haematomas), but all require neuro-intensive care. This is a specialised field that is rapidly developing. Until recently, control of intracranial pressure has been the focus of treatment of diffuse brain injury. However better outcomes are obtained if treatment is directed at maintaining cerebral perfusion pressure. This change reflects a growing understanding of the importance of cerebral perfusion that has been stimulated by new methods of cerebral monitoring. Techniques such as Transcranial Doppler (TCD), near-infrared spectroscopy (NIRS), cerebral function monitoring (CFAM), measurement of jugular venous oxygen saturation, direct measurement of brain tissue oxygenation, and invasive measurement of intracranial pressure (ICP) are allowing the development of treatment protocols specifically directed to the optimisation of brain blood flow. This multi-modality monitoring of the brain requires the patient to be treated in a neuro-intensive care unit, in a specialist neurosurgical unit.

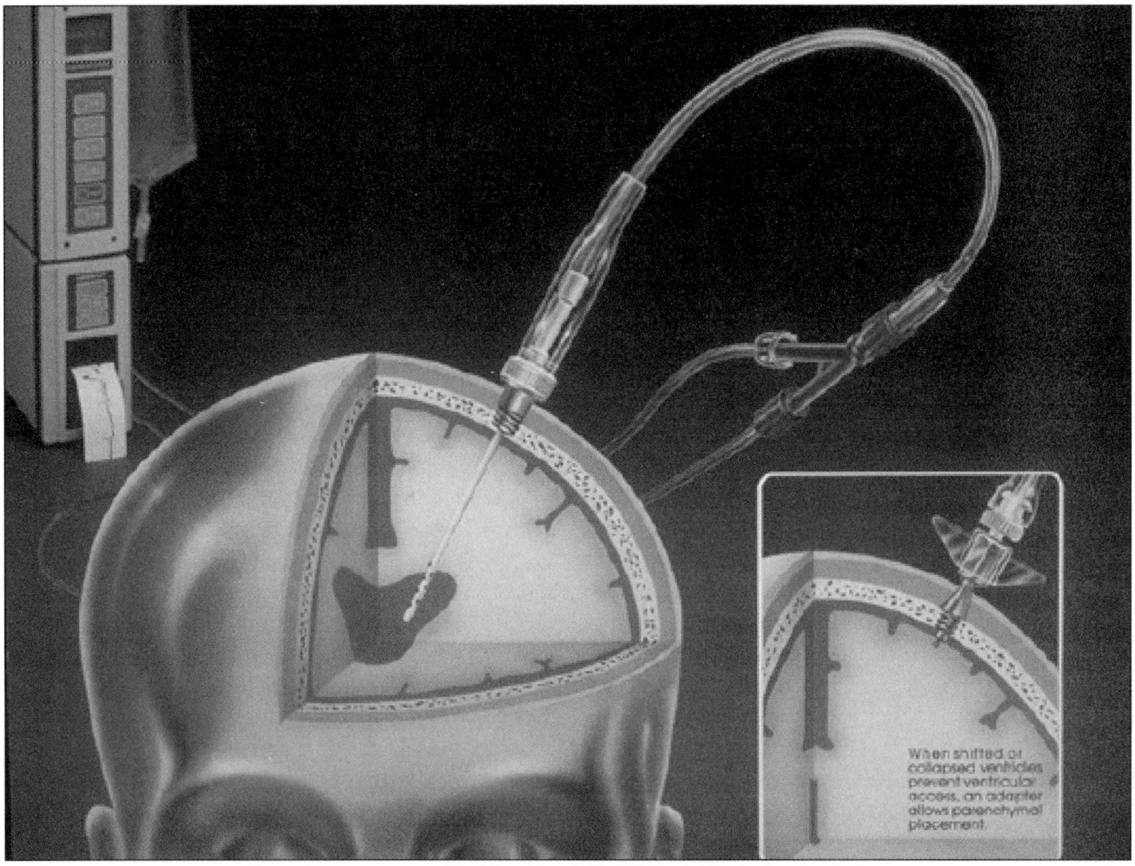

Invasive measurement of intracranial pressure using a Camino bolt

Modern management of patients after severe head injury is directed to maximisation of cerebral perfusion pressure (CPP) rather than reduction of intracranial pressure (ICP). Accurate measurement of ICP is still required. There is not a non-invasive method, so an intracranial pressure bolt is required. Severe head injury cannot be adequately treated without this type of monitoring. Bolts can measure pressure within a number of intracranial spaces. The HEMS trauma system uses Camino micro-ventricular pressure bolts which have the dual advantage of accurate reading and the ability to drain cerebro-spinal fluid.

The early rehabilitation of patients with neurological injury is vital to the long term recovery of such patients. The Royal London Hospital has a dedicated trauma physiotherapy service, supported by the active involvement of the neurophysiotherapists. The aim is the early neuro-rehabilitation of patients and the prevention of the adverse effects of multiple injury on neurological recovery. Patients are then transferred to a specialist rehabilitation centre when their clinical condition allows.

The Future

The best outcome after head injury is obtained by avoiding secondary insults to the injured brain and reducing the time between injury and definitive intervention. The basis of our care is that the damage resulting from a head blow, such as hypoxia, blood loss and raised intracranial pressure, all of which can be treated in the early emergency phase. The present integral nature of the HEMS/Neurosurgical care will therefore continue. The recent acquisition of a rapid spiral CT scanner in the A&E department, taking only twenty seconds to perform a whole CT head scan, will reduce the time between injury and definitive intervention, and it is anticipated that this will further improve outcomes.

The department of neurosurgery has a senior research nurse and a clinical research fellow who are involved in the continuing follow-up of HEMS patients and the development of multi-modality neurophysiological monitoring. Patients cared for by the HEMS system benefit from early specialist assessment and intervention with modern intensive neurosurgical treatment and monitoring. The early access and monitoring of the patient enables studies to be performed that may resolve some of the current controversies in head injury management.

***Acknowledgements**

Camino Laboratories, 5955 Pacific Center Blvd, San Diego, California 92121, USA.

Julia Harris, past Neurosurgical Registrar, Royal London Hospital, is now Senior Registrar in Accident and Emergency, St Mary's/Bedford Rotation.

Tim Coats, Emeritus HEMS Registrar, Research Fellow in Neurosurgery and Senior Lecturer in A&E department, RLH.

NAILS AND SCREWS – DEPARTMENT OF ORTHOPAEDIC AND TRAUMA SURGERY

Mark Paterson

Seventy per cent of the patients evacuated to the Royal London Hospital by HEMS have a significant musculoskeletal injury which requires the services of the Department of Orthopaedic and Trauma Surgery. Of these, about half have injuries in other systems which will involve other specialties, such as neurosurgery, vascular and general surgery, maxillofacial surgery and plastic surgery.

Of course, we have always been responsible for looking after patients with fractures, dislocations and other musculoskeletal injuries. Some of our patients have had many fractures, and the concept of the multiply-injured patient is one which was familiar to us before helicopters started to land on the roof of the hospital. The arrival of HEMS, however, has brought about a major change in the way musculoskeletal trauma is managed. In many ways, it has acted as a catalyst for much-needed reforms in the organisation of orthopaedic trauma. For example, before HEMS started, the concept of daily orthopaedic trauma lists was considered by many to be an unnecessary luxury. Many fractures were dealt with during the night by relatively junior orthopaedic and anaesthetic staff, simply because there was no time for these cases on routine lists during the day. HEMS emphasised the necessity for severe trauma to be managed promptly by experienced personnel. All orthopaedic consultants and senior registrars obtained the ATLS certification, daily trauma lists were instituted, and the department was organised in such a way as to enable senior staff to be available at all times.

Figure 1

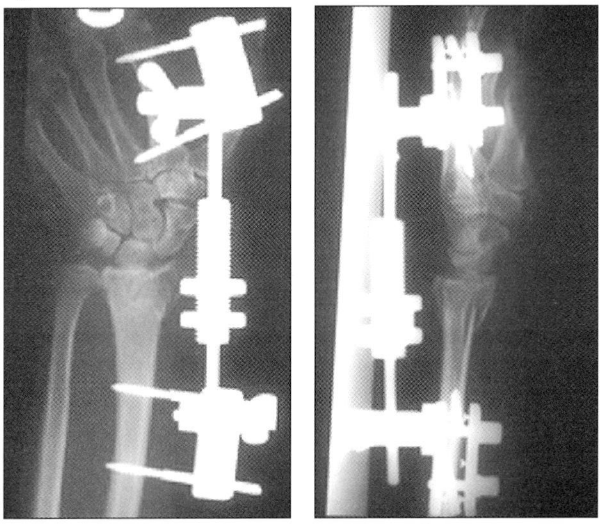

Photo: author

Traditionally, single fractures have often been treated by non-operative means, such as traction apparatus or casts. We have discovered that the patient who has suffered multiple injuries may well do better if his or her fractures are more rigidly fixed, either by so-called internal or external fixation. Stabilisation of fractures in this way greatly eases the task of others taking care of the injured person; nurses are able to move the patient safely and comfortably, plastic surgeons can retain access to soft tissues for inspection and treatment, and a confused, restless patient recovering from a head injury is less likely to injure himself further. In addition, there is now good evidence to show that if fractures are stabilised in this way, there is less risk of overwhelming respiratory complications in the polytrauma patient. This is because early fixation reduces the quantity of fat particles and other products of injured tissues in the bloodstream. Finally, some patients arriving via HEMS have devastating limb injuries which include damage to blood vessels and nerves; it is essential to have skeletal stability before delicate repair work on these structures is undertaken.

One of the simplest and quickest means of achieving a firm fixation is to apply an external fixator. After the fractured bone has been realigned, metal pins are drilled through the skin and soft tissues into the fractured bone and these pins are bolted to a frame lying alongside the affected part (Figure 1). One advantage of this kind of fixation is that the position can be changed relatively easily if the alignment needs to be improved. The frame or bar can be placed so that it does not interfere with access to the surrounding soft tissues. It is difficult to think of a bone which has not at some time had an external fixator applied. We commonly use fixators on all long bones, including the bones of the fingers. Pelvic fractures may be another indication for the use of an external fixator; this is an important indication which merits separate consideration.

Internal fixation means having to perform a surgical operation, but it does not necessarily involve exposing the fracture site. Sophisticated techniques have been developed which allow us to introduce strong metal rods along the internal medullary cavity and across fracture sites of long bones such as the femur and tibia

Figure 2

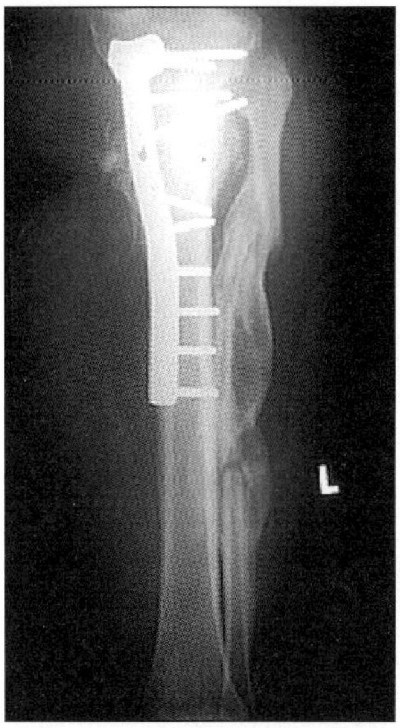

Photo: author

(Figure 2). These procedures require radiographic image intensification and a considerable degree of skill in order to manoeuvre the nail into the right position and lock it in place. Techniques such as this must be learnt by all orthopaedic trainees, and we are fortunate that Smith and Nephew have sponsored an Orthopaedic Bioskills Laboratory in our department, where trainees can practice their fixation skills on artificial bones in complete safety!

Although the femur and tibia are the bones most commonly stabilised in this way, the same technique is sometimes used for the humerus, and a similar principle is used for stabilising other smaller bones. Advantages include the ability to mobilise without the need for external casts or other supports, and this enables adjacent joints to retain a good range of movement. Until recently, these techniques were not thought suitable for use in open fractures with contamination, as the risk of introducing infection into the depths of the bone was considered to be unacceptably high. However, we now know that immediate and meticulous cleaning of the wound, with removal of all non-viable tissue (a procedure known as debridement), allows an intramedullary nailing technique to be used with confidence.

Established internal fixation techniques such as plate and screw fixation are still widely used (Figure 3). However, we have to be very careful to ensure that when we plate a fracture we do not create an unacceptable degree of additional damage to the bone and surrounding tissues. In order to heal, fractures need a good blood supply. They also need to be surrounded by those tissues which are going to supply them with the cells and materials for healing to take place. It is all too easy to strip away these necessary components in an enthusiastic attempt to obtain a secure fixation of the bone fragments. This may make the post-operative x-ray look good, but it will do nothing to improve the chances of the fracture healing.

During 1991-93 we used more external fixation devices than intramedullary nails.

This ratio has been reversed since 1994, as the indications for nailing have widened, reflecting our increasing experience and confidence. On average, we are now inserting three intramedullary nails each week, and placing one to two external fixators in the same time.

The increasing use of fracture fixation techniques such as these means that patients are no longer confined to bed by their injuries for weeks or even months. Although this is clearly good news for all patients, it is particularly important for those patients who have unfortunately sustained a head injury in addition to their skeletal injuries, in whom early mobilisation is an essential part of their rehabilitation. The disadvantages include the high cost of the implants, the technical difficulty in performing the surgery, and the consequences of complications such as infection.

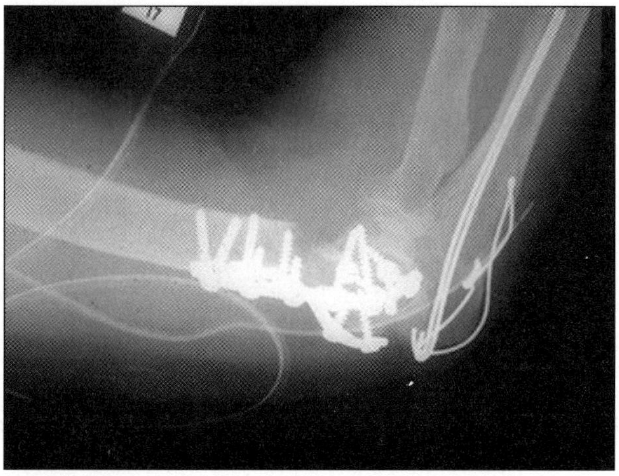

Photo: author

Figure 3

The principles of orthopaedic management in the care of the multiply-injured patient could be summarised as follows:

- aggressive debridement of open fractures
- early stabilisation of fractures
- close cooperation with other surgical specialties
- early mobilisation.

J Mark H Paterson FRCS is Head of Service of the Department of Orthopaedic and Trauma Surgery at the Royal London Hospital.

FRACTURES OF THE PELVIS

David Goodier

The pelvis is a bony ring structure comprising the sacrum (the lowest part of the spinal column) and the paired innominate bones joined to the sacrum posteriorly at the sacroiliac joints (SIJs) and each other anteriorly at the symphysis pubis.

The ring structure means that it cannot be broken at a single point without another part of the ring being involved (in the same way that a Polo mint cannot be broken in one place only).

Pelvic fractures can be divided into two major types: fractures of the acetabulum and fractures of the pelvic ring itself.

1. Acetabular Fractures

The acetabulum is the socket of the ball-and-socket that is the hip joint. It is lined with articular cartilage that is only 2mm thick in places and so a fracture that causes incongruity of 2mm or more will inevitably lead to abnormal wear and subsequent disabling arthritis of the hip joint. Prompt and accurate reduction of the bone fragments and internal fixation using plates and screws is the treatment of choice for displaced acetabular fractures, but this procedure is fraught with difficulty and requires an exceptionally high degree of operative skill and a surgical team familiar with the various fracture patterns. In the past such fractures were rare and tended to be referred to other institutions for treatment but the sheer volume of major injuries brought by the Helicopter Emergency Medical Service has allowed us to develop the skills necessary to treat the majority of these complex fractures.

2. Fractures of the Bony Ring

As far as anatomical reduction is concerned in fractures of the ring of the pelvis, this takes second place to the treatment of the associated injuries and complications inherent in such a severe injury.

The bony pelvis is a solid structure and the degree of violence necessary to cause a significant fracture is high; as such there are often synchronous injuries to other parts of the body that may be more immediately life threatening. In addition to this it must be considered that within the pelvis lie some major body parts such as the bladder, rectum and in women the uterus, as well as the major arteries, veins and nerves to these viscera and to the lower limbs. Any of these structures may be damaged in association with fractures of the pelvis and cause immediate threat literally to life and limb.

Haemorrhage

This is the most immediately life-threatening complication of pelvic fracture; a relatively minor fracture may cause the loss of half the circulating volume of blood, and the more severe injuries may cause rapid and complete exanguination despite aggressive transfusion.

The common iliac vessels divide to form the external and internal iliac vessels in front of the sacroiliac joints (a common site of injury) and these latter vessels provide multiple branches to the structures within the pelvis. Any of these vessels may be lacerated by bone fragments or literally torn apart by displacement of bones which themselves have a copious blood supply.

The key to reducing haemorrhage is early stabilisation of the pelvis where possible to allow blood to clot and so reduce further bleeding. As in most aspects of trauma care the earlier this is done the better – once a certain amount of blood has been lost, even if it is replaced by transfusion, the patient's own clotting factors will be diluted and clot will not form. The rapid transport of the patient to a centre where there is the expertise and facilities for dealing with this pathology is therefore vital.

The treatment of these injuries depends on the fracture pattern, which in turn depends on the severity and direction from which the impact was sustained. There are three main patterns of pelvic ring fracture and the treatment for each is different.

a) **Stable injuries**

In these there is minimal movement possible between the fragments so surgical stabilisation is not warranted.

b) **Rotationally unstable injuries**

These are further divided into :

i) External rotational injuries – this is the so-called 'open book' injury. The force is usually from the front and drives the iliac wings apart causing separation of the symphysis pubis anteriorly and hinging open of the sacroiliac joint posteriorly. Haemorrhage can be torrential from the common iliac vessels or their branches which are held open in front of the SIJ. The immediate treatment is to 'close the book' by bringing the iliac wings closer together and holding it closed. This may be done by a variety of methods such as plating across the symphysis pubis or, more commonly by constructing a simple anterior external fixator attached to pins driven into the iliac crests. This procedure may be undertaken in the resuscitation room but in keeping with the principle of 'taking the hospital to the patient' a belt with inflatable pressure pockets has been developed by staff in the Accident and Emergency department at the Royal London Hospital which may be applied at the scene of an accident and remain in place until definitive treatment is instituted.

Photo: Otto Chan

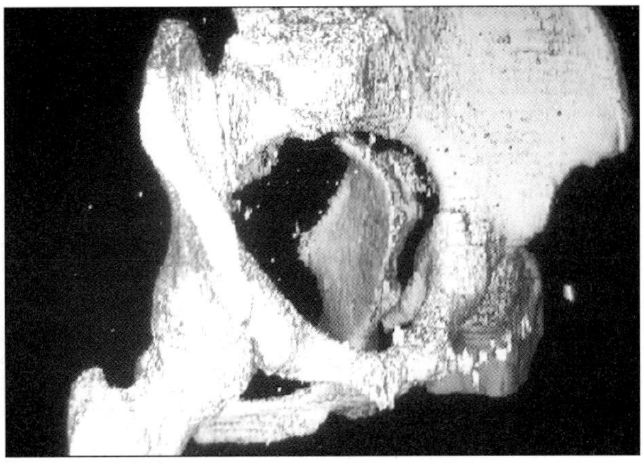

Figure 1: 3D CT showing fracture of left acetabulum

(ii) Internal rotation injuries – the 'stove in pelvis'. The force is from the side and the iliac wing is driven inwards causing fractures across the pubic rami anteriorly and either crushing in the sacrum or fracturing the iliac wing posteriorly.These injuries do cause significant haemorrhage but it is not likely to be controlled by simple methods such as the application of an external fixator unless the inward force is so severe as to force the opposite iliac wing outwards.

c) Translationally unstable injuries – in these the whole innominate bone has been detached from the rest of the pelvis and pushed either backwards (as an extension of the external rotation injury) or upwards (the vertical shear injury). Bleeding can be massive and difficult to control without securely fixing the innominate bone to the sacrum with screws etc as an anterior external fixator will not provide enough structural rigidity to control movement.

Figure 2: 3D CT of same patient. Inferior view showing acetabular separation

Photo: Otto Chan

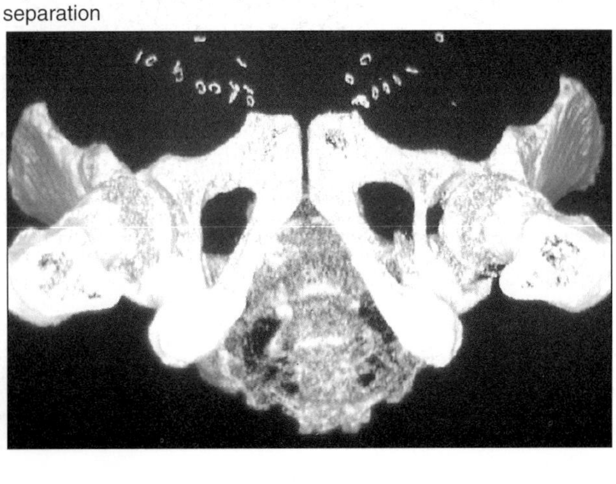

Other methods of haemorrhage control may be tried as an adjunct to these methods, most notably the use a radiologist familiar with interventional techniques to pass a catheter (under fluoroscopic control) into a bleeding vessel to create an embolus in it to stop the bleeding. With the equipment now available this can be done on the operating table in theatre if necessary.

Other Complications

As well as major bleeding, there are many other complications associated with fractures of the pelvis. The urinary bladder or the urethra may be lacerated or divided leading to extravasation of urine into the surrounding tissues which may in turn lead to potentially fatal sepsis.

Other viscera such as the rectum or vagina may also be lacerated; again if this goes unnoticed the consequences can be dire. These problems are only avoided by having a high index of suspicion and examining the patient with major trauma under the assumption that such injuries exist until evidence to the contrary exists.

The severity of these injuries is reflected in the statistics kept in the HEMS database: in the five years from 1991 to 1995 a total of 211 patients with pelvic fractures were treated, some 17% of HEMS patients. The average Injury Severity Score of these patients was 26, compared to 15 for HEMS patients as a whole, which is reflected in the mortality figures: 31% for patients with pelvic fractures, 20% for HEMS patients as a whole. A fractured pelvis is a dangerous injury.

Summary

Pelvic fractures can be rapidly fatal due to uncontrollable blood loss. They also act as a pointer to other trauma and life-threatening injuries because the kinetic energy involved is so high. The key to the management of the pelvic ring fracture is identifying the pattern of injury: this is itself a problem since the standard plain AP radiograph of the pelvis is often difficult to interpret even by experts and a CT scan used to be impossible in a briskly hemorrhaging patient. We are confident however that the recently installed Spiral CT scanner, actually in the A&E department itself, will alleviate these problems and allow us to 'fine tune' our management of this important injury.

David Goodier FRCS (Orth) is Senior Registrar in Trauma and Orthopaedic Surgery at the RLH.

MAXILLOFACIAL DEPARTMENT

Hugh Cannell, Peter Dyer

Maxillofacial injuries are classified as injuries either to the soft tissues or to the bones in an area extending from the forehead down to the collar bone. This means that almost any patient with injuries of the head or upper part of the body has maxillofacial injuries. These may include injuries that masquerade as a haematemesis, or cannot easily be seen because they are within the oral cavity. At the time of writing, of the 1172 HEMS cases about 222 had maxillofacial injuries. Only half had serious injuries but these were often so severe that they were life-threatening.

Maxillofacial injuries are normally dealt with at secondary survey according to the ATLS protocol. However, life-threatening injuries must be dealt with at once. The most common ones that threaten life are those which have affected the airway or have resulted in continuing haemorrhage.

The airway may be compromised in maxillofacial injuries under the following circumstances:

- Inhalation of loose teeth or fragments of bone.
- Loss of tongue control due to a comminuted fracture of the anterior part of the lower jaw.
- Displaced upper jaw which obliterates both the nasal and the oral airways. The airway may also be threatened by direct trauma to the soft tissues of the mouth, for example swelling of the tongue, or by direct damage to the airway passages – for example a fracture of the larynx.

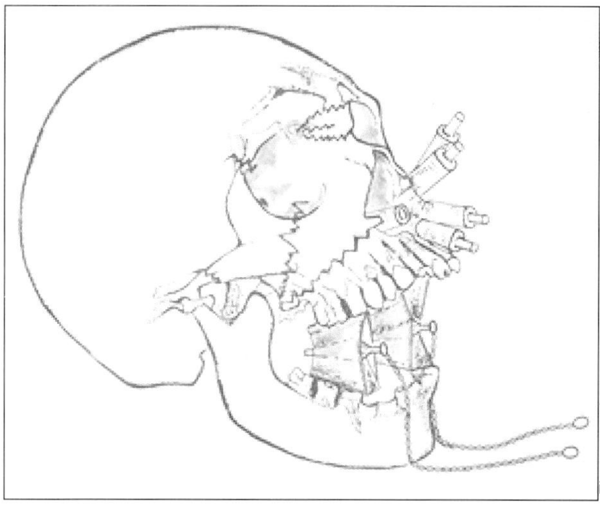

Figure: author

Figure 1: Insertion of nasal Epistats (shown below)

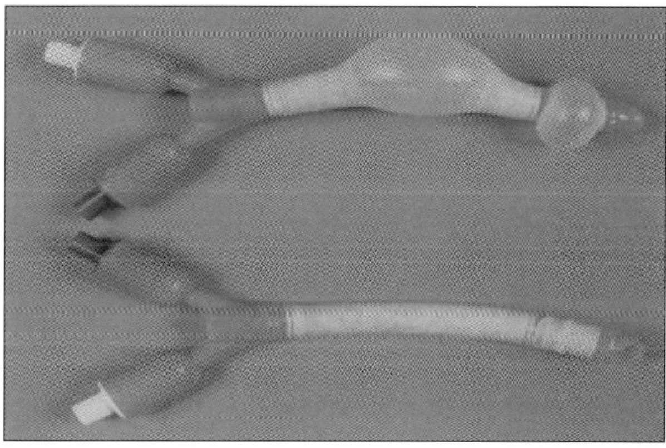

Photo: author

Haemorrhage from the oropharynx, mouth or nose may be life-threatening also. The risk of inhalation of blood is ever present in an unconscious patient and comminuted injuries to the face or gun shot wounds easily produce hypovolemia.

A useful development arising out of the arrival of multiply injured emergency patients from HEMS has been our technique for the emergency stabilisation of displaced facial bones. Many of these cases require urgent intervention due to airway embarrassment or haemorrhage. The technique is a simple one and derived from routine procedures with which many young doctors and dentists will be familiar. It is to bring forward and downwards a posteriorly displaced maxilla and then temporarily to stabilise the fracture. This is done by the insertion of two rubber mouth props wedged posteriorly as far as possible in whatever remains of the dental arches. The floating maxilla thus can be pushed firmly into its correct position and held there by an upwards force towards the anterior part of the skull. After this has been done, nasal epistats of the double rubber bulb type (*Epistats*, Xomed UK Ltd) are inserted through the nose. The rubber bulbs are then inflated with normal saline or sterile water, first posteriorly so as to occlude the top of the nasopharynx, and then in the nasal airway using the longer rubber bulbs. The bulbs exert a considerable downwards force. Thus the upward pressure exerted by the props wedged between the teeth, or the remnants of the teeth, forces the maxilla into its correct position, but allows the local pressure forces produced by the nasal epistats to control haemorrhage (Figure 1). The technique has now been widely adopted by accident teams and is taught as part of first aid to primary health care workers.

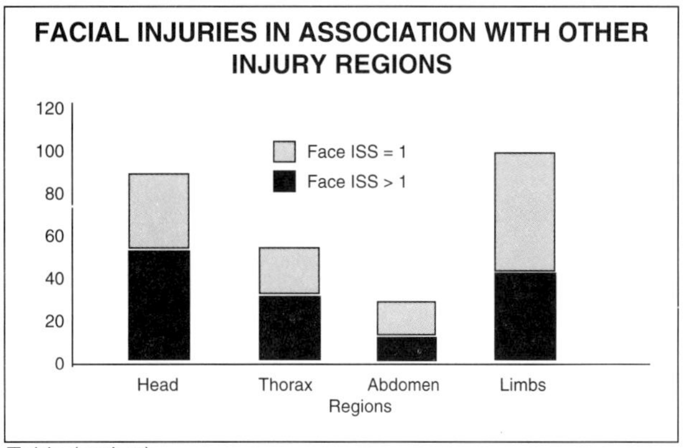

Table (author)

Although some maxillofacial injuries may occur in isolation, they are more commonly seen in association with injuries to the brain, limbs and abdomen. The maxillofacial surgeon has to take part as one of the emergency surgical team managing a multiply injured patient and the subsequent treatment (Table). For HEMS patients, particularly, he is likely to contribute at the emergency operative phase with the use of several types of interventions, in addition to those carried out at resuscitation.

Amongst the emergency interventions in 'the golden hour operating phase', have been further stabilisation of comminuted fractures affecting the facial bones. The stabilisation is performed to improve the airway further and tracheostomies are often performed. Haemorrhage control can be a stop and start business. It has been found that when a patient's blood volume has been increased, fresh haemorrhage may commence from an injured facial area due to the rich vascular networks. Combined operations with neurosurgical colleagues are often undertaken. High level, high maxillofacial injuries can then be approached from above, through the anterior cranial fossa and often by bicoronal incisions. Orbital decompression for acute continuing haemorrhage is also an occasional emergency operation.

Unfortunately the massive amount of swelling that so often accompanies trauma to the maxillofacial region, may delay definitive surgery. Secondary procedures are undertaken as soon as the patient's condition permits. Usually this is when the swelling has settled a few days after admission.

In the past, definitive treatment of maxillofacial injuries has often been delayed for up to a fortnight to allow the intracranial injuries to stabilise. However, recent changes in the management of head injuries have greatly improved outcome and now every effort is made to reduce and fix facial fractures within the first 72 hours. The majority of facial fractures are now treated using mini- or micro-plate internal fixation systems which allow the bones to be very accurately aligned. Previously, loose fragments of bone were discarded from compound wounds, but nowadays efforts are made to preserve every piece of bone. Better understanding of the anatomical relationships of tissues surrounding the eye has also led to improved treatment of fractures at the difficult mid-face region.

New imaging techniques, including 3D reconstruction of CT Scans have helped in the reconstruction and repair of some of these complicated facial injuries (Figure 2).

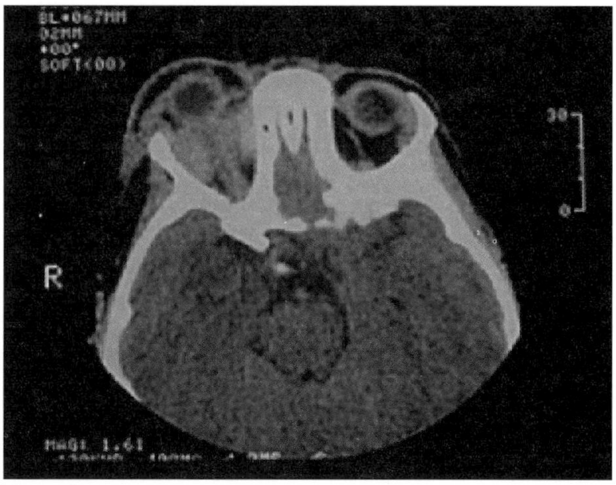

Photo: author

Figure 2:

Emergency maxillofacial operations are always undertaken by a senior registrar or consultant in the discipline. Fortunately the number of teams available means that a senior surgeon is always at hand to go to the theatre. The main aims are to operate and stabilise, or definitively fix the facial bones within the so-called golden hour. This is not always possible but when it is, this prevention of any future deformity is well worthwhile.

One of the problems associated with research into maxillofacial injuries has been comparison of the severity of the injuries with those to other parts of the body. Chief amongst the technical difficulties has been the very poor parameters by which all injuries are measured within the UK. We would agree with other authors in this volume who state that the Abbreviated Injury Score and its derivative the Injury Severity Score, have limitations for scientific and research purposes. We prefer to use the physiological Revised Trauma Score, together with an emphasis that the severely injured maxillofacial patient may indeed require interventions as soon as possible after admission.

Hugh Cannell O St J, RD & Bar, MD, MSc, FDSRCS, LRCP, MRCS is Honorary Consultant and Reader in the Department with special clinical and research interests in trauma to the face and jaws. Author of several articles on the multidisciplinary treatment of trauma, he developed the Royal London Hospital technique for temporary stabilisation and haemorrhage control referred to in this article.

Peter Dyer FFDRCSI, FRCS (Maxfac) is Senior Registrar in Oral and Maxillofacial Surgery at the RLH. He is co-author of a book entitled *The Handbook of Immediate Care*, Bailliere Tindall, London 1995. ISBN 0 7020 1881 3.

DEPARTMENT OF PLASTIC AND RECONSTRUCTIVE SURGERY

Lena Andersson

The plastic surgery team, available for trauma care consists of: three consultants, four registrars, four senior house officers, two house officers, plastic surgery trained nursing staff, occupational therapy and physiotherapy. Since the establishment of HEMS at the Royal London Hospital, the plastic surgery department has developed and is now fully established. Our special input is usually in conjunction with other surgical disciplines such as orthopaedic and general surgical departments. Many patients who receive help through HEMS may have multiple injuries, and in many such cases immediate plastic surgical expertise is required to achieve good end results by a multidisciplinary approach.

Plastic surgery is a sub-discipline that has evolved from general surgery over the years, and from a technical point of view, much of the trauma with which we deal originates from 'war surgery'. This can range from the very simple wound management to the most advanced soft tissue cover where a microvascular free flap is required. Due to constant developments within the plastic surgical field it is now possible to salvage limbs and areas of the body that may have been inconceivable even 10-20 years ago. In conjunction with the orthopaedic and general surgical teams we have been able to raise the level of management in salvaging soft tissue so that patients may now expect a higher quality of life following major trauma. For example, a limb that may have been partially damaged or amputated due to shotgun injuries, high velocity bullets, or handgun injuries, which all involve extensive soft tissue injury, would in the past not have been considered for reconstruction and this would have led to the loss of the limb. Today, however, with new plastic surgical techniques we are able to provide cover and reconstruct functionally, so that these types of injuries can be successfully treated.

It is absolutely crucial to have a HEMS service functioning in a hospital such as the Royal London Hospital, because if patients should survive severe trauma, a multidisciplinary way of handling matters is vital; it would not be possible to salvage fingers, hands and feet if the ischaemic time proved too long. In the management of much soft tissue trauma combined with fractures we work jointly with the orthopaedic department who apply external fixation to the fractures. This allows us to have access to treat the soft tissues and provide adequate cover. Some injures of a vascular and general surgical nature will expose vital parts of the body such as vessels and nerves, and if a soft tissue cover is not acutely provided it would, in many cases, lead to the vessels and nerves being so badly damaged that their function distal to the injury would not be possible to preserve. Therefore this immediate assessment in the resuscitation room with the HEMS team is of paramount importance to those patients who have vital structural damage.

To provide cover with only a skin graft sometimes is not enough if the reconstruction is to hold for the future. In

Figure 1: Injured axilla with exposed vessels and nerves leading to the arm, demonstrating major soft tissue loss (Intraoperative).

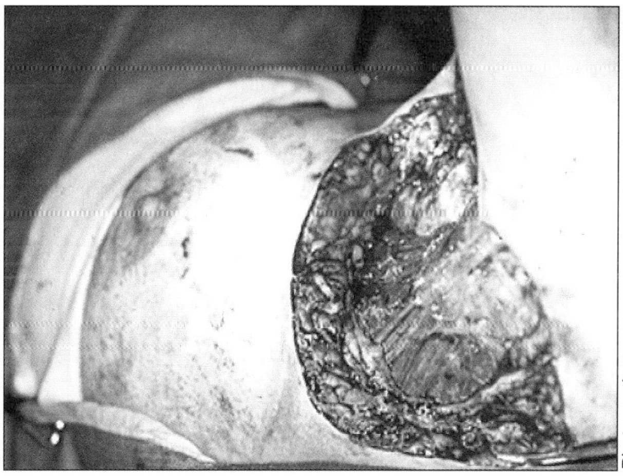

Photo: author

Figure 2: Post-operative appearance after one year with flap reconstruction from the back, enabling full range of movement and providing safe cover for nerves and vessels to the arm.

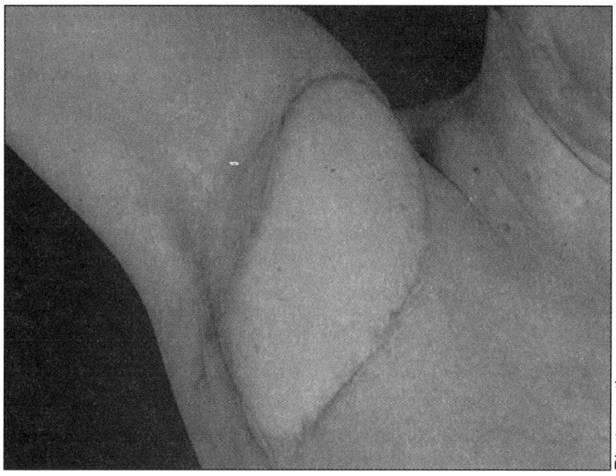

Photo: author

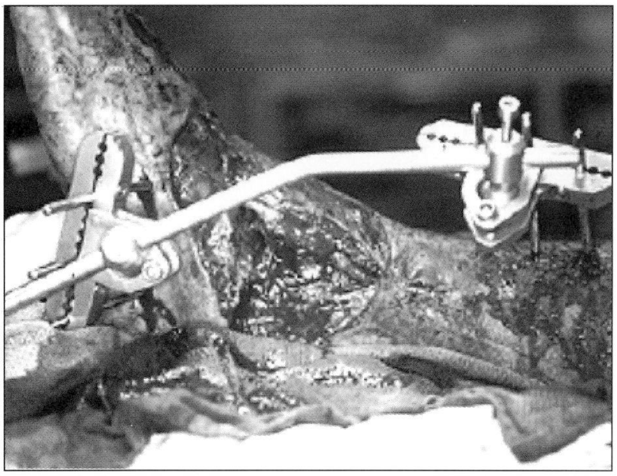
Photo: author

Figure 3: Traumatised foot after compression under lorry, showing exposed joint, tendons and external fixation applied by the orthopaedic team (Intraoperative)

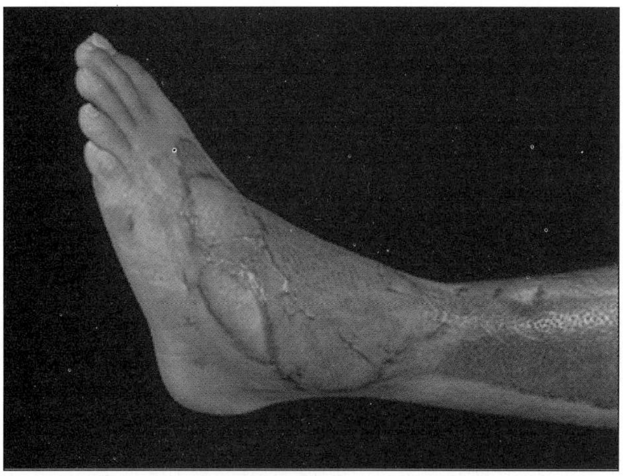
Photo: author

Figure 4: Post-operative one year after microvascular flap reconstruction from back and skin grafts from the thigh. The foot has ankle movement and the patient is able to walk.

many cases we use pedicle flaps which contain muscle, fat and skin or flaps which are lifted off from one part of the body and microvascularly connected to another part where the cover is required. Direct reconstruction of the most suitable kind is very beneficial to the patient from both a functional and aesthetic point of view.

Plastic surgery input with the HEMS and trauma team is also extremely valuable in reducing the hospitalisation time for many patients and returning them as soon as possible to professional and daily lifestyle. Over a period of four years we were involved in 140 lower limb traumas where it was necessary from a plastic surgical point of view to provide soft tissue reconstruction. Without the additional expertise of the plastic surgery department the rate of amputation would have been higher and a number of patients would not have been able to return to their previous lifestyle so soon.

The Greek word 'plasticos', meaning to mould and shape, is of major importance in any type of trauma since it is our aim from a functional, as well as an aesthetic point of view, to re-establish what was once present. The importance is not only to re-establish function and provide aesthetically good results in the long term but also to debride damaged tissue and reconstruct so that the patient's life can be saved in the initial stages. The principles of plastic surgical management in the care of the multiply injured patient are as follows:

1. Speedy initial assessment and aggressive surgical treatment of soft tissue damage.
2. Direct reconstruction as a definitive first operation instead of staged procedures to avoid unnecessary infection and delayed healing.
3. Multidisciplinary management of trauma patients should be smoothly integrated and discussed with other surgical specialities at each stage.
4. Restoration of function and aesthetic appearance as soon as possible to enable the patient to recover her/his original daily social and professional lifestyle in the least possible time.

Lena Andersson, MD, Dr med, Lead Consultant Plastic Surgeon, originally trained in the Karolinska Institute, Stockholm, University Hospital, Linkoping and the University Hospital in Zurich.

THORACIC SURGERY DEPARTMENT

Shaun Purkiss, Alan Wood

Thirty four percentage of the patients with which the Helicopter Emergency Medical Service (HEMS) is involved have a thoracic injury. The workload and potential involvement of thoracic surgeons in patient care therefore can be significant. Not all injuries sustained require expertise and treatment by a thoracic surgeon. This applies particularly to those injuries amenable to treatment in the pre-hospital resuscitation phase. They may include tension pneumothorax and haemothorax which can be managed by procedures such as needle and tube thoracotomy.

The helicopter emergency system at the Royal Hospitals Trust is based on similar systems in Europe and America. There are however important differences of emphasis in our East End service. This includes the permanent use of an on-board doctor, emergency physician, surgeon, anaesthetist. This facility adds an extra dimension to the field resuscitation procedures that can be provided in the pre-hospital phase of treatment. Many of these procedures can be considered life saving in the context of thoracic trauma. As a consequence, scene tube thoracotomy is a frequently performed operation by attending HEMS physicians for pneumothorax. Fortunately the equipment on HEMS is more appropriate and aesthetic than the coat hanger soaked in brandy and the Foley catheter provided by the national airline for a similar problem on a patient mid flight from Hong Kong.

The concept of the hospital being taken to the patient by HEMS has been taken to the extreme on occasions in the management of patients with thoracic trauma. A group of HEMS attending doctors, predominantly with a surgical interest, have performed a number of on-scene thoracotomies as part of the pre-hospital phase of resuscitation. This is an entirely original concept as previous experience with resuscitative thoracotomy has been reported in only those patients that have reached the hospital and had the procedure performed within an emergency room environment. This HEMS experience has achieved widespread media attention with a specific case report in the national newspapers and on 'This is your life' for one of the HEMS paramedics.

In this instance the victim suffered a penetrating cardiac injury to the chest, possibly from a knife. Initially the patient's condition seemed satisfactory, however, rapid deterioration occurred at the scene and signs of life became absent. Faced with a clinically dead patient an on scene resuscitative thoracotomy, using basic instruments and manual retraction of the chest wall, was performed. The penetrating wound was found to traverse the pericardium. On opening the pericardial sac a cardiac laceration was discovered which was closed using sutures and haemostasis was achieved. The heart stopped temporarily and cardiac output was maintained using cardiac massage. The patient was flown to the Royal London Hospital in a very quick transfer to the resuscitation room. The heart started beating again, but further surgery was required on other cardiac injuries. During this more controlled procedure the previously placed sutures were observed to be perilously close to the left anterior descending artery, the main blood supply to the left ventricle. The patient survived and the triumph was confirmed by the patient's discharge fourteen days after admission and the patient's own account to the cameras in the continuing media exposure.

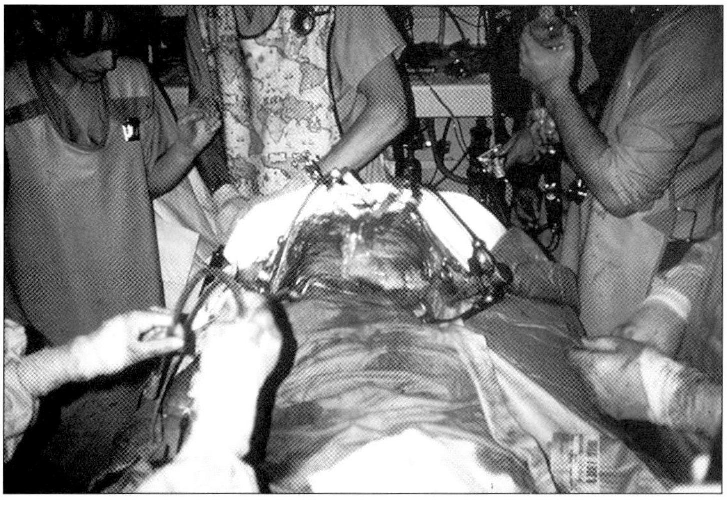

Photo: Alastair Wilson

Sadly this course of events has not been repeated in any subsequent HEMS patients. The debate continues as to whether this 'stay and play' should be adopted for similar patients in the future with immediate scene thoracotomy or the alternative, a 'swoop and scoop' to the nearest trauma centre. During the period 1991-1992, from a total of 1084 HEMS missions, 16 patients – of which only one was a female – with an age range between 9 and 38 years, were identified as having had the operation. Nine procedures were performed at the scene and 7 in the emergency department. The promptness of the medical service was confirmed by the fact that the average time of knife to skin was 16 minutes from the initial call to the London Ambulance Service. The median injury severity score of patients was approximately 30, indicating major trauma, and was not significantly different between those patients undergoing thoracotomy at scene or in casualty. The time spent attending patients who underwent thoracotomy at scene was 35 minutes, significantly greater than those in whom the procedure was performed in hospital (16.2 minutes). No patient however survived resuscitative thoracotomy with either the 'swoop and scoop' or the 'play and stay' approaches, but temporary improvements occurred more frequently in patients with penetrating injuries.

These results have demonstrated the limited efficacy of resuscitative thoracotomy and lends support to the 'swoop and scoop' approach. A low level of thoracotomies should continue however in Accident and Emergency departments.

American experience of emergency room thoracotomies has demonstrated similarly bad results. The patients that most often do the best are those that can survive to the operating theatre. The debate as to whether it is a worthwhile procedure will therefore continue. It is appreciated that this is a difficult area for stringent guidelines but the treatment must be considered high risk medical therapy which may eventually be curtailed by financial and legal intrusions into HEMS' medical practice. As a consequence, guidelines for each patient and the HEMS physician cannot be made and the decision to perform on-scene thoracotomy remains one of clinical judgement by individuals on patients and personal clinical preference.

It is likely that on-scene resuscitative thoracotomy should be reserved for low velocity penetrating thoracic injuries. The procedure should be performed only after securing the airway and failure of other resuscitative measures, on moribund patients following patient deterioration, or recently observed development of absent signs of life by the HEMS physician or attending paramedic. Unfortunately even with a selective policy resuscitative thoracotomy will remain a high cost, low yield procedure.

It is reassuring that not all patients with thoracic injuries have such a high profile and dramatic presentation as those requiring immediate thoracotomy. The spectrum of injuries can range from fractures of the thoracic cage to major organ and vascular disruption. In addition, thoracic trauma often occurs as part of a multisystem complex of injuries which may influence the eventual outcome. The impact of a thoracic injury on the prognosis of patients has been examined in HEMS patients. The overall mortality observed in a period covering two years was 26%. During the same period the mortality of patients with an element of a thoracic injury was significantly greater at 47.5%. In this group the mechanism of injury was predominantly blunt trauma (89%) of which 66% was the consequence of a road traffic accident. Eleven patients suffered a penetrating injury of which nine were inflicted by a knife. Interestingly the survival of patients who suffered a thoracic injury by a blunt mechanism was associated with the overall injury severity but not the severity of the thoracic injury. The associated head injury in this series of patients was observed to have the greatest impact on survival. In patients with blunt thoracic injuries 50% of the patients died. 74% of these patients had an associated severe head injury defined by a Glasgow Coma Score of less than 7 at the scene. In the patients that survived only 28% had a severe head injury. This suggested that in patients with thoracic injury, the severity of the associated head injury was the most significant determinant of survival.

Thoracic injuries, therefore, can be considered to be very common in HEMS patients but not all require the involvement of a thoracic surgeon. Most injuries can be managed along broad general surgical principles with attention to detail, especially in chest drain management. Thoracic surgical expertise is required in the 'second wave' after resuscitation by emergency room physicians. This may include the assessment of myocardial contusion and surgical management of major vessel or tracheobronchial injuries. The operative expertise to perform thoracotomy for those patients with significant haemothorax is valuable and thoracic surgeons should be involved in these tasks. Emergency room thoracotomy however remains controversial because of its unproven efficacy and as such should not demand the presence of a thoracic surgeon on site 24 hours of the day.

Mr Shaun Purkiss is Consultant Senior Lecturer at the Royal London Hospital.

Mr Alan Wood is Consultant Cardiothoracic Surgeon at the Royal London, St Bartholomew's and the London Chest Hospitals.

THE ROLE OF THE RADIOLOGIST

William Teh, Otto Chan

Trauma is a major cause of death, being responsible for 160,000 deaths/year in the USA and 15,000 deaths/year in the UK. Reviews have shown that errors in management are twice as common in patients who died compared with survivors. Patients are often over investigated and therefore are literally being 'x-rayed to death'. There is a tendency to over concentrate radiologically on obvious peripheral injuries e.g fractured ankle, thus delaying the management of more severe injuries such as visceral or mediastinal injuries. Serious injury in blunt trauma is often overlooked, especially aortic injuries and myocardial contusion. For instance, in patients under 40 years old, chest injury in combination with other injuries accounts for over half of traumatic deaths. A review of medicolegal cases where radiographic involvement occurred showed that in 55% of these cases the x-rays were not taken on admission 23% clearly missed the abnormality on admission, and 10% were thought to be technically inadequate x-rays. 54% of these patients had an altered level of consciousness which made the clinical history unreliable and 35% of these patients were intoxicated. The clinical examination is at best unreliable. Injuries to the heart, great vessels, liver and diaphragm are often overlooked. They are more often missed in unconscious head injury patients and patients who have suffered blunt chest and abdominal trauma. Often oversights are not only due to lack of knowledge but failure to consider the possibilities and exclude them.

The Radiologist and HEMS

At the Royal London Hospital, the radiology department forms an integral part of the HEMS trauma team. During the day there is always a radiologist carrying a trauma bleep who attends all trauma calls. The on-call radiologist is also always available at night to assist in any emergency through the hospital switchboard.

The role of radiologists is discussed under the following headings:

1. **Provide patient access to radiographers**: We aim to perform all ATLS recommended radiographs within 12 minutes of the patient arriving in the resuscitation room. The resuscitation room has a ceiling mounted Siemens

Figure 1:

a) Lateral cervical spine film shows an apparent fracture of the odontoid peg

b) Sagittal section confirms this

c) 3D spiral CT reconstructions showing clearly the fracture and orientation to the base of C2 and the lateral masses of C1

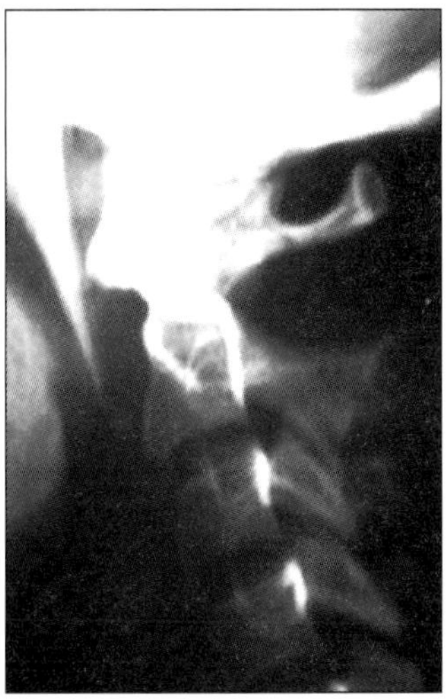

Figure 1a

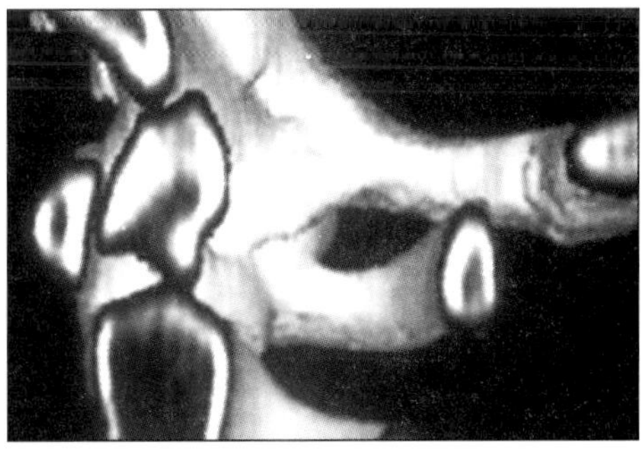

Figure 1b

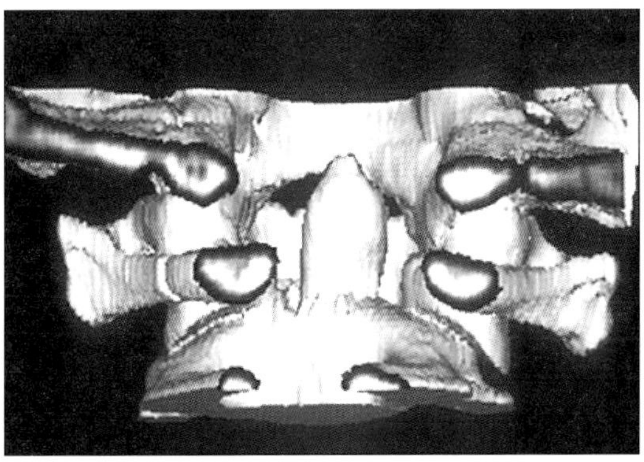

Figure 1c

Mobilette x-ray unit which allows most radiographs to be taken without the patient being moved. It has the advantage of being mounted along a longitudinal rail which not only allows access to all five bays but also frees up valuable clinical floor space around the patient. A Dupont film processor unit which processes films within 90 seconds is also installed within the resuscitation room.

The ATLS guidelines recommend the following radiographs:

- Lateral cervical spine
- Frontal AP chest radiograph
- Frontal AP pelvis radiograph

In addition, we routinely perform trauma oblique cervical spine radiographs as part of our trauma series. This has advantages of visualising the cervicodorsal junction as well as further assessment of spinal alignment and particularly the posterior elements without moving the patient. A slight modification to ATLS recommendations is that the chest radiograph is taken before the cervical spine views if there are acute life-threatening injuries in the thorax e.g tension pneumothorax or traumatic aortic injuries.

2. **Instant evaluation, interpretation and quality control of radiographs**: It is vital that all radiographs obtained are rapidly and correctly evaluated. Moreover, the radiologist can recognise the various technical factors which may limit the diagnostic quality of radiographs such as poor film screen contact, under or over penetrated films, patient motion, poor inspiration or rotation, and if necessary correct whatever factors possible by assisting the radiographers. The radiologist can assist the team leader by recommending additional radiographs and further imaging.

3. **Instant ultrasound in unstable patients**: All patients have an ultrasound of the abdomen and pelvis performed using the resuscitation room mobile ultrasound machine to look for free intra-abdominal fluid. Ultrasound has a sensitivity of over 90% with a 99% specificity in the detection of free intra-abdominal fluid. Organ injuries e.g liver, spleen and kidneys can also be assessed but ultrasound is unreliable. The main indication for performing ultrasound is in the detection of free intra-abdominal fluid in the unstable patient as the presence of fluid removes the need to perform a diagnostic peritoneal lavage (DPL). However ultrasound does have diagnostic limitations and DPL must often be used in conjunction with it.

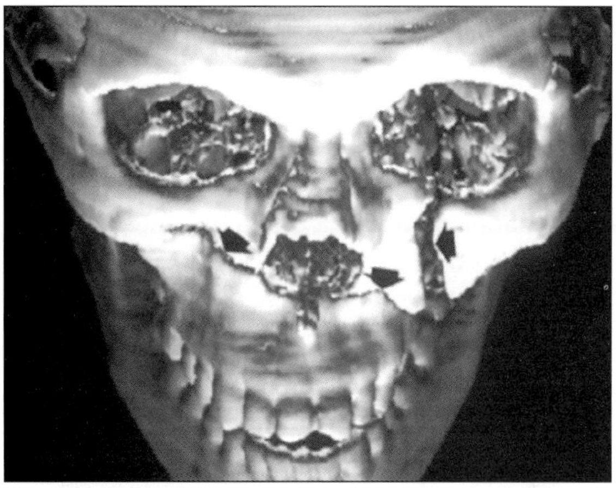

Figure 2
3D spiral reconstruction clearly demonstrates the fracture planes in a patient with oro-facio-maxilliary injuries

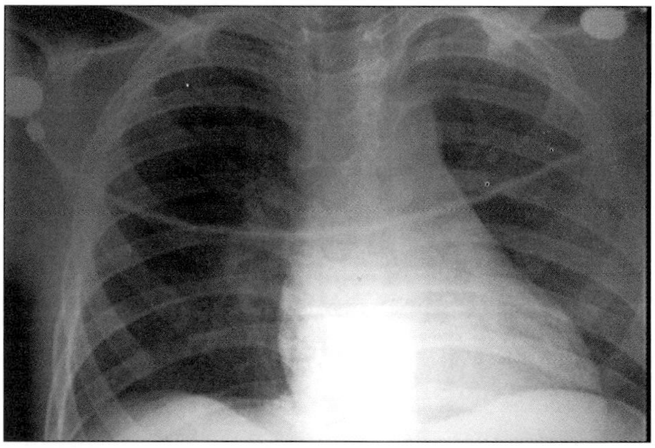

Figure 3a:
Plain chest x-ray – no definite pneumothorax seen though there is increased transradiancy of the right lung

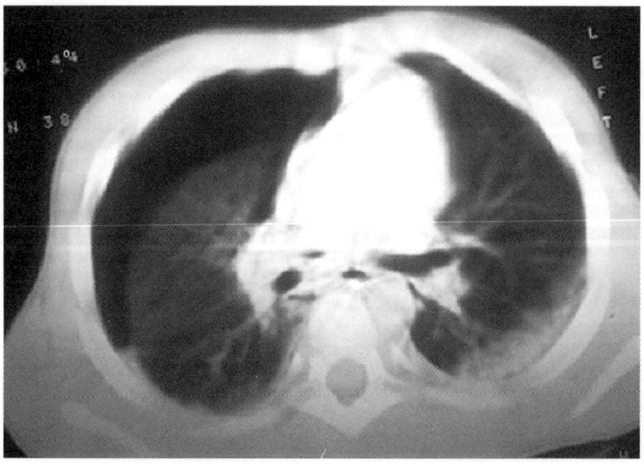

Figure 3b:
CT chest confirming a right sided pneumothorax

4. **Provide other imaging modalities**: If after discussion the team leader feels that further imaging is necessary, this is coordinated by the radiologist. There is a Siemens Somatom Plus 4A Spiral CT scanner in the A&E department which has considerably shortened the transport time of these potentially unstable patients. Priority is given to trauma patients and there is always instant access to CT. The siting of the scanner, instant availability of CT, rapid scanning time and immediate 'hot' reporting of these scans has considerably reduced the delay in imaging. A sophisticated workstation allowing rapid 3D reconstruction facilitates radiological evaluation which is particularly useful in facio-maxillary injuries.

5. **Magnetic Resonance Imaging (MRI)**: There is a 24-hour emergency MRI scanning service available. This is of great value in the assessment of patients with spinal cord injuries and permits a non-invasive method of visualising the spinal cord thus avoiding the need for CT myelography. Although not often necessary, MRI has become indispensable in the management of these patients.

Immediate diagnostic and preoperative angiography should be performed on all patients with suspected vascular injuries if haemodynamically stable. It should also be performed in patients with multiple pelvic fractures who are haemodynamically unstable. In these situations, a diagnostic study can be supplemented by embolisation procedures to aid stabilisation prior to definitive vascular surgery.

Non-operative CT directed conservative management of patients with solid organ and intra-abdominal injuries is now well established. There is a complimentary role for angiography and embolisation in such patients.

Conclusion

The role of the radiologist can be summarised by

- Quality control
- Providing the radiographer access to the patient
- Instant evaluation of ATLS recommended radiographs
- 'Instant' ultrasound examination to evaluate abdomen
- Providing advice on further imaging with additional views, CT or MRI
- Acting as coordinator for different imaging departments
- Providing instant 'hot' reporting.

William Teh is Senior Registrar and **Otto Chan** is Consultant Radiologist in the Department of Radiology at the Royal London Hospital. The illustrations shown were kindly provided by authors.

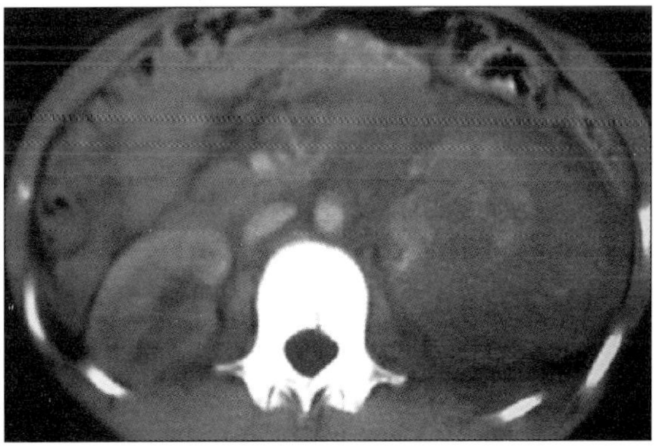

Figure 4b:
Spiral CT - fragmented left kidney with a large surrounding retroperitoneal haematoma.

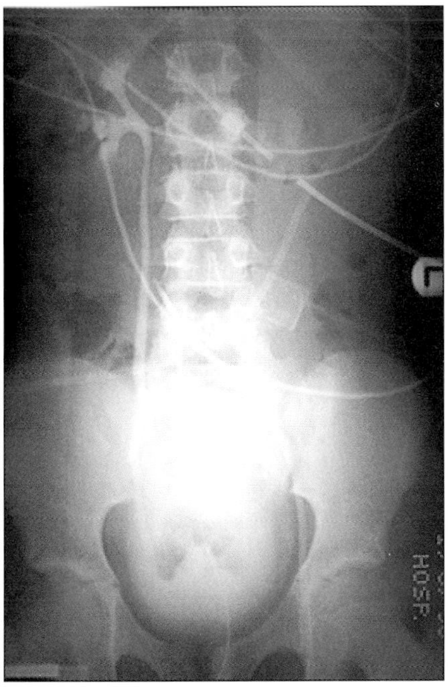

Figure 4a:
Limited on-table IVU – no excretion of contrast is seen from the left kidney in a patient with frank haematuria.

HAEMATOLOGY DEPARTMENT/BLOOD TRANSFUSION LABORATORY

Judith Chapman, Adrian Newland

For the trauma patient large volumes of blood and blood components are often required immediately the patient arrives in the emergency room or occasionally at the site of the incident. It is important that there is a good working relationship between the Emergency Medical Service (EMS) and the blood transfusion laboratory so that the laboratory is able to keep pace with the blood and blood component requirements of the medical team and for the effective management of the patient. The implementation of guidelines and procedures helps to avoid confusion and is vital for training new staff.

Communication with the EMS

It is essential that there is good communication between the laboratory and the EMS so that the laboratory is prepared for all situations. A dedicated telephone line between the A&E department and the laboratory is useful in this respect. The EMS should notify the laboratory in advance of the estimated time of arrival of a patient and also give the allocated code name and sex, a unique patient identification number and the nature of the injuries if known. In order to avoid confusion all requests for blood and blood components should be made through 'Nurse 1' of the trauma team and nobody else.

Patient Identification and Sample Labelling

Correct patient identification and sample labelling is a most important aspect of blood transfusion practice. All samples should be accurately labelled and include the unique patient ID as well as the signature of the person taking and labelling the blood. For legal reasons inadequately labelled samples cannot be accepted by the blood transfusion laboratory.

Organisation within the Laboratory

There is a dedicated trauma bench, trauma blood refrigerator and staff member. Laboratory computer terminals and printers are installed adjacently. There is an airtronics system for transport of specimens and blood products between the A&E department and the laboratory. This automated tube system saves time and the use of valuable staff.

Trauma patients are divided into three categories for blood requirements:

Category A patients are those who require group O RhD negative blood immediately.

Category B patients are those who require blood quickly but there is time to carry out a full ABO ad RhD group. These patients receive group compatible blood.

Category C patients are those where there is time to carry out a full ABO and RhD group and crossmatch before blood is issued.

As soon as the laboratory is notified of the imminent arrival of an EMS patient, sample identification numbers are attached to the telephone request form and the patient

Scheme for emergency blood use

	Bench Work		**Blood Issue**
Category A	Select O RhD negative units	→	Issue O RhD negative
	Full ABO and RhD group		
	Antibody screen		
Category B	Rapid ABO and RhD group		
	Select group compatible units		
	Full ABO and RhD group	→	Issue group compatible units
	Antibody Screen		
Category C	Full ABO and RhD group		
	Antibody screen		
	Crossmatch	→	Issue fully crossmatched units

details and request are entered in the laboratory computer. Blood grouping and antibody screening reagents are dispensed and tubes are labelled. A results worksheet is prepared with the sample number and patient identification. This preparation ensures speedy processing of the sample and the issue of blood once the sample is received.

Blood Availability

The trauma blood refrigerator is stocked with 40 O RhD positive, 30 A RhD negative, 20 O RhD negative and 10 A RhD negative units. It is always restocked immediately if blood is removed.

Blood Usage

From April 1993–March 1994, 313 patient samples were received. 69/313 patient samples were for group and save serum only and blood was requested on the remaining 244. Patients were grouped into three categories:

A: O RhD negative blood issued followed by group compatible blood.

B: O RhD negative blood issued but not transfused, group compatible blood only transfused.

C: Group compatible blood only issued and transfused.

Category A patients required significantly more group compatible blood and had a significantly higher percentage transfusion rate. The ability of the laboratory to provide group specific blood quickly has minimised the use of O RhD negative blood in the emergency room.

Massive Transfusion

Massive transfusion is when a volume equivalent to the patient's normal blood volume is given within 24 hours. Problems which can occur in patients receiving massive transfusions are due to the condition itself or to the effect of transfusing stored citrated blood. Problems which can arise are a shift to the left in the oxygen dissociation curve, thrombocytopenia, and a decrease in clotting factors, particularly those which deteriorate rapidly during storage, e.g factor V.

The Use of Blood Components

The use of blood components is indicated when a coagulopathy is observed. Causes of coagulopathy in massive blood transfusion include the consumption of platelets and clotting factors and the possible development of disseminated intravascular coagulopathy (DIC) in patients who are hypotensive or septic. The use of fresh frozen plasma (FFP) is only indicated when the prothrombin time (PT) is greater than 1.5 x control. The use of platelets is generally restricted to patients with abnormal bleeding and low platelet count.

Three Examples of Patients Requiring High Transfusion Support

Patient 1

Male aged 30 involved in a motor bike accident while travelling at 70 mph. Flung 50-70 metres across the central reservation of the motorway.

When admitted, small fractured C5, fractured radius/ulna and fractured femur.

Table 1: EMS use of FFP, platelets and cryoprecipitate, April 1993 to March 1994

248 patients	FFP	Platelets	Cryoprecipitate
Units issued	706	428	253
Units transfused	644	418	226
% transfused	91	98	89

Table 2: EMS use of blood in each category, April 1993 to March 1994

Patient Category	No. of Patients	O RhD negative		Group compatible	
		Issued	Transfused	Issued	Transfused
A	62	311	252	1707	1192
B	42	139	0	342	138
C	137	0	0	1060	426

The patient was treated as Category A by the blood transfusion laboratory. On admission he was transfused 4 units of O RhD negative blood. The laboratory issued a total of 46 units of blood, 15 units of platelet concentrates and 5 units of fresh frozen plasma. The patient was in ICU for 23 days, on a routine ward for 11 days and was then discharged.

Patient 2

35 year old woman fell in front of a train and suffered multiple injuries including a ruptured spleen, ruptured right internal iliac artery, punctured left and right kidney, fractured femur and skull fractures.

The patient was treated as Category A by the laboratory. She was given 4 units of O RhD negative blood and received a total of 39 units of blood, 15 units of platelets, 12 units of fresh frozen plasma, 20 units of cryoprecipitate. The patient died the same day.

Patient 3

53 year old woman who fell in front of a train and suffered right pelvic fractures, fractured right femur, scalp lacerations. She also received an above the knee amputation. The patient was treated as Category A. Six units of O RhD negative blood were issued on admission but only 2 were used, 6 units of group checked blood were then issued. Following the antibody screening results the patient was found to have anti-Kell. The units were recalled and tested, one unused unit was found to be Kell positive. During a 24 hour period the patient received 46 units of blood, 10 units of platelets, 10 units of cryoprecipitate, 27 units of fresh frozen plasma and 4 x 500ml bottle of 4.5% albumin. The patient survived.

Judith Chapman is Senior Scientist in charge of the Blood Transfusion Department at the RLH.

Professor A C Newland is Professor of Haematology at the RLH.

MASSIVE BLOOD TRANSFUSION FOLLOWING TRAUMATIC INJURY

Marie Healy

Acute massive haemorrhage is a medical emergency that necessitates immediate intervention to control the haemorrhage and maintain the circulating blood volume. Acute haemorrhage is the most common cause of shock in the trauma victim and exsanguination remains the leading cause of death in the operating theatre following trauma. Although the severity of the underlying injury is the primary determinant of outcome there are numerous strategies that can be employed to reduce morbidity and death. Massive transfusion is generally defined as the replacement of the patient's total blood volume by stored homologous blood in less than 24 hours (i.e approximately 10 or more units of blood in the average adult). However many patients will require in excess of two or more blood volumes in the first 24 hours.

The conventional management of haemorrhagic shock advocates the establishment of a secure airway, adequate oxygenation and ventilation, and rapid restoration of the circulating blood volume to maintain oxygen delivery and tissue perfusion until haemorrhage is controlled. The primary goal of diagnostic and therapeutic interventions in the initial resuscitation phase is to achieve control of haemorrhage (definitive care) as soon as possible following injury, while preserving vital organ function. Once the source of haemorrhage has been identified and controlled, the aim in the post-definitive care phase is to achieve supranormal circulatory goals and optimise oxygen delivery to the tissues. This is generally undertaken in the ICU and necessitates the use of a pulmonary artery flotation catheter.

Excessively aggressive fluid resuscitation prior to surgical control of haemorrhage may accelerate blood loss in selected patients, especially those with penetrating cardiac or vascular injury; inducing haemodilution and increasing the blood pressure in some stable but shocked patients may prevent the formation of, or prematurely dislodge, a protective thrombus formed at the site of injury. As a general rule, most patients who require a major transfusion will need early, sustained, aggressive resuscitation both prior to surgical intervention and throughout the perioperative period.

Initial Management /Venous Access and Monitoring

Baseline laboratory investigations that are undertaken at the first available opportunity include full blood count, blood group and crossmatch, coagulation screen and urea and electrolyte concentrations.

Rapid fluid administration is facilitated by the use of large gauge, short intravenous cannulae and wide bore administration sets, as the flow of fluid through a tube is proportional to the fourth power of the radius and inversely proportional to its length (Hagen-Poiseuille equation). Two 14 gauge peripheral intravenous cannulae are sited proximal to injured areas, preferably one above and one below the diaphragm in patients with multiple injuries, to secure access when there may be occult vascular disruption. Intraosseous cannulation and surgical venous cutdown are useful alternative techniques in paediatric and adult resuscitation, respectively, when intravenous access has failed. The additional placement of a large bore (8.5 French gauge) catheter (e.g Arrow Trauma Kit) into a central vein permits even more rapid fluid administration. These catheters are inserted percutaneously, using a Seldinger technique. The selected vessel is initially cannulated with a small needle to minimise trauma to surrounding structures and then, when correct placement has been ascertained, a guidewire is passed through the needle, the needle removed and the large catheter introduced over the guidewire. This avoids inadvertent cannulation of a central artery with a large catheter and trauma to adjacent structures. The most appropriate site depends on the nature of the patient's injuries. The internal jugular vein is best avoided if the cervical spine has not been cleared and femoral vein may be unsuitable if there is significant pelvic injury. The subclavian route is used with caution in those with significant coagulopathy because it can not be compressed if traumatic haemorrhage occurs.

Early arterial cannulation permits beat to beat blood pressure measurement, frequent blood sampling and blood gas analysis. Basic monitoring includes electro cardiography, oxygen saturation, end tidal CO_2, central venous pressure (CVP), invasive blood pressure, hourly urine output and core temperature. Conventional haemodynamic parameters, such as heart rate and blood pressure have a low specificity and sensitivity for diagnosing hypovolaemia. CVP monitoring is usually instituted as early as possible to help optimise fluid replacement and to administer inotropes, when indicated. More sophisticated monitoring tools which can be used to detect hypovolaemia, such as transoesophageal echocardiography and pulmonary artery catheterisation have practical limitations in an emergency situation. Markers of global tissue hypoperfusion, including serial base excess and lactate measurements are useful in assessing the adequacy of resuscitation, despite their lack of specificity.

It is important to bear in mind the mechanism of injury since additional injuries, some of which may be as yet undiagnosed, may be contributing to the shock state, such as haemothorax, pneumothorax, cardiac tamponade, myocardial contusion and spinal injury. Metabolic derangements, hypothermia, transfusion reactions, anaphylaxis and pre-existing disease may add to the diagnostic difficulty.

Transfusion Therapy

Red blood cell transfusion is indicated when the blood oxygen content is critically reduced by anaemia or haemorrhage.

oxygen delivery = cardiac output x oxygen content
oxygen content = haemoglobin concentration x % saturation x 1.34

Following acute haemorrhage the blood volume should be restored initially with crystalloid and/or colloid solution to maintain the intravascular volume. As a general rule three times the volume of isotonic crystalloid solution is needed to achieve a similar increase in cardiac output compared with colloid solution. Red cells are usually replaced when the blood loss approaches 20-30 % of the circulating blood volume. Red cell transfusion is instituted early when bleeding is likely to continue, and if there is coexistent myocardial or cerebral ischaemia or persistent hypoxaemia. The haematocrit is usually maintained around 30%.

Fully crossmatched blood should be used, if available, although this may take in excess of 45 minutes if atypical antibodies are found. Group specific (ABO and Rhesus matched) is usually available within ten minutes, ensures compatability in 98% of transfusions and is a safe alternative in a life-threatening emergency. Group O rhesus negative blood should only be used in exsanguinating haemorrhage when the blood group is not yet known. Care must be taken to avoid clerical errors, which are the commonest cause of fatal ABO-incompatible transfusion reactions. These usually occur in the operating theatre.

Coagulopathy

Many factors contribute to the coagulopathy associated with massive transfusion including the dilution and consumption of clotting factors and platelets, and hypothermia. A significant coagulopathy due to haemodilution alone is rare until at least 1.5 times the blood volume has been replaced with stored blood and other fluids. Disseminated intravascular coagulopathy (DIC) should be suspected when abnormal bleeding or marked derangments in coagulation tests and platelet counts occur earlier than would be expected from the degree of haemodilution. Prolonged shock, extensive tissue damage, brain injury and acidosis all predispose to DIC, with pathological activation of the coagulation system, consumption of clotting factors and platelets and secondary fibrinolysis.

The onset of an abnormal bleeding diathesis is generally considered to be best established clinically, by the presence of diffuse microvascular ooze (DMVO) from mucosal surfaces, traumatised tissues and venepuncture sites. It is prudent to begin clotting factor and platelet replacement prior to the onset of DMVO in high risk patients such as those with head injury when bleeding has not yet been controlled. In-vitro tests including the platelet count (PC), prothrombin time (PT), partial thromboplastin time (PTT) and fibrinogen concentration should be measured frequently to direct the nature and extent of appropriate replacement therapy.

Specialist advice from haematological colleagues should be sought to optimise the use of blood component therapy. The platelet count should be maintained at >50x 109/litre; fresh frozen plasma (12 mls/kg) is indicated when the PT or PTT exceed 1.5 times the control values. Cryoprecipitate is administered primarily to reverse hypofibrinogenaemia when the fibrinogen level is <0.8 grams/litre.

Hypothermia

Hypothermia (core temperature <35°C) occurs frequently following major trauma due to heat loss from pre-hospital and resuscitation room environmental exposure, transfusion of inadequately warmed fluids and visceral exposure during surgery. Hypothermia slows the enzymatic reactions of the coagulation cascade and interferes with platelet function. The PT and PTT are normally performed at 37°C which can lead to an underestimation of the degree of coagulopathy in hypothermic patients. Severe hypothermia reduces citrate and lactate metabolism, increases the affinity of haemoglobin for oxygen and induces myocardial irritability.

Core temperature should be monitored continuously during resuscitation and active measures taken to maintain normothermia. Patient exposure should be kept to a minimum and warming blankets used to prevent heat loss. All fluids should be warmed prior to administration; the resistance to flow is increased and the warming capacity reduced when standard 'blood warmers' are used to administer fluids at rates exceeding 5 litres per hour.

Automatically pressurised high capacity fluid warmers, which can be set up rapidly, are now widely available. We use the Level 1 500 model, which can warm cold packed red blood cells to temperatures >35°C at flow rates of 500 mls/minute.

Metabolic Complications

The citrate anticoagulant contained in stored blood and blood components is normally rapidly metabolised by the liver. It may accumulate when blood is rapidly transfused, especially in patients with hepatic hypoperfusion or injury and hypothermia. Potential complications of citrate toxicity include hypocalcaemia and hypomagnesaemia. Serum potassium concentrations should also be monitored regularly during massive transfusion.

Conclusion

Polytraumatised patients who require high-volume exchange transfusions present a complex clinical scenario where team work, experience and good communication are needed to ensure that all patients achieve the best possible outcome. The priorities include prompt surgical intervention, when indicated, the maintenance of haemodyamic and haemostatic stability and the prevention and treatment of the complications of massive transfusion, such as coagulopathy, hypothermia and metabolic disorders.

Dr Marie Healy is Consultant in Anaesthesia and Intensive Care at the RLH.

PSYCHIATRY AND THE TRAUMA PATIENT

John Joyce, Simon Fleminger

This chapter is in two parts: the first reviews the relationship between mental illness and deliberate self harm presenting to trauma services; the second part discusses psychological management of patients in trauma services.

1. DELIBERATE SELF HARM AND THE TRAUMA SERVICE

Deliberate self-harm accounts for at least 8% of all Helicopter Emergency Medical Service (HEMS) admissions to the Royal London Hospital. Methods of self-harm include cutting and piercing, hanging, shooting, crashing a motor vehicle or jumping. 40% of those who fall from a height or before a moving object are either psychiatrically ill or have a history of psychiatric illness or both.

Train Suicides

Farmer at Charing Cross recently reported that between 1977 and 1988, 4.8% of all suicide verdicts returned by Coroners in Greater London involved people jumping in front of moving London Underground trains. In the past ten years the rate of suicide on the underground system, as a percentage of all suicides in Greater London, has remained more or less constant but there has been a decrease in the case fatality rate in the past decade. Using the ratio of incidents to average annual passenger throughput, two stations had exceptionally high incidence rates, Mile End Station which is close to St Clement's Hospital, the psychiatric wing of the Royal London Hospital, and Tooting Bec which is close to St George's psychiatric unit. In both stations a high proportion of the victims were inpatients at the time of the incident (15.5% for Tooting Bec and at least 22% for Mile End). This phenomenon has been found at other stations which are close to psychiatric institutions. In fact they were unable to locate a station adjacent to a psychiatric institution which had a low number of incidents. This is consistent with the finding of a study in Brisbane of train suicides in the early 80s in which at least 57% had major psychiatric illness, 54% being inpatients at the time. The incidents at King's Cross, Embankment and Earl's Court stations involved a high proportion of people of no fixed abode.

This mode of attempted suicide is one which results in high mortality and disfigurement, considerable psychological trauma to patients and relatives and great psychological difficulties for those directly involved, such as train drivers and on-lookers. The chance of survival appears to be influenced by the presence or absence of a channel several feet deep between the rails. It is not absolutely clear why these channels were built, but they are normally referred to as 'suicide pits' by London Underground staff. The survival rate at stations which have the feature is 55%, but drops to 32% in stations without pits. It might be possible to reduce case fatality by digging more suicide pits or modifying rolling stock.

Jumping from a Height

The literature contains a number of studies of cohorts of people who successfully killed themselves by jumping or people who have attempted suicide by jumping. Between 50 and 100% of cases are reported to have a psychiatric illness. O'Brien (1978) and Cantor et al (1989) found a preponderance of diagnoses of schizophrenia whereas Prasad & Lloyd (1983) and Isbister and Roberts (1992) found a greater number of cases with depressive illness. The conclusions from these studies were somewhat inconsistent, but it seems likely that people who attempt suicide by jumping, successfully or unsuccessfully, often have a severe psychotic illness and tend to be young single men.

These previous studies in attempted suicide by jumping have been hampered by a relatively small sample size (mean n=18). Sample size may have influenced the findings of two studies that relied on cohorts recruited from psychiatric inpatient wards or specific referrals to a psychiatric service (Prasad & Lloyd 1983, Salmons 1984).

Follow up of Patients who have Jumped

Over a ten year period, of the 94 persons who had attempted suicide by jumping in front of London Underground trains in the late 1970s, later completion of suicide was not found to be higher than in previous studies of attempted suicide by other methods, despite the apparent seriousness of the methods. Two smaller studies have looked in more detail at outcome months to years following attempted suicide by jumping (Cantor et al [1989], n=16; Sims & O'Brien [1979], n=22); they found about 40% attempted deliberate self-harm again within a period of about five years. In both studies two patients subsequently killed themselves by jumping a second time.

Study of Patients Admitted from HEMS after Jumping from a Height or in Front of a Train

More and more people are killing themselves by jumping either from a height or in front of a train (Cantor et al 1998). The department of psychiatry at the Royal London Hospital provides a liaison service to HEMS. We have undertaken a retrospective case note study to identify the psychiatric and physical morbidity of the group who have self-injured themselves by jumping either from a height or in front of a train. We also looked at the costs they incurred to the service and their outcome at discharge from the Royal London. Our study has the advantage of being a large cohort (n=51) not exposed to referral bias with respect to psychiatric assessment.

In the first four years of the service 62 consecutive patients were noted on the HEMS database as belonging to this group and we were able to find the case notes of 51 of these patients.

Major psychiatric disorder ranked high on the list of principle diagnoses. The prevalence of affective disorder and schizophrenia were roughly equivalent with rates of 28% and 23% respectively. Substance abuse, either as a primary or co-morbid diagnosis, was present in 23% and alcohol dependence in 9%.

Of the patients who suffered moderate to severe injuries, Revised Trauma Score (RTS) ranged from 3.22 to 7.85 and 37% died. UK probability of survival ranged from 4.4 to 99.5. 46% had expressed definite suicidal plans or ideas, whereas 17% jumped with no warning at all. Almost one third (30%) were recorded as having made a previous attempt.

While in hospital on the trauma unit, 82% had significant mental symptoms, one third (32%) either expressed on-going suicidal ideas or required one-to-one continuous nursing observation.

Of those transferred or discharged, one third (30%) still had mental symptoms and 48% were moderately or severely physically disabled. The cost to the service of these patients included over 200 hours of theatre time and over 1,000 bed days.

Summary

Trauma from deliberate self-harm is common and often severe. As a consequence, many of the patients being looked after by a trauma service will have a history of severe mental illness. All trauma services must therefore have good liaison with psychiatry.

2. PSYCHOLOGICAL MANAGEMENT OF PATIENTS IN THE TRAUMA SERVICE

Historical Information

Broadly speaking patients who develop behavioural and psychological problems in the trauma unit do so either because they have had a mental illness which antedated their admission, or because they have developed mental symptoms as a consequence of the medical illness that caused their admission, or a mixture of both. It is therefore important to obtain as clear a history as possible of the patient's mental health leading up to admission. This will include establishing through witness accounts the evidence as to whether injuries were self inflicted, and to establish any previous history of self-injury. A history of previously prescribed and illicit drug or alcohol use is necessary.

Immediate Aftermath on the Trauma Unit

If it seems probable that patients have self-injured themselves, they should be encouraged to discuss their feelings about the self-injury once they have regained full consciousness. Many are amnesic for the event and have no recollection of suicidal thoughts preceding the event. Such patients are likely to deny that it was self-injury and may say that they must have been pushed. In such circumstances there needs to be a clear agreement with the relatives as to who is going to inform the patient, and when.

Sometimes, even though the patient is conscious, there is a latent period of a few days before mental symptoms, present before the admission, are observed on the ward. This is probably related to the profound psychological effect of admission to a trauma unit or ICU. The euphoric effect of narcotic analgesics, bland indifference resulting from brain injury, or the use of denial as a psychological coping strategy, may be other explanations for this latent period. But this quiescent period may be followed by extreme mental symptoms and staff should be prepared.

Patients with previous mental ill health may be particularly vulnerable to extreme agitation on attempts to wean the patient off mechanical ventilation. This is more likely to occur following medium or long term mechanical ventilation. It is important to ensure that any anxiety symptoms are not a consequence of hypoxia or hypercapnia. Quiet explanations of the procedure and reassurance that a short period of respiratory discomfort is to be expected may help. Mental relaxation, including hypnotic techniques of counting down into a relaxed state imagining a tranquil scene, may be of value. Lorazepam may be very effective when given one hour before weaning is due to start.

Some patients who demonstrate denial demand to leave hospital against medical advice. If this happens the family should be rapidly mobilised and the seriousness of the illness carefully explained to all. If the patient continues to demand to leave, get a psychiatric opinion.

Care in Hospital

All patients who have self injured themselves should be regarded as being at high risk of a repeated suicide attempt. The particularly dangerous time is around the time of transfer to a general ward. The patient should not be transferred to wards from which they can jump.

Fear and anxiety may cause panic and agitation which interferes with medical care. Quiet reassurance and explanation are often sufficient, but benzodiazepines may be necessary. However, benzodiazepines should be used cautiously in patients with a history of drug or alcohol dependence or a history of chronic anxiety.

Patients may cause concern because of overt symptoms of depression or because of general apathy and demoralisation. Often this will come to the attention of the physiotherapist who finds that the patient is not interested in rehabilitation. Apathy and psychomotor slowing are not always due to depression. On occasion these signs may be a consequence of organic brain disorder or may result from Parkinsonism due to neuroleptic medication. Nevertheless, it is generally reasonable to treat all cases of apathy with an antidepressant given that a treatable depression may be present even if an organic brain disorder is primarily responsible for the symptoms. Clomipramine, a tricyclic antidepressant, is useful when an antidepressant needs to be given by intravenous infusion.

Those with a psychotic illness should be reviewed by a psychiatrist.

Post Traumatic Stress Disorder

The early identification and subsequent treatment of post traumatic stress disorder (PTSD) may improve outcome. PTSD is characterised by exposure to a terrifying traumatic event, subsequent reliving of the event (nightmares, flashbacks, avoidance of memories relating to the event), and symptoms of hyperarousal and anxiety. These symptoms may be delayed in onset following the trauma, but in general a high level of distress immediately after the event is a good predictor of psychological problems one month later.

Upto 25% of the general population who experience potentially traumatic events develop post traumatic stress syndrome. About half of those who develop the disorder may still have it a decade later. Most studies find a dose response relationship between the severity of the stressor and the degree of consequent psychological distress. The vulnerability factors are low education and social class, pre-existing psychiatric problems and female gender, but in many there is no evidence of pre-existing mental vulnerability.

Mayou et al, in a study of the psychological sequelae of road traffic accidents, found that immediately following the accident 40% of subjects could be assigned to a high risk group on the basis of prominent anxiety symptoms, mood disturbance and/or horrific memories of the accident. One half of these subjects had significant mental symptoms at one year of whom one half were characterised by PTSD.

Once established, symptoms of PTSD may last for years and cause secondary problems, for example, alcohol abuse or the break-up of a marriage which themselves cause a downward spiral. Those at risk should therefore be identified as early as possible. Paradoxically it may be those who seem on the face of it to have no problems initially, may be at risk later on. The terrifying memory of the trauma results in avoidance of discussing and remembering the event.

These patients may be missed if staff are not willing to gently explore with the patient his/her feelings about what happened. This needs to be done in the patient's own time and they should not feel pressurised into talking about the event.

For some the best coping strategy is getting on with other things and simply trying to forget what happened. Nevertheless, simple questionnaires such as the Hospital Anxiety and Depression Scale and Impact of Events Scale, which take the patient only a few minutes to complete, may indicate that the patient is at risk. High scores on either of these two scales would suggest that the patient should be referred for a psychiatric opinion or for counselling.

Psychological debriefing is a structured intervention, designed to promote the emotional processing of traumatic events, through the ventilation and normalisation of reactions and preparation for possible future experiences. There is as yet no clear evidence that psychological debriefing helps in the prevention of post traumatic stress disorder but anecdotal evidence is encouraging.

Other specialist techniques include cognitive behavioural treatment approaches which are increasingly showing a superiority to other psychological methods. Drug studies have shown modest gains. However firm statements about the power of the different therapeutic procedures are probably premature.

Staff Support

There is considerable interest by the military in the value of debriefing for those working to rescue survivors of trauma or to recover the dead. Typical psychological debriefing takes place 2 -3 days after the trauma as a single group meeting lasting approximately two hours. However, it is less certain that such methods are of any use for those working in trauma services within the National Health Service.

In the less acute situation formal staff support groups, familiar to those who work in psychiatric settings, may be appropriate. Trauma services often have their own informal support mechanisms which may be very helpful for some, but should not be relied upon as the only source of support. Staff strain is a common experience in intensively pressured work settings of a trauma service. Access to psychological support should be available for all people working in this field so that when stressors (the loads placed on an individual) outweigh strengths (the individual's coping skills) and leads to strain (adverse effects on the individual), action can be taken.

A programme aimed at improving staff coping strategies which enables staff to recognise symptoms of strain and informs them of avenues of help, should be incorporated into the educational programme of the trauma service.

John Joyce is Senior Lecturer in the Department of Psychiatry.

Simon Fleminger is Consultant in the Department of Psychiatry at the RLH.

SECTION 8 K (ii): ESSENTIAL DEPARTMENTS AT THE RLH
REHABILITATION, PSYCHIATRY, FIM AND COUNSELLING

REHABILITATION

Julie Baldry-Currens, David Rushton

Rehabilitation following major trauma may be defined as a planned programme in which an injured person regains their optimum physical, psychological and social independence. The rehabilitation process starts immediately after acute admission to hospital and continues after discharge into the community. Evidence shows that early intervention is essential to prevent secondary complications and obtain maximal functional outcome.

Rehabilitation occurs in a variety of settings and incorporates many different clinicians and therapies as the patient progresses from the acute specialist trauma unit back into the community. Good rehabilitation practice is multi-disciplinary, based on full and continuing assessment of the patient's needs, having specified progressive goals and time-limits, with effective discharge planning and outcome measurement. Therapy incorporates a range of techniques, exercises and creative activity, specifically designed to help the patient relearn previously used skills, and to develop strategies which will both overcome and accommodate to new restrictions.

Continuity of Care

Each HEMS patient has a unique set of injuries and circumstances and therefore requires an individual rehabilitation programme. This will range from patients with orthopaedic lower limb injuries who may make a full recovery within a few months, to those likely to suffer significant long-term disability such as severe head injury and paraplegia.

The rehabilitation process involves complex assessment, discharge planning and ongoing support within the community. It is essential that continuity of care is provided for patients when leaving the Royal Hospitals. Some patients will return home, able to continue their rehabilitation programme as an outpatient in the various therapy departments, or receive domiciliary therapy within their home in special circumstances. Others will transfer to specialist rehabilitation facilities, and some may require placement in residential or nursing homes.

When HEMS patients live outside the geographical area of Tower Hamlets, it is usual for them to return nearer home once the acute phase of care has occurred. Extensive communication is therefore essential to ensure smooth transfer to the appropriate local authority.

The Rehabilitation Team

The multidisciplinary rehabilitation team for HEMS patients varies according to the clinical presentation of the patient. The full range of services (particularly physiotherapy, occupational therapy, speech and language therapy, social work, clinical psychology, dietetics, orthotics, wheelchairs and footwear) all may come into play as part of the rehabilitation process. These rehabilitation professionals work together with the patients and their families, in conjunction with nursing and medical staff, and other clinical teams such as the Pain Control Team. Injured children will often require input from many additional disciplines such as play specialists and teachers. Trauma and associated stress often has a devastating effect on both the patient and their family, who may require support and psychological de-briefing from the post-traumatic stress counsellor. Below is an outline of the specific contribution made by some of the therapy and social work professions:

Physiotherapists: Have specialised knowledge and skills in optimising respiratory function, preventing secondary musculo-skeletal problems and in the analysis and re-education of movement. The physiotherapy service has a designated trauma specialist who is supported by clinical experts in the fields of respiratory care, orthopaedic, neurological, paediatric and amputee rehabilitation. This ensures that each patient receives an individually designed treatment package provided by specialist physiotherapists, thereby maximising efficient use of resources.

Occupational Therapists (OT): Use an holistic approach to functional assessment and treatment programmes. There is no designated OT to the trauma team. Referrals are made to the OT service under service level agreements held with service directorates such as neurology, children's services and orthopaedics. All referrals made to the OT service are seen according to priority.

Speech and Language Therapists: Become involved with the assessment, diagnosis and management of swallowing and communication disorders in patients who have sustained a head injury. Initial contact is usually made as the patient begins to regain consciousness and aims to:

- assess the safety of swallow function and advise on appropriate feeding regimes.
- assist with specific swallowing and communication problems of patients with a tracheostomy
- assess the level of functional communication which may be affected by speech, language, voice and/or cognitive impairments.

Rehabilitation for specific communication deficits begins when the patient is medically stable and demonstrates an intention to communicate. Early intervention is less direct, aiming to assist family, nursing staff and other team members to communicate most effectively with the patient.

Social Work: An integral part of the social work role in trauma care is a needs led assessment (Community Care Act, 1990) which involves liaison and planning within the hospital multidisciplinary team and with community social services. A discharge plan is then formulated in consultation with the patient, their relatives and carers; for example returning home with domiciliary assistance from statutory and/or voluntary community service providers, or residential/nursing placement which is coordinated by social work in conjunction with the placement coordinator.

Social workers also support patients and their families emotionally, in coming to terms with the circumstances of their admission and the subsequent adjustments. Hospital based social workers continue to support and monitor patients and their families for three weeks after discharge (extended if necessary), or transfer their care to the appropriate local authority if outside Tower Hamlets.

Organisation of Therapy Services

In and outpatient therapy services at the Royal Hospitals and the local community are provided from within the Tower Hamlets Healthcare Trust. This unified organisation helps to facilitate the provision of coordinated rehabilitation as the patient moves out of the acute phase into recovery. The pressure on acute surgical beds means that there is an urgent and increasing need for a dedicated in-patient rehabilitation facility which would enable this seamless care concept to extend through the crucial early and middle rehabilitation phases. This need is also particularly felt when patients are brought in from outlying districts which may not have well-developed facilities for this phase. This service would undertake both active continuing physical and psychological rehabilitation itself, and the extensive liaison and detailed planning process leading to an agreed return to the community, as well as freeing beds for acutely ill patients.

This paper has been written with contributions from members of the multidisciplinary team. For further information regarding the specific roles of any discipline, please contact the individual department.

Julie Baldry-Currens is HEMS Rehabilitation Coordinator, Royal London Hospital.

David N Rushton is Professor of Rehabilitation at the Royal London Hospital.

MEASUREMENT OF DISABILITY: THE FUNCTIONAL INDEPENDENCE MEASURE (FIM)

Julie Baldry-Currens

Evaluation of Morbidity

Traditionally, evaluation of trauma care concentrates on assessment of mortality. Although calculations for probability of survival are complex, the 'end point' is clear – the patient either lives or dies. Assessment of morbidity, however, has received less attention, and no clear method has been devised for evaluating the quality of life for those who survive. Many factors must be considered, for example: the specific injuries that are residual (impairment), the extent of any functional limitation (disability), the affect of that disability on a persons social role (handicap), the cosmetic acceptability of residual scars etc. Although complex, and often controversial, outcome assessment is an essential component of trauma care evaluation. Such evaluation is helpful in assessing the value of a particular trauma system, to compare such systems, and to predict the type of recovery that trauma survivors could be expected to make.

Assessment of Disability

Over the last two decades, measurement of disability has gradually emerged as the most popular type of assessment. It is possible to state, for example, whether or not a person is able to walk, dress, and feed him/herself, and how much help, if any, is needed to perform a task. From this information it is usual to generate a numerical score. It is, of course, recognised that in a real life situation, a person would carry out a number of activities in a normal day which are far more complex and exciting than dressing. However, the purpose of this type of assessment is to look at basic everyday activities which are common to everyone, and which are usually performed without assistance.

Many different methods have been devised to assess disability, with literally hundreds of 'measurement tools' being used. Regrettably no one method has emerged which has a universal application or proven scientific qualities in all dimensions. However, one particular tool, the Functional Independence Measure (FIM), has attracted considerable interest internationally and was selected by HEMS as the tool by which disability would be assessed (*Hetherington & Earlam* see publication list) in HEMS.

Functional Independence Measure (FIM)

The FIM was devised in the 1980s by a large task force of clinicians and researchers from the American Congress of Rehabilitation Medicine and the American Academy of Physical Medicine and Rehabilitation. It was published in its current form by the Research Foundation by the State University of New York. Its premise is: *level of disability equates with burden of care.* All such

Figure 1: Function Independence Measure (FIM) © 1990 Research Foundation of State University of New York

Levels	
7 Complete Independence (Timely, Safely) 6 Modified Independence (Device)	NO HELPER
Modified Dependence 5 Supervision 4 Minimal Assist (Subject = 75% +) 3 Moderate Assist (Subject = 50% +) Complete Dependence 2 Maximal Assist (Subject = 25% +) 1 Total Assist (Subject = 0% +) /	HELPER

	ADMIT	DISCH
Self Care		
A. Eating		
B. Grooming		
C. Bathing		
D. Dressing – Upper Body		
E. Dressing – Lower Body		
F. Toileting		
Sphincter Control		
G. Bladder Management		
H. Bowel Management		
Mobility		
Transfer:		
I. Bed, Chair, Wheelchair		
J. Toilet		
K. Tub, Shower		
Locomotion		
L. Walk/wheel Chair	w / c	
M. Stairs		
Communication		
N. Comprehension	a / v	a / v
O. Expression	v / n	v / n
Social Cognition		
P. Social Interation		
Q. Problem Solving		
R. Memory		
Total FIM		

NOTE: Leave no blanks; enter 1 if patient not testable due to risk.

measurement tools require extensive testing, and FIM has undergone many aspects of evaluation which prove it is 'fit for the job'. It is intended as a generic measure of disability and can be scored by clinicians from any discipline, though preferably by the rehabilitation team involved with a patient's care. In addition to the standard version, one has been developed for children – the *WEEFIM*, and for telephone follow-up – the *FONEFIM*.

As shown in Figure 1, FIM consists of 18 items, of which 13 are classified as 'motor', and 5 'cognitive'. Each item is ranked according to what the person usually does, and is scored from 1 -7, according to the level of ability. For example, if someone is unable to perform a task and needs everything done for them, they will score 1, whereas if they are completely safe and independent they will score 7. The scores are added together and when compared over time, the scores will show how a person is progressing.

HEMS uses this measurement tool for all patients who stay in the hospital for longer than 48 hours, by discussion with the patient, their family and the clinical staff involved with the patient. Assessments are made between the second and third day of admission, and then again at discharge. If there are still some areas of difficulty, follow-up contact will be made at 3 months and then again, if necessary, at 6 and 12 months.

FIM is proving to be a very useful measure and, as the data collected grows, it is possible to see the improvements that both a single patient makes as they recover from their injuries, and the type of recovery patterns that groups of patients with similar injuries make. Additionally, it is possible to view the recovery of all patients, and from this information quantify the value of the HEMS system in reducing disability in patients with major trauma.

Julie Baldry-Currens is HEMS Rehabilitation Coordinator at the Royal London Hospital, London.

Photo: Mark Landon

This accident took place outside St. Clement's Hospital, a psychiatric hospital near the Mile End Underground tube station. The photograph emphasises that there are crazy people in motor cars who finish upside down outside hospitals.

POST TRAUMATIC STRESS AND COUNSELLING

Shirley Crossfield

Trauma care traditionally focuses on the physical injuries of a patient. It is indeed essential to resuscitate the victim and to ensure that they are physically out of danger, but once the patient begins to regain consciousness, the work of psychological rehabilitation begins. Every patient is unique, as is the capacity to cope with the trauma experienced. Psychological symptoms resulting from the trauma can emerge immediately after consciousness is regained. However, it can also remain hidden beneath the surface of consciousness for any period of time thereafter, whether it be measured in weeks, months or years.

Because the traumatic event usually occurs unexpectedly and often in shocking circumstances, many trauma survivors have reported that the process of living through their overwhelming events was so intense that it changed the way they felt about themselves and their place in the world.

Trauma survivors can experience overwhelming psychological reactions which they may find hard to control. These can range from rapid mood swings, feeling numb, angry or depressed. Many victims suffer from hallucinations of a paranoid type whereby they feel the medical staff or their loved ones are trying to harm them. They may experience physical symptoms such as palpitations, profuse sweating, sleep disturbances, flashbacks of the event and nightmares of a threatening sort. Many patients experience these symptoms known as Post Traumatic Stress Reactions which are a normal process and usually subside over a short space of time. For some, these symptoms last longer and develop into a syndrome known as Post Traumatic Stress Disorder, especially in victims who have lost a limb in the trauma or if there has been a death involved.

Trauma often leaves not only the patient but also the relatives and friends quite vulnerable and helpless because their world has been thrown out of balance. It is therefore essential that psychological aid is offered to help both the patient and relatives to:

- adjust to the trauma
- understand and make sense of what has happened
- to incorporate the trauma and its outcome as a positive part of the future.

After trauma, it is essential that a patient's rehabilitation programme incorporates professional counselling or therapy. If the patient does not adjust to the trauma, subsequent quality of life may be impaired and social integration affected.

Shirley Crossfield is a trained Trauma Counsellor who works for HEMS and Tower Hamlets community.

WHO OWNS TRAUMA? THE PATIENT

Frank Cross

The Background

The provision of emergency services in this country has been the subject of a number of enquiries and reports over the years; the main effect has been to improve Accident and Emergency (A&E) services, introduce the career consultant grade of A&E physician, and make A&E training compulsory at senior house officer level. The object of this article is to examine more recent changes in the organisation of trauma care, describe the recommendations of the most recent reports and assess whether or not these improvements will result in better trauma care in the future.

Hitherto the province of the orthopaedic surgeon, many doctors still think of trauma in terms of broken bones, and the appointment of a 'trauma surgeon' or 'trauma anaesthetist' in a hospital is generally thought of as a way of dealing with the fractured necks of femur. The *Journal of Trauma* is placed with the orthopaedic journals in the library. There is however a wind of change blowing, mainly from across the Atlantic, but much of it now originating in the UK.

1988 was a good year for trauma in the United Kingdom. There was a visit from an American trauma expert who commented on the provision (or lack of it) of trauma services in the UK, the '1000 deaths' study was published in the *British Medical Journal*, the Royal College of Surgeons introduced the ATLS course and published a report on trauma management, and preliminary plans were made to start three trauma centres. It is worth looking at these events in some detail since they have a direct bearing on the future of trauma management in this country.

1. Overseas advice

The overseas expert was Donald Trunkey, who visited four hospitals in the UK and was then invited to comment on the provision of trauma services. His conclusions were: a consultant general surgeon was needed to supervise the trauma operating; proper audit of outcome should be started; the number of higher surgical trainees should be reduced and proper teaching should be instigated at this level; surgical registrars should receive some formal intensive care training; more time and effort could be put into trauma research; and there should be regionalised trauma centres, run by general surgeons.

2. The '1000 deaths' study

This was commissioned to form the basis of the Royal College of Surgeons' report on trauma care. One thousand deaths from multiple trauma, 100 from each of ten hospitals, were reviewed by an independent panel of four surgeons and the question was asked: 'If this patient had been admitted to a fully-staffed and equipped American-style trauma centre, might death have been prevented?'. Twenty per cent of the deaths were judged preventable by all four panelists and a further 13% by three out of four. By any standards this is a poor result.

3. The Royal College of Surgeons' report

This looked at the results of the '1000 deaths' study, and by means of comparisons with results from trauma systems in the USA, France and Germany, together with a careful appraisal of the current trauma facilities in this country, made the following recommendations:

- Closure of all but one A&E department in each district.
- Establishment of trauma centres at regional or multi-district level with a 24-hour in-hospital service at consultant level.
- Enhanced pre-hospital training for ambulance crews, with improvements in communications.
- Consideration of alternative forms of transport such as helicopters.
- Establishment of a national trauma audit scheme based on the American Major Trauma Outcome Study (MTOS).
- More trauma research.

4. Advanced Trauma Life Support (ATLS)

The ATLS course of the American College of Surgeons was introduced into this country by Sir Miles Irving in 1988. There is an elected ATLS steering group under the wing of the Education Board of the RCS, and at one stage there was talk of the possession of an ATLS qualification being an essential requirement for the FRCS Part II examination – currently it is 'strongly recommended'. The course is a didactic management course, aimed at a doctor working alone, based on the careful assessment of a patient's injuries in the order most likely to be fatal (Airway, Breathing, Circulation etc); in addition to lectures there are practical skill stations where candidates can learn skills such as cricothyroidotomy and tube thoracocentesis. Role playing is used to practice the resuscitation of a badly injured patient (the 'moulage') and candidates are scored on their performance.

5. The trauma centre

The concept of the trauma centre was first developed in the USA after Trunkey showed that mortality from major trauma could be reduced from 74% to under 20% by concentrating both patients and resources into major hospitals geared to the management of trauma. This is expensive and not without its problems. For example, some American trauma systems have suffered in recent years from several hospitals withdrawing from the system for reasons connected with workload, cost, difficulty in recruiting physicians and a general recognition that dealing with major trauma, especially when crime related, is unpleasant.

The Current Situation

An examination of the current situation suggests that major improvements have been made and that these are likely to be long-lasting, if not permanent.

1. Pre-hospital care

Pre-hospital care is based on the ambulance service. A number of changes, particularly in the London Ambulance Service (LAS), have been made in order to improve patient care and response times, not just for trauma, but for all types of emergency. This has resulted in improved paramedic training (though not to American standards), the provision of rapid response non-conveying vehicles to speed the delivery of advanced trained paramedics to the scene of an accident, and conveyance of patients to the nearest appropriate, as opposed to the nearest available, hospital. LAS flirted briefly with Computer Aided Despatch (CAD). Despite the fact that this early system failed amidst a blaze of adverse media publicity, CAD will one day form the basis of ambulance service callouts countrywide, as it has done in the USA for some time.

There is little provision for the use of doctors at the scene of an accident. The only pre-hospital role for the doctor (apart from HEMS) is through the British Association of Immediate Care Specialists (BASICS) whose role is to attend accidents on a voluntary basis and whose training and organisation is improving to the point where some feel that a BASICS doctor should be available for every ambulance trauma callout.

2. Helicopters

Four helicopter emergency systems, started since 1988, are still running. The first of these was FirstAir, an ambulance service based system in Cornwall using an MBB B0105 which carries a paramedic but no doctor. The system was assessed over a period of one year (1 December 1990 – 30 November 1991) by the Medical Care Research Unit (MCRU), Sheffield, which concluded that the system was expensive, activation times were slower than for land-based systems but travel time to hospital was much shorter once the helicopter had arrived at the scene. The helicopter was at its best when the distance from the incident to hospital was the greatest. The second system is the Kent Air Ambulance which uses a police helicopter, an Aerospatiale SA355, to augment the ground ambulance system. Their early operations were described in a report which was widely circulated but not published, in 1991, which revealed that the system was being used for quite minor conditions such as back pain. Major trauma featured rarely in the report. The third system is also a paramedic system in the West Midlands, based in Coventry, which has flown over 1000 missions but has not been formally assessed.

The fourth system is based in central London, at the Royal London Hospital (RLH), on a rooftop helipad above a university hospital which always carries a doctor.

The Sheffield (MCRU) Unit has carried out an evaluation of HEMS. Unfortunately MCRU were only able to assess one third of the helicopter patients, comparing them with a similar cohort of similarly injured patients conveyed by paramedic-manned ambulances, and their conclusions are expressed as a statistical range rather than a firm figure. They think that HEMS save 12 lives a year, though this figure may be higher or lower.

3. Trauma centres

There are three trauma centres in the UK, only one of which is officially recognised as such by the government. This is Stoke-on-Trent, where A&E consultants live in at night in order to run the trauma calls and resuscitate patients who are then passed into the normal hospital system and generally receive their definitive care from on-site registrars in other specialties. The Department of Health has assessed this system by comparing it with two comparator sites, Hull and Preston, to see whether centralisation of resources improves the patient outcome. Unfortunately the comparator sites had also been upgraded and include on site neurosurgery. This reduced any measurable difference and the findings of the report were inconclusive.

The second trauma centre is in Oxford, at the John Radcliffe Hospital, where consultant orthopaedic and A&E surgeons live in at night and lead the trauma calls. Emergency surgery is initiated at consultant level. This system results in a higher senior registrar and consultant call-in from the other specialties. The drawback in Oxford is that neurosurgery is on a separate site and it is difficult to manage multiply-ill patients unless all the specialties involved are immediately available in the same hospital.

Until very recently there were two units in London which would have satisfied the American College of Surgeons recommendations for a Level I trauma centre, having all the main specialties available on a 24-hour basis on one site, and with university affiliation. One of these, St Bartholomew's Hospital, is now closed to emergencies which leaves the Royal London Hospital, three miles to the east, as the only Level I - type centre in London. The trauma is managed by consultant surgeons running the trauma calls and being immediately available on a 24-hour basis, in addition to which the A&E department is staffed at night by an A&E consultant. Other specialties are serviced at a senior registrar or consultant level.

4. The trauma team

Many hospitals receiving major trauma now have trauma teams. Most of the work showing that a trauma team actually makes a difference was done by Driscoll who showed that starting a trauma team could reduce resuscitation times by up to 75% in hospital resuscitation rooms. A trauma team basically consists of a team leader who should be a consultant or senior registrar supervising a number of team members drawn from the surgical, anaesthetic and neurosurgical junior staff. Resuscitation proceeds along ATLS guidelines. The team works in a concurrent manner, a method adapted from ATLS which essentially teaches consecutive resuscitation for the doctor working alone who has to do everything himself.

5. ATLS

ATLS has made deep inroads into the training program of the junior surgeon, and indeed the consultant, since 1988. There are now 112 provider courses a year available, and up until the end of 1994, 5027 doctors had successfully completed such a course. 1085 of these were orthopaedic surgeons, 1221 were anaesthetists, 1269 were A&E physicians and 956 were general surgeons. 824 were consultants, but the vast bulk of the trainees came from the registrar and senior registrar grades. There are only five instructor courses a year with 344 instructors, of whom 104 are in A&E, 90 are anaesthetists, 78 are orthopaedic surgeons and only 36 of which are general surgeons.

6. The Major Trauma Outcome Study (MTOS)

MTOS was started in this country in 1988. All trauma patients who either die in hospital or are admitted for more than three days, those transferred for specialist trauma care or admitted to an intensive care unit are entered into the study. There are now 120 centres which have admitted 40,000 patients into the database which is held at Hope Hospital, Manchester. Patients aged 65 years or over with fractured neck of femur are excluded. A probability of survival, calculated on the Injury Severity Score (ISS) and Revised Trauma Score (RTS), is produced for each patient; this is influenced by age and whether or not the trauma is blunt or penetrating.

The drawback of MTOS is the enormous number of variables. The calculation of the ISS depends on accurate scoring of the patient's injuries which may not be available until post mortem, and the way in which the score is calculated has given rise to considerable criticism . In addition, no allowance is made for permanent casemix variables at individual hospitals resulting from an unusually heavy trauma load. Nevertheless, MTOS remains a valuable tool for trauma audit.

7. Trauma committee

The External Affairs Board of the Royal College of Surgeons has established a trauma committee, which meets twice a year. It is served by representatives of all the major surgical specialties involved in trauma in the UK and is additional evidence of the Royal College's commitment to improvements in trauma care.

8. Research

This is perhaps the one area, apart from the MTOS study, where there has been little improvement since 1988. There is still little research into trauma care in the UK. Perhaps some clues as to who is interested in trauma research can be gleaned from the surgical journals. Certainly in this country orthopaedics predominates. The journal *Injury* which is published in this country aims to publish as broad a spectrum of trauma papers as possible. During 1994 it published 167 papers, about one third of which were case reports. 100 of the total originated from orthopaedic surgeons, 41 from all other surgical specialties combined and 26 from A&E departments. The *British Journal of Surgery* published 511 papers during the same period, of which 13 (2.5%) were about trauma. Seven of these originated in the UK. Perhaps the doyen of trauma journals is the *Journal of Trauma*, the official journal of the American Association for the Surgery of Trauma. In 1994 it published 340 papers, 95 of which originated outside the North American continent. Only eight of these came from the UK. The inescapable conclusion is that there is very little trauma research going on in the UK and certainly very little indeed originating from general surgeons.

The Future

The future of trauma care in the UK is far from clear, and depends very much upon whether the current or any future government recognise major trauma as being an area of health care worthy of investment; nevertheless, some target areas can be outlined.

1. Trauma centres

The setting up of further trauma centres will depend on the outcome of the Stoke evaluation which may well turn out to be flawed for the reasons already given. The message from the United States is unequivocal; taking patients to a proper trauma unit rather than to the nearest hospital improves the outcome in trauma.

2. Cost

Much depends on funding; the perception of trauma care is that it is expensive but deaths from trauma are also exceedingly expensive. It is vital not to confuse value with cost, and to provide the facilities needed for treating these people. It is recognised by everyone that spending money on prevention will reduce the number of trauma deaths in the medium term but this does not help today's trauma victim.

3. Training

Training in trauma care will become more important. General surgeons are particularly well equipped to deal with the initial management and resuscitation but their actual role in the A&E department appears to be diminishing as they are replaced by the A&E consultant and anaesthetist. Williams and Irving suggest that this situation could be improved by increasing the general surgeon's interest in trauma in four ways; improving basic training, adding intensive care training to the surgical curriculum, encouraging academic involvement and research into trauma and using general surgical consultants as role models for surgical trainees. Certainly there is evidence from the USA that including ICU training in the training of a trauma specialist makes the specialty more interesting for the trainee. Very few higher surgical training rotations in the UK offer this option.

Trunkey and Irving both recommend intensivist training for general surgeons. There is some evidence that this is happening, with provision for ICU training on a limited part-time basis in the Basic Surgical Trainee's (BST) curriculum and some trauma training for the Higher Surgical Trainee (HST) in the registrar grade. However, the majority of trainee surgeons in this country will not want a full-time intensivist training, and indeed with the recent changes in surgical training, involving both a shorter training span and shorter working hours, it is difficult to see how proper intensive care training can be fitted in to the busy training schedule unless the trainee surgeon takes a year, or perhaps two, off from his/her rotation, either at the BST/HST changeover or as part of a research sabbatical during the HST years. This would then be on a voluntary basis.

The removal of A&E from the compulsory training of the surgeon is bound to have some impact on A&E services, if not the training of the trauma surgeon. The inclusion of this post as a requirement for the FRCS was widely credited with improving the quality of A&E services countrywide; its removal has put A&E departments in a difficult position because they can no longer attract staff to what is a fairly unpopular post. Nevertheless, both from the point of view of the surgical trainee and the patient, this move is unlikely to make much difference. The trainee will receive training at a higher level anyway, and (it is hoped) the initial management of the seriously injured patient will be at a more senior level than previously pertained when the SHO, the most junior registered practitioner in the hospital, was expected to run the initial management of the most seriously injured patients.

4. Research

Current research into trauma is woefully lacking, and is probably the only one of the recommendations made both by Trunkey and the RCS report which has not been dealt with at a hospital level. There is enough trauma going through the A&E departments and Intensive Care Units of most large hospitals to enable surgical teams to collect good data and publish it.

Conclusion

Many major decisions on the provision of trauma services, including the provision of helicopter transport, will be made at a Trust Board level in today's NHS, and funding will be provider driven. It is important therefore that clinicians involved in trauma care should have proper input where these decisions are being made, and should be able to argue for trauma care as an investment in the health of the nation rather than as a drain on scarce healthcare resources.

This brings us to the question posed in the title of this article: 'who owns trauma?' Many think it is the orthopaedic surgeons, some think it is the A&E physician, some regard trauma as the last bastion of the general surgeon, but in fact none of these sections of the acute medical services can lay claim to the subject on their own. The successful trauma clinician is the doctor, regardless of his specialty, who is interested in trauma management and can argue both scientifically and politically for improvements in trauma care. It isn't the clinician who owns trauma at all, but the patient; it is to the injured patient that we owe the best possible care.

Acknowledgements: An extended version of this paper was published in the *Association of Surgeons' 1995 Yearbook.* Please see list of publications.

Frank W Cross, MS FRCS is Consultant General and Vascular Surgeon at the Royal London Hospital, London E1

SECTION 9: DATA, OUTCOME AND COSTS

Introduction

Richard Earlam

In the UK each year there are approximately 150,000 people injured each year and of these 15,000 die either before they reach hospital or in anyone of the 250 hospitals. With major trauma the fatal accidents die not from their actual injury but from the inability of the body to respond to such damage from the accident. This might appear to be just a play with words but it is a justifiable subdivision from the surgeon's point of view. There is an anatomical classification of injury – the Abbreviated Injury Scale (AIS) – and a pathophysiological scale – the Trauma Score or Revised Trauma Score (TRS) – which describes the body's response. As an example, for any given injury the body may respond differently; most statistics divide the population into young and old with the border at 55 years of age but clearly there is a graduated response that is worse as one grows older and 75 year old patients do worse than 25 year old athletes. Similarly the subdivision into 'blunt' and 'penetrating' injuries involves a different type of trauma e.g coming off a motor bicycle at 70 mph which can affect most of the body versus a stab in the chest which may only damage one lung. These anatomical and pathophysiological scores are the basis of measuring the severity of trauma which is applied in the Major Trauma Outcome Study (MTOS) in the USA and in MTOS-UK. The original purpose of this data collection was to select patients for audit and give a rough guide as to what the chances of survival were. The data was concerned with audit of mortality but the system has been hi-jacked to assess the competence of hospitals and by administrators, health economics and insurance firms to calculate prices and costs.

The fact that AIS came originally from the Automotive Industry in North America for measuring injury in car crashes so that they could improve motor car safety is, of course, an historical irrelevance. The first pathophysiological score was the Trauma Score (TS) which has now been simplified into the Revised Trauma Score (RTS). RTS has three physiological parameters – Glasgow Coma Scale (GCS, based on eye opening, motor and verbal responses), systolic blood pressure (so you need a sphygmomanometer) and respiratory rate (we hope you have a watch). TS has a scale from 16-1 (highest best, lowest worst) and RTS ranges from 7.84 to 0 (highest best, lowest worst). Figure 1 shows that when the pathophysiological response is less than 13 the mortality is 10%.

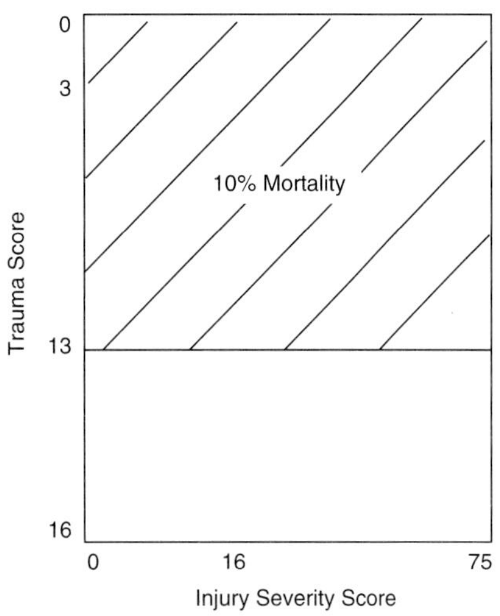

Figure 1:
Trauma Score less than 13

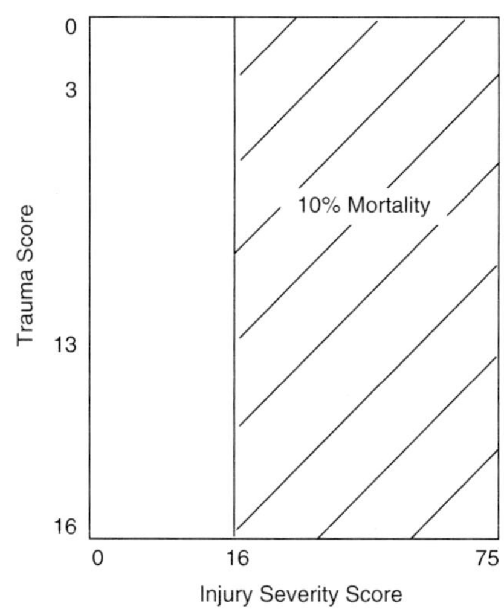

Figure 2:
Injury Severity Score more than 15

SECTION 9: DATA, OUTCOME AND COSTS

The anatomical injuries are measured with the Abbreviated Injury Scale (AIS 6-1, highest fatal, lowest minor). The six scales are calculated in each of nine anatomical services: i) head; ii) face; iii) neck; iv) thorax; v) abdomen and pelvic contents vi) spine, vertebrae; vii) upper extremity; viii) bony pelvis, lower extremity; and ix) external including burns. Over 2000 injury types are listed in the AIS book. Such injuries are also coded by the International Classification of Diseases ICD-9 and the latest edition ICD-10. The original nine AIS subgroups were then placed into six body regions and the highest score was taken for each of these anatomical groups. Then the sum of the squares of the three highest scores were added together to give the Injury Severity Score (ISS) and put in order from 75-0 (highest usually fatal, lowest less so). Empirically a score of greater than 15 was designated as **major trauma** which has a high mortality. Figure 2 shows, when the ISS is over 16, that the mortality rate is 10%. However those with an historical interest, observing that ISS is an ordinal rather than an interval scale and also is a non-linear progression lacking the figures 7 and 15, with 14 and 22 unusual and 9 and 16 common because you are summing squares, would perhaps like to consult the three ladies in Macbeth over the logic, because it smacks of witchcraft. They might possibly inform you that a simple ICD coding can also give a good indication of outcome and you probably get an equally satisfactory outcome measurement listing all the injuries and adding up the AIS scores. Summing squares was all right for Pythagoras but is illogical for trauma outcome measurements. However it is used in North America and we in the UK who do not have so much experience should use the TRISS Scoring System because it is the best we have (Figure 3). Here it will be evident that anatomical injury and pathophysiological response can be combined to give an assessment of 50% survival or deaths, thus combining the two previous 10% mortality thresholds (Figures 1 and 2).

Stoke-on-Trent have simplified their data by concentrating on major trauma (ISS greater than 15) and then subdividing according to blunt and penetrating, above or below age 55, and taking special note of head injuries which are a killer. Our figures are similar to theirs as you will see in Section 9A by Clive Kirk. He mentions that we cannot compare UK trauma patients with USA patients because we have less shooting and stabbing and more blunt and head injury patients. He also points out that if you transfer from one hospital to another, the patient population changes because some will already have died in the first hospital, so those transferred are a selected group. What nobody has done is a study of those who died at the scene or during transport by land ambulance. The faster and better the pre-hospital care the greater will be the number dying in hospital, usually in the emergency room, in spite of the very best care in expert centres. There is a case to be made out for compulsory investigation of all trauma deaths, with special attention to those who died *before* the ambulance men arrived and *before* they were transported to hospital, looking for preventable causes so that we can learn and improve.

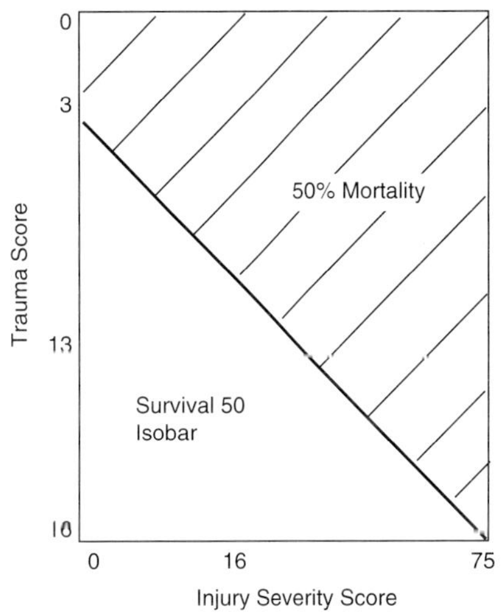

Figure 3:
The 50 Survival Isobar for the TRISS diagram

These paragraphs have concentrated on data collection and outcome for improving pre-hospital and hospital care. Good doctors are quite capable of performing their own assessment and really do not require a superimposed central bureaucracy of curious administrators. But prices and costs have to be collected for payment in today's NHS and the same flawed methodology has to be adopted. This is discussed by health economists in Section 9D and from the point of view of a purchaser in Section 9E. These are two very important articles by experts in their fields and it is clear that the subject of costs must not be avoided, yet on the other hand difficulties and limitations must be recognised.

PROPAQ FOR THE FRONT LINE.

Vital Signs Monitoring in the Air and on the Ground.

Small wonder. The Propaq® is the lightest portable vital signs monitor available. It's also extremely rugged, water resistant, and has long battery life.

Propaq delivers all the information you need and more: ECG (3 to 5 leads), SpO_2, end-tidal CO_2, respiration, apnea, noninvasive

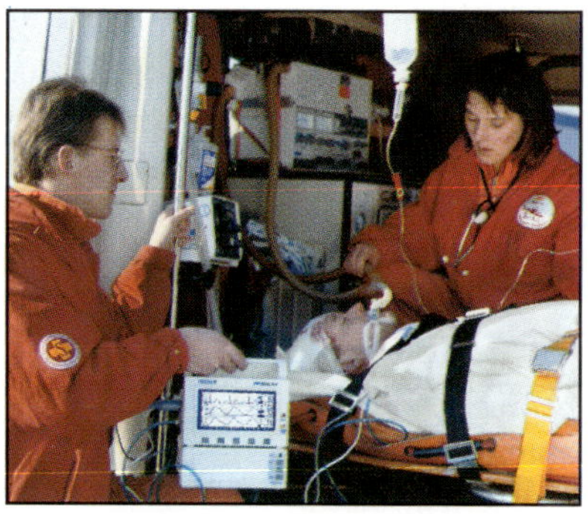

or invasive blood pressure and 2 temperature channels. Propaq is ready to go anywhere you do. For more information call Protocol Systems at 01264 720 828.

Put a Propaq on your team. And provide a higher level of care on the ground and in the air.

PROTOCOL®
SYSTEMS EUROPE

Harewood House, Wherwell Road, Longparish, Hampshire • SP11 7AH
+44(0)1264 720 828 (telephone)
+44(0)1264 720 514 (fax)
Internet: http://www.protocol.com

Germany Tel.: +49-89-4607080 • Fax: +49-89-4607087
France Tel.: +33-1-53675264 • Fax: +33-1-53675263

OUTCOME

Clive Kirk

The controlled rescue of patients from the scene of trauma, provision of early medical care, and rapid transportation to suitable facilities would appear to be obvious advantages of the HEMS system. There has been, however, considerable argument as to whether these factors do in fact produce a better outcome. The common sense approach is deemed inadequate so science and statistics have been called in to assist.

Unfortunately it is generally agreed that the tools, whereby trauma systems can be investigated and compared, are blunt. In addition, outcome has usually been measured in terms of death or survival, which is an all or nothing approach that leaves many questions unanswered. Quality of survival is obviously an important factor but as yet relatively little work has been published concerning the quality of survival after major trauma. Lastly HEMS is unique in the United Kingdom so direct comparison with other systems in this country is not possible. The patterns and quantities of trauma seen by similar systems in other countries tend to be very different making this approach equally difficult.

Notwithstanding these caveats, an attempt has been made to show the mortality of the seriously injured entering the HEMS system and to compare this with the experience of the pilot Trauma Centre established at the North Staffordshire Hospital in Stoke on Trent.

The definition of **serious injury** is a score of more than 15 using the Injury Severity Score (ISS). Figure 1 shows the total number of such patients arriving via HEMS at the Royal London Hospital.

Figure 1: HEMS Patients with ISS>15

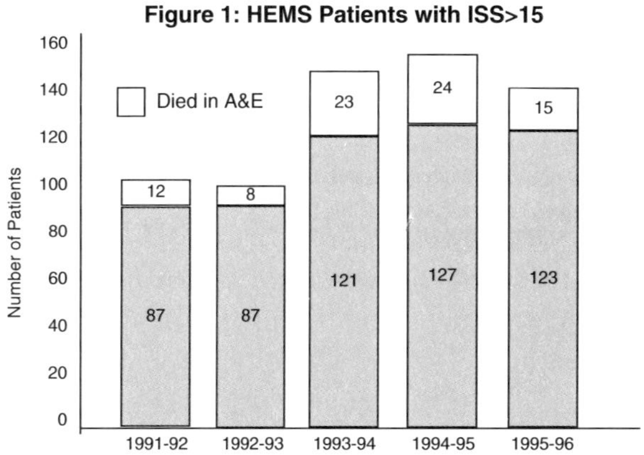

Figure 2 shows the breakdown of these patients with serious injury confined to a single region. It can be seen that head injuries predominate but that patients with one system account for only about a quarter of the seriously injured. Most patients in that category have had significant injuries in more than one body area. Figure 3 shows the percentage of patients with **critical injuries** which are defined as AIS >4. Again it can be seen that head injuries predominate and that over half the seriously injured patients are also critically injured using this definition.

Figure 2: Body regions in the seriously injured with isolated injuries only (ISS>15 and other regions AIS < 2)

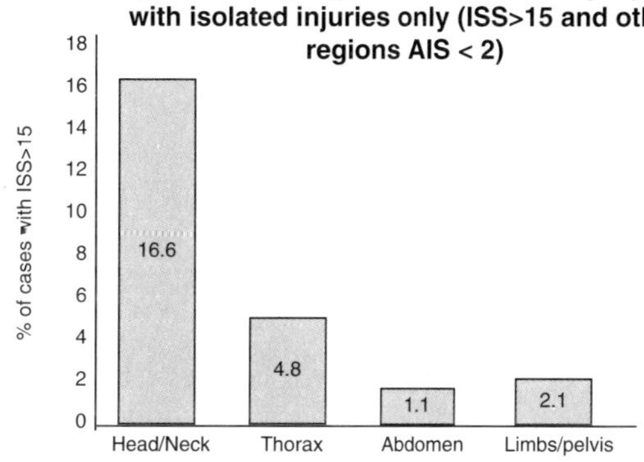

Figure 3: Body regions with critical injuries defined as AIS >4

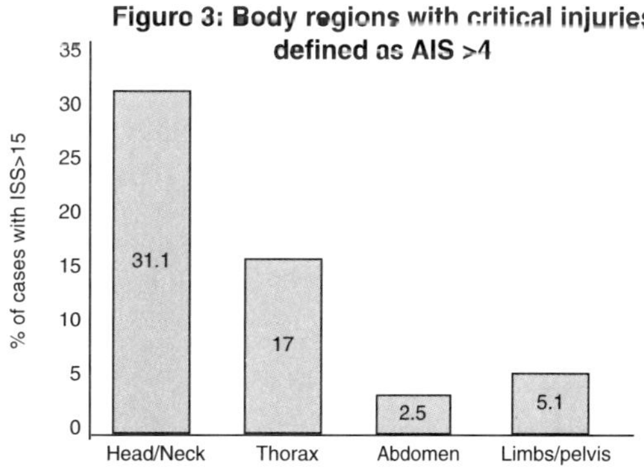

The difficulties in comparing outcomes between HEMS and other systems is the mismatch in injury severity, which is demonstrated by the relative proportions of patients in the national Major Trauma Outcome Study (MTOS-UK) and HEMS compared with probability of survival bands. The Trauma Research Group at the North Staffordshire Hospital have recently published their experience of patients with ISS>15 and we have attempted to compare our figures. In the period 1992-95 around 180 patients per annum with ISS>15 were admitted to the

Stoke unit. Between 1993-96 the number of HEMS patients with an ISS>15 received at the RLH were from 138 to 151 per annum.

Figure 4: Distribution of injury severity scores

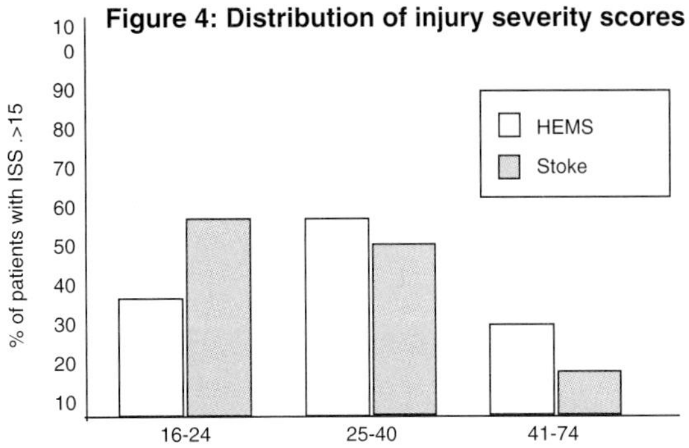

Figure 4 shows a mismatch in case mix with higher percentages of HEMS patients in the higher ISS bands. Another confusing factor is that the Stoke experience included some 35% of patients transferred in from other hospitals. These patients are to some extent self selecting survivors as they have got through the initial phase of treatment at the first hospital and the transfer journey. On the other hand all HEMS patients are primary admissions direct from the scene of injury. As can be seen in Figure 1, a significant number die in the A&E department at the RLH before definitive treatment can be accomplished.

The mortality figures are presented with and without these patients as an, albeit crude, attempt to adjust for the differences in referral pattern because those dying in A&E would not survive a secondary transfer. Bearing in mind these considerations Figure 5 shows the mortality rates in three ISS bands. As can be seen these are slightly higher in the HEMS series if all cases are included but reduce to very similar figures to those from Stoke if A&E deaths are excluded. Injury severity scores are only part of the picture; disturbances in consciousness levels and physiology are also important and these parameters together form the basis of probability of survival calculations.

Figure 5: Mortality in three Injury Severity Score bands

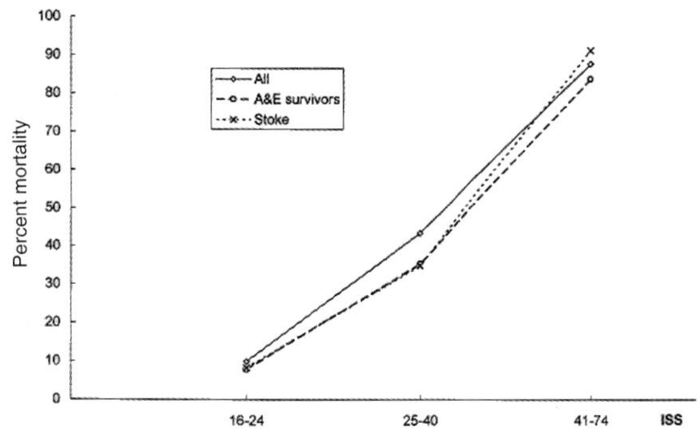

Based on this probability of survival bands Figure 6 shows the mortality rates comparing HEMS and Stoke. At the lowest risk level there is no difference as expected because these patients are unlikely to die. Similarly at the top end, when death is probable, no differences are detected. The intermediate groups however show a 10-15% decrease in mortality comparing HEMS with the Trauma Centre. Whilst care is needed in interpreting these figures it is evident that HEMS is doing at least as well as the only officially recognised Trauma Centre in the UK.

Figure 6: Mortality in probability of survival bands

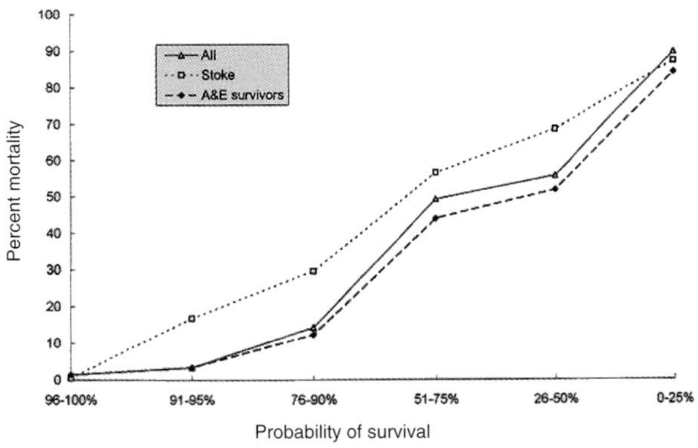

In their health care evaluation of the effectiveness of HEMS, the Sheffield group curiously suggested that the less seriously injured patients might actually do less well when treated by HEMS. Currently, for those patients admitted to RLH by HEMS, the death rate in patients with an ISS of less than 16 is 0.88%. This can be compared with 1.1% for RLH trauma patients overall and 1.7% in the national MTOS cohort.

Figure 7: Functional Recovery in HEMS Survivors using FIM (n=80)

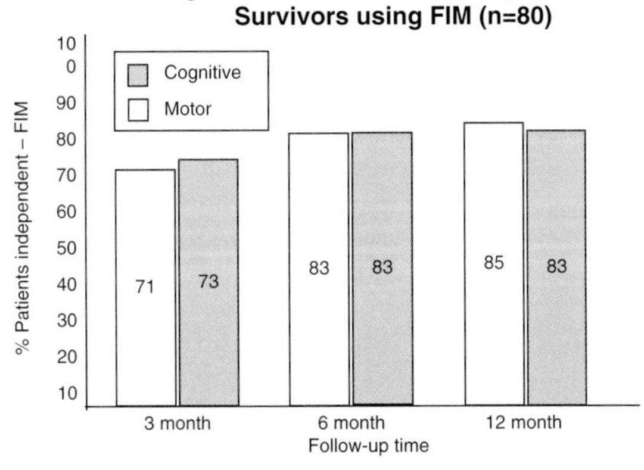

A start has been made looking at disability outcome using the Functional Independence Measure (FIM) (see Section 8 K (iii)). Figure 7 shows the outcome of 80 HEMS survivors at 3, 6 and 12 months. It is evident that 85% have reached full motor function and 83% full cognitive function at 12 months. Unfortunately there are no comparable figures from other centres available. It is absolutely essential that outcome measures of trauma care include both mortality and morbidity which is considered as both disability and handicap.

Clive Kirk is Data Manager for HEMS at the RLH.

DATA COLLECTION IN THE INTENSIVE CARE UNIT AND TRAUMA UNIT: APACHE II

David Goldhill, Stuart Withington

Data on all Intensive Care and Trauma Unit patients has been collected since 1990 at the Royal London Hospital with a computerised data collection system.[1,2] Standard agreed definitions are used when recording the information which is collected on a typeset form by marking boxes in the manner of a multiple choice paper. In addition some text fields are entered through the keyboard. The information consists of basic demographic data, time of hospital and ICU admission and the information necessary to calculate an APACHE II score.[3] In his original paper on APACHE II,[3] Knaus stated that 'This scoring system can be used to . . . compare the efficacy of intensive care in different hospitals or over time.'

The APACHE II score is derived from 11 physiological variables (Table 1) and the Glasgow Coma Score (GCS), the patient's age and chronic health status. The physiological variables score 0 if normal, and up to 4 points for abnormalities, apart from the creatinine which scores double points (up to 8) in acute renal failure. Of the maximum 71 points, 6 depend on the patient's age, 5 on previous chronic health, 12 on the Glasgow Coma Score and 48 on abnormalities in the physiological variables. The patient's predicted mortality is calculated from their APACHE II score, a coefficient based on the reason for ICU admission (diagnostic category) and an additional weighting for emergency surgery.

Table 1:
The 11 physiological variables contributing to the APACHE II score

	maximum points
Temperature	4
Mean arterial blood pressure	4
Heart rate	4
Respiratory rate	4
Oxygenation (either A-aDO_2 or PaO_2)	4
Arterial pH	4
Serum sodium	4
Serum potassium	4
Serum creatinine (with acute renal failure)	8
Haematocrit or haemoglobin	4
White blood cell count	4

The worst values of inspired oxygen concentration, PaO_2 and $PaCO_2$ are recorded and the number of points for oxygenation are calculated. All other physiological points are recorded by marking boxes indicating the range which encompassed the worst value of the variable. Nurses and doctors have the responsibility for collecting the data. They are trained and supported by a full-time regional audit coordinator. The forms are read by an optical mark reader (OMR) and the data entered into a computer database. Validation of the data begins with a visual check of the form. Simple error checking is incorporated into the OMR so that incomplete forms or those with mutually exclusive marks are rejected. Rejected forms are returned for completion. Further error checking takes place within the database to reject obvious errors such as patients discharged before admission, or duplication of records. Further checks are run within the database to identify anomalous data.

Although there are several pitfalls when interpreting APACHE II data[4,5] the method is widely used to stratify ICU patients and to predict outcome. Data for trauma patients is shown in Table 2 and Table 3.

The total number of ICU patients has decreased since 1992. This has occurred because some routine cardiac surgical patients were admitted to a High Dependency Unit during 1994 and in 1995 all cardiac surgical admissions ceased as cardiac services moved off site.

The general non-trauma ICU population is predominantly male and old (Figure 1) with 67% of admissions being males. The percentage mortality for the four years 1992-1995 was 19%. Among trauma patients there is an even higher percentage of males (76%) and the average age is much younger with most patients in their teens, 20s, 30s or 40s (Figure 2). The percentage mortality (18%) among trauma patients for the four years 1992-1995 was almost identical to that of the other patients.

Mortality increases with increasing APACHE II score (Figure 3). Hospital mortality is the chosen end point and approximately 35% of patients that die in hospital do so after discharge from the ICU. The APACHE II score is not adjusted for casemix. In other words the score does not take account of the underlying diagnosis. This is very important especially with trauma as patients with severe head injuries are less likely to survive than patients who

Figure 1: Sex and age distribution for non-trauma patients 1992-95

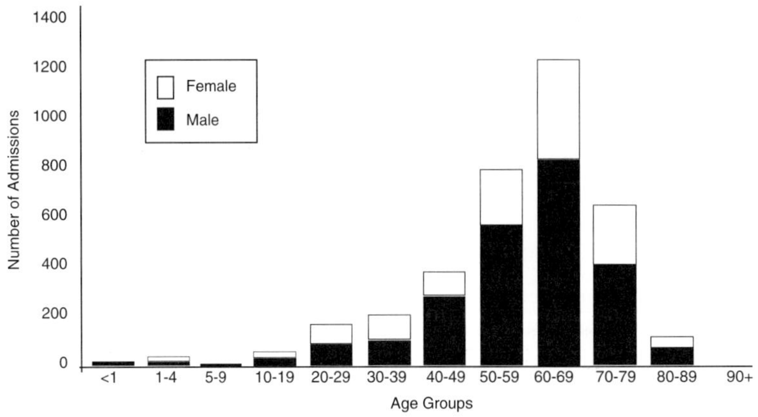

Figure 2: Sex and age distribution for trauma patients 1992-95

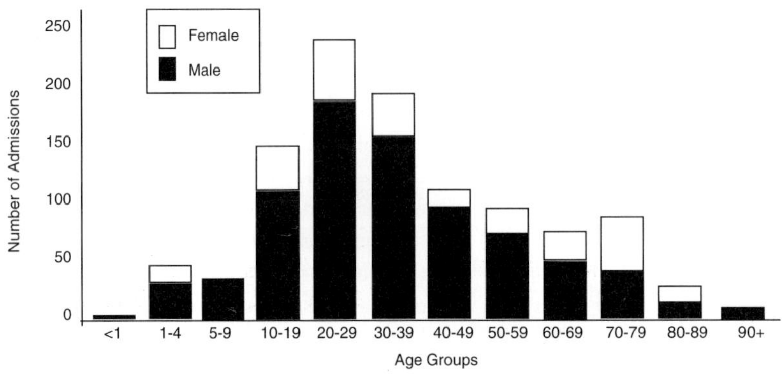

Figure 3: APACHE II Scores and outcome for trauma patients 1992-95

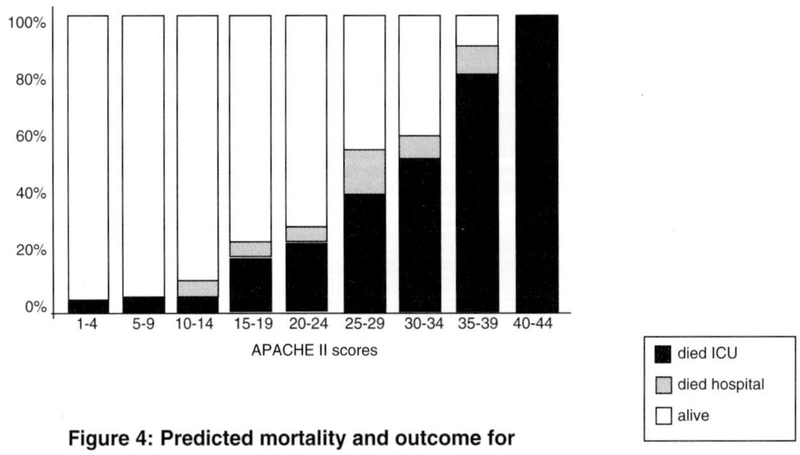

Figure 4: Predicted mortality and outcome for trauma patients 1992-95

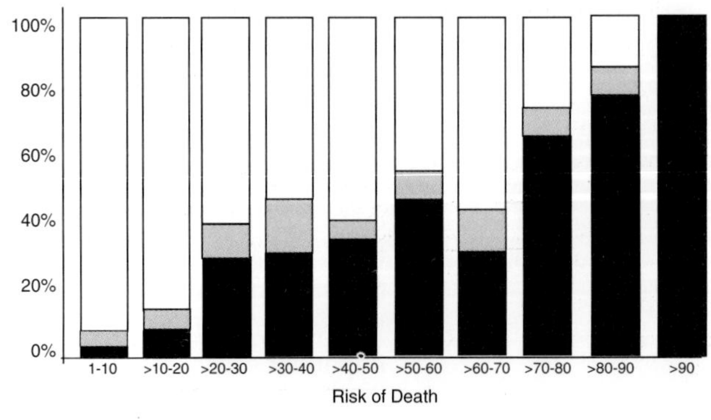

Table 2: ICU and Trauma Unit patients 1992–1995

	1992	1993	1994	1995
Total patients	1345	1314	1039	1000
Non-cardiac patients	572	702	680	767
Trauma patients	211	295	284	266
% of total	15.7	22.5	27.3	26.6
% of non-cardiac	36.9	42.0	41.8	34.7
HEMS patients	116	164	175	173
% of trauma patients	55.0	55.6	61.6	65.0

Table 3: Trauma patients fulfiling APACHE II criteria (16 years or older, first admission, no burns)

	1992	1993	1994	1995
Number	171	228	235	203
Average bed stay	4.1	4.6	4.9	5.9
Average APACHE II	12.0	12.0	15.0	14.0
Predicted mortality (%)	13.2	14.2	18.5	17.5
Observed mortality (%)	18.7	18.0	19.1	19.2
SMR	1.4	1.25	1.03	1.09

SMR = standardised mortality ratio (observed hospital deaths/predicted hospital deaths)

do not have major cerebral damage. This is why an equation incorporating the reason for ICU admission is used to calculate a predicted hospital mortality. It is then possible to compare the predicted outcome with actual (observed) hospital outcome.

Figure 4 shows observed mortality by bands of predicted percentage mortality. For example the band >20–30 summarises the outcome of all trauma patients with a predicted mortality of between greater than 20% and 30%. Although there are many pitfalls in interpreting APACHE II outcome data[4,5] we would expect, more or less, for there to be a 25% observed mortality for patients in this band. The observed hospital mortality is 40% so outcome is worse than expected. On the other hand in the band >60–70 we would expect, more or less, for there to be a 65% observed mortality for patients in this band. The observed mortality is 46% so outcome is much better than expected.

One way of summarising this data is to calculate the ratio of observed hospital deaths to predicted hospital deaths and this is called the standardised mortality ratio (SMR). The SMR for each year are in Table 3.

References

1. Withington PS, Goldhill DR, Ooi LG, Birch NJ. Optical Mark Reading, A new approach to audit for intensive care. Care of the Critically Ill 1992; 8: 74-7.
2. Goldhill DR, Withington PS, Birch NJ.The North East Thames Intensive Care Audit System. Theoretical Surgery 1993; 8: 1-5.
3. Knaus WA, Draper EA, Wagner DP, Zimmerman JE. APACHE II: A severity of disease classification system. Critical Care Medicine 1985; 13: 818-29.
4. Goldhill DR, Withington PS. Mortality predicted by APACHE II: The effect of changes in physiological values and post-ICU hospital mortality. In Press Anaesthesia 1996.
5. Goldhill DR, Withington PS. The ability of APACHE II to adjust for casemix difference. In press Intensive Care Medicine 1996.

David Goldhill and **Stuart Withington** are both consultants and senior lecturers on the ICU and Trauma Unit. They have recently edited a Textbook of Intensive Care published by Chapman Hall, London in Autumn 1996. ISBN 0 412 601 303.

OUTCOME FOLLOWING HEAD INJURY TREATED BY THE HEMS SYSTEM

Tim Coats

In the evaluation of patient outcome in a trauma system those with head injury are most likely to act as a sensitive marker of quality of treatment. It is well known that early definitive intervention and avoidance of secondary insults improves outcome following head injury. An integrated trauma system combines pre-hospital and specialist in-hospital management, providing a seamless continuum of care. The addition of helicopter transport allows triage from the incident scene to the most appropriate hospital. Such a system, by improving each component, ought to improve outcome following head injury.The application to the HEMS system of conventional forms of trauma audit such as the TRISS method used by the Major Trauma Outcome Study (MTOS-UK) is not valid because of variations in case mix and timing of Revised Trauma Score (RTS) measurement. We therefore have to look at other measures of success.

It seems likely that an integrated system, using early correction of hypoxia and hypotension combined with definitive intervention and avoiding the need for inter-hospital transfer, leads to a better outcome. There is a concern that this form of management may increase survival, but that the extra survivors will be severely disabled. The production of a large number of severely disabled survivors would not be widely regarded as a good consequence of advanced trauma management.

Long term severe disability has a profound personal, social and economic cost. Leaving aside the personal cost, the care of a severely disabled individual following head injury has an economic cost approaching one million pounds for a lifetime's care (assuming a life expectancy of between 25 and 30 years and a cost of approximately £30,000 per year). This figure will be greatly increased if institutional care is required.

Inclusion of the cost of disability amongst survivors is vital in any economic analysis of a trauma system. The cost of a single patient with long term disability approximately equals the annual cost of HEMS, so prevention of a single case of long term disability each year would pay for the system. Any analysis of cost/benefit that does not include such an important factor as the disability of survivors is incomplete.

The outcome following severe head injury (GCS < 8) measured by Glasgow Outcome Score (GOS) in 209 patients treated by the HEMS system is shown in Table 1. Comparison sets are available from other series, the best being the Traumatic Coma Data Bank which is a large American series of head injury outcomes from a group of neurosurgical centres. Outcome in the HEMS system is compared with the Traumatic Coma Data Bank (TCDB) in Table 2.

There is a greater mortality in the HEMS patients because this group has a greater injury severity, but amongst survivors there is less disability. The apparent increase in mortality for the HEMS group is explained by the greater severity of extra-cranial injuries. The fear that large

Outcome (GOS)	Number	Percentage
Dead	107	51%
Vegetative	1	0.5%
Severe Disability	15	7%
Moderate Disability	31	15%
Good Recovery	41	20%
Lost to Follow-up	14	6.5%

Table 1: Distribution of Outcome following Severe Head Injuries

	TCDB	HEMS
Dead	36%	51%
Vegetative	6%	0.5%
Severe Disability	16%	7%
Moderate Disability	16%	15%
Good Recovery	25%	20%
Lost to follow-up	1%	6.5%

Table 2: Comparison of HEMS outcomes with the Traumatic Coma Data Bank

numbers of severely disabled survivors may be produced by the intensive pre-hospital care of HEMS is unfounded.

Comparison of head injury outcome in different trauma systems is difficult because:

- Patients treated in the HEMS system have more **severe extra-cranial injuries** than other series. Previous reports are usually from neurosurgical tertiary referral centres and contain a higher proportion of isolated head injuries and patients who have late deterioration in level of consciousness.
- Pre-hospital resuscitation included **anaesthesia, intubation and ventilation in all patients**. This precludes the measurement of a post-resuscitation GCS. If comparison is to avoid the inclusion of patients with a depressed level of consciousness from extra-cranial causes, an anatomical criteria must be included in the definition of severe head injury.
- Mechanism of injury, and in particular speed of impact, has a profound effect on outcome. Patients treated by HEMS tend to have a **severe mechanism of injury** and profound immediate neurological consequences, because such cases can readily be identified in the ambulance control room. These patients are usually the more severely injured end of the spectrum and are more likely to die.
- There are more patients lost to follow up in the HEMS group because there are more patients of no fixed abode or vagrants. All those lost to follow-up were certainly not in the dead or disabled groups, and were not institutionalised in a hospital.

There is no database at present which includes details of mechanism of injury, timed measurements of pathophysiology, anatomical classification of head injury on CT scan, details of extra-cranial injury, details and times of interventions, and classification of outcomes that could form the basis of a comparison.

The HEMS system provides speedy treatment for the head injured patient within times that have been shown to be associated with better outcomes. The system also immediately corrects abnormalities of perfusion and oxygenation that produce secondary brain injury. The low level of long term disability is encouraging, but further studies, and the creation of a comparison data set, is required to define which of the different components of the HEMS system can be improved even more.

Tim Coats, Emeritus HEMS Registrar is Research Fellow in Neurosurgery and Senior Lecturer in Accident and Emergency at the RLH.

Photo: G Collins

The patient must always be resuscitated and rehabilitated but sometimes the transport cannot be repaired and must be recycled

ECONOMIC EVALUATION IN BRIEF

John Brazier, Colin Green

Background

The discipline of economics has been called the dismal science because of its association with resource scarcity. However, economists are only the messenger in this respect, and the focus of economics and its application is on making the most of available resources. It can be easily recognised that within health care, limited resources combined with the growing demand for health services create an increasing number of difficult decisions. The continuing technological advances in medicine, the growing expectations of the general population and the increasingly visible demographic changes are a few of the factors putting pressure on health care resources, and ultimately on those involved in decision making within health care. Nevertheless, decisions must be made. In the provision of trauma care, as in many other areas, the application of economics is concerned with assisting in the making of these difficult decisions.

Economics aims to promote the efficiency, or 'value for money', obtained from the numerous health services competing for limited health care resources.[1] In considering health services, as with most goods and services, it is important to understand their value for money prior to any purchase. For example, most people would not purchase an insurance policy without knowing the insurance coverage provided, as well as the price of the premium payable. Indeed it would be difficult to believe that most purchasers would not also compare one insurance policy with another, before deciding upon which option offered the best value for money. Economics follows this process of assessing efficiency and value for money in deciding which health services to purchase. This process of comparing costs and benefits is called *economic evaluation*.[2]

Economic evaluation compares the different uses of resources in terms of their costs and benefits. This is not the same as minimising costs (economists are not that cynical!). A cheap service which yields no benefit is a waste of resources, whereas an expensive technology saving many lives can be highly efficient.

Looking at cost is an important part of economic evaluation but economics does not centre around the financial cost of alternative services or treatments, since it is the economic cost that is of interest. The economic cost of devoting resources to any activity is the benefits foregone from using the next best service and this is known as the *'opportunity cost'*. Despite considerable advances in NHS financial systems, the financial consequences for an NHS Trust may not reflect these costs.

There are two important practical considerations in costing health care developments. Firstly, it is essential to consider the *marginal* costs rather than the more commonly used average costs. Average costs are simply the total cost divided by the level of activity (e.g cost per A&E attender). Whereas *marginal* costs are the costs arising from any change in activity, i.e the 'extra' costs. For example, the marginal costs of an extra 10,000 attenders at an A&E department are likely to be less than the average costs, this being due to the existence of fixed costs. The costs associated with the extra attenders will also depend on the type of case. One USA study found the marginal costs of minor injuries to be 39% of the average cost per attender.[3] A second issue is the importance of assessing all the resource consequences of a development, including primary care, social services, patients and their carers, and even the economy as a whole, from days off work, should also be assessed.

There are different techniques of economic evaluation. The simplest is where the health consequences of interventions are identical (e.g day case or inpatient stay for the same successful outcome of a minor operation), and here the appropriate technique is known as *cost-minimisation* analysis. Cost-minimisation analysis is concerned with a comparison of costs alone, where the decision relates to interventions which deliver the same outcome to the same patient. Cost-minimisation does not help the purchaser tackle the more difficult decisions concerning which patient group to provide for.

In practice there are few occasions where the consequences of interventions are the same and what is usually required is a comparison of interventions with differing costs and differing consequences. The comparison of alternative interventions that have differing health consequences, but where costs can be related to a single common effect, is known as *cost-effectiveness* analysis. Cost effectiveness analysis compares the costs of particular interventions to health effects measured in 'natural' units, such as life-years gained or cancer cases detected. These costs and effects are directly compared, usually in the form of a ratio showing the cost-effectiveness between two forms of treatment (e.g cost per life saved or cost per cancer case detected in breast cancer screening), with the service or treatment option showing the least cost per unit of effect being preferred. However, in some situations an intervention with a higher cost per effect ratio may be chosen if the extra cost is judged to be worthwhile. The presentation of results using ratios may be inappropriate if one treatment is shown to dominate another in terms of both costs and effects, i.e yield greater benefit, whilst also being less costly.

Cost-effectiveness analyses address some of the issues which relate to the allocation of limited NHS resources, yet many of the options upon which guidance is sought relate to the comparison of alternatives involving multiple outcomes (e.g life-saving surgery compared with a health improving drug therapy for arthritis), and here cost-effectiveness analysis is inappropriate. Where such wider reaching purchasing decisions must be made, a purchaser of health care will often need to weigh up different types of benefits available from different services, such as programmes within cancer, diabetes, and mental health. HEMS like many medical technologies has many different consequences, including disability and the health of survivors as well as the chance of survival. Where a purchaser must make decisions involving multiple outcomes of this nature, i.e quality of life improvements and quantity of life improvements, a common measure is required which can be used across programmes.

One method of economic evaluation which applies a common outcome measure is *cost-benefit* analysis. Cost-benefit analysis presents all benefits (outcomes) in monetary terms. However, attempting to conduct a cost-benefit analysis within health care carries with it a number of complex issues, for example, determining the monetary value to be attached to the life of an elderly person or a teenage child. Where a common measure of value is needed the more popular approach in health economics has been to value changes in health status, in terms of a non-monetary measure of a year in full health. States of health are valued on a scale from zero to one, where one represents full health, and hence zero represents a position where no value is obtained from health. There are a number of techniques available for deriving such an index, which is known as the Quality Adjusted Life Year (QALY).[4] This measure of health can be used to conduct *cost-utility* analysis and allows comparisons of efficiency between services promoting the quantity of life as well as its quality, in terms of cost per QALY.

In practice, although an economic evaluation which addresses multiple outcomes may be very useful, many studies do not summarise their results in terms of a

Table: Main Elements of the Costs and Health Outcomes of the London HEMS

COSTS	HEALTH OUTCOMES
Helicopter operations	Survival
Helicopter	
Maintenance	Residual disability (OPCS disability survey)
Pilots	
Medical and paramedical staff	General Health (Nottingham Health Profile)
Reception facilities	Post-traumatic stress disorder (symptom questionnaire)
Helipad	
A & E facilities	
Patient transfer facilities	
Hospital Care	
ICU stay	
Ward stay	
Outpatient attendances	
General Practice	
Community and social services	
Patient's and carer's time	

common measure of health status, such as the QALY. This being the case with the Sheffield evaluation of HEMS study.[5] Even those studies which are able to relate costs to a single common effect, as in cost-effectiveness analysis, may not be presented in this fashion. In fact, although the general framework of economic evaluation detailed here is commonly accepted and supported, what often tends to happen in the economic evaluation of health care is a form of *'partial evaluation'*. Due to the complex issues within the assessment of health care, and the uncertainties which exist within it, an approach is often adopted which presents the costs alongside the multiple consequences for health. This approach is known as *cost consequence* analysis. Whereas cost-effectiveness analysis and cost-utility analysis present results in the form of a ratio, cost consequence analysis present costs and one or more outcomes separately without integrating their results in the form of a ratio. The HEMS evaluation reported by the Sheffield Group is an example of a cost-consequences analysis, and the methods of this study form a case study.

The HEMS Study (Methods)

The assessment of HEMS provides an interesting case study on how to apply economic evaluation to developments in trauma services. The main elements of this evaluation are listed in the Table .

The benefits of HEMS in terms of the process of care, such as the time to seeing a doctor, time to hospital and the appropriateness of the receiving hospital, are only of value in as much as they improve rates of survival, and/or the long term health of survivors. It was therefore necessary to assess a wide range of outcomes, due to the heterogeneity in severity and nature of injury. Patients may survive with quite minor problems, or be left with major disabilities. Rather than attempt to measure and value all these outcomes on a single scale, it was decided to use two survey instruments and to describe outcomes across a range of dimensions. One was the OPCS survey instrument, which covers a broad range of disabilities,[6] and generates an overall 11-point index of severity. The other was the Nottingham Health Profile measuring health across six dimensions (mobility, pain, emotional function, sleep, social isolation and energy) on 100 point scales.[7]

The costing exercise estimated the incremental or extra cost consequences of the HEMS cases over and above the costs of an attendance by a ground ambulance. It included the costs of operating the helicopter (listed in the Table), the special landing and patient transfer facilities. The helicopter was also expected to have consequences for hospital and other services, since it may impact on survival and disability. Improved survival may, of course increase the costs to hospital, while lower levels of disability are likely to reduce hospital stay and hence costs. As an economic study, it was important to also follow up the consequences for other services, including primary care, social services and the patient's relatives.

Conclusion

Economic evaluation is intended to help people with difficult purchasing decisions. It does this by assessing the costs and benefits of the alternative ways of spending scarce resources. This chapter has outlined the key techniques and presented the recent HEMS evaluation as a case study. We hope to have shed some light on a subject which can seem impenetrable to the outsider. For those interested in taking the subject further, we recommend you look at the references below. Should you wish to include an economic component in a research study, it is advisable to consult a local health economist. It has become an essential component of health technology assessment; ignore it at your peril!

References

1. G Mooney. Economics, Medicine and Health Care. Harvester Wheatsheaf: London, 1992.
2. M F Drummond, G L Stoddart, G L Stoddart, G W Torrance. Methods for the economic evaluation of health care programmes, Oxford Medical Publication: Oxford, 1987.
3. R M Williams. The costs of visits to emergency departments. New Engl J Med334: 642-6, 1966.
4. A Williams. Economics of Coronary artery bypass grafting, British Medical Journal, 291: 326-9.
5. J E Brazier, J Nicholl, H Snook. The costs and effectiveness of London helicopter emergency medical service. J Health Services and Policy (accepted).
6. Martin J, Meltzer H, and Elliot J. The prevalence of disability among adults. OPCS Social Survey Division, HMSO, London, 1988.
7. Hunt SM, McEwan J, McKenna SP. Measuring Health Status. Beckenham Kent: Croom Helms, 1986.

John Brazier is Director of Health Economics, and **Colin Green** is a Research Associate in Health Economics within the Health Economics Section of the School of Health and Related Research (SCHARR), University of Sheffield.

SCHARR is a multidisciplinary research centre, located in The University of Sheffield's Faculty of Medicine. The staff of the School are drawn from a wide range of disciplines and backgrounds, embracing epidemiology, health economics, management sciences, medical sociology, medical statistics, nursing research, operations research, primary care, psycology, information science, public health, general practice and health care of the elderly. SCHARR offers an MSc programme in Health Economics and Management , an MSc programme in Health Services Research, and short courses on the principles and methods of health economics.

The publications relating to helicopter services written by members of SCHARR are listed in the 'further reading list' books by the authors of articles in Trauma Care.

PURCHASING HEMS IN THE INTERNAL MARKET

Peter Greengross

Introduction

Although the NHS reforms were instituted because of concern about waiting lists and the resources available to fund the service, the subsequent fundamental changes that occurred mostly affected the way in which resources are allocated and how their use is monitored, rather than the level of funding per se. At the heart of the reforms was the introduction of the 'purchaser-provider split'. Essentially, the separation of commissioning from the provision of services enables resources to be allocated according to need, rather than reflecting historical development. This is widely recognised to be a sound, and potentially more equitable basis from which health services can develop to meet future needs and, ultimately, improve health. However, the system can only function effectively if purchasers are independent of the institutions providing care and are thus free to shift resources between different providers. The 'internal market' thus introduces competitive pressures into the NHS, with an expectation that efficiency will improve, but it is tightly managed because any health care market is inherently inefficient and because political pressures distort it.[1]

Allocating Resources

The total NHS budget for England and Wales is about £33 billion for 1996/97 of which, after top-slicing for nationally funded services and Family Health Services, about £25 billion is allocated for Hospital and Community services. 29% of this total is allocated to the two Thames regions.[2] Resources are allocated to individual Districts using formulae based on an age-sex modified population count with weighting factors to reflect socio-economic deprivation. The annual budgets for individual Authorities therefore vary widely and, in London, the range is from £120 million to £430 million. Districts are responsible for purchasing the full range of Health Services, and in theory they should plan services after a needs assessment has been completed.

The need for any type of health-care is derived from a need for health, and has been defined by Stevens and Raftery[3] as 'the population's ability to benefit'. As such it depends on both the incidence and prevalence of a condition and the effectiveness of any services or interventions that the health service can provide. The resources available to improve health are restricted in the face of unlimited demand. Choices therefore have to be made between competing demands. It is clearly pointless to provide services that are not effective, but equally, from a utilitarian perspective of achieving the maximum benefit for the greatest number, it is unethical to provide a certain, albeit effective service if alternatives can benefit more people for the same or at less cost. Hence the enormous attention being focused on cost-effectiveness at both national and district level.

Purchasing Health Care

Although in theory purchasers are free to allocate their funds as required, in practice they are subject to political pressures, and the need to take a long term view of health care delivery. Most funds are committed to existing services and in reality, changes in contracting occur almost exclusively at the margin and only when extra funds are available. Sources of extra revenue include increases in central funding, special initiatives such as the Tomlinson London Initiative Zone (LIZ) monies, or the release of funds from hospital re-developments. However, such sources will not be realised in 1996/97. The 1.1% increase in central funding announced in the 1995 Autumn Budget used unrealised assumptions about inflation and NHS spending in the previous year, and the true increase is closer to 0.3%. LIZ monies were specifically allocated for primary care initiatives, and have all been awarded. The extra funding lasts until 1998/99, when problems of recurrent funding will emerge.

In such a climate, there are enormous pressures on Health Authorities to restrict expenditure. The Sheffield Report[4] calculated the cost of HEMS at £1,150,000 annually, with additional hospital costs associated with patients transferred to the Royal London Hospital. The total is tiny in global terms, especially when divided between the 16 funding Health Authorities, but it is a new expense and, as discussed above, purchasers are bound by very tight financial constraints. As Richard Earlam discusses elsewhere, in the past, Health Authorities have been billed for HEMS patients individually and, unpredictably, on a cost-per-case basis. Such bills are anticipated by retaining about 10% of resources for activities which are 'subject to risk'. Such events include extra-contractual referrals

(ECRs) and variable elements in contracts to cater for over- and under-performance. New funding arrangements for HEMS have been introduced to remove the element of risk and to fix bills at a rolling average of the previous three years usage. This should reduce some of the pressure on purchasers in funding the service.

One of the main criticisms levelled against the NHS reforms is that administrative costs have increased disproportionately due to the requirement to set contracts and monitor them annually. The Government has targeted such costs in an effort to release funds. DHA administrative costs are about £10 per person resident within a District, but there is huge variation and costs tend to rise with the size of the Authority. For 1996/97 these must be reduced by 5% before inflation, so probably 8% in reality. Additionally, the annual efficiency index dictates savings of 3% in costs to be met by purchasers, and essentially this is achieved through provider efficiency gains.

Who Should Purchase HEMS?

HEMS is a regional service, but is now exposed to the same semi-competitive pressures as other health services in the Capital. Funding, which initially was top-sliced from the regional budget, is now shared between and allocated by DHAs. There are inherent problems in devolving the commissioning of tertiary services to District level, not least because the prevalence of disease (or incidence of trauma) is rare and clinical events unpredictable.

It is tempting to argue that HEMS, along with many other tertiary services such as paediatric cancer, plastic surgery and transplant services, should continue to be funded at Regional level despite the fact that such arrangements no longer exist. Such a situation would acknowledge the special nature of such services, might facilitate needs assessment, and would avoid the increased administrative costs associated with multiple purchasers operating independently. The disadvantages of purchasing these services separately are that the resources are subject to political pressures and that the relative cost-effectiveness of the services is not accounted for with respect to more routine care. In other words, various assumptions have to be made regarding the effectiveness of the service and value for money. As Brazier and Green discuss in Section 9D, the opportunity costs foregone by purchasing HEMS may outweigh any benefits derived from the service. For these reasons, purchasers are developing novel ways of commissioning such services, for example by nominating 'lead' authorities to negotiate on their behalf, or by creating informal commissioning groups.

Conclusions

The new unified authorities have increased responsibilities and expectations are greater. They are now expected to manage GP Fundholding, should be increasing public consultation and are obliged to fulfil the roles of the old Regional Authorities. Simultaneously they are subject to tough financial constraints and many London Authorities are currently committed to overspend on their budgets. There are multiplying political pressures including a need to improve mental health services, develop care in the community, reshape cancer services, reduce waiting lists and re-orientate maternity services. HEMS is expensive and its impact is disputed. It is perhaps not surprising that, whatever its merits in an ideal world, some purchasers feel the need to meet other priorities in the rather turbulent and cash-stricken NHS of the 1990s.

References

1. Ham C, Maynard A. Managing the NHS Market. BMJ 308:845-7, 1994.
2. Appleby J. Financing the NHS. NAHAT 1995/96 Annual NHS Handbook 10th Ed 1995, JMH Publishing.
3. Stevens A, Raftery J (Eds). Health Care Needs Assessment. Radcliffe, Oxford 1994.
4. Nicholl JP, Brazier JE, Snooks HA, Lees-Mlanga S. The Costs and Effectiveness of the London Helicopter Emergency Medical Service. Medical Care Research Unit, University of Sheffield. July 1994.

Acknowledgements

I am grateful to Peter Commins, Finance Director, Brent and Harrow District Health Authority, for providing financial data and for helpful comments.

Peter Greengross, FRCS, Emeritus HEMS Registrar, is now a Senior Registrar in Public Health Medicine, North Thames. He is currently seconded to the Royal Free Hospital, London.

COSTS

Richard Earlam

'... who knows the price of everything and the value of nothing'.
Oscar Wilde (1854-1900)

1. Pre-hospital Costs of HEMS

It is essential that the public knows that HEMS was set up with the highest standards possible, established by copying other foreign countries' systems and obtaining the best. In my opinion this would never have been achieved without the help of Lord Stevens and the *Daily Express*, who paid for the helicopter (£1.4 million) and half of the running costs for first three years (£3 million). To this day there is still suspicion in central government about the service which was the first in the UK but we were the last country in the European Community to have such a system.

In Table I is a list of the main **capital** requirements relating to HEMS, some of which are pre-hospital and some are in-hospital. The latter can be regarded as helicopter service related but they are actually essential improvements which should have been there in the first instance, e.g an emergency room, for the benefit of all seriously ill and injured patients not just the 300 brought in by HEMS each year.

Table 1
Capital Improvements Associated with HEMS

1988	Helicopter	£1.4 million
1990	Helipad control room and lift	£1.2 million
1990	Emergency room Siemen's overhead x-ray Dupont processor of films	£250,000 including £125,000 given by the Wolfson Foundation
1994	Emergency theatre rebuilding	£500,000
1996	CT scanner in the A&E department Siemen's Somaton Plus 4	£500,000

The **running costs** were £665,000 in 1991-92 and in the four year period 1992-95 were over £1 million a year. The workload of approximately 1500 call outs per year is reduced to about 1000 useful missions including work at the scene, accompanying patients to other hospitals by land ambulance and HEMS emergencies to other hospitals which could be charged for. All secondary transfers are free in that no charge has been levied. The total pre hospital cost amounts to £1000 per patient as compared with the mean figure of £10,000 for the cost of inpatient trauma care at the Royal London Hospital. The pre-hospital care bill is 10% of the total medical care and in practice should be considered an integral part thereof. In the USA private insurance reimburses US $1500 for emergency helicopter transport of a patient, so our costs are similar.

The HEMS pre-hospital budget figure of about £1 million gives the 12 million people either on or inside the M25 the chance to have an air ambulance at the scene of their accident in less than 15 minutes with a doctor, a specially trained ambulance man with paramedic skills, every available road side facility for resuscitation, the ability to choose the most appropriate hospital and fly there in under six minutes. The helicopter can fly off within three minutes of a call from the London Ambulance Service central control, because pilot, co-pilot, doctor and paramedic are always there on full duty with a control room operator in the hospital every day of the week in daylight hours. This front line team needs back up so there are many other staff each of whom are essential – four pilots, four HEMS doctors (all with higher degrees and diplomas of specialisation), London Ambulance Service men with special training, control room personnel in HEMS and LAS control room, data collectors, firemen and management support. It is known that one intensive care unit bed requires seven separate nurses to look after its patient for 168 hours each week 52 weeks per year. Similarly HEMS requires many staff for a 365 days per year service, but this is a demanding job in a dangerous situation with a higher mortality rate than an ICU. In a normal year the helicopter crew will attend just under 1,000 incidents in which about 80 are certified dead at the scene of the accident. No patient has died in the helicopter during transport, but in the first 1,000 brought to the Royal London 156 (68% of the total deaths) died in the emergency room or theatre within the first day of hospital treatment. These patients are seriously ill with a potential mortality during their stay in hospital of 23%, they deserve the best care and indeed they are offered the best pre-hospital care for £1000. This round figure is easy to grasp.

2. The Cost of a Death

The cost of a death to the NHS is zero because ongoing costs then stop and for this particular 'patient episode' the cost is reduced. In terms of providing medical and nursing care prior to death the bare minimum of care and costs would be the ideal in a macabre world run by economists. It is therefore essential that the patient and the medical profession whom they trust should insist on providing the optimum amount of care rather than the minimum. There will always be arguments about money between the professional staff and government whether it be the politicians (they decide the overall budget level with a political decision and it is always too little), the civil servants (Treasury and DHS), and now the purchasers who distribute money for services provided by hospitals. The cost of a death is however not borne by the Department of Health, but by other departments of the Government who provide social security payments for the dependents and by the Treasury who lose tax.

There are various cost estimates for a premature death from trauma. The usually quoted figure comes from the Department of Transport because road traffic accidents are their business but they only have one weapon to deal with this and that is by road improvements. It always requires a certain number of deaths before any new road work can be 'justified'. They do have some interest in motor car safety but are not involved in prevention (e.g alcohol abuse) or medical care. They assess the societal cost of a premature death at between £500,000 and £750,000. Such estimates are the same or higher in other countries. In the USA the loss of a child's life from burns is around £1.5 million. The trouble is that no one can calculate the true cost let alone put a value on the sadness of the bereaved. It is no use going to law because bias arises and if the judge alone decides, there will be a figure which will certainly be below that suggested by the jury who put down a sum which they consider the death or disability to be worth.

In 1988 the Department of Transport adopted a new calculation method by asking the public (at last an individual) how much they would pay to avoid a death; so it then depended on the circumstances of death. Curioser and curioser – this method came up with the value of £750,000 for a road traffic accident (less than 4000 per year in the UK) but on the railways it was more than £2 million (Economist, 16 March 1996, page 29). Such was the perceived risk of travelling on British Rail, where a passenger could do nothing to avoid death. But in the prospectus of Railtrack the deaths in 1995/6 were 13 passengers and 6 workers, which appears somewhat safer than travelling by road.

It is essential to keep a clear mind amidst this confusion. At the RLH we accept the cost of a premature death as £500,000 (minimum figure) and agree with the estimate by the Sheffield Group that we save one life a month, so we save £6 million per year in addition to the happiness and satisfaction given to all concerned. HEMS was not set up either to make money or save money. Its main purpose is to give the best possible service for accidents in London regardless of cost. If money has to be taken into account, the helicopter costs £1 million a year and the hospital care £3 million but the lives saved alone retrieve £6 million. Good value indeed.

3. The Cost of Permanent Disability

It is as equally difficult to estimate the cost of permanent disability as it is to put a figure on the cost of a premature trauma death once it has occurred or the amount of money which should be spent to prevent it. Death is a fixed point easily measured that will occur in all of us, but what is premature? Do we all expect to live to 76? Is it true that if we eliminate the risks of smoking, men would live as long as women? Do the tobacco companies pay for the premature deaths in men? And whom should we blame and send the bill to for the excess of deaths from trauma amongst men compared with women? Measurement of disability is extremely complicated and there are arguments about the best methodology. We need a great deal of optimism to develop even better methods of disability assessment and we need more humility if we think we can measure everything. Even if we had a perfect measure for disability, the problem remains of assessing its permanence and the length of time it will last before anybody can put a price on it.

The author is optimistic and that is why Helen Hetherington was supported by HEMS: a) to choose the Functional Independence Measurement (FIM) for assessing our patient's recovery, and b) to assess the amount of permanent disability (see publication list under Hetherington). The importance of long term disability is that health economists see this as an unnecessary and unacceptable additional cost against a trauma service. It is an important fact of life that the more patients treated for trauma the higher will be the number who are disabled, but that is no indication for withdrawing treatment or not trying to save their life in the first instance. An old adage, which is wrong, was that permanent disability occurred in two to three times the number of those who died. With a mortality of 25% that would mean that 75% had permanent disability. This is totally false. 85% of our patients have a normal FIM score on follow up at six months and only 15% have any disability at all, although of course they will still have the mental trauma of the accident. A six month follow up of 100 patients treated by HEMS revealed six permanently disabled – 2 paraplegic, 2 quadriplegic and 2 persistent vegetative states after a severe head injury. I personally would not like to be treated by an economist if the rugby scrum collapsed and I became paraplegic. Such patients are frequently flown into central London before being transferred to specialist centres such as Stoke Mandeville. There must be no cost or money influence on the treatment of paraplegics which must never fall below the optimum. The LAS and HEMS are meticulous in careful treatment of the cervical vertebrae with collars in all accidents, because an unstable cervical vertebral fracture does not always lead to a permanent paralysis. It is suggested that the cost of treating a paraplegic or quadriplegic after discharge from hospital can not be made as a charge against a trauma care service.

This leaves two persistent vegetative state patients per 100 for analysis. Head injury outcome can be improved. Better care at the scene, improved speeds of transport, triage to neurosurgery centre, quick CT scanning and decompression of blood collection by surgery within the first hour or two all improve the results as demonstrated by Tim Coats in this section. When brain damage is so severe that there is no possible chance of recovery and the EEG waves are flat, brain death can be diagnosed. A specialist team, totally separate form the doctors who are looking after the patient, decide when brain death occurs but tests must be repeated carefully and the whole process takes about 24 hours. This is absolutely necessary before any organs can be transplanted. But there are two patients per 100 who will have brain injuries severe enough for them to be unconscious yet not brain dead. With this uncertainty about future recovery and in the presence of waves of activity on the EEG such patients must be looked after in hospitals and they will eventually be cared for in specialist centres such as the Royal Home at Putney. The costs there for permanently institutionalised head injuries run at £48,500 per annum which is approximately £1000 per week.

D. Cost-Benefit Analysis

Behind every doctor in the NHS seems to stand an accountant, an auditor, a data collector, a coder, many administrators and a health economist (12 departments now established to sort out the NHS). Doctors have an unwritten contract with their patients to provide the best for the patients (please not the terms client nor customer) because that presumably is what has been requested by them. It becomes difficult when this contract between doctor and patient is complicated by the presence of a third party who pays the money (Milton and Rose Freidman, Free to Choose, Pelican, London 1980). This may be the government or an insurance company, both of whom extract a handling charge (their profit, wages or job) and have the main aim of spending less money rather than insisting on good service. Hence the importance of health economists in advising governments and purchasers on how to buy the best value. They are armed with controversial methodologies based on costs. Outcome, which is basically death or disability or even in many cases just a 'feel good' factor, is in itself extremely difficult and controversial to measure. The great problem is how to measure this in monetary terms because cost (in money) must have the same measurement as outcome (in money) for correct analysis. The cost of a death can be measured but is not necessarily the same as the cost of a death avoided and it is not the same as the cost of a life.

One of the original terms used was 'cost-effective' but since cost and effect (not efficiency) were measured in different ways it has been replaced by 'cost-benefit'. An original critique of the term 'cost-effective' (Doubilet P, Weinstein MC, McNeil BJ, New Eng J Med 314:253-5, 1985) divided usage into four criteria:

1. Cost effective = cost saving i.e. lowest cost
2. Cost effective = effective i.e. no mention of money costs
3. Cost effective = cost saving with an equal or better outcome (but excludes any programme that does not save money)
4. Cost effective = having an additional benefit worth the additional cost
   a. less costly and at least as effective
   b. more effective and more costly
   c. less effective and less costly

Effective was changed to benefit because the money value of the latter was presumed to be easier to work out. The problem is that outcome, which equates with benefit if it is better, is extremely hard to measure. Although the RLH chose Functional Independence Measure (FIM) as a method of measuring disability it is appreciated that there are hundreds of available scores, which should alert the suspicious to the fact that none actually are perfect and all have their limitations. It has been slowly realised that there is a difference between the term disability, which applies to what the patient is unable to do or want to do, versus handicap which is what society perceives is the position of the disabled, how he copes and how they accept him. Paraplegia is a disability but some paraplegics complete the marathon in a wheelchair or compete in the Olympics, so what is the handicap? It is encouraging to know that there are no acceptable financial methods for measuring handicap yet it is the most important outcome. Nevertheless with flawed methods of measuring disability, costs in monetary terms are still assessed.

Quality of Life (QALY) measures are another tool, dependent on a) how you define quality and b) how you calculate quantity because nobody knows how long they are going to live and nobody but the actuary, who always wins, knows how long the company will pay your pension. Armed with QALYs the helicopter trauma service has been assessed as being less valuable than a heart transplant by health economists. I personally do not know the cost of a heart transplant but it is an effective operation and I would want one too, and would buy it by getting to France slower. The purpose of these irreverent remarks is to sow seeds of unrest, concern and worry about health evaluation methodology and on the 'evidence based' source reallocation programmes.

It appears that the individual is at last being recognised by the health economists because 'willingness to pay' is recognised as an acceptable approach. This has the disadvantage that it is income related i.e the difference between a Formula One Grand Prix driver versus a student with a clapped out Mini, no airbag and no ABS. But nothing is perfect and anyway most decisions on how the government spends our money are political or irrational. £3 billion will be spent on improving the railway from London to the Channel port in order to save half an hour on the journey. A cheaper solution by a Times reader for saving the same time at no cost, was for each train to start off half an hour earlier. The television series 'Call Red' with 6 episodes cost £4.5 million to produce which could run the helicopter service for four years. One must not get too agitated – after all, its only money and not lives which are at risk.

5. Conclusion

HEMS measures all injuries for anatomical damage (Abbreviated Injury Scale – AIS) and patho-physiological response (Revised Trauma Score – RTS) to give TRISS scores (Trauma Score and Injury Severity Score) and contribute our results to the Major Injury Outcome Study (MTOS UK). All patients are monitored for disability by Functional Independence Measurement (FIM) and followed up by a rehabilitation coordinator. It is not surprising that permanent disability occurs but HEMS does not accept this as a disadvantage although health economists and purchasers of health care may do so. The costs of deaths and the charges for permanent disability must be put into perspective. The aim of medical care and nursing is to provide the best service, reduce the mortality and consequently lessen the disabilities. Measurement and costing of these deaths and disabilities are controversial and inaccurate in spite of our best efforts. So the results in monetary terms must be treated with some suspicion and reservation. Finally it must be emphasised that there are many benefits from HEMS (Table 2) which can not be measured by money and yet must be added to any cost-benefit analysis.

Table 2
Intangible Benefits of HEMS

1. **Lives saved** — approximately one per month, 12 per annum; minimum cost £500,000 each = £6 million per annum
2. **Disability reduced** — persistent vegetative states less than expected; full recovery of lesser head injury damage
3. **Ambulance man** obtaining enhanced training for pre-hospital care and paramedic training. Pre-hospital Trauma Life Support (PHTLS) training.
4. **LAS central control** able to triage and establish faster and more effective response.
5. **Other Emergency Services** – Police and Fire Brigade – help to improve care, communication and cooperation.
6. Increased standards of care in the **emergency room**, theatres and acute services due to reorganisation, consultant involvement, increased numbers and interest.
7. Increased standards of **junior medical care** due to a) Advanced Trauma Life Support (ATLS) courses, b) trauma calls (2 per day), c) consultant involvement, d) volume and e) specialisation in trauma care. This includes training 8 new HEMS registrars each year.
8. Increased standards of **nursing care** in A&E department, emergency room, Intensive Care Unit, Trauma Unit with Advanced Trauma Nursing (ATNC) and Trauma Nurse Care Courses (TNCC).
9. Subsequent better care for **non-helicopter land ambulance emergency cases**.
10. Focus for **learning and teaching**: nurses/doctors/paramedics/ambulance man.
11. **Research** in a University Teaching Hospital.
12. Establishment of a Level 1 **Trauma Care System** as an example for others to follow. Interest and specialisation improve results.

SECTION 10: PERSONNEL, SELECTION AND TRAINING

Photo: Peter Mahoney

Major incident 'table top' exercise on the helipad involving HEMS registrars and Dr Judith Fisher

SELECTION AND TRAINING OF THE HEMS REGISTRAR

Peter Mahoney

Introduction

HEMS started attending major accidents in May 1989 and began operating from the helicopter pad on the roof of the Royal London Hospital in September 1990. The first doctor was appointed in September 1989.

Doctors are selected for HEMS by interview. Preference is given to those with experience of pre-hospital care and an interest in trauma management.

To be eligible to apply for a position with HEMS, doctors must be of registrar grade and hold a higher professional qualification.This means they have completed five years at medical school, a year as a house officer and, on average, a further five years in senior house officer and registrar positions. They must also have passed the membership or fellowship qualification in their chosen speciality. Suitable qualifications include Fellow of the Royal College of Surgeons (FRCS), Fellow of the Royal College of Anaesthetists (FRCA) and Member of the Royal College of Physicians (MRCP). Ideally they should have passed the Advanced Trauma Life Support (ATLS) course, a two and a half day course administered by the Royal College of Surgeons, that trains people in the practical and theoretical management of patients in the first hour after major injury.

HEMS Training

Doctors are appointed to HEMS for six months. The first month is dedicated to training. This covers five major areas:

1. Aircraft Familiarisation

As this is the first time many doctors have worked with a helicopter they need to understand how and when to approach the aircraft, how to exit the aircraft and where the danger areas are. Understanding aircraft safety is particularly important when entering or leaving the helicopter on sloping ground where blade height is greatly reduced.

2. Communications

Writing in 1976 after the Moorgate tube train crash Winch et al commented that at every major exercise and incident in the preceding 30 years, the main criticism had been failure of communications.

The HEMS medical crew carry both radios and mobile telephones, the latter pre-programmed with accident and emergency department 'blue' telephone numbers. A day is spent early on in the training month at the LAS central control room so that the communications system can be seen first hand. This is followed by formal training in radio procedure.

3. Anaesthetic skills for non anaesthetists

HEMS registrars include anaesthetists, accident and emergency specialists, surgeons and physicians. One of the main areas where aggressive pre-hospital management is producing better patient outcome is head injury. HEMS teaches doctors to give a 'field' anaesthetic to these patients, including endotracheal intubation and drugs to control intracranial pressure. Non-anaesthetists are given sessions in the operating theatres supervised by a consultant anaesthetist to learn how to give a suitable anaesthetic.

HEMS Paramedic Training Course

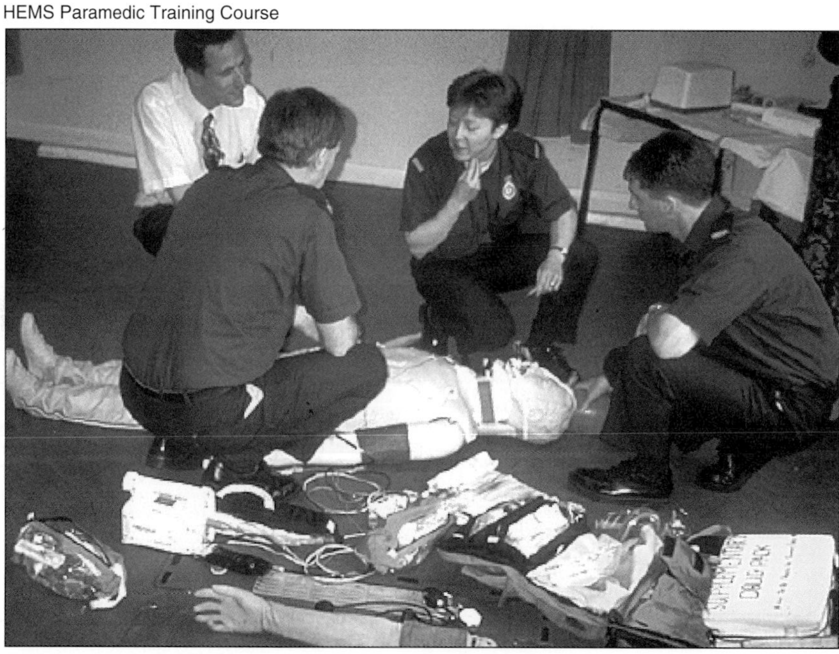

Photo: author

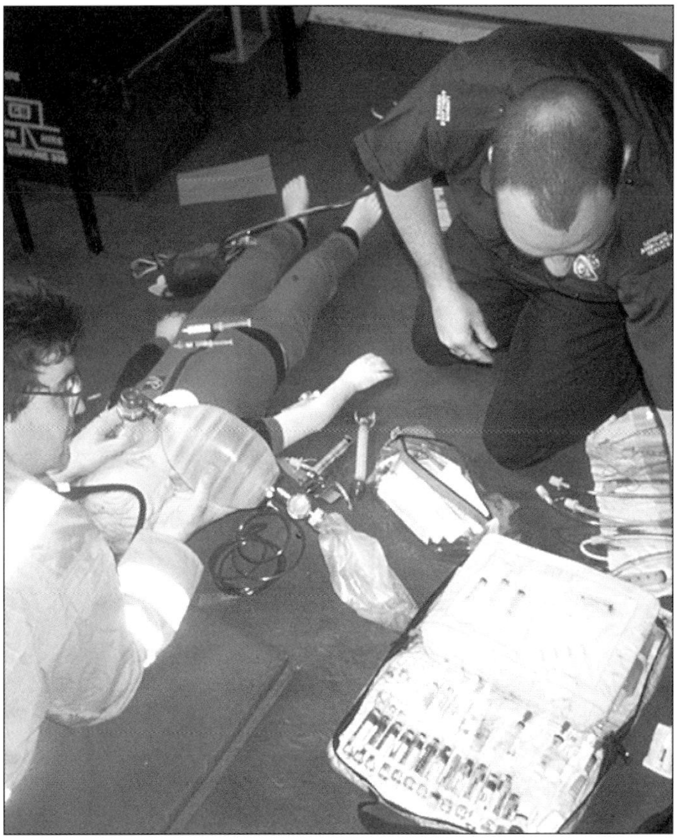

Photo: author

HEMS Paramedic course moulage test

4. Extrication and hazardous location training

This is carried out at a number of locations. A day with the London Fire Brigade's Extrication training team introduces the doctor to techniques of vehicle cutting and how medical procedures can be safely carried out alongside the fire brigade teams.

A day at the London Underground training centre teaches the doctor how to ensure traction that current is off when dealing with a casualty on the tracks and how to safely remove them.

Further training is given in confined space rescue by specialists in this area.

5. Major incident planning

The helicopter is likely to be tasked to a 'Major Incident' on average once a year and, if first on scene, the HEMS registrar may need to adopt the role of Medical Incident Officer prior to the arrival of more experienced personnel.

This aspect of training is addressed by table top exercises and attendance at Major Incident Management courses.

Conclusion

A national survey of Accident and Emergency departments published in 1992 concluded that arrangements for on site medical services are inadequate in most hospitals

The HEMS pre-hospital care training month ensures that the HEMS registrars are able to work safely and efficiently in the pre-hospital environment.

Dr Peter Mahoney, FRCA, Emeritus HEMS Registrar, is Senior Registrar in Anaesthetics in Nottingham.

Photo: author

Fire Practice.
The author concentrates on the helipad with Jim Seager, the fireman

TRAUMA NURSING

Jill Williams

When the Helicopter Emergency Medical Service was established it was unclear what skills were necessary for nurses to become experts in Trauma Care.

Our original thoughts were to develop staff to be able to work in all areas where trauma victims are nursed. This included Accident & Emergency, Theatres, Trauma Unit, Intensive Care, Neurosurgery, Orthopaedics, General Surgery and Rehabilitation. It became apparent that we were trying to have a *'Jack of all trades, master of none'*, and that most nurses were ultimately returned to their preferred speciality. For instance, Accident & Emergency nurses do not sit comfortably in an Intensive Care or Theatre setting.

The majority of the nurses that we employ in critical care areas have a post-registration qualification. We felt what was really needed was nurses with an appreciation of all aspects of trauma care.

In line with the current approach in nursing education for nurses to gain a BSc (Hons) Nursing, we decided to develop two modules in trauma care at level 3 which would form a trauma pathway to gaining a degree. These modules will be open for nurses with a minimum of four years' post-registration experience in a critical care field. They should also have undertaken an ENB course at level 2 and be able to demonstrate that they had undertaken or observed a recognised trauma nursing course. These modules will be open to other healthcare professionals although they will not be taking the pathway to gaining a nursing degree.

The rationale for module 1 was identifying the need in the field of trauma care for an overall perspective of the continuum of care, preventative, acute and rehabilitative. The aim of this module is to develop an understanding of the importance of a multi-disciplinary approach to trauma. This embraces the 'Road to Rehabilitation' concept, trimodal distribution of death, physiological response to treatment and its impact on the care given in other clinical areas, the psychological and social effects of trauma. It will also seek to provide people with the appropriate skills and knowledge of trauma care relating to the pathophysiology and psychology of injury from pre-hospital to discharge. The specialist nurses or health professionals will develop their role within the framework of holistic trauma care alongside other healthcare professions and agencies involved in the care of the trauma patient. It also aims to ensure that the nurses or healthcare professionals have an overall perspective of the web of trauma care.

The rationale for module 2 focuses more on the non-acute aspects of health promotion, rehabilitation and networking. This module aims to make the nurses explore strategies which are aimed at prevention and rehabilitation while continuing to address issues arising from the acute phase. This should enable the specialist nurse to evaluate critically the continuity and depth of care through his or her understanding of other health-care professionals and agencies who are involved in:

- The prevention of accidents.
- The care of the trauma patient in the acute and high dependency places of hospitalisation.
- The rehabilitation of the trauma patient.

By extending knowledge in this way, the specialist nurse will have the ability to facilitate communication links within the network of trauma care.

During the course the nurses will be gaining a significant amount of clinical experience. They will be given an overview of advanced trauma life support, the trimodal distribution of death and accident prevention. They will also be given an opportunity to appreciate the different mechanisms of injury and to learn some advanced skills such as intubation, cut downs and cannulations. They will be given some insight into major incident and disaster planning, triage, pre-hospital care, the role of paramedics, transport of patients and the mode of travel. They will look at the acute and long-term facilities available, such as Trauma Units, at acute bed management, high dependency beds and acute beds. They will also be looking at the need for rehabilitation beds and care. They will explore different models of nursing and models of other disciplines, look at professional accountability, nursing and medical diagnosis and the scope of practice. There will be some emphasis in biological sciences which will include the advanced physiology of trauma, airway and ventilatory disorders, haemodynamics of trauma and sepsis. They will also look at applied psychosocial sciences such as the sociology of trauma, social class, age and gender, women and families, culture and ethnicity and substance abuse. There will be some teaching on organ donation and brain stem death and the ethical debate regarding trauma. They will be looking at the psychology of trauma such as domestic violence, urban violence and post-traumatic stress disorder. They will develop communication skills with regard to team building, counselling for bereavement and a top down, bottom up organisational communication strategy.

In the second module, they will be gaining some knowledge of the epidemiology of trauma and undertake some applied research. There will be teaching about health promotion, such as national and international policy, Health of the Nation and WHO. They will also look at accident prevention, health and safety at work, ergonomics and work related trauma, road safety and car design, and voluntary and charitable organisations. They will gain an understanding of rehabilitation, particularly with regard to spinal injuries, head injuries and the problems related to altered body image. There will also be some work done in biological sciences such as indolent fractures, brain damage and paralysis. There will be some applied psychosocial sciences which will include attention/perception, accident prevention, trauma facilities and advanced communication skills. There will also be an element of management within the course which will include skill mix, budget management, funding, contracting and purchasing.

It is hoped that this course will begin to develop real specialists in trauma care who understand the need for a multidisciplinary approach and who care for patients and their families in a complimentary manner throughout the whole of their hospitalisation and rehabilitation period.

The first course commenced in October 1995. I must acknowledge the work that has been done by my colleagues who were responsible for designing and developing modules. They were *Ann Ferguson* (Lecturer, ENB 199), *Eileen McDonnell* (Course Director, BSc Hons, ENB Higher Award APL-APEL), *Val Dimak* (Lecturer, Curriculum & Development), *Gillian Bradbury* (Senior Nurse, Trauma Unit, Royal London Hospital), *Nina Parkinson* (Senior Nurse Manager, Accident & Emergency Clinical Group, Royal London Hospital), *Mr Bill Blowes* (Lecturer in Biological Sciences), *Mr Mervin Jakeway* (Lecturer in Applied Psychology).

Jill Williams is the Manager of the A&E department and HEMS at the Royal London Hospital, Whitechapel.

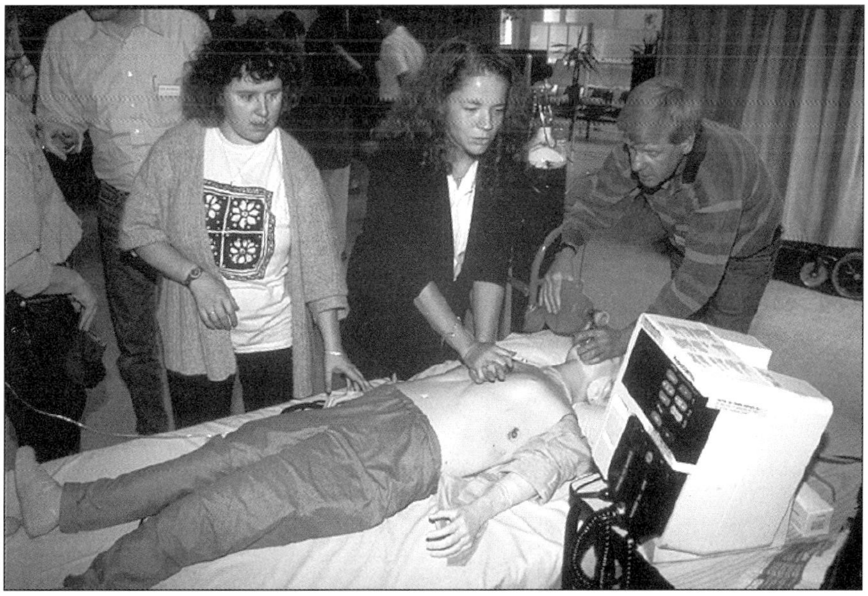

Photo: Mark Whitbread

Training with a mannikin

PARAMEDICS

Ian Canning

The HEMS medical team is made up of a paramedic and a Registrar grade doctor, this partnership bringing together advanced medical skills and experience in the pre-hospital environment. The paramedics that make up half of the HEMS medical team are seconded from the London Ambulance Service (LAS) for between six months and one year.

The standard training for ambulance service personnel begins with a three week Induction foundation course learning the principles of basic ambulance aid and a three week driving course. There follows a nine week Technician's Course which teaches anatomy and physiology and now covers the use of a semi-automatic defibrillator, nebulisation therapy and glucagon administration along with all operational protocols, an example of this being the use of all ambulance equipment. This is followed by a minimum four week operational training during which the trainee is supervised in operational work by a trainer. Satisfactory performance during this 19 week course qualifies the trainee as an Ambulance Technician.

After one year of operational experience an application can be made to become a paramedic. A pre-entry examination requires 60 hours of distance learning as recommended by the University of Hertfordshire. This is achieved by a period of studying in the student's own time, using a supply of books/workbooks which prepares them for the examination. The examination consists of a half-hour multiple-choice paper, a two hour written paper, a practical session covering CPR, assessment of a patient that is conscious/unconscious and if successful an interview with the Training Manager. Successful applicants undergo a four-part course. This is standardised nationally by the Institute of Health Care and Development, formerly the National Health Service Training Authority (NHSTA).

The first stage is preceded by 60 hours of distance learning, followed by 40 hours of formal tuition and a Stage 1 assessment which consists of a half hour multiple-choice paper, a two hour written paper and practical sessions, which must be passed to go on with the next stage of the training. The next stage consists of 20 hours of distance learning and 120 hours of formal tuition, followed by the Stage 2 examination. The theory learnt in the classroom is put into practice during 160 hours spent in hospital attachments. This time is spent in operating theatres, coronary care, intensive care and Accident and Emergency departments. Skills practised are venous cannulation, intubation, cardiac rhythm recognition, basic airway control, and patient assessment and observation. In the near future a Stage 4 will be introduced. This stage will place a paramedic with a mentor for a period of six months, enabling the new paramedic to gain confidence and adjust to new responsibilities.

The LAS and the University of Hertfordshire are in the process of developing courses that will lead to a paramedic degree, giving the paramedic further scope for development.

Requirements for Application to HEMS

Paramedics have to have a post-qualification of two years experience. They also need to be physically fit, weighing 85 kg or less and be able to demonstrate the application of first class paramedic skills.

There are a large number of paramedics applying for secondment to HEMS and because of this a process of shortlisting takes place which identifies the appropriate paramedics to be offered interviews.

The successful paramedics (4-6) then undertake a HEMS/London Ambulance Service Paramedic Training Course over a two week period. While under secondment they will be trained in all aspects of HEMS procedures and while additionally incorporating training sessions to outside parties. The course includes a welcome and introduction with a tour of the Royal London Hospital and over a period of ten days covers various skills and procedures. These include advanced life support/paediatric advanced life support, pre-hospital anaesthesia/analgesia, airway management, management of chest injuries, and the role of HEMS in a major incident. The paramedics are made familiar with the Thomas Pack and contents including drugs, Propaq and the use of fluids. On the course they also cover shock, head injury, abdominal trauma, hypothermia, electrocution etc. Near completion of the course they take part in a practical circus which includes needle chest decompression, chest drainage, needle/surgical cricothyroidostomy, cutdowns and intra-osseous infusion. At the end of each day a review session is held and a course debrief is undertaken at the end of the course.

Also included within this two week course will be an Advanced Trauma Life Support Observer's Course. HEMS courses are constantly reviewed and updated as required.

Ian Canning is a London Ambulance Service trained paramedic who is the HEMS Liaison Officer.

Operational Responsibilities and Duties

(a) Ensure that all necessary equipment including communications are available, serviceable and correctly stowed.

(b) On receipt of a call take personal responsibility for the collection of intravenous fluids and ensure anaesthetic drugs are available.

(c) On arrival at scene advise control of patient's condition and whether any additional equipment or assistance is required in accordance with Central Ambulance Control (CAC) protocols.

(d) Assist the Medical Officer on scene to stabilise the patient and carry out any medical procedures to ensure an appropriate level of patient care. Undertake liaison activities on scene between medical staff and land based London Ambulance Service (LAS) staff.

(e) Appraise pilot and CAC of patient's intended destination and method of conveyance to designated hospital. Additional duties also include the covering of the Audi car (MEDIC 1) if and when the helicopter is off line.

(f) On completion of a call take responsibility for the retrieval and cleaning of all HEMS and LAS equipment so as to ensure that the aircraft and equipment are ready to respond to the next call.

(g) Be prepared to receive any visitors to the Helipad at the Royal London Hospital and to display a professional image at all times.

Control Room Duties

(a) The paramedic assesses all tickets received from the Special Incident Desk, ensuring that Priority A calls result in the immediate despatch of the helicopter.

(b) On receipt of Priority B calls the paramedic will interrogate the caller to ascertain the potential for a multi-system injury.

(c) The paramedic will institute appropriate pre-arrival instructions and update the medical crew via Channel 7.

(d) Under the direction of the Control Room Commander (CRC) provide liaison between CAC and the HEMS operation.

(e) Ensure that the CRC is aware at all times of the aircraft's availability and identify any associated problems.

(f) The identification and tasking of appropriate calls for HEMS and assisting the Motor Cycle and Paramedic Response Units.

(g) On activation of HEMS advise the appropriate Police Force of incident details and location. In addition ensure that the appropriate control sectors are aware of the aircraft's activation. This will also include outer-counties control when the aircraft is activated to the surrounding areas of the LAS.

(h) Maintain record of HEMS activations within the Control log together with any other CAC documentations.

(i) Liaise with CAC to develop a tasking and audit profile.

FIRECREW TRAINING

Jim Seager

Due to the anticipated number of aircraft movements and the fact that the helicopter operates from a raised helideck, it is a CAA requirement that at least two qualified airport fire fighters are on duty during all operational hours. To meet this requirement four full time fire fighters are employed by the Royal London Hospital. Contrary to popular belief the crew are not on attachment or secondment from the LCDFA, City Airport or any other agencies. The minimum standard of competence required is that the fire fighter has received training at a recognised CAA training school and completed an intense two day helicopter fire fighting course. The successful fire fighter will receive a certificate stating the fact enabling him or her to work at (Low Category) Special, Category 1 and 2 airports. It should be noted that the highest airport category in the UK is 9, but most helicopters (with the exception of the large Chinooks, Sea King and EHIOI types) are grouped in Category 1.

Initial training is provided by the CAA International Fire Training School at Teeside Airport, Cleveland. The school has some of the most modern training facilities available presenting realistic, real fire scenarios to students and experienced firecrews alike. The two day course commences with lectures on safety, chemistry, equipment, fire fighting tactics and techniques before the fire fighter is allowed onto the fire ground. Having been equipped with a fire tunic, trousers, boots, gloves and helmet the ten minute journey by coach to the fire ground can be a daunting time for some new comers. Aircraft incidents involving fire are usually large and intense. There is no comparison if you have only used a hand held extinguisher on a waste paper bin fire. The reflected heat screen is the first rig the fire fighter confronts. A 20ft x 10ft wall of flame fed by high pressure fuel lines is not for the faint hearted. This piece of kit gives fire fighters the experience and confidence to work in close and contend with the intense heat generated by large aircraft type fires. Other training rigs simulate engine and undercarriage fires, running fuel fires and a variety of full size aircraft mock-ups which can be set alight and used for fire fighting and rescue exercises. The latest rig is a simulated raised helideck/helicopter mock-up – very appropriate for HEMS fire crews.

Jim Seager and Mark Landon practise fire-fighting on the helipad

Photo: G Collins

Final selection of the firecrew has as much to do with having the right personality as well as having fire fighting experience. It is most important they are able to work in a small knit team atmosphere, get on with other staff and are willing to muck-in with most tasks as required. The firecrew must receive continuous fire training, however, hot fire practice on the helideck is not feasible for obvious reasons. To maintain their currency, the crew are grateful to the firecrews and management at Fairoaks Airport and Wycombe Air Park, who allow them to use the airport fire grounds and equipment at least every three months. On a day to day basis the crew are limited to performing hose drills, equipment familiarisation drills and maintenance checks on the deck.

With 1800 litres of premixed AFFF (Aqueous Film Forming Foam), an endless supply of mains pressure water, 250 litres of 6% foam concentrate and 100 kgs of Halon, in the unlikely event of an accident on the helideck the fire crew have more than ample supplies of fire-fighting media with which to deal with any given situation.

Jim Seager has been Fire Officer on the helipad at the RLH for the last three years. Before that he managed the Daily Express Air Display Team.

RESUSCITATION OFFICER

Mark Whitbread

'... and lay upon the boy mouth to mouth
...the boy's body grew warm'

2 Kings 34

Introduction

Is there life after death? A certain proportion of our population would definitely say yes! These people are those who have been successfully resuscitated! From early biblical times there are accounts of people being restored to life after death and these were called miracles. But is it actually possible to make miracles happen? Yes, it is possible through proper training and education in the methods of resuscitation life support and the key person is the resuscitation officer.

The role of the Resuscitation Officer

Defined in the Oxford English Dictionary, resuscitation is *'Revival from apparent death'*. It is now established and, in a number of places, accepted that Trusts/Health Authorities should employ full time resuscitation officers to enable the 1987 Royal College of Physicians report into the training and organisation of resuscitation from cardiopulmonary arrest to be fulfiled.

A thorough knowledge of all aspects of resuscitation, both theoretical and practical, is essential for the resuscitation officer. There are many articles and books being published on the subject all the time and it is vital that he/she keeps up to date with all new information.

A resuscitation officer may be chosen from a nursing, technical or paramedic background, but all should have previous experience in the field both as a teacher and regular participant in active resuscitation. It is essential that a resuscitation officer be part of an established resuscitation and trauma team so that his his/her presence at an arrest is recognised and contributions welcomed. The resuscitation officer is in the ideal position of ensuring that people learn from such an event and can thereby use information gleaned as a teaching platform. I strongly believe that resuscitation officers should attend cardiac and trauma calls wherever possible since attendance at these incidents not only gives the resuscitation officer the chance to keep up his/her practical skills, but also to contribute to the team effort of caring for the patient and providing support, encouragement and guidance for colleagues from the most junior to the most senior. The salary scale should reflect this expertise and the resuscitation officer's grade should be that of a senior nurse or senior paramedic instructor.

The four main duties of a resuscitation officer are:

- Training
- Equipment
- Audit
- Research

Training

Training is the obvious role, and it can be split into three levels:

- Basic Life Support +/- AED
- Basic Life Support with adjuncts including defibrillation
- Advanced Life Support

Cardiac/Trauma Life Support Training

- **Basic Life Support**
  Mouth to mouth ventilation including the triple airway manoeuvre
  Mouth to mask ventilation
  Cardiac massage – one and two person CPR

- **Basic Life Support with Adjuncts**
  Use of oxygen
  Bag-valve-mask ventilation
  Use of suction equipment
  Use of oral airways
  Defibrillation

- **Advanced Life Support**
  Defibrillation
  Rhythm recognition
  Drugs
  Intubation with and without C-spine immobilisation
  IV access
  Paediatric Life Support

All levels of Life Support Training should include mock scenarios.

It is of course absolutely essential that medical, nursing and paramedical staff receive the appropriate level of life support training for their needs.

Basic life support is when resuscitation is carried out without the use of any equipment except perhaps a simple mask device such as the 'Laerdal Pocket Mask'. This level of support should be taught to all unqualified health care professionals such as student radiographers, and pre-clinical medical students, P20 00 student nurses etc.

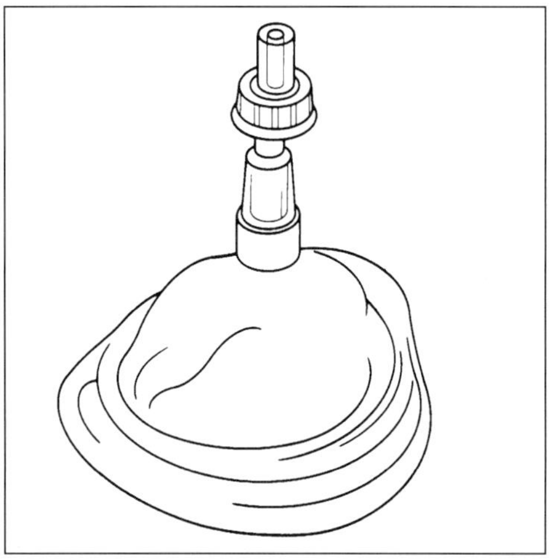

A simple ventilation device: Laerdal Pocket Mask

Basic life support with adjuncts implies the use of airway suction equipment, oxygen and, in some health authorities, defibrillation. These levels should be taught to qualified nurses and clinical medical students.

Qualified medical staff and nursing should be competent in all aspects of **advanced life support** and those doctors dealing with trauma resuscitation should hold current advanced life support (ATLS, ALS, APLS, PALS) certification. Pre-hospital personnel, i.e paramedics, should be taught to an advanced level and should have close links with their local hospitals. Extended training should be carried out both in regional schools and hospitals. Medical staff input should be used to a far greater extent in the training of paramedics than it is at present, thus promoting improved standards of patient care.

Equipment

To enable the resuscitation officer to carry our effective life support training, a wide range of equipment is essential. These range from the basic resuscitation 'Annie' mannikin to the more sophisticated models such as the Airway Management mannikin. It is the resuscitation officer's responsibility to ensure that all training equipment is cleaned and well maintained, ready to use. Patient equipment, such as pocket masks and bag-valve-mask devices, that are in use by staff should also be well maintained and checked regularly. All staff should be able to use the equipment in the correct manner and effectively. This should include how to turn oxygen on and how the various pieces of equipment are connected together.

Audit

Collected information on the treatment and general management of cardiac and trauma calls has many beneficial points. A general overall picture of the standard of resuscitation can be drawn and deficiencies in the system can be corrected without undue delay. In my experience the best way to collect the information is to use a simple form which contains basic details and the overall management of the incident. This should be completed by a senior member of the medical team and then returned to the resuscitation officer so that once the information has been collected and collated it can be presented at various meetings of medical and nursing staff within the hospital.

'Survival from in-hospital cardiac arrest nearly doubled following ACLS training.'

Lowenstein, 1986

Research

Research plays an important part in the resuscitation officer's role. There is much more information to be gathered in the field of resuscitation and the resuscitation officer is in the ideal position to instigate this. He should always be aware of the possibilities for research and be available to assist others when asked. Examples of current research include the measurement of end-tidal carbon dioxide during CPR.

Conclusion

In this article I have briefly outlined the role of the resuscitation officer. The job in itself is a 'hands on' affair and cannot only be seen as an academic or administrative role. The importance of regular involvement in all resuscitation efforts cannot be stressed too highly, because it is well know that frequent practice is necessary to maintain practical skills and dexterity. The resuscitation officer has a great responsibility to oversee all facts of resuscitation within a hospital or district, to establish response to emergencies, to ensure that the correct equipment is available for use and to organise effective training and repeated retraining for staff.

Further Reading

Evans T R. Royal College of Physicians Report in Training and Organisation and Resuscitation from Cardiopulmonary Arrest, 1987.

Lowenstein SA. Benefits of Training Physicians in ATLS. Chest 1989 : 512-6 1986.

Mark Whitbread is Senior Resuscitation Officer at the RLH.

THE ADVANCED TRAUMA LIFE SUPPORT (ATLS) COURSE

David Skinner

Introduction

Advanced Trauma Life Support (ATLS) courses were originally conceived and developed in Nebraska, USA, in 1977. At that time some good came out of a personal family tragedy. An American surgeon was piloting his light aircraft with his wife and children onboard. The aircraft crash landed, the surgeon was injured, as were his four children, and his wife was killed. He was transported to the nearest hospital with emergency facilities and the poor management he and his children received from the inexperienced junior doctor at that hospital incensed him. He decided that the system for managing patients with major injuries must be changed.

He developed a pilot ATLS course using local colleagues and in 1978 the course was taken over by the Committee on Trauma at the American College of Surgeons and further refined and developed. The course was propagated throughout the United States, Canada and Latin America, with regular revisions, until the first ATLS Instructor course was held outside the Americas at the Royal College of Surgeons (RCS) of England in November 1988.

ATLS Provider Course

There are essentially two sorts of ATLS course. The Provider course – which lasts two and a half days – is an intense theoretical and practical course designed to equip a doctor with the necessary skills for managing a patient with major injuries in Trunkey's so-called 'Golden Hour'. The prime objective is to enable the relatively inexperienced doctor to recognise life-threatening injuries and correct them, as well as subsequently documenting all other injuries sustained by the patient. The philosophy of 'do no further harm' is stressed throughout the course and it is assumed that the doctor managing the patient has limited facilities, and indeed, little time to use them even if they were available. A heavy reliance is, therefore, placed on clinical skills and simple practical manoeuvres.

When a doctor is accepted onto an ATLS Provider course he is sent a standard ATLS manual, produced and printed in the United States under the auspices of the American College of Surgeons, and distributed in the United Kingdom by the RCS. The doctor is expected to complete a pre-test, having read the manual, before attending the course so that all the lectures on the course which cover the entire text of the manual, are a revision. Practical skill stations include airway management, x-ray interpretation, examination of the head injured patient using a life-size model with a variety of injuries, and advanced intravenous techniques. The practicalities of various manoeuvres, such as chest drain insertion and surgical airway techniques are practised on human cadavers or sheep chest and neck preparations. This latter practical skill station ensures a high level of competence in the practical techniques of various life saving manoeuvres. It is often the first time that a senior house officer has inserted a chest drain and prepares him well for such a manoeuvre in the resuscitation room with a real, injured patient.

The whole ATLS course stresses a dogmatic approach to the patient and teaches one simple, safe method of managing patients with major injuries. Whilst recognising that there may be other systems or approaches to the management of the patient with major injuries, the ATLS method has been shown to be safe over more than a decade of use in the United States. The course concludes on the last afternoon with an assessment. Successful completion of an ATLS course requires the participant to have attended all the lectures and skill stations, as well as achieving 80% in an MCQ paper and a pass grade on the 'moulage' station.

The Moulage*

The moulage station is something entirely new to British practitioners and is generally regarded as the focus of the whole course. It is fair to say that it stimulates a level of anxiety comparable to that experienced when managing a real patient in the resuscitation room. A distinguished ATLS instructor recalls that his first moulage assessment on his own Provider course was more stressful than getting married, taking the Final Fellowship and, indeed, going to war. Essentially, it involves the practical management of a simulated casualty, made to look as if they have sustained major injuries and briefed to behave as if they are experiencing a variety of life-threatening problems. The simulation is realistic and the anxiety induced in the candidate is necessary, not only for realism, but also to reinforce the message that it is essential to have a simple system which remains effective in spite of stress, and allows a logical approach to the patient without forgetting any part of the patient's assessment or treatment.

ATLS Instructor Course

The Instructor course is attended by those who wish to teach the ATLS philosophy, having successfully completed a Provider course and performed above average in both the MCQ and moulage stations. These courses are held at the RCS and the core ATLS knowledge is assumed. The whole emphasis of the Instructor course is to teach the doctor how to teach others on future ATLS Provider and Instructor courses. It is only recently that some members of the medical profession have accepted the view, long held by educationalists, that there is a right way and, very definitely, a wrong way to impart knowledge. If doctors are impressed by the ATLS Provider course they are doubly impressed by the revelations of an ATLS Instructor course, not least by their own inadequacies so readily exposed and comparatively easily corrected. The Instructor course lasts for two days and when the candidate has confirmed his retention of the core material, by completing a further MCQ and moulage, the major part of the assessment, which is continuous throughout the course, is conducted by the educator.

Each Provider and Instructor Course currently held in the UK takes 16 candidates. These are all doctors. They are currently being drawn from all specialties involved in the care of patients with major injuries and, whilst an attempt was made to influence more senior members of the specialities, SHOs now form the largest single group on most courses. The RCS ATLS Committee requires doctors who have successfully completed an ATLS course to repeat an MCQ and moulage after four years, if necessary using a revised manual, as this is updated every four years. Instructors all have to be reassessed.

Policy of Update and Revision

Although it was perceived when the course was introduced to the UK that changes would be necessary because of different practices, this has not proved necessary thus far and the instructors, as well as the RCS, agreed to use the American manual verbatim until the next revision was produced. The Americans take the task of revision very seriously and nothing is said in the manual that has not received careful consideration. UK suggestions for changes are readily accepted as are those from other countries teaching ATLS.

The ATLS System

Participants on the Provider course are told that the manual contains very little about the management of trauma that they do not already know. What it does do, however, is offer a system which ensures that injuries are dealt with in the correct order and the patient safely managed. Naturally those who have been managing trauma in their own way for many years, often very successfully, find the concept of a different system hard to stomach.

Although many hospitals now operate a trauma team system, support from more senior staff in general surgery, anaesthesia and orthopaedics may be five, ten or even fifteen minutes in appearing. If the doctor is ATLS trained, most life threatening problems will have been identified and some corrected in this time. There is only Trunkey's 'Golden Hour' to save some of these patients and transport time may already have devoured 50% of this period. It is important that in the few minutes remaining the first doctor recognises that airway problems are more important than documentation of a compound fracture of the tibia and fibula and that correction of a pneumothorax and hypovolaemia have a higher priority than radiographic confirmation of numerous long bone fractures.

If a hospital's trauma team does not have one system to work to, their approach will be disorganised and not in the patient's best interests. The various tasks required in the Primary Survey (A – Airway with C-spine control, B – Breathing, C – circulation with haemorrhage control, D – Disability, E – Exposure) can easily be allocated to those doctors and nurses present so that all aspects of this initial assessment are dealt with simultaneously, under the direction of a team leader, in a very short space of time.

Almost all doctors attending an ATLS course leave with a high level of enthusiasm for the system and on their course evaluation forms agree that this brief course will change their management of patients in the resuscitation room – implying a change in practice and attitude has truly taken place.

Current Situation

Although many doctors still have difficulty securing a place on a local course, persistence usually ensures a place within six months. Instructors are supported in gaining leave to teach by the chief medical officer and this policy has allowed 77 ATLS courses to be completed in the first six months of 1996 with a total of more than 150 by the end of the year. More than 7000 doctors have achieved Provider status and 560 Instructor status. The programme continues to expand, strongly supported by the RCS England.

Involvement of Nurses and Other Medical Personnel

Nurses involved in the care of patients with major injuries have been generous in their assistance, particularly during the moulage stations, and are often drawn from the ranks of up to ten 'observers' allowed to attend each ATLS course. The ATLS Committee at the RCS England agreed that as nurses are very much equal partners in the team management of a patient with major injuries, they should have access to the same course as their medical colleagues. Negotiations between the RCS and representatives from the Royal College of Nursing have resulted in a historic agreement whereby nurses will attend ATLS courses, side by side with doctors. The first four UK ATLS Nurse Instructors attended the November 1990 Instructor Course at the RCS and six nurses then attended the inaugural joint doctors and nurses ATLS Provider course at St Bartholomew's Hospital in February 1991. The manual for doctors and nurses is identical and all the lectures are, therefore, also the same, but the slightly differing role of the nurse in the resuscitation room is reflected in different skill stations. Other nursing requirements have made it necessary for them to precede the standard ATLS course by one day and extend it for a further day at the end. Therefore the nurses' course lasts for five days and is known, in its entirety, as an Advanced Trauma Nursing Course (ATNC). Most importantly the nurses' course is recognised by both the RCS and the Royal College of Nursing.

Conclusion

Howard Champion, a prominent American trauma surgeon, has gone on record as saying that the improvement in trauma care in the United States over the last decade is not the result of magnificent new buildings or equipment but simply due to the enormous number of doctors who have been trained on ATLS courses. I have no doubt that a similar improvement is occurring for the same reason in the UK and that the Royal College of Surgeons (RCS), led on this occasion by Professor Miles Irving, should be congratulated for their hard work in ensuring the smooth introduction of ATLS to the British medical and nursing professions.

Dr David Skinner is Accident and Emergency Consultant at the John Radcliffe Hospital, Oxford. He was formerly A&E Consultant at St Bartholomew's Hospital and Chairman of the RCS Committee that introduced ATLS into the UK.

He is Senior Editor of the ABC of Major Trauma, BMA Publishing Group, ISBN 0 7279 0917 7. It is now in its Second Edition.

* 'Moulage' is derived from the French word *mouler* meaning to mould or cast.

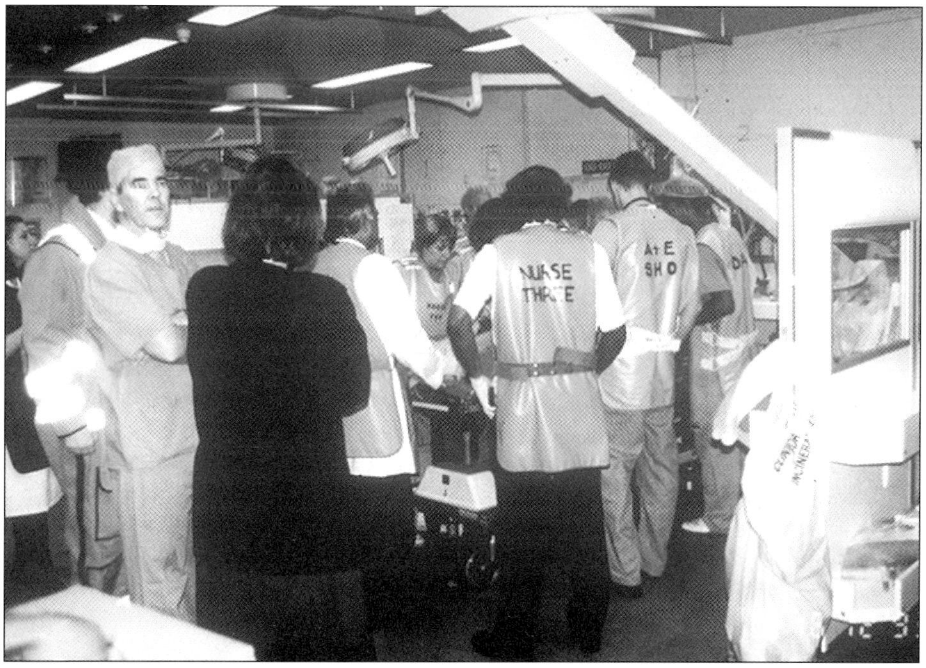

Photo: G Collins

The trauma team in the emergency room at the RLH. Originally the ATLS courses trained individuals to act alone in sequence. But if all the team have been trained by ATLS or ATNC methods, the basic skills, combined with organisation, enable simultaneous actions which are faster and more effective.

THE FUTURE OF TRAUMA TRAINING IN THE UNITED KINGDOM

Jim Ryan

Introduction

The Royal College of Surgeons of England sponsored *Working Party Report* on the management of patients with major injuries, detailed the deficiencies in current trauma care and highlighted two main requirements for improved care in the future. These are:

- The need to get the seriously injured patient to hospital alive.
- On arrival the prompt provision of expert anaesthetic and surgical care throughout the hospital management phase.

To achieve both of these objectives there is clearly a training requirement for all concerned, and not just medical and nursing personnel working in the resuscitation or crash rooms of our hospitals. Delivery of optimal care involves a continuum of care from point of injury through acute hospital care and rehabilitation and involves various agencies who, historically, have not worked or trained together as a team. To date the only organisation that has attempted to assemble and train medical personnel in a continuum of working to a common doctrine is the Defence Medical Service. The Doctrine is for all in the Armed Forces – Navy, Army and the Royal Air Force. This organisation is now in almost terminal decline as a result of Treasury demanded cost cutting exercises, but we can perhaps learn from their experience.

A military trauma tent during the Gulf War

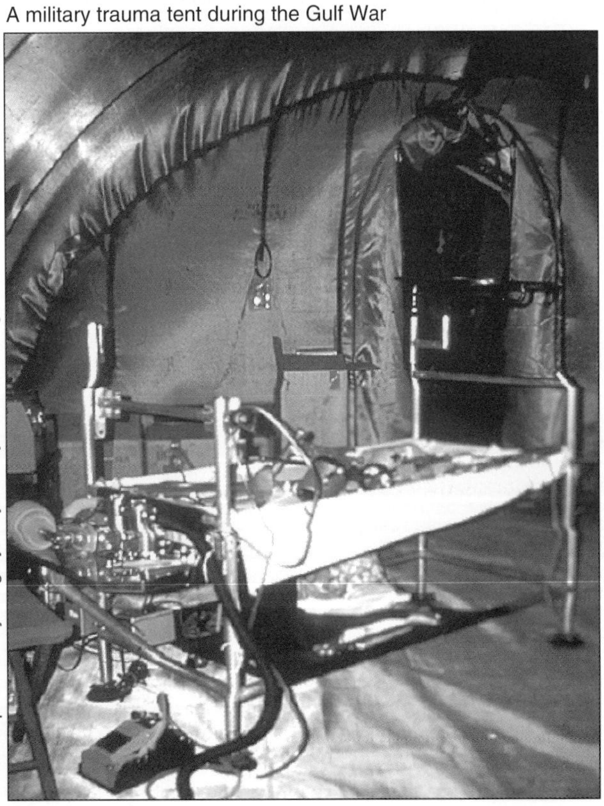

Photo: Dept of Military Surgery, Royal Army Medical College

The way forward must be towards the development of a trauma care system, supported by an agreed doctrine and training programme. We should not be afraid of doing so. A Trauma Doctrine would be merely the formal expression of knowledge, most of which is in the public domain and generally agreed. The Advanced Trauma Life Support Working Party, the Pre-hospital Trauma Life Support group, and BASICS Education are current examples of groups working to agreed management doctrines. Although these groups have much in common, there are noted differences which require to be addressed.

It is of particular note that no doctrine or agreed system exists for management beyond the initial phase and this is, in this author's view, the great 'Black Hole' of trauma management in the United Kingdom. Steps have been taken to rectify this problem. The Royal College of Surgeons of England have set up a Care of the Critically Ill Working Party under the Chairmanship of Professor Brian Rowlands. The task is to design a two/three day course covering management in the period beyond initial assessment and resuscitation and details care in the ICU or HDU setting. The course will use the ATLS model of lectures, skill stations and clinical role play and is designed to dovetail with ATLS management. Thus, the designers of this new course appreciate the concept of a continuum and have accepted the ATLS doctrine and the course is being written to dovetail with it. This represents the start of a wider task which will be to 'marry' existing courses and to design courses for areas where none currently exist. However, it does not extend into care in the operating theatre.

The Way Forward

A new working party with particular responsibility for training is required (you will doubtless say 'not another working party!') with membership drawn from all groups involved. These must include representatives from pre-hospital groups, accident and emergency, intensive care, anaesthetics and surgeons from the front-line specialties. The group will need to be hosted by a national college or institution, or might stand alone like the Dutch Trauma Society. Their first task would be to amalgamate existing training organisations, identify differences in ideology and approach and produce a single document detailing management and training needs for paramedics, pre-hospital doctors, emergency room and definitive care personnel. The Committee on Trauma of the American College of Surgeons have already produced a document dealing with most of these issues (see Further Reading).

Amalgamation of existing organisations, doctrines and training should not pose particular difficulty once rivalries and concepts of ownership have been dealt with. The philosophy of shared care and shared training needs must be accepted at the outset. Strategies for pre-hospital personnel might involve co-location of ambulance units alongside Accident and Emergency units large enough to train all grades of staff involved in early management. Pre-hospital paramedics must, in my view, be trained alongside their A&E department colleagues so that a seamless continuum of training and care is possible.

I now turn to, what I believe to be, the most difficult nut to crack – getting the acute 'front line' specialties involved. Currently, there is no agreed training package in the United Kingdom. National courses do exist in France, Scandinavia and the United States. Howard Champion, working under the auspices of the International Association for the Surgery of Trauma and Surgical Intensive Care, is developing an internationally based Definitive Surgical Trauma Care course and has invited the United Kingdom to participate through the Royal College of Surgeons of England Committee on Trauma. There is an urgent need to develop the theoretical basis and practical skills necessary to provide definitive surgical care for critically injured patients in the United Kingdom setting and it should be designed to dovetail seamlessly with existing initiatives such as PHTLS, ATLS and the Care of the Critically Injured course. This raises questions of who should be trained and what should they be taught. The question of who should be trained is for others to debate, but what should be taught will be discussed below.

Training in Technical Aspects of Operative Care

It is generally accepted that surgical training in the United Kingdom is excellent and internationally recognised, yet training in decision making and techniques in the field of trauma are generally deficient. Major, life threatening, multisystem injury in this country is relatively rare, penetrating injury from firearms is rarer still, with the consequence that surgeons on completion of their higher professional training will have had very little exposure to management. We urgently need a theoretical and practical course for surgeons, already trained in the generality of surgery and in the specialties, to teach them the skills of decision making and practical application of psychomotor skills – in short, how to assess and operate upon the victims of trauma. It should not be for beginners and should help to move away from the concept that major trauma is for the new trainee to cut his or her teeth on. Perhaps what we need is the involvement of old surgeons with no teeth left!

The emphasis should be on complex, multi-system injury where urgent intervention is required. The critically injured patient is never more at risk while awaiting handover, particularly on completion of resuscitation in the A&E department and now in transition to 'in house' team care. A distinguished colleague refers in this context to *TEMP* – the Temporary Evaluation and Monitoring Period while awaiting a consultant. Another of his aphorisms states: '5 minutes in a helicopter, 20 minutes in the resuscitation room, 10 days in hospital, and a life time to recover'. Particular emphasis will need to placed on this dangerous handover/ takeover period.

Other topics for inclusion might include any or all of the following:

- Surgical intervention in the face of continuing haemodynamic instability.
- Haemorrhage control at laparotomy (packing, balloon tamponade, for example)
- Vascular access for haemorrhage control
- Operative decision-making in the face of multiple organ injury
- Timing of interventions and prioritisation for multi-system injury
- Management of specific site or organ injury
    - liver
    - spleen
    - pelvis
    - major vessels
- Staged procedures – 'damage control' laparotomy followed by planned definitive procedure
- Use of external fixators
- Vascular repair and shunts
- Neuro-trauma
- Paediatric trauma
- Trauma in pregnancy

The list above serves only as an example. A final list would doubtless be more exhaustive. Any course should ideally be designed along the lines of existing courses and methods. A model course should include an agreed core of theoretical knowledge delivered as a series of didactic lectures and available in manual form for pre-course reading. This should be followed by a circus of practical skill stations with pass/fail criteria and the course should conclude with a series of clinical and practical scenario assessments for test and quality assurance purposes. Time and cost are critical factors and will need approval by training organisations and, not least, hospital trusts. Costs might be recovered from life assurance and accident insurance organisations using a risk reduction argument.

Teaching psychomotor skills in a realistic way poses problems, particularly where Home Office rules preclude the use of live animals. Nevertheless, fresh animal and human cadavers can be used within existing legislation. This problem will recede with time as the teaching of required skills will be greatly facilitated in future years by advancing technology, including interactive computer programmes and virtual reality systems. Already in development are virtual reality simulators for laparotomy and thoracotomy. Realistic training will require 'real time' manipulation of high resolution images fed in from CT and MRI data. One of the problems being addressed is the concept of realistic tactile feedback from the 'structures' being manipulated. Such systems, we are assured, will be available within three to five years and will revolutionise all surgical training including trauma.

In concluding this section it is possible to visualise a virtual reality workshop encompassing management of a single trauma victim from a pre-hospital scene by paramedics, transferring the victim to the resuscitation room, on to theatre and then to ICU, all in real time.

Quality Assurance and Audit

It is still difficult to provide meaningful audit data proving the benefit of trauma systems and specific trauma training in terms of improved survival and reduced morbidity. However, it is possible to utilise local audit filters to examine in isolation particular processes of care such as time taken to institute particular interventions. What is required is matched audit incorporating all processes from point of injury to discharge and rehabilitation. Such an enterprise is under way in the Netherlands following the promulgation of the ATLS programme in January 1995.

The development of an all embracing trauma care training programme must result in improved outcome and this must be measurable. It follows that concepts of quality assurance, clinical audit and quality improvement must be understood and accepted. This should not pose difficulty because many of the existing groups such as PHTLS, ATLS and BASICS Education have designed their programmes around these concepts.

The ultimate aim must be to prove objectively for once and for all the value of a systems and training approach. Until then, cynics will continue to cast doubt and even suggest that by improving survival, particularly for head injured patients, long-term morbidity is actually increased with a considerable cost benefit.

Summary

Trauma or injury is a unique clinical problem demanding novel solutions. We need to develop a different paradigm when considering training for the management of multiply injured patients. Trauma is unique in terms of place and time. The place varies from the field setting to the A&E department, the operating room and the Intensive Care Unit. The time relates to the sense of urgency and crisis. This raises special training problems for varied and diverse groups of individuals across the spectrum of care.

Considerable effort has already been expended in training medical personnel in the retrieval, safe transport and initial resuscitation of the victims of trauma. There are perhaps too many groups involved in these aspects and cooperation, if not amalgamation, is urgently needed. However, a major problem, as yet unaddressed, is the organisation and training of medical and nursing personnel in later management and, in particular, operative intervention. Management for the victims of trauma is not for amateurs and should be left to properly trained teams carrying out sufficient procedures to maintain skills. This has logistic implications beyond the remit of this paper. I am concerned with training those who will be involved in the future. An agreed system is demanded and should be part of a comprehensive programme involving all. Whatever system is put in place, concepts of quality assurance, peer review and on-going audit of delivered care must be understood and accepted.

Further Reading

1. Report of the Working Party on the management of patients with major injury. Commission on the Provision of Surgical Services. The Royal College of Surgeons of England, 1988: London.
2. Resources for Optimal Care of the Injured. Committee on Trauma, American College of Surgeons, 1993: Chicago.

Professor James M Ryan MB MCh FRCS RAMC(V), is Leonard Cheshire Professor in the Leonard Cheshire Department of Conflict Recovery at University College Hospital, London. His book – Ballistic Trauma: Clinical Relevance in Peace and War, Ed Ryan JM, Rich N, Morgans BM, Dale R, Cooper GJ, published by Arnold, London – Winter 1996. ISBN 0 340 581 14X.

THE FACULTY OF PRE-HOSPITAL CARE AT THE ROYAL COLLEGE OF SURGEONS OF EDINBURGH

Richard Fairhurst

Dr Ken Easton, the founding father of the British Association of Immediate Care (BASICS) recognised as early as 1949 that if pre-hospital care was to make an impact on trauma it must be multidisciplinary, and the skills of all involved must be increased and formally assessed. To this end BASICS promoted the appointment of Accident and Emergency consultants, paramedics in the Ambulance Service, and rescue equipment to the Fire Service.

From the beginning, ad hoc training courses were run for doctors, but it was realised that these courses should be standardised and accredited by an academic body. After a great deal of work the Royal College of Surgeons of Edinburgh, through Mr R Myles Gibson, agreed to co-operate with BASICS in developing a Diploma in Immediate Medical Care. The first Diet was in 1990 and the Diploma is now established as the standard for doctors involved in pre-hospital care. The examination lasts for two days with projected material, multiple choice paper, short answer paper, triage paper, followed by four 30 minute moulages in Advanced and Basic Life Support, Medicine, Trauma, and Major Incidents.

In 1993 the College agreed to co-operate with BASICS, The Royal College of Nursing Accident and Emergency Association and the NHS Ambulance Service to develop and run a Pre-hospital Emergency Care Course (PHEC). Demand for the course escalated with requests from such diverse bodies as the Football League, the Fire Service, and practice nurses.

In 1994 BASICS proposed to the College a Faculty to oversee and develop this activity. This was warmly received, and The Faculty of Pre-hospital Care at the Royal College of Surgeons of Edinburgh was formally launched on 11th January 1996.

The Faculty is unique in encompassing doctors, nurses, paramedics, Voluntary Aid Society members and other pre-hospital care providers. All members will have equal status within the Faculty, but their primary qualification will be reflected in the post nominal e.g MFPHC (Paramedic) or MFPHC (Nurse) to prevent blurring of professional identification.

The membership of the Faculty will be achieved by each professional group by an ascending staircase. For a doctor this may be: post-registration experience – PHEC (or ATLS + ACLS) – five day Immediate Care Course – Diploma in Immediate Medical Care – log book of pre-hospital care experience – viva on log book.

The Faculty has a Management Board supported by Committees where much of the development work is done. The current committees are: Research and Development, Education and Assessment and Publications and Public Relations.

'Pre-Hospital Care' is the official Journal of the British Association of Immediate Care and The Faculty of Pre-hospital Care at The Royal College of Surgeons (Ed) will be published 3 monthly, starting in 1997. Royal College of Surgeons (Ed), Nicholson Street, Edinburgh EH8 9DW.

Dr Richard J Fairhurst, FFAEM, DIMC.RCS(ED), Consultant in Accident and Emergency Medicine, Chorley and South Ribble NHS Trust, Publications and Public Relations Committee Faculty of Pre-hospital Care Member.

THE FUTURE OF PRE-HOSPITAL MEDICINE

Gareth Davies

In the UK today some 5000 people die each year on the roads. Health Authorities spend up to £1.4 million per 100,000 population on ambulance service provision. Despite this investment clinical outcome measures are virtually non-existent. Services are judged on response times and little else, diverting our attention from the real issues of quality pre-hospital care. As ambulance systems develop around such targets, we may well be constructing services that ultimately will never provide appropriate pre-hospital trauma care or, at best, are incredibly over-priced. Definitive care for the multiply injured patient is simply more than getting them to hospital and into the operating theatre as soon as possible. By definition the disease requires a multiplicity of therapeutic interventions and end points. Our goal for the future is to deliver these end points in a timely, quality controlled fashion. The challenge is to do it in a cost effective manner.

Philosophies of Pre-hospital Care

There are two fundamental philosophies of pre-hospital trauma: 'scoop and run' and 'stay and play'. In the former, patients are removed from the scene and taken rapidly to hospital with only minimal intervention. This is a common feature in many North American models of pre-hospital care where ambulance providers are non-physicians. The alternative view, stay and stabilise, brings the hospital (and doctor) into the streets and is a fundamental feature of the HEMS operation and many European models of pre-hospital care.

Why the Divide between US and European Models?

In the US it is rare to see doctors acting as ambulance providers and treating patients in the streets. This position is largely historical, though the safety record of many of the flight programs in the early 1980s undoubtedly made the insurance and indemnity fees of pre-hospital physicians untenable in the commercial market of North American health care.

To some degree the type of work encountered in the US has also influenced the model of pre-hospital care. The high incidence of penetrating trauma (shootings and stabbings) requires an element of minimising scene time and getting the patient to theatre as soon as possible. However even this could be debated as a simple function of system sophistication. There are already several case reports of a pre-hospital thoracotomy producing neurologically intact survivors from previously 'fatal' situations.

Despite this evidence research has identified that medical interventions, when used in the pre-hospital setting by non physicians, do not dramatically enhance survival. That such a position exists suggests that either the treatments were misconceived or they were simply not meeting their end points, i.e a lack of quality control in the system. To propose that a vacuum of care, for example the denial of anaesthesia and controlled ventilation to a severe head injury, is a therapeutic model is illogical. If we believe that such treatment is physiological then it is incumbent on physicians to ensure its delivery in a timely quality assured manner.

The Myths

As the philosophy of trauma care has slowly divided into two camps, myths have arisen that only serve to distort the clinical issues. One of the most prominent of these is scene time. To presume that time spent at scene is time wasted is a nonsense. What is important is that patients receive appropriate care at the appropriate time. If the patient is stabbed over the liver then it is important that such a patient gets to theatre as rapidly as possible. Measuring the scene time is useless and diverts attention from other potential delays in patient care, for example a stay in A&E. In the French SAMU model such patients are seen by a pre-hospital physician and taken directly to theatre. Time spent on scene relieving the pneumothorax and maximising oxygen delivery is hardly wasted and meets the needs of the patient as they arise. For blunt trauma the case for on scene treatment is even stronger.

That most trauma patients require salvation from hypovolaemic shock in theatre is a common belief. Though such a statement may be true with high volumes for a penetrating injury it can not be presumed in blunt injury. With the advent of better imaging and more aggressive interventional radiology, the need to rush to surgery is becoming ever less evident.

Another favourite misconception is that the chaos of the pre-hospital environment precludes the delivery of quality interventions so these are best accomplished in the tranquil surrounds of the resuscitation room where, after a denial of care, patients could be seen by a multitude of unknown doctors endeavouring to produce a coordinated response to the process of the dying patient. Such a presumption is both bold and ignorant.

So What should be the Model of Care?

Major trauma is a rare disease. On average an ambulance man would expect to see one or two major cases per year (ISS> 15). Skill utility in this environment is therefore a very real problem. As such it would be wrong to expect ambulance staff to provide the the sort of care patients could have in hospital; a position supported by much of the literature on pre-hospital care. To deliver appropriate care with a high degree of quality control, centralisation of skills and equipment is essential. At first glance the cost of equipping a helicopter with a doctor may appear high. However, when comparing this with the cost of training and equipping every ambulance to deliver the same level of care, it becomes apparent that value for money is high.

It is not simply about putting a physician in the streets. There are many skills which physicians do not have at their disposal such as extrication and communications, skills which the ambulance services have well developed. It thus becomes obvious that the ideal functional pre-hospital unit should be a closely knit team of both physicians and ambulance staff where the various skills can be used together.

The Need For Tasking Efficiency

For cost effective use of special resources, such as a physician-equipped aircraft, accurate tasking is essential. Though there is little research on this issue commercially available packages are available which aim to identify the sicker patients. The degree of quality control within these packages varies enormously and most only identify high numbers of patients in high risk categories. Thus their sensitivity is high but specificity is weak. However, when special resources are tasked it is important they are tailored to local needs. Data should be prospectively collected, routinely analysed and despatch criteria adjusted accordingly. This together with advanced technology will allow progressively more accurate tasking of resources.

Conclusion

Despite the level of resourcing, performance indicators for ambulance services are lacking. Development of meaningful quality indicators represents a major challenge in the delivery of pre-hospital care. Trauma, like many other diseases, is not the domain of one particular group. It is vital that the acute-phase physicians move hand in hand with other health care providers, to work alongside purchasers in developing quality standards and a service that meets the needs of the patient. Care should be viewed as a continuum, from assessing 999 back to prevention. Only when the disease is viewed and perhaps even bought from this perspective will we produce real value for money and a quality service.

Gareth Davies, Emeritus HEMS Registrar, is Consultant in the A&E department of the RLH.

Air Hanson

ADVERTISEMENT FEATURE

McDonnell Douglas Helicopter Systems

MD 900 - The Explorer

THE NOTAR SYSTEM ADVANTAGE

Few ideas can be truly called revolutionary but, in the field of helicopter design, the first flight of the NOTAR concept demonstrator from **McDonnell Douglas Helicopters**, marked the start of a revolution. The first NOTAR helicopter, the MD-52ON was a development of the highly successful MD-500 Series. What set the MD-52ON apart from other rotorcraft was the anti-torque system. With the NOTAR system, the tall rotor is replaced by a fan-driven air circulation control system within an enclosed tall boom. The result is a helicopter which provides unparalleled safety, quiet and performance. With the elimination of the exposed tail rotor, the 52ON was easier and more pleasurable to fly. Its manoeuvrability and hovering performance were without equal. It flew higher and faster than its competitors, yet was able to carry a greater payload. This was revolution in motion and McDonnell Douglas patented the system, which is now featured on the MD-600 as well as the larger twin engined MD-900 Explorer.

The NOTAR System consists of an enclosed articulated fan driven by the main transmission; the circulation control tail boom, direct jet thruster and vertical stabilisers. Low pressure air, forced through two tailboom slots, causes the main rotor downwash to hug the contour of the boom. This effect provides the majority of the anti-torque force required in a hover, by creating a lateral lift that counteracts main rotor torque. Remaining anti-torque and directional control are provided by the direct jet thruster, controlled by anti-torque pedal input. The result is anti-torque control power, without the disadvantages of the tail rotor blades, such as excessive noise and potential damage or injury due to an exposed tail rotor. In addition the NOTAR system prolongs the structural life of aircraft components and reduces maintenance by eliminating vibrations caused by a high speed tail rotor. In the air ambulance configuration, the quieter cabin and the lack of vibration has obvious advantages for both patients and medical attendants. The elegance of the system lies in its simplicity as well as the inherent safety of its operation.

21st Century Rotorcraft: *The twin-turbine MD Explorer, which features the Notor anti-torque system, is the first new twin-turbine helicopter to enter production in nearly a decade*

The significance of NOTAR safety: No hull damage from tail rotor related accidents

- No dramatic centre of gravity shift with loss of gear box (no gear box)
- Reduced pilot workload
- Less sensitive to wind direction
- Enhanced safety in confined areas
- No third party liability from walking into almost invisible tail rotors
- No drive shaft, hangar bearings or 90" gear boxes
- Easy access to all components
- Polypropolylene fan blades are FOD tolerant
- Flyable with loss of fan drive
- Reduces vibration noise and drag
- Simplifies maintenance and associated costs
- Greater reliability

The Managing Director of one of America's largest air medical service units described the Explorer as the *replacement helicopter for the HEMS industry.* Judging by the number of agencies now selecting Explorers for air medical missions, the statement was well judged.

Andy Richardson, Sales Director, UK

McDonnell Douglas Helicopters are exclusively represented in the UK by Air Hanson, who will be pleased to supply further information.

Air Hanson Ltd, Business Aviation Centre, Blackbushe Airport, Camberley, Surrey GU1 9LG

Tel: 01252 890089 Fax: 01252 876447

SECTION 11: THE FUTURE

Introduction

Richard Earlam

Nobody can plan for the future without a good knowledge of past history and the present situation. Other countries or systems will be at a different stage of development than one's own so it is always essential to wander the earth 'just looking'. In America with businesses they say there are three options for the future: the same, smaller or bigger. The first option never occurs because you are either bust and go bankrupt or you become larger and take over the others. In trauma care this does not occur because luckily there is only a small pool of trauma which hopefully will become even smaller by prevention and secondly there is an optimum size above which efficiency does not improve, experience is already large enough and the enlargement has already changed the work ethos of the recipient hospital. About 300 of the 2000 potential major trauma victims in the LAS area come to the RLH through HEMS and the same amount go elsewhere; the remainder are taken to their nearest hospital by land ambulance. 300 trauma patients per annum is quite enough for any one hospital in the UK otherwise overload and tiredness creep in. It is rewarding but exhausting work for the helicopter crew and doctors, for the A&E department and the Intensive Care Unit. They require time between the severely ill patients arriving for recovery. We originally suggested that Greater London needed one trauma centre for each of the four Thames regions. Now there are only two divisions, north and south of river Thames, so two main hospitals for receiving major trauma united with all the other A&E departments by land and air seems a suitable compromise for the future.

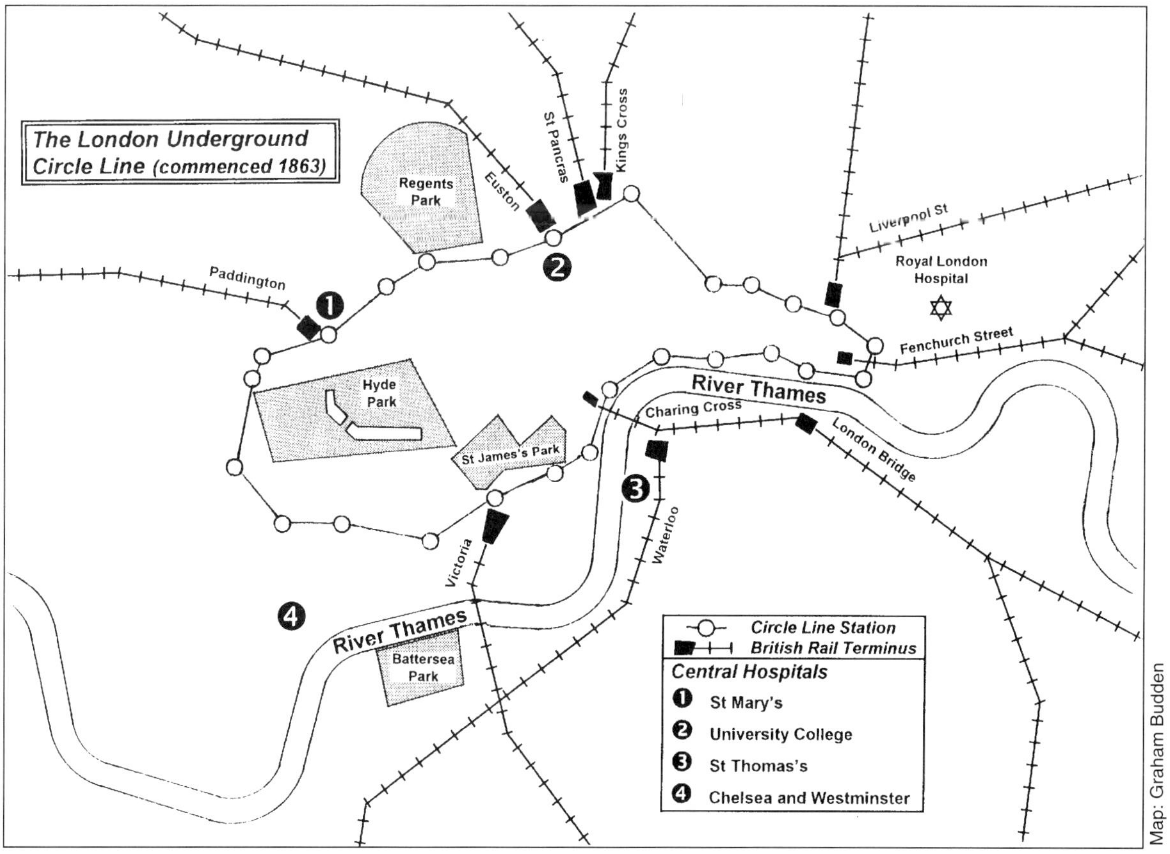

SECTION 11: THE FUTURE

The map of the Circle Line of the Underground in London showing how the underground tube circle joins the terminuses of the original mainlines, tells a short story.

Transport is the clue to why cities exist where they are today and populations follow transport and trade. The river Thames was the reason for the Roman town of Londinium being built on raised ground above the flood waters on the north bank near where St Paul's cathedral is now. In early days many Roman towns, like Chester, Winchester, Colchester and York were founded upstream and not at the head of an estuary for the sole purpose of protection from raiders by sea; London is no exception. Marine transport originally united England by coastal trade. This was followed by canals in the 18th century and railways in the 19th century. Roads, straight ones and well built, existed in Roman times but were ignored by the natives until Ernest Marples opened the Preston motorway bypass in the 1950s, about 1500 years after the legions had left. So London and its development was originally based on the river and this was tidal to well beyond Hampton Court. The lowest bridge was London Bridge above which no large sailing vessel could pass, only barges and wherries. Later the obstruction was Tower Bridge which could go up and down but the majority of ocean going ships docked below downstream. You are wondering what this historical lesson is all about. The London Hospital developed in the East End as a large hospital when there was a large population and 500,000 dockers. They and the ships have departed. Another large hospital of even greater ancestry started its early life to the north of the lowest river crossing to look after the pilgrims going to Canterbury. Times have changed.

Back to the map we must go to see the main line terminuses of the great railways: London Midland Scottish (LMS), Great Western (GW), London North Eastern Railway (LNER) and Southern Region (SR). There they ended because historically each one had one slice of the cake – one segment of the circle. In the 1860s the Victorian engineers went underground, not totally, but cut and not cover. They built a railway link from Farringdon Road in the City to Paddington in the west and then later burrowed more underground with tunnels or cut and cover to complete a circle to join the main line stations. It is interesting how much some of the central London Hospitals relied on such rail transport for their patients to come, and somebody cleverly said that one reason for Harley Street being a medical centre was rail and underground communication. The lesson to be learnt is that the solution for transport in the 19th century lay in the appreciation that burrowing underground was feasible when the roads were inadequate.

A solution for the 20th and 21st century is to use the airspace above as well as roads and the tube underneath. The roads are now clogged probably in a worse manner than at the peak of horse and carriage travel in the last century. There are now more horses in England than during the height of horse driven transport in Victorian days, but luckily they do not all come into central London now. Speeds in central London are a mere 7 mph with the occasional grid lock in an emergency disaster situation. A helicopter service must not be for anything other than emergencies and it must be complementary to the land ambulance system. But what is clear from the map is that hospitals are dotted around in a haphazard historical way so transport must respond by using any of the available methods. The future for pre-hospital transport lies in the proper integration of population, transport and hospitals.

This Section contains other futuristic ideas such as quicker and more efficient helicopters with no tail rotor, an assessment of the feasibility of flying a helicopter service at night, the increase in safety of flying with new regulations and the possibility of using new technology for training and education. Finally there are two articles on research and education by a group in the University of Munich and our own Professor of Surgery and Anaesthetics. It is the duty and responsibility for Universities to think, research and teach so these two articles are a most important guide to the future of trauma care not just in London but everywhere.

NOTAR HELICOPTERS – LOOK NO TAIL

David Gurney

The Aerospatiale Dauphin (Figure 1) used by HEMS is 15 years old and is slowly being superseded by new technology. Al Rock, HEMS Chief Pilot, and Dr Gareth Davies, HEMS senior registrar, have recently been to America to look at a possible replacement, the McDonnell Douglas Explorer (Figure 2).

Notar is an abbreviation for No Tail Rotor. This is one of the most recent technical advances we have seen in the helicopter. But why have McDonnell Douglas dispensed with the tail rotor and how? To understand this you first have to understand a little about how a helicopter flies.

Helicopters are weird and wonderful beasts which defy the laws of gravity and have been described as a whirling conglomeration of mechanical parts which happen to be in the air at the same time. The helicopter, although commonly powered by jet engines, still produces it's forward thrust from the main rotor. The jet engines are used only to power the rotors and any forward thrust from the jet exhausts is negligible.

Figure 1: G-HEMS – a European SA365N or Dauphin

Figure 2: McDonnell Douglas Notar MD900 or Explorer

Newton's third law states 'For every action there is an equal and opposite reaction'. But friction tends to mask the effects of this law. When the engines turn the rotor blades on a helicopter they are also trying to turn the helicopter in the opposite direction. This is fine while it is on the ground, because the friction of the wheels or skids on the ground stops the aircraft from spinning around. Consequently the rotors turn and the helicopter doesn't. However, when the helicopter lifts into the air it no longer has any friction reaction from the ground and some force is required to counter balance the turning force. There are several solutions to this problem (Figure 3).

The most obvious solution are two rotors turning in opposite directions, allowing the turning forces to cancel each other out, as in the Chinook (Figure 4), or Osprey (Figure 5). The advantage of this system is that all the available power is used to produce lift, making it particularly good for heavy lift helicopters. The disadvantage is the complexity of the rotor system and drive linkage. The two rotors are normally interlocking and a mechanical failure of the synchronisation system is likely to result in the rotors mincing each other to bits, with disastrous consequences.

The Fairey Roto-Dyne used tip jets to power the rotor. This works by pumping the compressed gases from the jet engine down the inside of the rotor blades where it is then exhausted through nozzles or jets at the tips. This removes the need for any anti-torque device, but in reality it proved to be very inefficient and incredibly noisy.

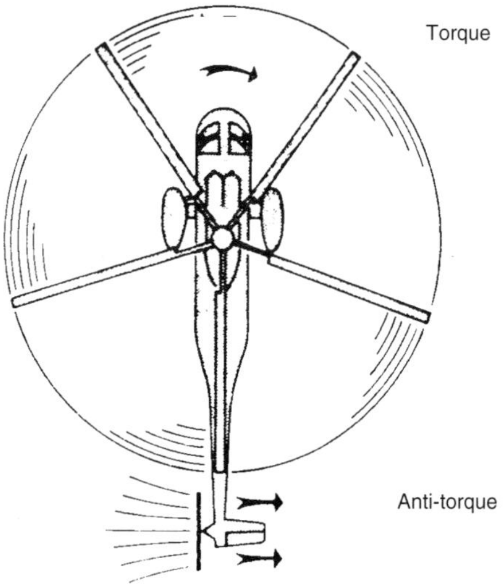

Figure 3 The Torque Problem

Figure 4: Chinook

Figure 5: Osprey

The most common solution is the tail rotor. It spins at a fixed ratio to the main rotor and the pitch of the blades is controlled by the pilot's foot pedals. The pilot must adjust the tail rotor, in synchronisation with the power demands made on the main rotor, to balance out the torque reaction from the engines. The tail rotor is the cheapest and simplest solution to the anti-torque problem of the helicopter. However, one major disadvantage is that it is usually mounted at head height and rotates at very high speed, making it quite difficult to see. Consequently it has been responsible for many fatal accidents. The Dauphin has an enclosed tail rotor called a fenestron. This is safer, but not infallible.

The tail rotor is the most dangerous hazard to the general public, so a helicopter without one would be an advantage to any HEMS operation.

The Explorer has a hollow anti-torque boom with an inboard fan driven by the engine at one end and a louvered nozzle at the other. The nozzle rotates and is controlled by the pilot's foot pedals in the same way as a tail rotor. This enables the pilot to adjust the anti-torque reaction and allows directional control in the hover. In this system the tail rotor has been replaced by the inboard fan. This has the advantage of being more compact, quieter, lighter (no tail rotor drive shaft or gearbox) and considerably safer. This is just half of the solution however. The hollow boom has horizontal slots cut in it on one side and you have to understand how a wing works to understand how fiendishly clever this is (Figure 6).

Both helicopters and fixed wing aeroplanes produce their lift in the same way. The secret is in the shape of the wings and the rotor blades which are very similar.

Figure 7 shows the cross-section of a typical aerofoil in flight. The airflow going over the top of the wing has further to go than the airflow going underneath the wing. Hence the airflow has to go over the top of the wing

Figure 6: The Notar System

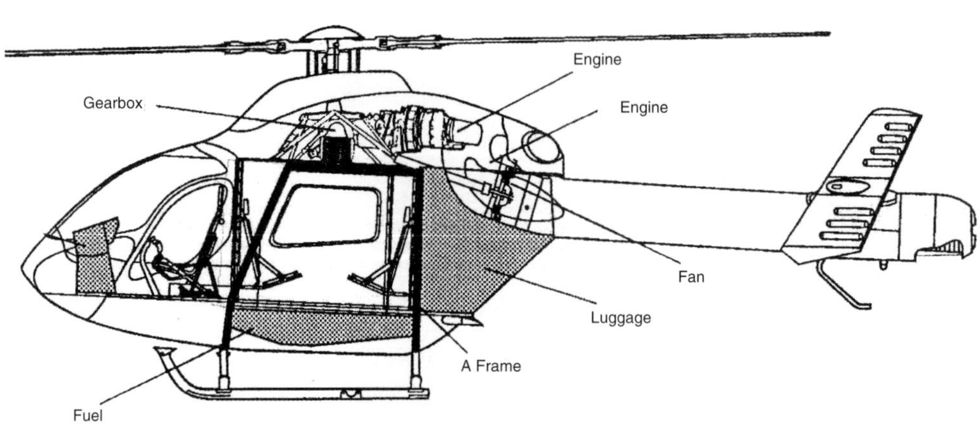

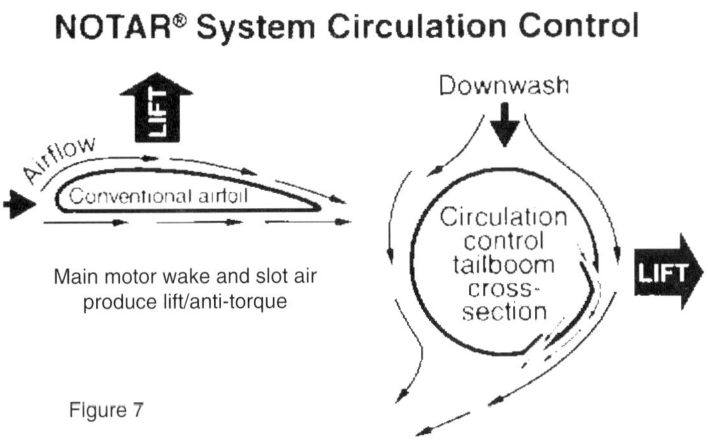

Figure 7

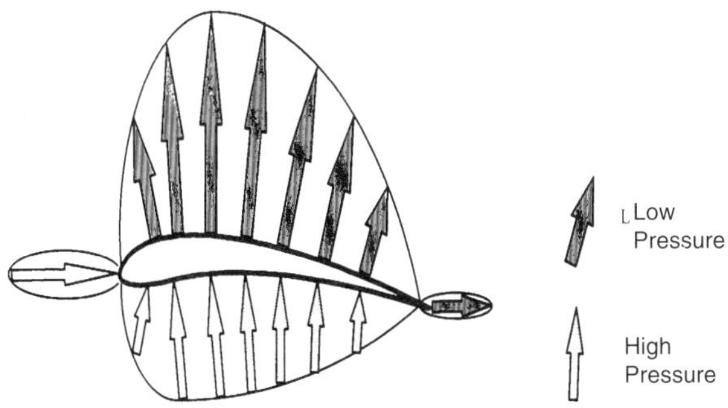

Figure 8: The Pressure Distribution on a Typical Aerofoil

Figure 9: Airflow Over the Boom

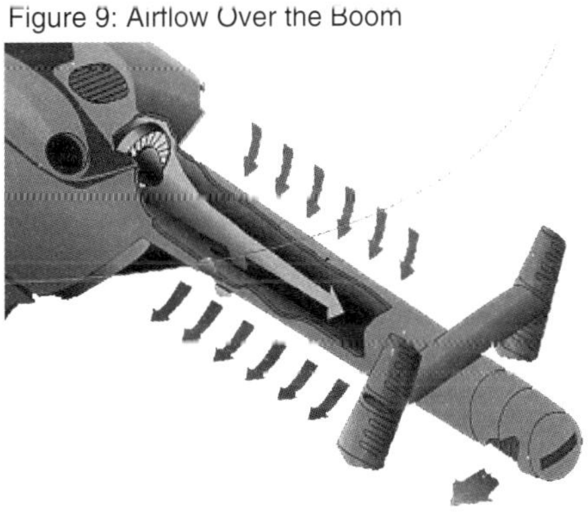

faster than the airflow going underneath and, by the laws of physics, the faster the airflow goes the lower the air pressure drops. The resulting pressure distribution over the wing is shown in Figure 8. This is where a wing gets its lift from, it is literally sucked upwards.

The horizontal slots in the Notar's tail boom encourage the airflow to follow the circular cross section on one side of the boom, Figure 9. This results in a similar airflow to that of a conventional wing and in effect turns the boom into a wing producing lift. The only difference is that the boom is using the down flow of the rotor to produce a horizontal force which acts as anti-torque.

The clever bit is that the amount of anti-torque produced by the boom is proportional to the speed of the airflow over the boom. This in turn is proportional to the amount of lift the main rotor is producing, which in turn is proportional to the amount of anti-torque required to keep the helicopter from spinning around, so the system is largely self-correcting. Whatever power demands the pilot puts on the main rotor produces proportionately more or less anti-torque from the tail boom, thereby automatically maintaining directional stability. The pilot therefore has less work to do with the pedals at low speeds. McDonnell Douglas have produced a quiet, lighter, safer and more stable aircraft, undoubtedly a step in the right direction.

David Gurney, BSc in Aeronautical Engineering, is a HEMS pilot.

NIGHT FLYING IN THE HEMS ROLE

Richard Shuttleworth, Mark Landon, Ian Field

When it was decided to set up an air ambulance for London in the late 1980s it was envisaged that it would, ideally, give coverage for all of the population of London all of the time. However there is a major factor which has prevented this from being achieved so far – *darkness*. The modern helicopter is perfectly capable of being flown in the dark and is fully instrumented for flying in cloud. So why, as the HEMS pilots are frequently asked, does the service only operate in daylight?

There is justification for a night capability as there are instances of major trauma at night. There are identifiable peaks and troughs in the expectation of incidents throughout the whole day and, although most happen in the normal day when people are active, a significant number occur at night. If HEMS is to be fully appreciated by the public and taken seriously by the medical profession as an essential part of the trauma care system it should be available all the time.

Safety

Before the service was set up in its present form the Civil Aviation Authority (CAA) examined its proposed method of operation in great detail. Parliament has, over the last 80 years, laid down in the Air Navigation Order rules specifying how any aircraft can operate within the United Kingdom and the rules for Public Transport Operations are very strict. The primary concern of Parliament, and thus the CAA, is *safety*.

It took some time to get permission to operate the service during the day and the service was eventually granted some dispensations which exempt us from certain Rules of the Air in very specific instances. Without these exemptions the service could not operate at all. Thus it had been decided that in the interests of saving lives there was an acceptable slight lowering of the very high safety standards normally required. The advantages were considered to outweigh the increase in risks. At the present time with the latest technology the CAA will not allow air ambulances to operate in the primary role at night.

What are the Risks and Problems?

Landing Sites: During the day G-HEMS lands in a great variety of locations almost all of which are not pre-selected but are identified visually from the aircraft as it arrives overhead the incident scene. There are a number of factors which a pilot must consider before attempting an approach which are equally relevant at night. Obviously, at night, it is not possible to identify a safe 'ad hoc' landing site in the same way. Thus it would be necessary to operate to pre-surveyed ones which would also have to be acceptable to the CAA. These sites would have to be considerably larger than any day-time ones with fewer obstructions and therefore there would be far fewer suitable places to land in London. In many cases we would not be able to land close to the accident at all negating one of the advantages of HEMS – namely speed of reaction.

All pre-selected sites would have to be surveyed for new obstacles regularly with a very large extra administrative load resulting.

Illumination of the selected sites is essential from both ground and air but as yet no suitable light other than the Spectrolab Night Sun has been identified. This unfortunately has an unacceptable weight penalty for G-HEMS and its requirement to operate to Group A especially during the summer. Night Vision Goggles have not been tried but they have their own limitations when there is ambient light about such as street lights, head lights etc. They suffer from 'blooming' and pilots also require regular practice with them.

The Metropolitan Police would need to be trained in helicopter night operations such as providing a pool of light with car headlights positioned according to wind direction. We have an excellent 'T' and Glide-path Indicator which can be positioned well in advance of a pre-decided landing or after the first landing of a prolonged operation. In our primary role this is unlikely to be used often, but it would be used for a major incident at night. Having landed we would require greater security assistance from the police for the helicopter.

Distance to Scene: A landing close to an accident is necessary if the response times are to be kept short but this could not be guaranteed at night. We would have to rely much more on police or other transport on the ground. The police will have their own role to fulfil. There will no doubt be some critic of the HEMS concept who would use slower response times in their arguments against it.

Conversely, ground ambulance response times improve at night as road traffic is reduced.

Environmental: With a reduced number of landing sites there will naturally be a likely greater use of each one even though the total number of tasks may be less at night. Until there is a much quieter model of helicopter (such as an up-rated McDonnell-Douglas Explorer) many of the local residents may not accept landings in the middle of the night much more than once and this would generate possible anti-HEMS feeling. We have already been asked why we disturb people at night when, in fact, it was the police helicopter. If the Fire Brigade get a helicopter the problem will worsen. How would one explain a hoax or 'not required' call to an angry local who has been awakened at 3 a.m? Waiting for more information would increase response times even further.

Aircraft availability: One aircraft could not possibly be available for 24 hour cover so there will be a requirement for a suitable second aircraft with consequential increases in maintenance costs including overtime at night.

Manning: The CAA has laid down firm rules for the maximum hours a pilot can be on duty over a specific period and has rules for flying hours as well. The only solution is to employ more pilots with its associated increase in cost. With increased hours of operation there would be a consequential need for more Operations Staff and Firemen.

Limited night operations: There are limited options that could be achieved without a great increase in cost. One is the duty day going to 12 hours every day of the year. However the comments regarding night landing sites would still apply.

Cost: Any of the above factors will increase the cost of the HEMS operation although there may be better financial recoveries as all patients requiring to be transported by air would have to come back to the Royal London Hospital, which has the only night-approved landing pad. It is perfectly possible to go to a secondary role at night from an aviation point of view should it be deemed necessary, but there would be an increase in costs as above regarding a spare/second helicopter, manning, maintenance and flying hours. At the moment HEMS does not do many transfers during the day because they keep it from its primary role.

Weather: The rules for minimum cloud ceiling and visibility are more restriction at night but it is possible that they could be relaxed in the urban environment if the CAA so decided.

Summary

A night operation is possible in a limited form but bearing in mind the cost and safety requirements and the present limited level of night landing technology, the question must be asked as to whether there is enough trauma at night to justify the operation of HEMS at night. The answer lies very much in the hands of those who finance the system.

Richard Shuttleworth, **Mark Landon** and **Ian Field** are all active HEMS pilots. Richard joined us in 1988 and has flow over 6000 hours; he was in the Royal Navy from 1962-74 and with the Royal Oman Police in the Sultanate of Oman from 1976-88.

JAR-OPS – A NEW WORLD: The Civil Aviation Authority (CAA) and the Joint Aviation Authority (JAA)

Graham Jeffs

In the United Kingdom the Civil Aviation authority (CAA) ensures safety standards for all fixed wing aircraft and helicopters. They act with the authority of an Act of Parliament and under statutory laws enforce their high standards of safety and air navigation. The CAA have no authority in Europe or in the European Community (EC). In the USA there is a similar controlling body, the Federal Aviation Administration (FAA), but the International Civil Aviation Authority (ICAO) is a world wide organisation on which most national authorities base their rules. However attempts are now being made through the Joint Aviation Authority (JAA) to unify European regulations, but although all members of the European Community are members of the JAA, not all have equal voting rights and some other non-European countries are members. Over 20 nations partake in these discussions. The relationship between JAA and the EC has not yet been established on a legal or statutory basis, whereas in the UK the CAA advice is based on law. Nobody can just buy a helicopter, add a doctor or an ambulance man, and call themselves a Helicopter Emergency Medical Service. The CAA control standards and have absolute authority for licensing such helicopter services. A major move towards a common set of European operating requirements was made on 1 April 1995 when the Joint Aviation Requirements (JAR-OPS) operating rules for commercial aeroplanes and helicopters were adopted. Harmonisation of aviation requirements is nothing new. For the last two decades, European aviation authorities have been working on common aircraft certification codes with the US Federal Aviation Administration.

As a natural development of this, work had recently started on harmonising some of the operational codes. In 1989 the Joint Aviation Authorities (JAA) formed an operations committee to develop a set of operating requirements for aeroplanes and helicopters conducting commercial air transportation. With the imminent arrival of the EU third liberalisation package, which guarantees de-regulation and free competition in the European marketplace, it was obviously important that all the European states should complete to a common set of operating requirements to help eliminate any commercial advantage that might accrue should the existing different national codes be retained.

The JAA operations committee have developed two operating codes: JAR-OPS Part 1 for commercial air transportation by aeroplanes and JAR-OPS Part 3 for commercial air transportation by helicopters. Areas covered by the regulations are as diverse as fuel policy, aerodrome operating minima, flight crew and cabin crew qualification and training, carriage of dangerous goods and performance requirements. Work on the development of the codes was concluded at the beginning of April 1995 when JAR-OPS Parts 1 and 3 were officially adopted by the JAA Committee. Operators now have time to work up to full implementation of the new requirements. Large aeroplanes and all helicopter operators must comply with the new requirements by 1 April 1998 and small aeroplanes operators by 1 April 1999. These rules will apply to all HEMS operators. In developing the codes it was necessary to form a large number of study groups to work on the text of the requirements and to ensure that an adequate level of safety was maintained.

ICAO's Annex 6 details minimum operating standards and the JAR-OPS committee used it as a 'base document' for the new requirements. The CAA members on the JAR committees ensured that the new regulations adequately reflected the United Kingdom's existing requirements.

The main difference between the existing national regulations and JAR-OPS is that new regulations are slightly less restrictive. However, the CAA's Safety Regulation Group (SRG) Flight Operations Department is satisfied that existing safety standards have been maintained. United Kingdom operators have received the new regulations fairly well. They are used to prescriptive rules due to SRG's existing systems, but the same is not true for some foreign operators, especially where their existing national regulations had been more lenient. For some overseas operators, JAR-OPS will prove more restrictive and may involve extra costs. As a result, some major European states, including France and Germany, have had difficulty explaining to operators that the long term JAA goal of a level playing field is worth pursuing. SRG has concerns about this as the agreed long term goal of the JAA is for common certification and operating procedures for all 23 member states. It is therefore essential that all states apply the regulations in the same way. To achieve this, all states must have an adequate means of inspecting the operations Air Operator Certificate (AOC) holders based in their country and the JAA must ensure that common standards of inspection are applied in all member States. Inspection and audit procedures currently used by the flight operations will not significantly change under the new regulations. It is becoming increasingly evident that there is a need to increase the inspection powers over certain foreign operators where it is obvious that minimum international standards are not being applied.

In the long term, as part of the JAA operational standardisation team, SRG's Flight Operations Department will be involved in the monitoring European authorities implementation of the JAR-OPS standards. The aims are to ensure that member states have fully implemented and complied with JAR-OPS by the applicable implementation date. Team members will be drawn from the JAA member nations and will be tasked with ensuring that the requirements are implemented consistently.

Although JAR-OPS Parts 1 and 3 have been adopted they do not become law until they are appended to Annex 2 of EU Council Regulations 3922/91. This is not expected to happen until 1999 and until that time the requirements have no legal standing in the UK. In the interim, operators will be allowed to operate under JAR-OPS by means of exemptions from the Air Navigation Order which have been drafted by the Authority's legal department. In the long term, JAR-OPS rules will also be introduced for General Aviation and these will be contained in JAR-OPS rules will also aeroplanes and Part 4 for helicopters. One area not included in the adopted version of JAR-OPS Part 1 and 3 are flight time limitations schemes. Although the proposals were similar to the existing United Kingdom scheme detailed in CAP 371, they were not well received in a number of European states, or by some operators or by the pilot and cabin crew associations. Although the new proposals did give some relaxation for on the day limits for pilots hours, compared to existing United Kingdom legislation, the new proposals, were actually much more restrictive for many European nations. The topic is still under discussion in JAA forums and it is hoped that by the end of 1996 the two schemes will be adopted.

To ensure a smooth implementation of the procedures, SRG has formed a Joint SRG/Industry JAR-OPS implementation study group in which the industry can discuss any problems with the new rules with the Flight Operations Department. The hidden benefit of the JAR-OPS work is much closer contact with the other JAA authorities, plus an insight into how they conduct their work. Now that the requirements have been adopted the role of the CAA Flight Operations Department in relation to JAR-OPS has been realigned. It is now our job to ensure that United Kingdom operators start to adopt the new procedures and that we monitor their progress in changing over to JAR-OPS. The CAA are planning to devolve some responsibility for regulation to the AOC holders. By doing this we aim to make the United Kingdom industry much more accountable. AOC holders will be required to implement internal safety and quality management systems which will enable them to audit their own operations. We hope this change in philosophy will enable the Flight Operations Department to become less prescriptive and give more assistance to operators for self regulation, but always with adequate supervision from SRG and we look forward to HEMS integration into the JAR OPS system.

Captain Graham Jeffs is a Flight Operations Inspector in the CAA. For the last 26 years he has been a helicopter pilot, firstly in the Royal Marines and then as a civilian pilot in the North Sea, in police operations with the Metropolitan Police and in air ambulance operations prior to joining the CAA.

PURCHASING AND REIMBURSEMENT OF HEMS COSTS

Richard Earlam

The pre-hospital and hospital costs of HEMS have been discussed in Section 9F. In general terms they must be divided into capital and running costs and someone has to pick up the bill for these two components of trauma care. The economics and assessment of the necessity for emergency care is discussed in Section 9, but this article will concentrate on the two problems of:

- Pre-hospital care and transport payment
- Hospital costs at the Royal London Hospital.

Under alternatives for spending money economists and accountants will always discuss buying 'the next best service'. So for pre-hospital care this entails an analysis of the costs of the London Ambulance Service. It must however be emphasised that HEMS must not be considered a competition or an alternative to a land ambulance service; it should be treated practically as an additional and supplementary system which must be fully integrated with the ambulance control room, ambulances and ambulance personnel.

On the other hand the hospital costs present a different problem. These are not extra costs because extra patients are not produced. This is not exactly true because HEMS saves lives and these extra patients, who would otherwise have died, must be looked after. But all would have had to be looked after in the NHS somewhere in some hospital, so the main difficulty is ensuring that the finance follows the patient in the most efficient and appropriate fashion.

1. Land Ambulances and HEMS – Pre-hospital Care and Transport

Until helicopter emergency medical services were introduced during the Korean and Vietnam wars and then for civilians in America, Germany and France, casualties were brought to hospital by any means of transport possible with carts, horses or cars. Originally any horse-drawn wagon would be used to carry a patient, whether it was a haywain or a brewer's dray. The London Hospital is surrounded by the relics of famous local breweries such as Charrington and Turner in Whitechapel, and surgical wards are named after their generous donations. With the arrival of motor cars a separate pre-hospital emergency transport system developed. Historically it was always separated from the fire and police services – the other two emergency services. This separation also existed in France and Germany where in Napoleonic times Les Pompiers – the firemen – were the elite combined in the social structure of each community with artisans forming the voluntary or professional frontline staff and the local mayor being in charge. On the other side the ambulance service developed from the portering staff at the hospital where they were originally based and then over the years the ambulance stations, totally separate from fire services, were built geographically separate from the local hospital itself, yet still regulated to deliver patients locally. Nowadays in the UK, if you wish to find the reason for an illogical and irrational way of doing something, always delve into history. The art form is to modernise without completely destroying the past, its associations and its strengths.

The London Ambulance Service (LAS) provides pre-hospital care and transport for 7.5 million people in inner and outer London (see map). This area abuts on to the local county ambulance services. The fact that one area was founded on the Greater London Council boundaries and the other was based on what a duke could inherit or grab to call his own county is based on historical facts with which we should enjoy living. HEMS uses the M25, a modern phenomenon, the largest parking lot in Europe, as a measure of its potential service area which it can reach in 8-10 minutes. This area has a 12 million population, covered by land ambulances of the LAS as well as county ambulances. Obviously HEMS can easily fly further than the M25 in 2-4 minutes.

The LAS developed into a pre-hospital transport service which in effect had two functions: a) emergency, and b) taxi. It has now completed the demerger and runs a smaller proportion of its non-emergency work as the patient transport section. This was a political decision based on the concept that an incredible amount of money was wasted by hospitals recalling patients to unnecessary outpatient visits to be seen by junior doctors instead of staying at home to be looked after by their experienced general practitioners.

The emergency pre-hospital land ambulance component costs £84 million each year. For this sum of money the taxpayer obtains 350 frontline A&E vehicles in 70 ambulance stations (mean 5 ambulances per station). There are 1800 front line ambulance man, of which 600 have paramedic training, and 300 support staff to give a total of 2100 personnel for the frontline ambulances. There are 200 administration and 200 control staff. These central staff also look after the patient transport system (500 staff and £12 million costs). But the work load is huge and the number of calls per day is 2000 which makes the central control room of the LAS the busiest in the world. Ambulances have to be sent out to collect patients from accidents, home or other hospitals and then deliver them either to the 70 A&E departments in the LAS geographical area or to hospitals for direct admission. Until HEMS was started all emergency patients were taken to their own local and nearest hospital. But in the last five years a system has been developed for sifting out the major injuries from the mass of calls. This is like looking for a needle in a haystack. HEMS may be called from 0-5 times a day for selected injuries. But the overall annual workload for 365 days and nights each year is 730,000 calls and it is calculated that about 2000 of these may have major trauma, but it is very difficult to be accurate about this figure. Sifting or triage is a big enough problem and has to continue at the same time as the 350 ambulances in the 70 ambulance stations each take about 30 patients a day to their correct destination. In each ambulance station the ambulances wait to go out in the equivalent of a taxi rank queue to do 5 or 6 calls per day. Major trauma is not a common incident and occurs in 1:182 emergency calls. Paramedics (600 out of 1800 frontline ambulance man) will be expected to do about one emergency endotracheal intubation per year. Although it is the long term aim of the LAS to have a trained paramedic on each frontline ambulance, this has not yet been achieved and one has sympathy with the LAS over the enormity of task.

It is difficult to calculate the cost of a land ambulance but with a total LAS bill of £84 million and 350 vehicles the annual cost of a front line vehicle is £240,000. They are charged out for pop concerts at £100 per hour. Another calculation is that the LAS cost per patient carried is £127.16. The cost of HEMS taken as the round figure for pre-hospital care including medical staff, pilots, paramedics, fuel, running costs of the helicopter for 400 hours of flying time and 1500 call outs each year is £1 million. £1 million as a percentage of £84 million is 1.2%. This figure is reflected in another calculation based on cost per head of population covered. The LAS costs £11.20 each year and HEMS costs 13 pence.

In economical theoretical thinking it is necessary to calculate what one could buy with the same amount of money as the £1 million that HEMS costs. There are two answers: a) 4 extra ambulances based on LAS costs per land ambulance – £240,000 each, or b) on a hire basis (e.g pop concert or football match) = 1.1 ambulances.

2. Hospital Costs at the RLH

There is an essential difference between costs and charges as anybody knows who has been into a shop or a restaurant. In the USA trauma centre charges are anything up to 25% or 50% greater than the costs. But in spite of this there are no Level 1 trauma centres in about half the

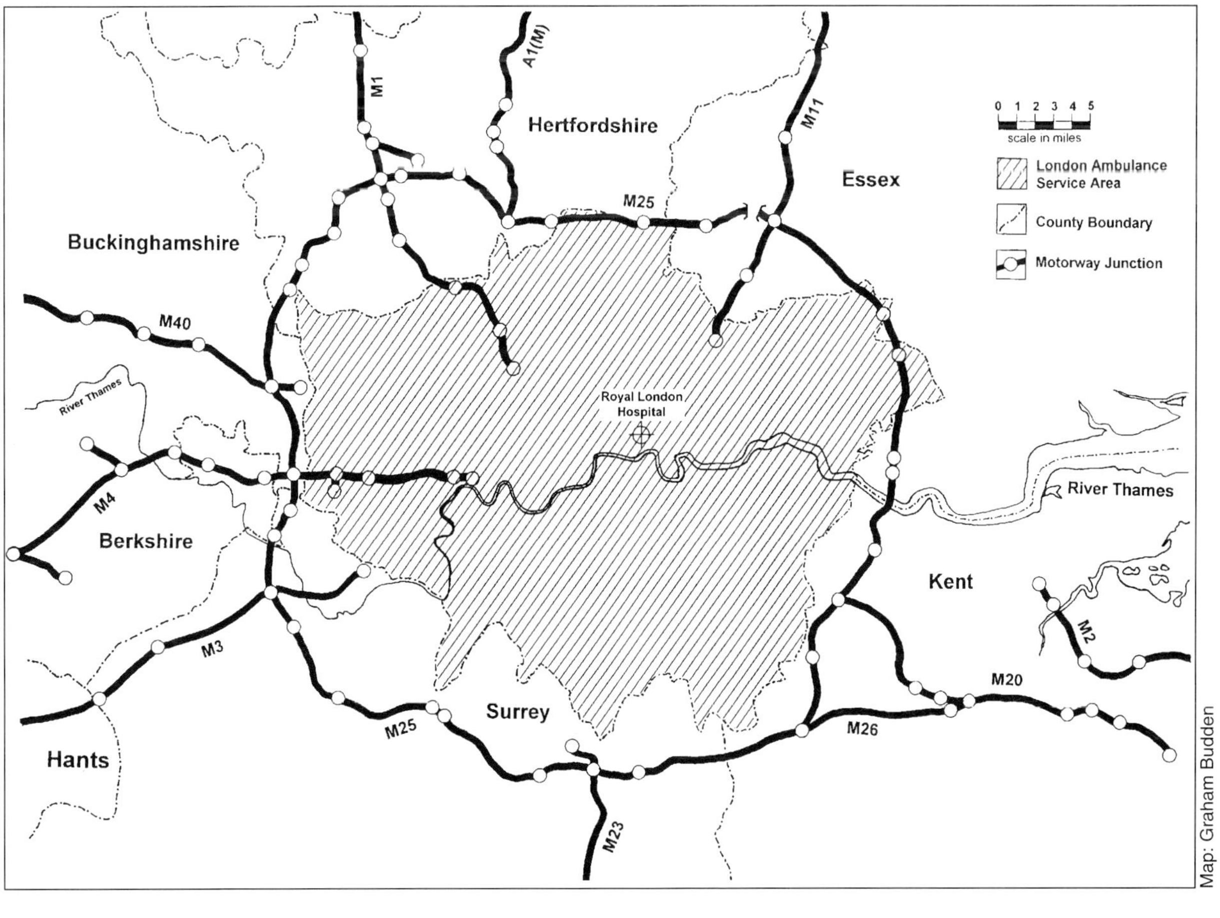

states in the USA, almost none make a profit and many close each year as those who read the Journal of Trauma soon learn. The Royal London Hospital does not make a profit on its emergency or trauma care; on the contrary the true cost of looking after these patients is usually lost in the budgets of the different acute specialities, each of whom in their different ways subsidise the service.

The capital costs of improving the emergency services at the RLH have all been paid for. Some were funded by the HEMS budget, some were provided by the government and the Wolfson Foundation kindly donated money to the emergency room. Such changes are not specific for a helicopter service which involves only one patient per day (300 per year) but on the contrary are considered essential for the adequate treatment of all our emergencies and the 80,000 local inhabitants who attend the A&E department each year. The hospital running costs have been calculated in various ways which will be discussed under Phase I (1989-92), Phase II (1992), Phase III (1993-95) and the latest Phase IV (1996-). These have changed as the NHS changed together with its radical reorganisation.

Phase I (1989-92) Direct Grant

This occurred in the early days when Regions, Teaching Hospitals, Boards of Governors and supraregional specialities existed. It was realised that HEMS, serving the 12 million population within the M25 orbital ring road was in effect a supraregional specialty involving all four Thames Regions. But since it was a pilot project, needed assessment and was not an established regional nor supraregional specialty, it would be funded with a direct grant of £1 million from the DOH. This money was skimmed (legal in this case) from the monies allotted to the 14 Regions, Scotland, Wales and Northern Ireland. The money was used to fund a new temporary Trauma Unit of four beds, one established ICU bed and the remainder went to assist the acute specialties and the A&E department for their additional work. Staff were directly employed so that the normal activity of each department was unaffected.

Phase II (1992) Costs per day for the ICU, Trauma Unit and acute wards

Central administration changed when Regions were phased out and District Health Authorities developed. Internal markets inside hospitals were initiated and plans for the future purchaser/provider split were organised. Supraregional specialties were abolished and replaced by regional centres who would charge for tertiary referrals (basically from consultant to old regional to supraregional specialists) as Extracontractual Referrals (ECRs) paid on a per case basis. In effect haemophilia treatment and its 20 or so UK centres were the last of the developing specialties to be allowed existence in 1993 (HSG (93)30). In June 1992 the DOH announced that the internal costs of HEMS were to be put into the market retrospectively. It was agreed that to recover our costs we would charge District Health Authorities a bed day cost which varied from ICU, Trauma Unit down to the average acute surgical ward cost. Because some of the cases involved a very high cost the Health Authorities were unhappy about their individual costs which might be occasionally high due to the exceptional severely injured with an expensive care cost. The total in-hospital costs at this stage amounted to about £2 million for the 200 patients brought in by helicopter. The mean cost was £10,000 but obviously some were below this and a few above. Since Health Authorities wished to have controllable budgets they did not like paying for the occasional catastrophe. They preferred that the insurance risk should be borne by the hospital under a block contract so that they could limit their risks and plan budgets.

Phase III (1993-95) Front loading of costs on to ICU and Trauma Unit

In order for the Health Authorities to plan their costs the DOH ordered us to charge only for ICU and Trauma Unit bed days which are always expensive, but in fact the Health Authorities got a bargain. In Clive Kirk's article (Section 2C) the first 1000 cases occupied 15000 bed days of which 4000 were ICU or Trauma Unit days. 630 of the 856 patients admitted and who did not die on the first day (126 had no charge) went to the ICU and Trauma Unit. This was the best buy of the year for the purchasers because a) they obtained 11000 bed days in an acute ward in a teaching hospital for free and b) the patients could stay there forever and never be transferred back home to a nearby hospital. Subsequently even the Health Authorities purchasers were unhappy with this because they occasionally had big bills for difficult cases who stayed longer in the ICU. During this phase the costs in the RLH increased to £3 million per annum with the number of HEMS patients increasing to over 300, but this still left the average cost of £10,000 per patient. At this time with the internal trading budget in place and a tightly controlled budget HEMS ceased to employ people directly as before but transferred the risk to the acute specialties by paying them for activity and work done rather than directly for salaries. In 1995 339 HEMS patients were brought into the RLH, 36 (11%) died in the A&E department and no charge was made for them and 110 (32%) were not admitted to the ICU or Trauma Unit. This made a total of 43% for whom no bill was sent. The consequence is that costs of the 57%, who were paid for, appears high. This method had none of the advantages of a mean cost nor a block contract and provided no incentive for the Health Authority to accept the patient back nearer home. The function of HEMS is to save life and not to provide the complete continuing care after initial stabilisation.

Phase IV (1996-) The new contract based on average workload per district

There are 16 districts including our local purchasing authority who contribute patients to HEMS. A new agreement has been arranged to replace Phase III so that

Table
Possibility of Insurance Reimbursement
Based on Mechanism of Injury in 1000 patients carried by HEMS

Transport (574)	Road traffic accident: car, motorcycle, pedestrian (third party)	yes
	Cyclists	?
	Railways (travel)	yes
	Horseriders (sport)	yes
	Aircraft (travel)	yes
	Watersport (sport)	yes
Falls (175)	Either on building site (employer)	yes
	Or home (household Insurance)	yes
Assaults (112)	Either criminal injury (victim)	yes
	Or criminal (himself)	no
Self harm (78)	Probably no insurance possible	no
Struck by falling object (23)	Who was responsible or were all acts of God?	no
Machinery (15)	Worker's/Employer's insurance	yes
Miscellaneous (23)		?

each district pays a quarterly sum based on the average activity of the last three years. Patients living outside of the 16 health authorities will be charged in two ways: a) £11,300 if they go to ICU b) as the usual ECR cost for the specialty under whose care they are e.g general surgery (average cost £1,510). In effect this irons out the discrepancies caused by some high individual costs which now are not borne by either the hospital nor the purchaser on an individual basis but accepted as a common insurance risk.

3. Insurance Principles

The present system of reimbursement may be successful but it is conceivable that in the future further money may be demanded from individuals through their own other insurances. The welfare state may not be able to exist in its present form supported only from taxation or NHS contributions. This occurs at the moment with payment for prescriptions and historically commenced with patients having to contribute to spectacles, dentures and wigs. In every case there are exclusions based on age (young children, old pensioners), chronic illness or a means test. Insurance principles apply whether run by the NHS, because for example it is nobody's fault that he has haemophilia, or by private insurance which will be for all types of illness. There has been a tendency to make national services into local systems by limiting the access of residents in one district to services in that district regardless of standard. In education this can cause problems if the local school is extremely bad and cannot be improved; it could also apply to hospitals, because we do not live in a perfect world where all schools and hospitals are equally excellent. Methods must exist for patients, who have paid their central government taxes, to obtain the best surgical treatment in exactly the same manner as if that patient had private insurance. Is it up to the politicians or the people to decide how the standards of their schools and hospitals should be maintained? Should it be by competition or compulsion?

Is there any possibility that patients involved in road accidents or other activities should have their care paid for by their own home or motor car insurance, employer's cover at work, holiday and sport cover? On the first 1000 patients brought into the RLH by HEMS, there is a list of mechanisms of injury (Section 2C). The majority could be covered by an extension of their present third party (Table) insurance made compulsory to include medical care for both the injured and the third party. At the moment it is unthinkable and unacceptable politically but we are heading for bankruptcy in the NHS and need supplementary income from any source. Watch this space – it is the future.

TRAINING IN THE USA: MULTIMEDIA FOR EMS

Peter Mahoney

Introduction

Multimedia technology is any technology capable of presenting combinations of text, sounds, pictures, animations and/or full motion video. This becomes 'interactive' when it accepts user input and presents further information conditional on that input. The material can be stored and accessed by a variety of media such as computer disk, video (laser) disc and compact disc read-only memory (CD-ROM).[1]

Commercially available programs for Emergency Medical Services cover topics as diverse as HAZCHEM management, infection control and defibrillation. One manufacturer even offers to come to the purchasers location, shoot video footage, and incorporate this, along with local protocols, into the programme.[2]

The advantages of multimedia computer systems for EMS training are portability, consistency in the scenario presented to different students, and immediate feedback on student performance. The disadvantages are that the quality of the programs and their educational content varies greatly.

Examples of Systems in Use

The State of Idaho EMS system has used interactive training for a number of years to provide continuing education for EMS providers in isolated rural communities. The first system was teleconferencing via a bridging terminal. In the early 1980s Mobile Trauma Training Units (special vans fitted with trauma mannikins and extrication trainers) were developed which toured around outlying areas. In 1990 one of these was converted to take eight interactive video disc training stations.[3] The most recent program to be introduced is an adult airway management trainer which links an intubation mannikin with video disc and CD-ROM players via a computer. The student watches video demonstrations of airway management techniques and then practices them on the mannikin. The computer confirms if the technique was performed correctly and, if not, where the errors occurred. Feedback from students has been favourable for all of these systems.

The intention is to install trainers in ambulance stations so people can work through the programs during their spare time.

Use of computer-linked mannikins has been taken further in Florida where some paramedics are being trained using a critical care patient simulator. These have been developed mainly for anaesthetic and intensive care training and can be programmed to simulate a number of anaesthetic emergencies. Invasive and non-invasive monitors can be interfaced with the system. There are two such simulators currently being marketed in the USA. 1994 costs were around $180 000 per unit.

New Horizons

Virtual reality prototypes have been developed to simulate laparoscopic surgery and further simulations of other medical procedures, such as central venous cannulation, are planned. Procedure simulations are likely to have a role in US paramedic training, particularly where paramedic schools are linked to large universities.

A further development is the linking of telemedicine and virtual reality technologies whereby hospital based practitioners can 'see' the accident scene via head sets worn by medics on scene.

The Department of Emergency Health Services of the University of Maryland, Baltimore County (who run a three year paramedic degree course) are assessing how the Internet can be used to enhance their program.

Conclusions

Multimedia and other computer based systems are being successfully used in EMS education in the USA. There may be a role for similar systems in the UK but they would need to be designed and adapted for UK training requirements.

References

1. Locatis, C. An interactive multimedia technology primer. Educational Technology Branch, Lister Hill Center for Biomedical Communications, National Library of Medicine, 1993.

2. Brown MS. Let's get hyper! Interactive multimedia in EMS. Journal of Emergency Medical Systems, 1994, 54-61.

3. Anderson, PB, Bennet, R S, Henderson, JV et al (1990). Interactive Technology: EMS training goes on line in Idaho. Journal of Emergency Medical Systems, 1990, 35-8.

ARBEITSKREIS NOTFALLMEDIZIN UND RETTUNGSWESEN (ANR): The Centre for Emergency Medicine and Rescue Service, Ludwig-Maximilian University of Munich

Christian K Lackner, Stefan Schmidbauer, Leonhard Schweiberer

The pre-hospital emergency medical services (EMS) and the trauma surgeon in the early clinical setting must not only intervene rapidly and accurately to reverse a progressive trauma process, but must do so while simultaneously prioritising and coordinating the care of other patients. Trauma treatment in the pre-hospital setting often begins before the exact diagnosis is known, so decisions must be made rapidly on the basis of limited information. Diagnostic tests, treatment and disposition decisions must be accurate and efficient to optimise patient outcome and cost-effectiveness. If tangible improvements in the process of trauma decision making are to be made, a sustained commitment to acute trauma medicine and closely related research is needed urgently. Pre-hospital emergency care was designed around the concept of a system of inter-related events that combine to offer a patient the best care possible outside the hospital. However, in contrast to the actual operations of EMS systems, acute trauma research has not typically used system-based models as the method for evaluation.

General Problems

Initially in 1993 specific steps were taken to develop and enhance acute trauma research support both outside (on-scene) and within hospital trauma centres. Special emphasis was placed on acute trauma research training of trauma investigators, promotion of collaborative acute trauma research efforts, and management of clinical information. New methods of assessing valid and meaningful patient outcomes were devised and pre-existing barriers to acute trauma research funding rectified. Enhanced support for pre-hospital and acute clinical trauma services is of utmost importance for the academic and clinical growth to create a supportive environment for researchers. Although not every academic general or trauma surgeon can be expected to pursue acute trauma research, all researchers should strive to maximise their potential. Pre-hospital medicine investigators should pursue advanced training to enhance their acute trauma research skills and development as mentors to future investigators.

Acute trauma research is facilitated by concentrating resources in initially small numbers of trauma research centres at existing facilities (e.g major trauma centres with helicopters or physician-staffed EMS vehicles), allied centres or academic institutions where a critical mass of specific investigators can be recruited. Resources should be concentrated on those medical students and residents with genuine interest in acute trauma research to ensure proper exposure, training mentoring, and development. Young acute trauma researchers should be encouraged to pursue training in identified centres of excellence.

Acute Trauma Research at Work

Promoting and increasing collaboration among acute trauma researchers at different sites and among other acute trauma research disciplines within institutions is crucial. Trauma specialists and researchers in all disciplines definitively share interests in a variety of pre-hospital, clinical and fundamental acute trauma research questions with trauma investigators. Pre-hospital EMS physicians can contribute a practical approach based on patient-centered experience, as well as a perspective on the social forces that influence clinical conditions. Basic scientists and specialists in other fields are invaluable sources of technical skills and knowledge that permit meaningful investigation of fundamental questions. Collaboration with social scientists and health economists enhance studies of the effectiveness, appropriateness and cost-benefit of acute trauma care. Collaborative acute trauma research with epidemiologists, social workers, and public health officials facilitates development of preventative strategies to limit the recurrence of major injuries. Multidisciplinary acute trauma research enhances the spirit of cooperation between clinical disciplines, and improves the emergency care rendered to traumatized patients. Nevertheless, 'trauma is a surgical disease' and has to be treated and evaluated by surgeons.

Need for New Data bases

There is a great demand to develop new systems to manage pre-hospital and early clinical information. A common database like the MTOS in the USA and MTOS (UK) have major epidemiological problems while acquiring more and more data. A proper and reliable method of describing the type and severity of injuries is by comparing e.g traumatized populations with Injury Severity Score (ISS) > 15 and other regions Abbreviated Injury Score AIS < 2 or AIS > 4. Mortality and morbidity studies should always include age in major trauma patients which by definition is an ISS greater than 15. The same ISS-score should be used for patients to assess the w-statistic for the probability of survival or death. The database could serve as a national and as a community-based resource for improving analysis, education and management of pre-hospital and emergency room care and could facilitate meaningful population-based acute trauma research. It could also serve as a data repository for common and important problems in major trauma. A sophisticated common database could answer many questions unanswerable with current data-management systems and could serve as an accurate monitoring system in total quality management efforts while including essential elements of a pre-hospital and early clinical trauma care record and an electronic information infrastructure to record and share data on a regional, national international basis.

Need of New Methods

For the question of whether pre-hospital ATLS care has any effect on patient outcome to be answered, proper systems analysis-type methods must be developed. The complexity and multidimensional nature of the HEMS acute trauma research topics demand the development of effective systems. We realised the weaknesses of component based acute trauma research models in HEMS evaluation and try now attempt to provide a conceptual 'systems-analysis' framework that can be used for future acute trauma research. Incorporation of this multi-discipline approach into HEMS acute trauma research is essential if there is to be any hope of finding answers to many of the important questions that remain in the arena of out-of-hospital health care. Systems analysis acute trauma research models come from a wide variety of studies. These models are typically found in the areas of engineering, economics, behavioural science, public administration, public health, mathematics, social science, and epidemiology. They are designed to evaluate complex and inter-related questions that contain many dissimilar and independent data elements. Typically, different institutions and disciplines are involved, and principle investigators frequently do not directly participate in the actual data collection process. The acute trauma research environment is often complex and uncontrolled and contains several sources of information. The desired data elements are often difficult to obtain with a high degree of accuracy, and outcome parameters are complex. The mathematic models needed to evaluate these data are complex. The current body of pre-hospital acute trauma research largely comprises component evaluations, and the literature of studies using systems-based methods is scant. The use of this model in the evaluation of pre-hospital care often leads to inaccurate conclusions. These inaccuracies are often due not to investigator errors but rather to the fundamental limitations inherent in this method. Attempting to isolate the issues to the actual delivery of trauma care for a specific patient population with a specific traumatic process can be very complicated, if not possible, in the pre-hospital or early clinical setting.

Organisation of ANR

The German title 'Arbeitskreis Notfallmedizin and Rettungswesen (ANR)' has been translated into the English words Centre for Emergency Medicine and Rescue Service but this does not do justice to its organisation or aims. The words centre or institute are not capable of an exact translation so the concept of a group of people interested in research and training bound together by a common purpose of improving standards of trauma care is more important than their title. This group was brought together in 1993 by Professor Leonhard Schweiberer, Professor of Surgery at the central University Hospital in Munich. From the surgical point of view however, it also includes experts from Grosshadern which is a relatively new and large University Hospital outside Munich and a community hospital Harlaching where the original Christoph I rescue helicopter service started. Additionally on the ANR committee are representatives of other specialties and most importantly the University of Munich including the Deans. Other members of the ANR come from all those people interested in trauma care, emergency medical services including the Fire Service, the ADAC, health insurance companies (private and public), other hospital personnel and various University disciplines such as Law and private individuals. Politicians at the high level of Bavarian Minister of State, Bayerische Innenministerium, whether for Health, Social Services, or Education are also closely involved. The committee of ANR has wide representation from these groups.

Aims of ANR

These come under the two main headings of research and training. Since correct trauma care is so complex, it is easier to understand how many people are involved if it is subdivided into: i) prevention, ii) treatment iii) rehabilitation. Treatment is then separated into a) pre-hospital and b) hospital care which are also multidisciplinary disciplines with a great amount of crossover in regard to expertise and personnel. No one person can be an expert in all these components of good trauma care, so a loose multidisciplinary group with good communications is essential to include every aspect of care wherever it occurs and including each different type of hospital and each emergency service.

Research supported by ANR is in general terms multidisciplinary and can occur anywhere in the trauma care life saving chain RETTUNGSKETTE, so it is not only in the central University Hospital but anywhere that cares for trauma patients. It can also be done by anyone. The important contribution of ANR is as an umbrella of organisation and expertise. In 1995 ANR was involved in about 30 different projects varying from specific anaesthetic procedures such as intubation to on-line data information provision in emergency situations. Training is provided for all levels of personnel involved in trauma care from medical students, therapists through to qualified doctors. Special emphasis has been placed on 'teaching the teachers'. The teaching centre was opened in January 1994. Even in these early days up to 130 courses have been run in one year, with over 2000 who attended. Workshops have been organised and in 1995 a polytrauma management week was held. All this has progressed so far with relatively little expenditure and a great amount of dedication and free work from many staff.

Much has been achieved in the three years since ANR was started. It remains as an independent facility of the Ludwig-Maximilian University of Munich organising those people, who are presently in post and not appointing new staff, to improve standards of trauma care by research and teaching, using all modern techniques including telecommunication. This, after all, is one of the basic tenets of a University and ANR offers expertise to all people caring in any way for trauma victims whether they or their departments are members of the University or not. The influence of a University must not be limited by artificial borders when important events occur outside the hallowed institutions. Alexander von Humboldt, a key figure in the development of German Universities, would be pleased, if he lived today, with the initiative of ANR as a contribution to society outside the normal boundaries of a University.

Professor Leonhard Schweiberer is Professor of Surgery at the Klinikum Innenstadt, Nussbaumstrasse 20, 80336 Muenchen, and chairman of Arbeitskreis Notfallmedizin und Rettungswesen e.V.(ANR) an der Ludwig-Maximilians –Universitat Muenchen.

Dr Christian K Lackner and **Dr Stefan Schmidbauer** both have the position of Oberarzt in the Department of Surgery, University Hospital of Klinikum Innenstadt Munich.

Photo: Alastair Wilson (1989)

The epidemic of road traffic accidents commenced in the last century and hopefully has reached its peak now although the number of motor cars continues to increase.

THE ACADEMIC FUTURE FOR TRAUMA

Tony Goode, Leo Strunin

The Background

The tempo of modern living seems to increase by the day and manifestations of it are more traffic congestion, more accidents at work and in the home, an apparent increase in violent crime with an increasing pressure for the injured to be restored to full health and back to work as soon as possible. Traditionally, accident and emergency departments in the United Kingdom have been 'Cinderellas', relatively starved of staff and resources in the face of an apparently ever increasing demand for their services. Similarly, the training for staff has been haphazard, with a wide national variation in standards and offering a poor career structure.

At last the tide is turning at both national and local level. A specific postgraduate faculty, the Faculty of Accident and Emergency Medicine, was instituted in 1992, with parent bodies in the Royal Colleges of Surgery, Medicine and Anaesthesia to structure, coordinate and improve postgraduate training nationally. In reality, undergraduate and postgraduate teaching will only be as good as the expertise and enthusiasm available at the individual hospital, but it is vital for the future. This depends on what we do now and how well it is done.

An active clinical base is fundamental for success, accompanied by a vibrant, busy department with enthusiastic knowledgeable and accomplished staff are the foundation from which all will flow. Teaching and research along with clinical expertise are the requirements to support the future and to guarantee quality to best manage the present day increase in trauma – properly described as a modem epidemic.

Teaching

The sooner the trainee is exposed to the rigors of an accident and emergency department with its noise, commotion, anxiety, responsibility and drama, the better. Medical students must be attached to the accident and emergency department early in their clinical teaching course, it is invaluable to learn how to manage difficult problems, to make clear and responsible decisions involving life and death and to learn by example from more senior staff. To this end, the time and duration of undergraduate teaching in emergency management should be reviewed so that there is a guarantee of the student's understanding of resuscitation, the ability to recognise the relative urgency of management of individual conditions and from this, a confidence in their clinical abilities providing a basis for postgraduate education.

In medical practice, a doctor ideally never stops learning from the day of graduation until the last day of practice. Indeed, specialist knowledge and expertise is learnt after graduation. Although there is now a national Faculty to set standards, the realisation of that goal is only as good as the individual hospital and its staff. Like watching a performance at the theatre or an opera what one sees is only a fraction of what is going on while behind the scenes many are involved in providing the whole. So it is in the management of major trauma that almost any or every department in the hospital may be involved and a knowledge of what is required and when is critical. Traditionally, teaching hospitals have had this concentration of expertise with both university and clinical staff, so as well as learning by active participation they have had the necessary structured teaching which is essential. Time has to be formally set aside for lecture courses, specific teaching in particular areas of expertise and thought given to awareness of weaknesses, such is the guarantee of future success.

Examples of courses in specific areas include:

For adults.:

- Advanced Life Support (ALS) under the aegis of the European Resuscitation Council
- Advanced Trauma Life Support (ATLS) under the aegis of the Royal College of Surgeons

For children:

- Paediatric Advanced Life Support (PALS)
- Advanced Paediatric Life Support (APLS)

These courses are run for providers and from these are selected candidates to go onto instructor courses for training the next generation. Protocol driven teaching tends to generate some adverse comment, especially from senior members of the medical profession, in respect of the rather didactic nature of the instruction and examination. It is essential, therefore, that the course material be reviewed on a regular basis and that the instructors are of proper calibre. Therefore, in order to run such courses and provide a recognised and structured environment probably requires a combination such as is found in the Royal Hospitals Trust in its close cooperation with St Bartholomew's and the Royal London School of Medicine and Dentistry. An additional factor has been the introduction of the Helicopter Emergency Medical Service (HEMS) at the Royal London Hospital. Since the inception of HEMS both hospital and university staff have given freely and voluntarily of their time to provide proper teaching as well as clinical support. The multidisciplinary nature of trauma can be gauged from the wide participation of departments ranging from all types of surgery, anaesthesia and nursing, to haematology, radiology and psychiatry. The patients occupy their own specific trauma theatre and provide a major part of Intensive Care medical practice.

Research

If proper and appropriate teaching is the life blood to support the day to day care of patients, it is only half of the structure. Equally important is research as this both shows us the way to improve patient care and ensures that the teaching is up to date and capable of presenting the options for the future clearly and responsibly. A particular requirement of university teaching hospitals is research. Again this must be structured to ensure quality coherence and in these financially constrained days the best clinical research is evidenced based and makes use of randomised controlled trials wherever possible.

HEMS has resulted in a concentration of severely injured patients at one centre which is unique in the United Kingdom in that triage is done on scene by a trained doctor who then decides where the patient will go, travels to the hospital of choice and the fate of the patient is known by long-term follow up. This unique resource has already generated substantial research activity as can be seen by the bibliography in this publication. However, much of this has been focused on the role of the helicopter, patient data collection and protocols, comparison with other trauma services and some outcome data. All of this is important, but fundamental research into trauma as an entity has been lacking.

If we are to make any substantial inroads into the devastating effects that trauma can have on both the individual, the family and the state, then we need a much more broad based and long-term approach. A Trauma Research Institute is a possible way forward.

The Trauma Research Institute

In the past the Medical Research Council (MRC) funded groups to address specific clinical problems where they felt that progress could be made but was not occurring due to a combination of lack of recognition and resources. Examples include liver disease, immunology, lung disease and many others. Funds were given for five years in an academic setting, a strong group was recruited and the pressure was then on the researchers to prove their worth. If successful the University then would take over the group. Many of the established clinical research departments we take for granted today were started in this fashion. Restraint in university funding has led to the decline of this mechanism. However the Higher Education Funding Council (HEFC) has always encouraged the formation of suitably large research groups of a multidisciplinary nature and examples include research into diabetes, rheumatology and dentistry. The time has now come for a similar approach to trauma research and the case load and clinical/research expertise is available in the Royal Hospitals Trust/St Bartholomew's School of Medicine and Dentistry.

This publication should be used as the spring board for launching the Institute. All the necessary information is present, the problems are delineated, the resources currently available are detailed and everything is present in one area. Indeed if the current negotiations for a Private Finance Initiative (PFI) are successful then the Whitechapel site of the Royal Hospitals Trust will essentially be rebuilt over the next 5-7 years. Pari-passu the School of Medicine and Dentistry is also being rebuilt and expanded on the same site.

We therefore have a unique opportunity. The HEMS initiative has brought together an unrivalled concentration of individuals interested in trauma. As a result within the ring of the M25 Motorway, a population of some seven million is available for study as trauma affects their daily lives. We must grasp this chance since trauma may affect any of us but is still one of medicine's Cinderellas.

Professor A Goode is Professor of Surgery and **Professor L Strunin** is Professor of Anaesthetics in the St Bartholomew's and The Royal London School of Medicine and Dentistry, Queen Mary and Westfield College, University of London.

HEMS PUBLICATIONS AND PRESENTATIONS, 1988-96

1. Earlam RJ, Wilson AW
Helicopter Emergency Medical Services – HEMS One.
Ann RCS Bull 71: 60-4, 1989

2. Earlam RJ, Wilson A
London Hospital Helicopter Emergency Medical Service.
Lancet 24 Dec 1988

3. Earlam RJ
Luftrettung Europaweit: England, in
10. Rettungshubschrauber (RTH) Fachtagung (ADAC)
Garmisch-Partenkirchen, Germany 11 Oct 1989

4. Earlam RJ
Selection of patients for trauma care management.
Roy Soc Med Surgery/AE Meeting. 29 Sept 1989

5. Wilson AW
Helicopter Demonstration (HEMS).
Symposium – Early intervention in major trauma
RSM 1989

6. Botha A
A South African view on the RLH Helicopter Emergency Medical Service.
London Hospital Gazette 16: 33-4, 1991

7. Wilson AW, Coats TC, Cross FW
Pre-hospital Care. In: Trauma Management
Ed. Rowlands B. 1994

8. McAvinchey RP, Bhagat K, Kirk C, Wilson A, Hately W
Analysis of lateral cervical spine x-ray in the assessment of 134 consecutive multiply injured trauma patients from the Helicopter Emergency Service.
Brit J Radiol Abstract 65: Congress 60, 1992

9. Cross FW
Trauma Care. A mid-Atlantic perspective.
Surgery 97: 2323, 1991

10. Kirk CJC, Earlam RJ, Wilson AW, Watkins ES
A helicopter emergency service operating from the Royal London Hospital: The first year.
Brit J Surg 80: 218-21, 1993

11. Earlam RJ (Editor)
The RLH/Daily Express Helicopter Emergency Medical Service. Published by Saldatore, Bishops Stortford, pp67
ISBN 0948047 02X 1992

12. Coats T, Wilson AW
Utilization of HEMS.
J Roy Soc Med 85: 725-6, 1992

13. Botha AJ, Earlam RJ, Wilson AW, Dalton AM, Spalding TJW, Warren C Hodkinson S
The Royal London Hospital Helicopter Emergecy Medical Service – first phase 1990.
Ann RCS Eng, 74 (suppl 5): 130-4, 1992

14. Sparling R
Flying doctors in London.
BMJ 304: 647, 1992

15. Wilson AW, Dalton M
Medical Helicopter Systems – recommended minimum standards for patient management.
(Working Party Chairman: Bristow A)
J Roy Soc Med 84: 242-4, 1991

16. Coats T, Wilson A, Cross FW
On scene medical decision-making and over triage.
Brit J Surg. 80: 1291-3, 1993

17. Cross F W
The surgical management of the severely injured patient.
Chapter in General Surgical Operations
Ed. Kirk G, Williamson R. Churchill Livingstone, Edinburgh 1994

18. Cannell H, Silvester K C, O'Regan MBO
Early management of multiply injured patients with maxillofacial injuries transferred to hospital by helicopter.
Brit J Oral & Maxillofacial Surgery 31: 207-12, 1993

19. Dalton AM, Botha A, Spalding T, Hodkinson S, Warren C, Hodgson R.
Helicopter doctors.
Injury 23: 249-50, 1992

20. Wilson AW
100 Deaths in NE Thames – Ashbeams
The need for a Helicopter Emergency Medical Service.
The Coroner's paper (abstract 1988)

21. Wilson AW, Cross FW
Helicopters. Editorial
J Roy Soc Med 85: 1-3, 1992

22. Wilson AW, Driscoll P
Transport of injured patients.
Chapter in ABC of Major Trauma, BMJ, 1991

23. Cross FW, Coats TJ, Kirk CJC
Care of road traffic victims in a district general hospital.
Ann RCS Bull 74: 437-8, 1992

24. Wilson AW
A new Scoring System for injury – Comment.
Theoretical Surgery. 1990

25. Skinner D, Driscoll P, Earlam RJ (Editors)
ABC of Major Trauma.
Published by British Medical Journal, pp 117, 1991
ISBN 0 7279 0291 1

26. Baxter I
Determination of a costing and charging system for the Helicopter Emergency Services situated at the Royal London Hospital Trust.
Accountancy Thesis. February 19922

27. Cross FW
Helicopter transport for trauma patients.
Injury 23: 69-72, 1992

28. Botha AJ, Earlam RJ, Wilson AW
The Royal London Hospital Emergency Medical Service (HEMS).
Injury 23: 211 (abstr) 1992

29. Withington PS, Goldhill DR, Ooi LG, Birch NJ
Optical mark reading: a new approach to audit for intensive care.
Care of the Critically Ill 8: 74-7, 1992

30. Melville CR, Coats TJ, Wilson AW, Cross FW
Pre-hospital care and ATLS training.
Care of the Critically Ill 8: 100 -2, 1992

31. Xeropotamus N, Coats T, Wilson A W
Pre-operative surgical airway management: one year's experience from the Helicopter Emergency Medical Service.
Injury 24: 222-4, 1993

32. Deakin R, Deakin C
Thames Medivac.
Aerospace 21: 16-9, 1994

33. Pre-hospital operations protocol for RLH.
HEMS January 1990

34. In-hospital protocol.
January 1992

35. Melville C, Coats T, Wilson A
Hospital Major Incident Plan. The Royal London Trust.
May 1992

36. Organ Transplantation Protocol.
In house RLH protocol 1992

37. Coats T J, Newton A
Call selection for the Helicopter Emergency Medical Service – Implications for ambulance control.
J Roy Soc Med 87: 208-10, 1994

38. Earlam R
Trauma centres. Editorial
Brit J Surg 80: 1227-8, 1993

39. Hetherington H
OT pilot project.
Therapy Weekly. 19:4, 14 Jan 1993

40. Coats TJ, Wilson AW
The effect of a helicopter trauma service on the workload of accident and emergency departments.
J Roy Soc Med 87: 513-4, 1994

41. Wilden JN
Resuscitation in severe head injuries.
BMJ 307: 1009, 1993

42. Cross F, Kirk C, Coats T, Wilson A
On scene medical care: the limitations of Triss.
Injury 25 (Suppl 2) 5-B 17 1994

43. Coats T, McAnena O, Kirk C, Cross F
Physiological changes dues to pre-hospital ATLS.
Injury 25 (Suppl 2) 5-B17, 1994

44. Coats T, Kirk C, Cross F
Physiological changes as an audit tool in pre-hospital care. Injury 25 (Suppl 2) 5-B17-8, 1994

45. Wilmink A, Samra G, Watson L, Wilson A
Vehicle entrapment rescue and pre-hospital trauma care.
J Acc Emerg Med 1: 297, 1994

46. Heath K J, Samra G S, Davies G E, Wilmink A B, Wilson A W
Blood pressure changes in head injury patients during pre-hospital anaesthesia
Injury 25 (Suppl 2) 5-B7-B8, 1994
Presented at British Trauma Society 1st October 1993
JRI Oxford by Karen Heath won the BIOMET prize

47. Purkiss S F, Williams M, Cross F W, Wood A J, Graham T R
Scene or Emergency room resuscitative thoracotomy for patients with severe trauma. Is is worthwhile?
Eurosurgery presentation.
Brit J Surg Suppl Sept 1993.

48. Purkiss S F
Resuscitative thoracotomy for trauma.
Association of Cardiothoracic Surgeons 22
Bristol Jan 1993

49. Purkiss S F, Williams M, Graham T R, Cross F W, Wood A J
Efficacy of urgent thoracotomy for trauma in patients attended by a helicopter emergency medical service.
J Roy Coll Surg Edin 39: 289-91, 1994

50. Wilden JN, Sutcliffe JC, McAvinchey R, Kirk CJC, Hetherington H et al
The outcome of head injuries rescued by a helicopter emergency medical service in a metropolis.
Brit J Surg 80: S104, 1993

51. Wilden JN
Rapid resuscitation in severe head injury. Editorial
Lancet 342: 1378, 1993

52. Wilden JN, Sutcliffe JC, McAvinchey R, Kirk CJC, Hetherington H, Turvey SE, Wilson A, Wylie IG, Watkins ES
The effect of early management of head injuries on outcome.
Proceedings of Congress of Neurological Surgeons p67
Abstract 1993

53. Walsh M S
The management of penetrating injuries of the anterior triangle of the neck.
Injury 25: 393, 1994

54. Baghat K, Earlam R J, Hately W, McAvinchey R, Brown I W, Blakeney C G
Ceiling mounted radiographic equipment for trauma management in the emergency room.
Brit J Surg 82: 71-3, 1995

55. Vaizey C J, Jacobson M J, Cross F W
Trauma in pregnancy.
Brit J Surg 81: 1406-15, 1994

56. Hetherington H, Earlam RJ
Rehabilitation after trauma and the need for coordination.
Injury 25: 527-31, 1994

57. Hetherington H, Earlam R J, Kirk C J C
The disability status of trauma patients measured by the functional independence measure and their use of rehabilitation services.
Injury 26: 97-101, 1995

58. Hetherington H, Earlam R J;
Measurement of disability after multiple injuries: The Functional Independence Measure.
Eur J Surg 161: 549-55, 1993

59. Pratt P G, Wood A, Bhagat K K, Dyer P, Cannell H, Chan O
The emergency strategy of facial fractures in polytraumatised patients: the HEMS experience.
Abstract: Brit. Ass. Radiology July meeting. 1995

60. Coats T J, Wilson A W, Xeropotamous N
Thoracic drainage in pre-hospital trauma management.
Injury 26: 581-5, 1995

61. Wilson A W
Utilization of the Helicopter Emergency Medical Service.
J Roy Soc Med 86: 557, 1993

62. Cannell H, Dyer P, Paterson A
Maxillofacial injuries in the multiply injured.
Eur J Emerg Med 3: 43-7, 1996

63. Chapman M A, Oni J
Motor racing accidents at Brands Hatch.
Br J Sports Med 25: 121-3, 1991

64. Cannell H, Paterson A, Loukota R
Maxillofacial injuries in multiply injured patients.
Brit J O M Fac Surg In press (1996)

65. Coats T J, Newton A
The trauma chain.
Poster presentation: Pan European Congress of Emergency Medicine
Padua, Italy, August 1994

66. Coats T J, Kirk C J C, Wilden J N
Matching injuries to trauma facilities.
Injury 25: 204-5, 1994

67. Coats T J
Shock
In: Pre-hospital care. Ed. Graeves, Dyer and Porter 1996

68. Coats T J
Helicopters.
In: Prehospital care. Ed. Graeves, Dyer and Porter 1996

69. Coats T J, Wilson A W
Aeromedical evacuation.
In: Emergency care: a textbook for paramedics.
Ed Graeves, Hodgetts and Porter (in preparation 1995)

70. Cross F W
Who owns trauma?
Ass. Surg. Great Britain and Ireland 75th Anniversary Yearbook Rowan Group, Isleworth, Middlesex, 85-95, 1995

71. Cross F W
Trauma surgery in the UK/
World Journal of Surgery In press (1994)

72. Cross F W, Kirk C J C, Coats T J, Wilson A W
Case-mix in a Helicopter Emergency Medical Service.
Injury 25 (Suppl 2) 5-B17, 1994

73. Wilson A W
Transport of injured patients.
Chapter in ABC of Major Trauma, BMJ publications.
Ed. Skinner D, Driscoll P, Earlam R J, 1991

74. Martin T E
Resolving the casualty evacuation conflict.
Injury 24: 514-6, 1993

75. Martin T E
Transportation of patients by air.
Chapter in Aviation Medicine. Ed. Harding RM, Mills F J
BMA Books 3rd Ed 1993

76. Wilmink A B, Kirk C J C, Wilson A W
Pre-hospital management of acute spinal injuries – an appraisal.
J Acc Emerg Med 1: 296 (abstract), 1994

77. Goldhill D R
Outcome prediction with TRISS and APACHE II presented at the European Congress on Intensive Care Medicine.
Clinical Intensive Care in press (1996)

78. Crooks D A
Pathogenesis and biomeochanics of traumatic intracranial haemorrhages.
Virchows Arch A Pathol Anat Histopath 418: 479-83, 1991

79. Sobeh M S, Westacott S, Blakeney C, Ham R J
Balloon angioplasty catheters for endovascular tamponade after vascular trauma.
Injury 24: 355-6, 1993

80. Jahangiri M, Hyde J, Griffin S, Magee P, Youhana A, Lewis T, Wood A
Emergency thoracotomy for thoracic trauma in the accident and emergency department: indications and outcome.
Ann R Coll Surg Engl 78: 221-4, 1996

81. Jenkins B J, Badenoch D F, Fowler C G, Blandy J P
Long term results of treatment of urethral injuries in males caused by external trauma.
Brit J Urol 70: 73-5, 1992

82. Chumas P D, McNaught A B, Jacomb-Hood J H, Butler P
Cervical arterial disection following trauma.
Br J Neurosurg 5: 313-6, 1991

83. Mahoney P, Hadjimichael P
Emergency helicopter systems.
Care of the Critically Ill 12: 131-5, 1996

84. Nicholl J P, Brazier J E, Snooks H A
Effects of London Helicopter Emergency Medical Service on survival after trauma.
BMJ 311: 217-22, 1995

85. Deakin C D, Davies G, Wilson A W
Simple thoroscotomy avoids chest drain insertion in pre-hospital trauma
J Trauma 39: 372-4, 1995

86. Deakin C D
Bilateral periorbital haematoma (raccoon eyes) following thoracic crush injuries: Case Reports.
J Trauma 38: 816-7, 1995

87. Goldhill D R, Withington P S, Birch N J
The North East Thames Intensive Care Audit System.
Theoretical Surgery 8: 1-5, 1993

88. Goldhill D R, Withington P S.
Mortality predicted by APACHE II: the effect of changes in physiological values and post ICU hospital mortality.
In press Anaesthesia (1996)

89. Goldhill D R, Withington P S.
The ability of APACHE II to adjust for casemix difference.
Intensive Care Medicine 22: 415-9, 1996

90. Younge P A, Coats T J, Gurney D, Kirk C J, Evans S
Using TRISS to measure the performance of the Helicopter Emergency Medical Service (HEMS) trauma system in groups with different probablities of survival.
J Acc Emerg Med 12: 75, 1995

91. Fenton R
A helicopter emergency medical system is needed here.
Irish Medical Times 28th May 1996

92. Dalton A M
Use of blood tranfusions by medical emergency medical services: it is safe?
Injury 24: 509-10, 1993

93. Morley A, Hadjimichael P G, Mahoney P F
Cervical spine control during pre-hospital tracheal intubation of trauma victims.
Anaesthesia 50: 661-2, 1995

94. Morley A P, Hadjimichael P G, Mahoney P F
The Helicopter Emergency Medical Service: a role for the trauma anaesthetist.
ITACCS newsletter 5:19-23, 1995

95. Deakin C, Davies G
Defining trauma patient sub-populations for field stabilisation.
Eur J Emerg Med 1: 31-3, 1994

96. Deakin C D, Hicks I R
AB or ABC: pre-hospital fluid management in major trauma.
J Acc Emerg Med 11: 154-7, 1994

97. Greengross P
Service is part of a continuum of care.
BMJ 311: 1164-5, 1995

98. Botha A
A trauma surgery/intensive care research fellowship in Denver, Colorado, USA.
Ann R Coll Surg Engl. Supplement 78: 35-6, 1996

99. Morley A P
Pre-hospital monitoring of trauma patients: the experience of a Helicopter Emergency Medical Service.
Brit J Anaesth 76: 726-30, 1996

100. Maclean A D W, Kirk C J C, Coats T J, Cross F W
Design of study predisposed to Type II error.
BMJ 311: 1165, 1995

101. Wilmink A B M, Samra G S, Watson L M, Wilson A W
Vehicle entrapment rescue and pre-hospital trauma care
Injury 27: 21-5, 1996

102. Keogh S P, Wilson A W
Survival following cardiac arrest with on-scene thorocotomy for a stabbed heart.
Submitted to J Trauma 1995

103. Mahoney P, Hughes G
Training in the USA – multimedia for EMS
Royal College of Anaesthetics training day lecture
May 1995

104. Hadjimichael P G, Mahoney P F
Outcome after pre-hospital anaesthesia for head injuries.
Association of Anaesthetists. Winter meeting Jan 1996

105. Mahoney P F, Hadjimichael P G
The role of the helicopter in UK Trauma Services.
Trauma anaesthesia and intensive care seminars.
Association of Anaesthetists presentation 1995

106. Mahoney P F
Helicopter evacuation: in R Coll Anaesthetists Symposium. Medical management of major incidents and disasters. 1995

107. Greaves I, Dyer P V, Porter K M
The handbook of immediate care.
W.B.Saunders, London, 1995.
£17.95 ISBN O 7020 1881 3

108. Coats T J
Time of death after injury – measure of quality care?
Annual conference Faculty A/E Emergency Medicine Nov 1995

109. Coats T J
Changes in physiology due to pre-hospital care
Invited paper. Association of Surgeons, London, June 1995.

110. Knowles C H, Chou N, Coats T J, Wright K, Sutcliffe J C
Pupillary response and outcome following severe blunt head injury.
Poster presentation. FAEM Scientific Meeting 1995

111. Coats T J, Sutcliffe J C, Baldry J, Wilson A W
Disability following treatment of severe head injury by the London Helicopter Emergency Medical Service.
Poster presentation. FAEM Scientific Meeting 1995

112. Gray S J, Kirk C J C, Keogh S, Coats T J, Fisher J
Childhood falls: the experience of the London Helicopter Emergency Medical Service.
Poster presentation. FAEM Scientific Meeting 1995.

113. Coats T J
Time of death following injury – a measure of quality of care?
Poster presentation. FAEM Scientific Meeting 1995

114. Keogh S, Gray J S, Kirk C J C, Coats T J, Wilson A W
Children falling from a height in London.
Injury Prevention. in press (May 1996)

115. Wright K, Knowles C H, Coats T J, Sutcliffe J C
Time between injury and surgery in patients with intracranial haematoma treated by an integrated trauma system.
Injury. in press (May 1996)

116. Wilden J N
Helicopters do not care for patients.
BMJ 311: 1165, 1995

117. Baretta, Sutcliffe J
A prospective comparison of subdural pressure transducers in ventilated neurosurgical patients.
Brit J Neurosurg Submitted 1996

118. Davies G, Deakin C, Wilson A W
Effect of a rigid cervical collar on intracranial pressure.
Injury submitted 1996

119. Hamlyn, Richards, Sutcliffe J
Subdural haematomas in boxers.
Lancet submitted 1996

120. Goldhill D R
Major Trauma Chapter in: Case Studies in Intensive Care.
Armstrong R F, Salmon J Editors Oxford University Press to be published 1996

121. Goldhill D R, Withington P S
Editors: Textbook of Intensive Care. Chapman Hall, London, to be published 1996

122. Skinner D, Driscoll P, Earlam E
Editors: ABC of Major Trauma. Second Edition
BMJ Publishing Group, BMA House, Tavistock Square, London WC1H 9JR. 1996
ISBN O 7279 0917 7

123: Watkins E S
Life at the limit.
Macmillan, London 1996
ISBN 0 333 65774 8

APPENDIX B

FURTHER READING

BOOKS PUBLISHED BY OUR CONTRIBUTORS

Earlam R J (Editor)
The Royal London Hospital, Daily Express, Helicopter Emergency Medical Service.
Saldatore, Millars One, Southmill Road, Bishop's Stortford, Herts CM23 3DH. 1991. ISBN 0 948047 02X.

Goldhill D R Withington P S (Editors)
Textbook of Intensive Care.
Chapman Hall, 2-6 Boundary Row London SE18 HN.
ISBN 0 412601 303 .1996.

Greaves I, Dyer PV, Porter KM
The Handbook of Immediate Care.
WB Saunders, London 1995. ISBN 0 7 020 1881 3.

Kugler G
Air Rescue Service in the Federal Republic of Germany.
ADAC – Luftrettung GmbH, Am Westpark 8, 81373 Muenchen, Germany.

Kugler G
Die RTH – Stationen des Oeffentlich rechtlichen Luftrettungsdienstes in der Bundesrepublik Deutschland.
ADAC – Luftrettung GmbH, Am Westpark 8, 81373 Muenchen, Germany.

Martin T, Rodenburg H
Aeromedical transportation: a clinical guide
Ashgate Distribution Services, Gower House, Croft Road, Aldershot GU 11 3HR. October 1996.
ISBN 0 291 398421 1. £43.00 including p&p.

Neal Wendy
Disastrous Consequences London Disasters 1830-1917.
Hisarlik Press, available from Basics London, Eastwood Medical Centre, Eastwood Road, South Woodford, London E18 1BN. 1992. £15.95 including p&p. ISBN 1 8 743 12 001.

Nicholl J P, Brazier J E , Snooks H A, Lees-Milanga S
The costs and activity of the London Helicopter Emergency Medical Service.
Medical Care Research Unit, Sheffield University, Beech Hill Road, Sheffield S10 2RX. 1994.

Brazier J E, Nicholl J, Lees-Milanga S, Beeby N
The costs and performance of the medical activities of the Sussex police helicopter unit.
Medical Care Research Unit, Sheffield University, Beech Hill Road, Sheffield S10 2RX. 1994.

Nicholl J P, Brazier J E, Beeby N R
The costs and effectiveness of the Cornwall and Isles of Scilly ambulance service helicopter unit.
Medical Care Research Unit, University of Sheffield, Regent Court, Regent Street, Sheffield S1 4DA. 1994.

Nicholl J, Snooks H, Brazier J
The costs and effectiveness of helicopter emergency ambulance services.
Information for purchasers in England and Wales.
Medical Care Research Unit, SCHARR, University of Sheffield, Regent Court, Regent Street, Sheffield S1 DA.1995.

Oakley PA (Co-editor)
Trauma System Review (1992-95). North Staffordshire Hospital.
Correspondence to Professor John Templeton, North Staffordshire Hospital NHS Trust, Princes Road, Hartshill, Stoke-on-Trent, Staffordshire ST4 7LN. 1996.

Ryan J M, Rich N, Morgans B M, Dale R, Cooper G J (Editors)
Ballistic trauma: clinical relevance in peace and war.
Arnold, London, Winter 1996. ISBN 0 340 581 14X.

Skinner D, Driscoll P, Earlam R (Editors)
ABC of Major Trauma. First Edition, 1991.
British Medical Journal, Tavistock Square, London WC1H 9JR. ISBN 0 7279 0291 1.

Skinner D, Driscoll P, Earlam R (Editors)
ABC of Major Trauma. Second Edition, 1996.
BMJ Publishing Group, BMA House, Tavistock Square London WC1H 9JR. ISBN 0 7279 0917 7.

Watson L
RTA persons trapped.
Greenwave, 17 Head Street, Halstead CO9 2AT. 1990.
ISBN 0 951 6860.

Watson L
Advanced vehicle entrapment rescue.
Greenwave, 17 Head Street, Halstead CO9 2AT. 1995.
ISBN 0 951 6860 11.

Watson L
How will supplementary restraint systems effect rescue.
resQmed, 9 Fifth Avenue, Bluebridge, Halstead CO9 2SZ. 1996. ISBN 0 951 6860 38.

Watkins ES (Author)
Life at the Limit.
Macmillan, 25 Ecclestone Place London SW1. 1996.
ISBN 0 333 65774 8. £16.99.

LIST OF ADVERTISERS

We would also like to thank Laerdal Medical for their contribution to this book

APPENDIX D

HEMS REGISTRARS

1989

Mark DALTON

1990

Abrie BOTHA
Simon HODKINSON
Timothy SPALDING
Caroline WARREN

1991

Tim COATS
Colin MELVILLE
Rebecca SPARLING
Mike WALSH
Mark ALEXANDER-WILLIAMS

1992

Peter BROMLEY
Jo CHALLANDS
Terry MARTIN
Jane McNEIL
Teun WILMINK
Timothy WHITBREAD

1993

Gareth DAVIES
Charles DEAKIN
Peter GREENGROSS
Karen HEATH
Gurdip SAMRA

1994

Steve BREE
Andrew CLAXTON
Matthew DAWSON
Phil HADJIMICHAEL
Sean KEOGH
Andy MORLEY
Panayiotou STELLIOS
Paul YOUNGE

1995

Mike MACHESNEY
Patrick MITCHELL
Peter MAHONEY
John SCOTT
Victor INYANG

1996

Ronan FENTON
Patricia WARD
Julie BAK
Duncan GREY
Ioannis TSAGURNIS
Taj HASSAN
Katherine HENDERSON
Mike BROWNING
Jake COLLINS
Karim BROHI

Also Flew

Frank CROSS
Ken BOFFARD
Brian GREENWAY
Alastair WILSON
Judith FISHER
Gillian BRADBURY

Trauma Care • HEMS • London

Further copies are available from:

Saldatore Ltd
Millars Three, Southmill Road, Bishop's Stortford
Herts CM23 3DH

Tel/Fax 01279 651130